D1713000

The Vitality of the Lyric Voice

Studies on China, 6

A series of conference volumes sponsored by the Joint Committee on Chinese Studies of the American Council of Learned Societies and Social Science Research Council

For titles in the series see page 407

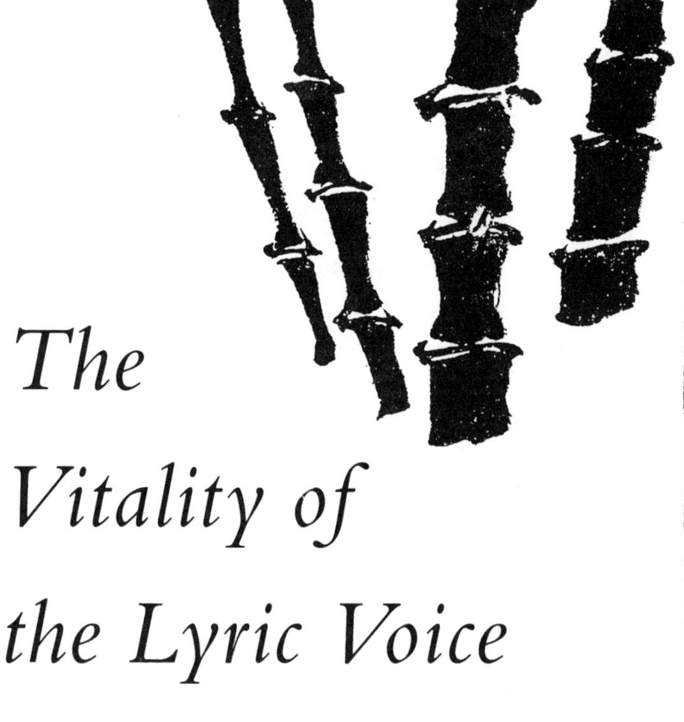

The Vitality of the Lyric Voice

Shih Poetry from the Late Han to the T'ang · *Edited by Shuen-fu Lin and Stephen Owen*

PRINCETON UNIVERSITY PRESS

Published by Princeton University Press, 41 William Street, Princeton, New Jersey 08540
In the United Kingdom: Princeton University Press, Guildford, Surrey

Library of Congress Cataloging in Publication Data will be found on the last printed page of this book

ISBN 0-691-03134-7

Publication of this book has been aided by a grant from the Paul Mellon Fund of Princeton University Press

This book has been composed in Bembo by Asco Trade Typesetting Ltd, Hong Kong

Clothbound editions of Princeton University Press books are printed on acid-free paper, and binding materials are chosen for strength and durability

Printed in the United States of America by Princeton University Press, Princeton, New Jersey

To Hans H. Frankel

Contents

Foreword ix

I. Theoretical Background 1

Profound Learning, Personal Knowledge, and Poetic Vision
Tu Wei-ming 3

Some Reflections on Chinese Poetic Language and Its Relation to Chinese Cosmology
François Cheng 32

The Paradox of Poetics and the Poetics of Paradox
James J. Y. Liu 49

The Self's Perfect Mirror: Poetry as Autobiography
Stephen Owen 71

II. Concepts and Contexts 103

Description of Landscape in Early Six Dynasties Poetry
Kang-i Sun Chang 105

The Decline and Revival of *Feng-ku* (Wind and Bone): On the Changing Poetic Styles from the Chien-an Era through the High T'ang Period
Lin Wen-yüeh 130

Verses from on High: The Ascent of T'ai Shan
Paul W. Kroll 167

The Nature of Narrative in T'ang Poetry
Ching-hsien Wang 217

III. Forms and Genres 253

The Development of Han and Wei *Yüeh-fu* as a High Literary Genre
Hans H. Frankel 255

The Legacy of the Han, Wei, and Six Dynasties *Yüeh-fu* Tradition and Its Further Development in T'ang Poetry
Zhou Zhenfu 287

The Nature of the Quatrain from the Late Han to the High T'ang
Shuen-fu Lin 296

The Aesthetics of Regulated Verse
Yu-kung Kao 332

Contributors 387

Index 391

Foreword

Under the sponsorship of a predecessor committee of the Joint Committee on Chinese Studies, of the American Council of Learned Societies and the Social Science Research Council, with funds provided by the National Endowment for the Humanities, the Ford Foundation, and the Andrew W. Mellon Foundation, a conference on the "Evolution of *Shih* Poetry from the Han through the T'ang" was held at the Breckinridge Public Affairs Center of Bowdoin College in York, Maine, from 9 to 14 June 1982. It was the first symposium of its kind on Chinese poetry ever to be held in the West. For four and a half days, thirteen scholars met in that lovely retreat—Breckinridge Center—to discuss eleven papers and two oral presentations on classical Chinese poetry. The twelve essays collected in this book represent the fruit of that cooperative endeavor.

Poetry is one of the imperishable glories of traditional Chinese civilization. By the turn of our century, it had a history already three thousand years old. Moreover, throughout the last two millennia, poetry has been the most esteemed form of literary expression for the educated elite in China. In organizing a conference on so vast and important a subject, naturally we found it necessary to limit ourselves to one phase of the development of only one major genre. Thus our conference was devoted to the evolution of *shih* poetry during the period from the second to the tenth century, the period that began with the sudden flowering of *shih* poetry in five-character meter and culminated in the glory of the T'ang, the golden age of classical Chinese poetry. The historical development during this specific period became the synchronic repertoire of classical poetry in the millennium that followed. That repertoire is held together by a single, unified definition of the form: *shih yen chih* 詩言志 or "poetry articulates in language what preoccupies the mind." This old Chinese definition dating from the ancient period was canonical, and initiated a tradition dominated by the expressive lyric. However, just as Chinese cosmogony initiates the universe in a unity which divides itself into the vast complexity of balances, categories, and particulars of the world we inhabit, so the unified canonical definition of poetry manifests itself in a historical diversity which goes beyond the simple definition without denying it.

In order to survey the repertoire of the form and to confront its complexity honorably, we assembled our own diversity of scholars, hoping in a congenial Babel to reunite all those points of view which might give some vision of the whole. We gathered scholars from the United States and Europe, and from the People's Republic of China and Taiwan. These scholars represented a full range of expertise in the historical period of our concern. Moreover, they represented traditional Chinese scholarship, traditional Western philology, intellectual history, and various more recent modes of Western literary scholarship. Our aim was not an artificial unity, but a structure diverse enough to match the mosaic of both the subject and the kinds of discourse that have grown up around it. We are also fully aware that the study of poetry is a complex and difficult task. The process of reading, understanding, and interpreting poetry often requires attention to features not only of the poetic text itself but also of the largest textual dimension, the dimension of culture. Therefore, by bringing together a diversity of scholars, we hoped to embrace the various aspects of cosmology, epistemology, literary history, religious tradition, and aesthetic convictions and ideals which, we believe, are relevant to an appreciation of the poetry under discussion.

In the first section, "Theoretical Background," are gathered essays which provide points of departure, concerns which touch on classical Chinese poetry in all its periods and genres. Each of these essays is, in its own way, a search for the origins of poetry. One way to discover such origins is to investigate the intellectual milieu in which poetry became a high literary form. It was during the period from the end of the second century A.D. through the third century that classical poetry was fully transformed from a folk lyric into a sophisticated and self-conscious literary form. That same period is the subject of Tu Wei-ming's "Profound Learning, Personal Knowledge, and Poetic Vision." Tu traces the new style of thought of that period from its philosophical roots to such pragmatic concerns as "personality appraisal," and from there to the developing concerns of classical poetry.

Another kind of search for origins looks to assumptions in the intellectual tradition which transcend the historical moment. Thus François Cheng looks to the recurrent patterns of Chinese cosmology to create a semiotic model for the Chinese lyric. Cheng's "Some Reflections on Chinese Poetic Language and Its Relation to Chinese Cosmology" describes a semiosis that is often concerned with gaps and empty spaces, a constant peering beyond the circumscribed realm of the expressible. It is precisely the tradition of this concern which is taken up in James J. Y. Liu's "The Paradox of Poetics and the Poetics of Paradox." Liu follows the abiding theoretical concern, expressed in language, for what lies beyond the competence of language; he then considers the poetics which grew up to address such yearning for the ineffable. One aspect of the ineffable is the Way; another is the exact quality of inner life. The ultimate paradox of poetry may be writing of oneself, in which the self known in reflection and writing becomes disjoined from the self in the act of reflection and writing. This consequence of the expressive lyric—the doubling of the self and the concern for authenticity—is the subject of Stephen Owen's "The Self's Perfect Mirror: Poetry as Autobiography."

The second section, "Concepts and Contexts," includes essays which in some way treat the terms and frames of reference through which we know classical Chinese poetry. Here we are brought to reflect on the role which indigenous concepts and borrowed Western concepts play in the epistemology of reading. Kang-i Sun Chang's "Description of Landscape in Early Six Dynasties Poetry" traces the pairing of description and the conceptual vocabulary which developed together in the actual writing of poetry. In her essay translated from the Chinese, "The Decline and Revival of *Feng-ku* (Wind and Bone)," Lin Wen-yüeh follows the fortunes of that elusive concept through five centuries and shows how the values around the concept helped shape the practice and history of poetry. Ching-hsien Wang works with the concept of "narrative," relating it to indigenous Chinese terms, and showing how "The Nature of Narrative in T'ang Poetry" differs in important respects from the usual expectations which surround the term. Not only do the individual terms of poetics lead to consequences in composition and reading, the matter of poetry too is a body of values and lore which stand behind the text and suffuse it. In "Verses from on High: The Ascent of T'ai Shan" Paul W. Kroll describes the body of religious Taoist images and associations which grew up around Mount T'ai and how the lore of the mountain became an essential part of understanding the poetry of the great mountain.

In the third section we find four essays on the major forms of *shih* poetry. The roots of *shih* poetry can be traced to the *yüeh-fu* of the Han, which were originally folk ballads and folk lyrics. The *yüeh-fu* remained one of the largest and most independent subforms of classical Chinese poetry, even after its original musical setting was lost. "The Development of Han and Wei *Yüeh-fu* as a High Literary Genre" by Hans H. Frankel treats that crucial and formative period in Chinese poetry when the folk lyric was first taken up and transformed by literary writers. The conception of *yüeh-fu* as one of the primordial forms of poetry made it particularly important in literary history as a form to which writers turned to reform and rejuvenate poetry. This later period of *yüeh-fu* writing is treated here in a brief summary of a longer paper written in Chinese by Zhou Zhenfu, "The Legacy of the Han, Wei, and Six Dynasties *Yüeh-fu* Tradition and Its Further Development in T'ang Poetry."

Perhaps the most common and characteristic forms of T'ang poetry were the quatrain (*chüeh-chü* or "broken-off lines") and the eight-line *lü-shih* or "regulated verse." Shuen-fu Lin's "The Nature of the Quatrain from the Late Han to the High T'ang" traces the evolution of the form and the distinctive aesthetic values which grew up within it. In contrast to Lin's diachronic description of the formation of the aesthetics of the quatrain, Yu-kung Kao in "The Aesthetics of Regulated Verse" gives a synchronic description of the underlying aesthetic values of the genre and offers a sophisticated account of the role of form in aesthetic experience.

The dozen essays contained in this volume cannot claim to be "comprehensive," covering all aspects of a millennium of poetry, but they do claim to be representative, both of the subject itself and of the ways in which it is studied. We hope that, from the breadth of our diverse approaches through the depth of each individual investigation, we have provided a better perspective with which to appreciate *shih* poetry during the first millennium of its development.

In addition to the authors whose works appear here, the participants in the 1982 conference included Professor Maureen Robertson of the University of Iowa. We deeply regret that she has not contributed an essay on T'ang literary criticism as originally planned; nonetheless, we are grateful to her for the various contributions she made at the conference. To Professor Ying-shih Yü of Yale University, we wish to express thanks for his participation at the planning meeting for the conference held in the fall of 1981. We must also express our appreciation for the assistance of three graduate students present at the conference. The two rapporteurs, Anne Behnke and Alice Cheang, carefully prepared a detailed transcription of the recorded presentations and discussions which were put to good use by the authors in the revision of their papers. And the conference would not have run as smoothly as it did without the help of the conference assistant, Arthur Tobias.

We are indebted to Ann Anagnost and Diane Scherer, staff members of the Michigan Publications on East Asia at The University of Michigan, for preparing the manuscript with a word processor. We are especially grateful to Diane Scherer, who far exceeded her duty as our editorial assistant to offer us help in proofreading and correcting numerous errors and inconsistencies.

We are thankful to R. Miriam Brokaw and Margaret Case of Princeton University Press for their continuous encouragement and professional advice. We are particularly grateful to R. Miriam Brokaw, former Associate Director and Editor of the Press, for her strong interest in our work since the very beginning and for her careful copy-editing of this volume.

An earlier version of Paul W. Kroll's essay was published in *T'oung Pao* 69.4–5 (1983), 223–260. We are grateful to E. J. Brill, which produces *T'oung Pao*, for permission to include a slightly revised version of the article that appeared in that scholarly journal.

In preparing the present symposium volume, we have received support from the Committee on Studies of Chinese Civilization of the American Council of Learned Societies and the Center for

Chinese Studies at The University of Michigan. We must record our profound gratitude to these two institutions for their generous financial support without which the original conference and the present book would not have been possible.

Shuen-fu Lin and *Stephen Owen*
June 1985

I. Theoretical Background

Tu Wei-ming

Profound Learning, Personal Knowledge, and Poetic Vision*

Kuo Hsiang 郭象 (d. 312), commenting on the idea of the "music of Heaven" 天籟 in the *Chuang Tzu* 莊子, observes in a distinctively Wei-Chin 魏晉 (220–420) style of thought:

> The music of Heaven is not an entity existing outside of things. The different apertures, the pipes and flutes and the like, in combination with all living beings, together constitute Heaven. Since non-being is non-being, it cannot produce other beings. Before being itself is produced, it cannot produce other beings. Then by whom are things produced? They spontaneously produce themselves, that is all. By this is not meant that there is an "I" to produce. The "I" cannot produce things and things cannot produce the "I." The "I" is self-existent. Because it is so by itself, we call it natural.[1]

* I am deeply indebted to Stephen Owen, Yu-kung Kao, and Maureen Robertson for their searching criticisms and inspiring suggestions.

[1] Kuo Hsiang 郭象, *Chuang Tzu chu* 莊子注, 1:15b, in *Erh-shih-erh tzu* 二十二子 (rpt. Taipei: Hsien-chih ch'u-pan-she, 1976), vol. 1, p. 152. Strictly speaking, the authorship for *Chuang Tzu chu* should be identified as Hsiang Hsiu 向秀 (fl. 250) and Kuo Hsiang. The controversy over the real author of the text is far from being settled. The accusation that Kuo Hsiang may have plagiarized Hsiang Hsiu is yet to be proved. See Hou Wai-lu 侯外廬 et al., *Chung-kuo ssu-hsiang t'ung shih* 中國思想通史, 5 vols. (Peking: Jen-min ch'u-pan-she, 1957), vol. 3, pp. 208–217. For this translation, see Wing-tsit Chan, *A Source Book in Chinese Philosophy* (Princeton: Princeton University Press, 1969), p. 328. It should be mentioned that the word *t'ien* is here rendered as "Heaven" rather than "Nature." For a comprehensive study on Kuo Hsiang, see Shu Sinn Whor 蘇新鋈, *Kuo Hsiang Chuang-hsüeh p'ing-i* 郭象莊學平議 (Taipei: Hsüeh-sheng shu-chü, 1980). See also T'ang I-chieh 湯一介, *Kuo Hsiang yü Wei-Chin hsüan-hsüeh* 郭象與魏晉玄學 (Wu-han: Hupei jen-min ch'u-pan-she, 1984).

This style of thought purports to understand things as they are in themselves, not merely as they appear to our ordinary sense perceptions. It takes as its point of departure the immediate apperception of concrete things *sui generis*, without the intervention of any external perspective in either being or non-being. A thing, no matter how it has come into existence, is intrinsically self-sufficient. It is there to be and to express. It is independent, autonomous, and spontaneous, definitely not produced by a willful design. To say that it is produced is to undermine the self-sufficiency and to reduce it to a mere creature. A thing does not and cannot acknowledge an external source of origin; its participation in nature is a form of self-contentment. It must manifest itself as an "I," pure and simple. As all things become self-sufficient "I's," equality pervades the universe. For Kuo Hsiang, this is the meaning of Chuang Tzu's "equality of things" 齊物.[2]

Kuo Hsiang's interpretation of the philosophy of Chuang Tzu in terms of the self-sufficiency of all beings appears to be incompatible with Wang Pi's 王弼 (226–249) interpretation of the philosophy of Lao Tzu, which presents non-being as the ultimate reality underlying all things.[3] As Wing-tsit Chan notes, "while Wang Pi emphasizes non-being, Kuo emphasizes being, and while Wang Pi emphasizes the one, Kuo emphasizes the many. To Wang Pi, principle transcends things, but to Kuo, it is immanent in them."[4] However, this apparent contrast between non-being and being, one and many, and transcendence and immanence must not lead us to the mistaken conclusion that Wang Pi and Kuo Hsiang actually subscribe to two incompatible metaphysical projects. Indeed, as Wing-tsit Chan further notes, "Kuo Hsiang and Wang Pi are similar in that both consider that the sage rises above all distinctions

[2] Kuo Hsiang, *Chuang Tzu chu*, pp. 13a–15b.

[3] Wang Pi 王弼, *Lao Tzu chu* 老子注, vol. 1, pp. 1a–b, in *Erh-shih-erh tzu*, pp. 5–6. For a general discussion on Wang Pi as a thinker, see A. A. Petrov, *Wang Pi (226–249): His Place in the History of Chinese Philosophy* (Moscow: Academy of Sciences, 1936). Mr. Petrov's B.A. thesis, which appears as Monograph XIII of the Institute of Oriental Studies in Moscow, is written in Russian. For a summary of his arguments, see Arthur F. Wright's review in *Harvard Journal of Asiatic Studies* 10 (1947), 75–88.

[4] Wing-tsit Chan, *Source Book*, p. 317.

and contradictions. He remains in the midst of human affairs although he accomplishes things by taking no unnatural action."[5] To philosophize in the spirit of the sage seems to be a shared orientation of the two distinctive modes of thought in the Wei-Chin period. And it is in this sense that Wang Pi and Kuo Hsiang can very well be said to belong to the same intellectual discourse.[6]

Historically the emergence of the Wei-Chin style of thought, as represented by the commentary works of Wang Pi and Kuo Hsiang, signifies a new epistemic era commonly known as the age of "profound learning" 玄學.[7] Since the character *hsüan* 玄, rendered here as "profound," is laden with fruitful ambiguities, there is pervasive reluctance among scholars of Chinese thought to fix its meaning in a narrow context. Against the background of the first chapter of the *Lao Tzu* 老子 in the commonly accepted sequence of the text, *hsüan* evokes sensations of an ineffable but mysteriously potent reality forever beyond the grasp of ordinary human perceptions. To comprehend the philosophical import of "profound learning," in terms of its internal structure, a radical restructuring of our conceptual apparatus is necessary. The temptation to adopt or to invent an ahistorical approach or to resort to a method of

[5] *Ibid.*

[6] Other prominent thinkers in the same intellectual discourse include Ho Yen, Hsi K'ang, and Ko Hung 葛洪 (fl. 317). See Hou Wai-lu et al., *Chung-kuo ssu-hsiang*, pp. 95–325. Also see Mou Jun-sun 牟潤孫, "Lun Wei-Chin i-lai ch'ung-shang t'an-pien chi-ch'i ying-hsiang" 論魏晉以來崇尚談辯及其影響, Inaugural address (Hong Kong: The Chinese University of Hong Kong Press, 1966).

[7] For background information, see Mao Han-kuang 毛漢光, *Liang-Chin Nan-Pei Ch'ao shih-tsu cheng-chih chih yen-chiu* 兩晉南北朝士族政治之研究, 2 vols. (Taipei: Shang-wu yin-shu-kuan, 1966), vol. 1, pp. 1–66; Ho Tzu-ch'üan 何茲全, *Wei-Chin Nan-Pei Ch'ao shih-lüeh* 魏晉南北朝史略 (Shanghai: Jen-min ch'u-pan-she, 1958), pp. 29–73; Han Pu-hsien 韓逋仙, *Chung-kuo chung-ku che-hsüeh shih-yao* 中國中古哲學史要 (Taipei: Cheng-chung shu-chü, 1960), pp. 70–137; and Fang Li-t'ien 方立天, *Wei-Chin Nan-Pei Ch'ao fo-chiao lun-ts'ung* 魏晉南北朝佛教論叢 (Peking: Chung-hua shu-chü, 1982), pp. 220–240. For a succinct discussion on the "profound learning" in English, see Erik Zurcher, *The Buddhist Conquest of China* (Leiden: E. J. Brill, 1959), pp. 86–92. For an overview of the discourse of the period, see Richard B. Mather, "The World of the Shih-shuo hsin-yü," in Liu I-ch'ing 劉義慶, *Shih-shuo hsin-yü* 世說新語, trans., Richard B. Mather (Minneapolis: The University of Minnesota Press, 1976), pp. xiii–xxx. Mather translates the title as *A New Account of Tales of the World.*

illogicality is strong; indeed, the fear that any interpretive strategy is inadequate and that any articulated position is by definition misguided is overwhelming. "Profound learning" itself can be understood as an historical phenomenon with a discernible pattern. An inquiry into the basic assumptions of such a pattern may shed some light on its internal structure, a structure which presumably cannot be comprehended by a single path alone.

T'ang Yung-t'ung 湯用彤, in a seminal essay on "profound learning," conceptualizes the emergence of the Wei-Chin style of thought as a shift of overall philosophical focus from cosmology to ontology. In his view, a defining characteristic of "profound learning" is the ontological mode of questioning.[8] While the Han 漢 (206–220 B.C.) scholars, notably Tung Chung-shu 董仲舒 (ca. 179 to ca. 104 B.C.), were primarily interested in cosmological issues, the Wei-Chin thinkers turned their minds to theories of being. T'ang's creative application of the two primary categories of learning in western metaphysics, cosmology and ontology, to the transition of Chinese thought from Han to Wei-Chin, is heuristically illuminating. To be sure, this dichotomy can be questioned as too neat to accommodate the complexity of the historical situation. We suspect that there must have been Han scholars who raised fundamental questions about ultimate reality. Take Yang Hsiung 揚雄 (53 B.C. to A.D. 18), for example. He observes that "the Supreme Profundity deeply permeates all species of things but its physical form cannot be seen."[9] His major philosophical work, entitled the *Classic of the Supreme Profundity* 太玄經, leads one to wonder if his attempt to probe the "great mystery" did not impel him to address issues that Wang Pi's ontology later addressed.[10]

[8] T'ang Yung-t'ung 湯用彤, "Wei-Chin hsüan-hsüeh liu-pieh lüeh-lun" 魏晉玄學流別略論, in his *Wei-Chin hsüan-hsüeh lun-kao* 魏晉玄學論稿 (Peking: Jen-min ch'u-pan-she, 1957), pp. 48–61.

[9] Yang Hsiung, *T'ai-hsüan ching*, ch. 9 (SPTK ed.), pp. 7:5a. For this translation, see Wing-tsit Chan, *Source Book*, p. 291.

[10] For a systematic inquiry into Yang Hsiung's life and thought, see Hsü Fu-kuan 徐復觀, "Yang Hsiung lun-chiu" 揚雄論究, in his *Liang-Han ssu-hsiang shih* 兩漢思想史, 3 vols. (Taipei: Hsüeh-sheng shu-chü, 1976), vol. 2, pp. 439–562; the section on *T'ai-hsüan* (pp. 485–498) is particularly relevant. Hellmut Wilhelm has provided an excellent discussion of the underlying structure of Yang Hsiung's metaphysics. See his *Heaven, Earth and Man in the Book of Changes* (Seattle: University of Washington Press, 1977), pp. 126–150.

However, as T'ang Yung-t'ung persuasively argues, the underlying structure of Yang Hsiung's metaphysics is the "mutual responsiveness of Heaven and man,"[11] whereas the ontic weight in Wang Pi's thought is the idea of "original substance" 本體. Thus, the same character *hsüan* assumes two different shapes of meaning because of the divergence in metaphysical context.

The metaphysical context of Yang Hsiung's "supreme profundity" is imbued with cosmological concerns: the way of Heaven, the passive and active natural forces, the cosmic transformation and human destiny. In this sense, Yang Hsiung fully participated in Tung Chung-shu's linguistic universe. The preoccupation of Tung with the meaning of the five phases, the correspondence of man and the numerical categories of Heaven, the historical cycles, and the transcendent justification for politics and morality continued to figure prominently in Yang's world view.[12] Wang Pi, by contrast, was involved in a significantly different metaphysical context. The issues discussed, the methods employed, and even the questions raised all seem to have undergone a major transformation. If a salient feature of the Han metaphysicians was system building, the Wei-Chin metaphysicians replaced the spirit of construction with the spirit of "digging." For the Wei-Chin thinkers, no blueprint for the construction of a philosophical edifice was available, nor even thought necessary or desirable. It seems that the prevailing ethos was to probe the underlying structure and principle of things instead of casting one's gaze outward in search of the grandiose design of the universe.

This archeological digging necessitates a deepened self-awareness or, more appropriate perhaps, an ever deepening self-awareness. To philosophize in the spirit of the sage entails the authentic possibility of analyzing things in a perspective fundamentally different from that which our ordinary human capacity, under the constraints of sensory perceptions, can appreciate. Yet, the sagely perspective in this connection is not merely a technique of seeing

[11] T'ang Yung-t'ung, "Wei-Chin ssu-hsiang te fa-chan" 魏晉思想的發展, in his *Wei-Chin hsüan-hsüeh lun-kao*), pp. 122–123.

[12] See Hsü Fu-kuan's critical analysis of Tung Chung-shu's *Ch'un-ch'iu fan-lu* 春秋繁露: "Hsien-Ch'in ju-chia ssu-hsiang te chuan-che chi t'ien-te che-hsüeh te wan-ch'eng" 先秦儒家思想的轉折及天的哲學的完成, in Hsü Fu-kuan, *Liang-Han ssu-hsiang shih*, vol. 2, pp. 295–438.

but a mode of knowing which also invokes hearing, sensing, tasting, and, indeed, embodying. This, I believe, is implicit in Wang Pi's insistence that "there is a great constancy in Tao and there is a generality in principle"[13] 道有大常, 理有大致. For the only way to *know* Tao as the "ultimate of greatness"[14] 大之極 is to experience it from within:

> Non-being is inherent in the one. But when we look for it in the multiplicity of things, it is like Tao which can be looked for but not seen, listened to but not heard, reached for but not touched. If we know it, we do not need to go out of doors. If we do not know it, the further we go, the more beclouded we become.
>
> If we know the general principle of things, we can know through thinking even if we do not travel. If we know the basis of things, even if we do not see them, we can point to the principle of right and wrong.[15]

The above statement, simple as it appears to be, is laden with far-reaching implications. However, it is important to note that the overall tone, despite the obviously paradoxical move from the first to the second part of the statement, is direct, confident, and assertive. There is no semantic nuance. Nor is there any sign of skepticism or negativism. The mental attitude is one of hope and optimism, even though the caution against the delusion of an intellectual grasp of the one "in the multiplicity of things" makes us wonder whether or not the whole epistemological enterprise implies subtle maneuvers and wary tactics.

We must hasten to mention that Wang Pi's rejection of "the multiplicity of things" as the primary field of inquiry in his philosophical project is not at all in conflict with Kuo Hsiang's idea of the spontaneous self-sufficiency of all beings. Kuo Hsiang certainly

[13] Wang Pi, vol. 2, 6a, in *Erh-shih-erh tzu*, p. 49; quoted from Wing-tsit Chan, *Source Book*, p. 323.

[14] Wang Pi, vol. 2, 2a, in *Erh-shih-erh tzu*, p. 41; quoted from Wing-tsit Chan, *Source Book*, p. 322–323.

[15] Wang Pi, vol. 2, 6a-b, in *Erh-shih-erh tzu*, pp. 49–50; quoted from Wing-tsit Chan, *Source Book*, p. 324.

does not subscribe to the view that the multiplicity of things as they appear to be is where the great principle of equality manifests itself. It is true that the sagely abode is in the myriad things, "but it does not mean that he does not wander freely."[16] The reason that a sage can wander freely *in* the midst of the myriad things is precisely because he is, in the ultimate sense, no longer *of* it: "The mind of the sage penetrates to the utmost the perfect union of yin and yang and understands most clearly the wonderful principles of the myriad things. Therefore he can identify himself with changes and harmonize with transformations, and finds everything all right wherever he may go. He embraces all things and thus nothing is not in its natural state."[17]

We encounter here the same direct, confident, and assertive tone. There is no trace of the "cloud of unknowing,"[18] no indication of doubt and, above all, no rhetorical device to suggest that reality is so elusive that human intelligence can never reach it. Of course it is one thing to say that the all-embracing capacity of the sagely mind "appreciates the nature of all things, partakes in the creative and transforming process of the universe, and fulfills the fame of Yao and Shun,"[19] but it is quite another to say that our limited human intelligence can also perform this godlike function. After all, it is only the sage "who identifies himself with the profoundly mysterious state and understands its wonder to the utmost."[20] Did Kuo Hsiang or Wang Pi mean to suggest that they were really sages simply by the fact that they attempted to philosophize in the spirit of the sage? Obviously they did not stipulate sagehood as a precondition for understanding what they were talking about. Nor, for that matter, did they imply that they themselves had somehow become sages. The attempt to philosophize in the spirit of the sage, far from being an *a priori* claim to a privileged position, is predi-

[16] Kuo Hsiang, 1:9b, in *Erh-shih-erh tzu*, p. 140; quoted from Wing-tsit Chan, *Source Book*, pp. 327–328.

[17] Kuo Hsiang, 1:10a, in *Erh-shih-erh tzu*, pp. 141; quoted from Wing-tsit Chan, *Source Book*, p. 328.

[18] Adopted from the title of a book on Christian life, *Cloud of Unknowing*, ed. Ira Progoff (New York: Dell, 1973).

[19] Wing-tsit Chan, *Source Book*, p. 328.

[20] *Ibid.*

cated on the assumption that it is an authentic human possibility to do so.

Surely, "with a tired body and a frightened mind,"[21] we often fail to appreciate things in perspective, for we try hard to avoid the sagely way and to take as evidently true the limited and fragmented vision of ordinary people. We simply cannot bring ourselves to the task of "harmonizing all the changes throughout ten thousand years";[22] we believe that it is impossible to accomplish and foolish to try to undertake such a task. The sage, on the contrary, "proceeds with utter simplicity and becomes one with transformation and always roams in the realm of unity."[23] The underlying reason that the sage is capable of such magnificent "creativity" is the natural order of things itself:

> [A]lthough the irregularities and confusions over millions of years result in a great variety and infinite multiplicity, as [the] "Tao operates and given results follow," the results of the past and present are one. And as "things receive names and are what they are," the myriad things are one in being what they are. Since there is nothing which is not what it is, and since there is no time in which results are not brought about [this mysterious function of the Tao], it may be called purity.[24]

To philosophize in the spirit of the sage is, therefore, nothing other than to understand the naturalness, spontaneity, and simplicity of the Tao in itself. Needless to say, this mode of understanding is universally open to the human community and is what we mean by ontological thinking. The difference between Wang Pi and Kuo Hsiang is thus two distinctive styles of ontological thinking. In fact, the points of convergence between them loom large when they are contrasted with the Han styles of cosmological thinking.

Admittedly the generalization about Wei-Chin ontology, based upon the family resemblance between Wang and Kuo, is a matter

[21] Kuo Hsiang, 1:31a, in *Erh-shih-erh tzu*, p. 183; quoted from Wing-tsit Chan, *Source Book*, p. 330.

[22] *Ibid.*

[23] *Ibid.*

[24] *Ibid.* It should be noted that the character *ch'un*, rendered by Wing-tsit Chan as "simplicity," is here changed to "purity."

of emphasis. It is not meant to serve as an exclusive explanatory model. Nevertheless, T'ang Yung-t'ung's interpretation of the ontological character of "profound learning" is vitally important for directing our attention to the main thrust of the Wei-Chin spiritual orientation. It is also useful as a guide for setting up our agenda for further exploration.

The ontological turn[25] enabled the Wei-Chin thinkers to raise fundamental questions about reality. As a result, issues of substance and function 體用, form and spirit 形神, root and branch 本末, one and many 一多, and being and non-being 有無 took on particular significance.[26] The philosophical project, simply put, was to comprehend the substance, the spirit, the root, and the one without losing sight of its manifold functions, forms, and branches. Since ultimate reality, or the Tao, is only approachable through a process of detachment, any artificial attempt to assert what the Tao seems to be is inevitably self-defeating. The only way out, then, is to adopt a sort of implicit *via negativa*; such a move, in its most radical development, logically leads to envisioning the Tao as non-being. Ultimate reality so conceived is identical to "nothingness," not the nothingness that negates all things but that which symbolizes the inexhaustible potency and generativity of the Tao.

Wang Pi's famous notion of "embodying nothingness" 體無, in the light of this ontological turn, should not be construed as an appeal to mysticism, for it directly addresses the issue of the best possible way of knowing the Tao. Thus, from Wang Pi's philosophical perspective, the ineffable Tao is knowable through experience. Implicit in this approach is a hierarchy of perception which, for both theoretical and practical reasons, can be generally differentiated into four levels of sophistication and subtlety. First, there are

[25] The expression "ontological turn" is used in the same way as the "linguistic turn" has been used by interpreters of the particular philosophical development in the Anglo-American academic circle under the influence of Ludwig Wittgenstein.

[26] For a general discussion of the so-called, "pure conversation," see Chou Shao-hsien 周紹賢, *Wei-Chin ch'ing-t'an shu-lun* 魏晉清談述論 (rpt. Taipei: Shang-wu yin-shu-kuan, 1966), pp. 24–233. The newness of this ontological agenda is beyond dispute. Wing-tsit Chan, for example, states in reference to Wang Pi's commentary on the thirty-eighth chapter of the *Lao Tzu*: "This is the first time in the history of Chinese thought that substance (*t'i*) and function (*yung*) are mentioned together." See Wing-tsit Chan, *Source Book*, p. 323.

ordinary people who perceive the multiplicity of things as they appear without any inclination to see the unity beneath them; secondly, there are those, like Chuang Tzu, who having perceived the Tao resort to elaborate linguistic strategies, including "wild words" 狂言 to shock the world so that ordinary people can sense the flavor of the Tao; thirdly, there are masters of the Tao, like Lao Tzu, who know well that the Tao is ineffable and yet choose words to express the inexpressible; and, finally, there are the sages, like Confucius, whose "silent appreciation" 默契 of the Tao is so intimate that they become totally internal to the Tao, i.e., they embody the nothingness of the Tao.[27] Confucius' silent appreciation, Lao Tzu's suggestive articulation, Chuang Tzu's elaborate depiction, and the unawareness of ordinary people constitute a wide spectrum of possibility in our relationships to the Tao.

Whether or not Wang Pi was unique among the Wei-Chin thinkers in identifying Confucius' "exemplary teaching" 身教 as superior to Lao Tzu's "teaching by words" 言教, the value structure embedded in the hierarchy of perception, as Mou Tsung-san 牟宗三 has pointed out, was quite pervasive.[28] The belief that language is deficient and descriptive language is most inadequate in apprehending the Tao was widely held. Furthermore, the assumption that the intimate experience of the Tao is extra-linguistic was taken as self-evident. The classical formulations of the subtle relationship between "word" 言 and "meaning" 意, in the "Appended Remarks" of the *Book of Changes* and in the *Chuang Tzu*, were often invoked to show the instrumental value of words in capturing the sagely meaning and their corresponding inadequacy in realizing a true experiential encounter with the Tao.[29] The central theme in the Wei-Chin recommendation for dissolving this

[27] For an analysis of Wang Pi's idea of "embodying nothingness," see Mou Tsung-san 牟宗三, *Ts'ai-hsing yü hsüan-li* 才性與玄理 (Hong Kong: Jen-sheng ch'u-pan-she, 1963), pp. 119–125. Also see Tu Wei-ming 杜維明, "Wei-Chin hsüan-hsüeh chung te t'i-yen ssu-hsiang—shih-lun Wang Pi 'sheng-jen t'i-wu' i-kuan-nien te che-hsüeh i-i" 魏晉玄學中的體驗思想—試論王弼"聖人體無"一觀念的哲學意義, in *Yen-yüan lun-hsüeh-chi* 燕園論學集, ed. Editorial Board in Memory of T'ang Yung-t'ung (Peking: Peking University Press, 1984).

[28] Mou Tsung-san, *Ts'ai-hsing yü hsüan-li*. p. 119.

[29] See T'ang Yung-t'ung, "Yen-i chih pien" 言意之辨, in his *Wei-Chin hsüan-hsüeh lun-kao*, pp. 26–47.

dilemma is to use words to capture the sagely meaning and to forget them as soon as it is captured.[30] There were of course those who took exception to this recommendation, notably Ou-yang Chien 歐陽建 (d. 300), who advocated that "words exhaust meaning" 言盡意,[31] but the main thrust of the Wei-Chin thinking on the matter was true to the spirit of Chuang Tzu's instruction: "the fish trap is forgotten once the fish is caught" 得魚忘筌.[32] To put it differently, words are convenient means to catch the sagely meaning, the intent of which is to direct us to gain personal knowledge of the Tao. If we are not critically aware that "words do not exhaust meaning" 言不盡意 and that words cannot in themselves really represent the Tao, we can be easily trapped in words to the extent that we are incapable of making the distinction between "substance" 體 and "function" 用. This is like committing the categorical mistake of confusing the fish trap with the fish.

Implicit in this line of reasoning, however, is a deep-rooted faith in the power of the human mind, not its discriminative cognition but its holistic "intellectual intuition" 智的直覺, to comprehend the Tao from within.[33] To "embody nothingness," in this particular connection, signifies the ultimate human capacity to open oneself up to a realm of the Tao which is not accessible to the ordinary sensory perceptions. Any form of knowing that requires the intervention of the trappings of words and signs falls short of reaching that realm. Confucius' silent appreciation of the Tao is thus a paradigmatic expression of what true knowledge means. The fact that all of us, including Lao Tzu and Chuang Tzu, have not yet been able to live up to the sagely model does not at all deny its

[30] *Ibid.* Also, see Yüan Hsing-p'ei 袁行霈, "Wei-Chin hsüan-hsüeh chung te yen-i chih pien yü Chung-kuo ku-tai wen-i li-lun" 魏晉玄學中的言意之辨與中國古代文藝理論, in *Ku-tai wen-hsüeh li-lun yen-chiu* 古代文學理論研究, no. 1 (Shanghai: Ku-chi ch'u-pan-she, 1980), pp. 125–147, and Tu Wei-ming, "Ts'ung i tao yen" 從意到言, *Chung-hua wen-shih lun ts'ung* 中華文史論叢, no. 17 (Shanghai: Ku-chi ch'u-pan-she, 1981), vol. 1, pp. 225–261.

[31] Mou Tsung-san, *Ts'ai-hsing yü hsüan-li*, pp. 243–254.

[32] For the reference, see *Chuang Tzu yin-te* 莊子引得, in *Harvard-Yenching Institute Sinological Index Series* (Peking: Yenching University, 1947), 75/26/48 (ch. 26).

[33] See Mou Tsung-san, *Chih te chih-chüeh yü Chung-kuo che-hsüeh* 智的直覺與中國哲學 (Taipei: Shang-wu yin-shu-kuan, 1971).

verity. Actually, it is likely that for generations to come no human beings, in practical terms, will ever experience the Tao at the same level of immediacy and intimacy. Yet, ontologically, to embody nothingness and to experience the Tao from within is an authentic possibility realizable with varying degrees of sophistication and simplicity by all members of the human community.

The hierarchy of perception and equality of potential provide the two necessary axes for locating the central significance of the Wei-Chin ontological turn of thought. The profound learning, as long as it focused on three of the most recondite texts in the classical heritage, was inevitably restricted to a small coterie of brilliant minds. Indeed, the ability to enunciate the hidden meanings in the *Book of Changes* 易經, the *Lao Tzu*, or the *Chuang Tzu* was so rare that only a few in a generation were gifted enough to cultivate the facility and the art to do so. The whole project was thus tinged with elitism of taste, if not of social origin. However, within the universe of literati culture, power, status, or even age was no longer the important criterion of influence. A penetrating insight of a literatus on the occasion of a ritualized debate, a casual conversation, a group discussion or a dialogue, could elevate him to the coveted position of an arbiter of taste, able to exert a shaping influence on the style and content of the discourse in vogue.[34] This illustrates the convergence of the two distinguishable movements of the period: "pure conversation" 清談, as exemplified in *A New Account of Tales of the World* 世說新語, was, in a way, a concrete manifestation of how the insights in "profound learning" were translated into a grammar of action and creatively applied to the vicissitudes of life of the

[34] This is of course not to undermine the importance of the political factor in the development of Wei-Chin thought; see Ho Ch'ang-ch'ün 賀昌群, *Wei-Chin ch'ing-t'an ssu-hsiang ch'u-lun* 魏晉清談思想初論 (Chungking: Shang-wu yin-shu-kuan, 1946), pp. 25–53. However, to understand the significance of "pure conversation" as a style of thought, it is vitally important to avoid the fallacy of reducing the philosophical enterprise to a mere reflection of political struggle of the period. Actually, we may well contend that "pure conversation" as an intellectual movement contributed to a new definition of power and influence. See Ho Ch'i-min 何啓民, *Wei-Chin ssu-hsiang yü t'an-feng* 魏晉思想與談風 (Taipei: Shang-wu yin-shu-kuan, 1967), pp. 46–102.

time;[35] similarly, "metaphysical discussion," far from being an isolated quest for objective truths through cool reasoning, was motivated by a strong desire to probe the ultimate principle and to experience fully the multiplicity of the human condition.

Understandably, the word "pure" in "pure conversation" and the word "profound" in "profound learning" assumed particular shapes of meaning in the discoursive context in which they were employed. The contrasting device, often used by historians to fix the meanings of these two terms, is of limited explanatory power. To be sure, "pure" is contrasted with "turbid" 濁 and "profound" with "shallow" 淺, but to define pure conversation and profound learning in terms of their opposites is misleading. For one thing, the highly cherished values in pure conversation have little to do with the idea of purity. If a personality was characterized as pure, as in Kuo T'ai's 郭泰 (128–169) famous judgment of a contemporary literatus, it did not necessarily commend respect among the pure conversationalists. Nor did a personality depicted as "turbid" imply a criticism, especially if one's turbidity evoked images of the turbid waters of the Yangtze or the Yellow River.[36]

On the surface, the pure conversationalists and the profound learners found their identity by detaching themselves from the mundane and shallow business of politics. Often, their quest for purity and profundity is interpreted as a thorough rejection of *realpolitik*. However, either by choice or by default, the celebrated members of these movements were perceived to have a great deal of attraction for the literati and thus were thought to have presented a serious threat to the ruling minority. Their attempt to explain

[35] Ho Ch'ang-ch'ün, *Wei-Chin ch'ing-t'an*, pp. 54–104. See Richard Mather, *New Account of Tales of the World*, pp. xiii-xxvi. It should be noted that Mather's emphasis on the philosophical conflict between "naturalism" 自然 and "moral teaching" 名教 is not at all incompatible with the view that the "ontological turn" is relevant to both.

[36] The contemporary literatus of whom Kuo T'ai thought highly was Huang Hsien 黃憲. Huang's ability to evoke sensations of expansiveness was sharply contrasted with another literatus whose purity conveyed to Kuo no more than a sense of limited personal integrity. See Fan Yeh 范曄, *Hou-Han shu* 後漢書 (SPPY ed.) biography 43, 83:4a. For a discussion of Kuo T'ai's art of appraising personalities, see Chou Shao-hsien, *Wei-Chin ch'ing-t'an*, pp. 36–39.

ordinary phenomena in the spirit of the Tao and their intention to live the life of an authentic person created an alternative mode of existence potentially capable of undermining the values of conformity and stability advocated by the state.[37] As a result, their seemingly apolitical use of language was thought by their contemporaries to have far-reaching political implications. The fate of the "Seven Worthies of the Bamboo Grove" 竹林七賢, notably Hsi K'ang 嵇康 (222–262), clearly indicates the complexity of the relationship between speculative conversation and political action at that time.[38]

The interplay between language and politics, an issue too intriguing to be fully explored here, impels us to inquire further into the messages of the Wei-Chin thinkers in both the "pure conversation" and the "profound learning" groups. We can no longer accept the single causal arguments and assign clear-cut motivations to any of our heroes or antiheroes. Nor can we take a compartmentalized methodology and isolate a "philosophical statement" as if it had a totally different ancestry. The synchronic structure of the discourse shared by thinkers of the same epistemic era must be noted, lest we should commit the fallacy of interpreting a text as a natural object without history and culture. The following quotation from Ho Yen 何晏 (d. 249), in the light of the above cautionary note, is still an ontological assertion, except that its meaning overflows into other dimensions of the human condition: aesthetics, ethics, and politics.

> Being, in coming into being, is produced by non-being. Affairs, as affairs, are brought into completion by non-being. When one talks about it and it has no predicates, when one names it and it has no name, when one looks at it and it has no form, and when one listens to it and it has no sound—that is

[37] For background understanding, see Étienne Balazs, "Nihilistic Revolt or Mystical Escapism: Current of Thought in China During the Third Century A.D.," in his *Chinese Civilization and Bureaucracy*, trans., H. M. Wright and ed., A. F. Wright (New Haven: Yale University Press, 1964), pp. 226–254.

[38] For a general discussion on the Seven Worthies of the Bamboo Grove, see Ho Ch'i-min, *Chu-lin ch'i-hsien yen-chiu* 竹林七賢研究 (Taipei: Shang-wu yin-shu-kuan, 1966). For Hsi K'ang's life, see Donald Holzman, *La vie et la pensée de Hi K'ang* (Leiden: Brill, 1957).

Tao in its completeness. Hence it is able to make sounds and echoes brilliant, to cause material force (*ch'i*) and material objects to stand out, to embrace all physical forms and spiritual activity, and to display light and shadow. Because of it darkness becomes black and plainness becomes white. Because of it the carpenter's square obtains a square and the compass draws a circle. The compass and square obtain forms but Tao has no form. Black and white obtain names but Tao has no name.[39]

Ho Yen's depiction of the Tao as nameless, formless, and soundless precisely because it is the source of all things is a treatise on metaphysics, but it also contains aesthetic and ethical, not to mention political, implications. At this fundamental discoursive level, the so-called "personality appraisal" 品題人物, another distinctively Wei-Chin style of thought, can also be construed as part of the same isomorphic system. This line of thought may appear to be in conflict with the common assumption that since the need for the categorization of human talents is motivated by pragmatic, administrative considerations, the upsurge of interest in this subject in the last decades of the Eastern Han 東漢 (25–220) and the period of the Three Kingdoms 三國 (220–265) was basically a political phenomenon.[40] In actuality, however, as several intellectual historians have already pointed out, "personality appraisal" as a genre of cultural analysis predates literary criticism and art connoisseurship and, therefore, may have provided rich symbolic resources such as vocabulary, syntax, grammar, pragmatics, and semantics for later scholars. Two centuries later, these scholars, notably Liu Hsieh 劉勰 (ca. 460–532) and Chung Hung 鍾嶸 (469–518), creatively tapped the symbolic resources in the heritage of "personality appraisal" in pursuing their analytical enterprises in a most

[39] This portion of Ho Yen's *Tao-lun* 道論 is preserved in Chang Chan's 張湛 commentary on the *Lieh Tzu* 列子. See *Chang-chu Lieh Tzu* 張注列子 (Japanese Kansei ed., 1791), 1:6a–b. This translation is quoted from Wing-tsit Chan, *Source Book*, p. 324.

[40] See T'ang Ch'ang-ju 唐長孺, "Wei-Chin ts'ai-hsing lun te cheng-chih i-i" 魏晉才性論的政治意義, in his *Wei-Chin Nan-Pei-Ch'ao shih lun-ts'ung* 魏晉南北朝史論叢 (Peking: San-lien shu-tien, 1955), pp. 298–310.

original, fruitful way.[41] It is therefore to be expected that literary criticism and, for that matter, art connoisseurship seem to have shared the same vocabulary, syntax, grammar, pragmatics, and semantics with the genre of "personality appraisal." This is of course not to suggest that Liu Shao's 劉邵 *Treatise on Personalities* 人物志 in the third century actually foreshadowed Liu Hsieh's *Refinements of the Literary Mind* 文心雕龍 and Chung Hung's *Judgments on Poetry* 詩品. For one thing, since Liu Shao's work was not at all widely circulated, it was unlikely that Liu Hsieh or Chung Hung had had access to it. Nor is this to suggest that the sort of debates on human talents 才性 that Chung Hui 鍾會 (225–264) and his adversaries were engaged in, as indicated in his *Essay on the Four Fundamentals* 四本論, in fact set the precedents for literary criticism and art connoisseurship in China. Indeed, it may also be far-fetched to suggest that Hsü Shao's 許劭 (150–195) *Monthly Comments* 月旦評 started the whole movement of "personality appraisal" in the first place.[42]

A broadly conceived influence study, combined with a nuanced inquiry into the subtle connections of the various streams of thought in the Wei-Chin period, will give us a flow chart of the "productive" relationships among the major intellectual enterprises that defined the age: "profound learning," "pure conversation," and "personality appraisal." Suffice it now to address the possible linkage between the ontological reflection of the Tao and the conceptual apparatus that was deemed necessary for "personality appraisal." The purpose is to see if the idea of "personal knowledge" can serve as a linchpin upon which the seemingly divergent Wei-Chin concerns can be shown to have actually en-

[41] See Hsü Fu-kuan, "Wen-hsin tiao-lung te wen-t'i lun" 文心雕龍的文體論 in his *Chung-kuo wen-hsüeh lun-ts'ung* 中國文學論叢 (Taichung: Min-chu p'ing-lun-she, 1966), pp. 14–15. There are numerous other examples to substantiate the claim that the vocabulary used in "personality appraisal" continued to influence ideas and concepts in literary criticism and art connoisseurship.

[42] For Hsü Shao's biography, see *Hou-Han shu* (Shou-p'ing ed.), biography 58, 98:8a–b. It should be noted that the so-called *Monthly Comments* may have been a common expression indicating that comments on famous personalities from him were made monthly or in ten-day periods. There is no evidence that "Yüeh-tan p'ing" actually referred to a journal-style publication.

tered into a fruitful dialogue. For this hypothesis to work, it must satisfy the two basic conditions of being philosophically tenable and historically sound.

"Personal knowledge," envisioned in the present context, possesses three interrelated characteristics: holism, centeredness, and dynamism. First of all, as a mode of knowing, it is a combination of "knowing that" and "knowing how," for it involves both verifiable information and acquired skill. To know a person is a form of pattern recognition. We need to know a great deal of objective facts about the person to form a reliable impression. The impression I have about a particular person is subject to change as more information is gathered. Pieces of information are put together in the way jigsaw puzzles are constructed. However, if I rely upon this mechanical method, the most I can achieve is a more or less complete profile of the person. I cannot presume to know the person. The only way I can hope to achieve that is to observe him, to talk to him, and to socialize with him. This already requires some "know-how," not just the art of human interaction but also analogical thinking, empathetic appreciation, self-knowledge, and a host of other internalized skills. Even then, if I am aware of the complexity involved, I may still feel reluctant to say that I really know the person. However, if, in a limited context, I express the view that I know the person, I mean to suggest that, in an holistic sense, I have some personal knowledge of what the person is. A salient feature of "personality appraisal," accordingly, is the ability to grasp the whole personality and to give it a comprehensive appreciation and evaluation. The famous depiction of Ts'ao Ts'ao 曹操 (155–220) by the aforementioned master personality appraiser, Hsü Shao, is thus a holistic expression.[43] Although we do not know through what kind of procedure Master Hsü made his insightful observations on his contemporaries, it is reasonable to assume that his personal knowledge was acquired through a manifold approach, including in-depth studies of model personalities in history, comparative physiognomical analyses, consultations, cross-references, inter-

[43] *Ibid.*, 98 : 8a. The five-character couplet depicting Ts'ao Ts'ao as a villain in time of peace and a hero in a chaotic age 淸平之姦賊，亂世之英雄.

views, and, perhaps most important of all, experiential encounters.[44]

The tact of grasping a personality holistically resembles the art of knowing the Tao. If we take seriously the dichotomies that the Wei-Chin thinkers brought to bear on the fundamental questions about reality, the tact involves many delicate maneuvers: to find a way to appreciate the "substance" of the person without losing sight of his observable "functions" in society, to acquire a taste for the "spirit" without ignoring the importance of the "form," to search for the "root" that nourishes the personality so that its branches can be properly appraised, and to grasp the unity, the one that underlies its manifold expressions. It may not be totally off the mark to say that we sometimes have to apply the "negative method' to fully comprehend what a person really is, even though no personality can ever attain total transparency comparable to the "non-being" of the Tao. Notwithstanding the vagueness of the whole approach, from a methodological point of view it makes good sense to distinguish the surface manifestations of a person's behavior and the deep motivational structure, constituted by a sense of values, dispositions, beliefs, and other factors, that makes the personality of the person. The classificatory scheme employed in the *Treatise on Personalities* is, strictly speaking, not a diagram for mapping out various personality types. It is, by and large, a methodical discussion of the facts and principles of understanding human beings in their concrete existential situations. As Mou Tsung-san notes, it is concerned with human talents 才性, physical appearances 體别, dispositions 性格, and styles 風格.[45] In other words, it intends to understand the whole person, body and spirit.

To carry this analogy further, the tact of apprehending the spirit as well as the body of a person is not a roundabout way of

[44] Although there is little information on this in Hsü Shao's biography, the emergence of practices such as passing judgment on notable people 臧否人物, starting and spreading around ditties about famous personalities 風謠, attaching labels to distinctive personality traits 題目, and formulating standards for evaluating scholar-official performances 淸議 clearly indicates that it is reasonable to assume that "personality appraisal" had become a sophisticated art. See Hou Wai-lu, et al., *Chung-kuo ssu-hsiang*, vol. 2, pp. 364–397.

[45] Mou Ts'ung-san, *Ts'ai-hsing yü hsüan-li*, p. 44.

circumventing the subject matter but a direct experiential encounter with the inner core of the personality. This requires one's ability to hit the mark, the bull's-eye, without recourse to any abstract scheme of cyclic definitions. Indeed, the tact is significantly different from the conventional definitional approach whereby one moves from a large circle of species and genre and gradually fixes the precise location of the subject matter within it. The definitional approach is necessary if we want to find out the social role, the party membership, or the religious affiliation of the person. It can also tell us a great deal about the personality traits of the person. But it cannot help us to know the person in the sense of having acquired a personal knowledge of him. To do that, the Wei-Chin thinkers seem to argue, we must learn the art of piercing through the heart of the matter and then rounding out the task from within. This is predicted on the power of our intellectual intuition to know not only what a thing appears to be but what a thing is in itself. This seemingly outrageous claim was taken for granted by the Wei-Chin thinkers as an authentic possibility for all members of the human community, even though, in practice, only the finest minds, namely the sages, can fully realize it.

This mode of knowing is tantamount to an immediate comprehension of the Tao from within. To search for the Tao by a gradual path of classifying and analyzing its manifold functions is like trying to find the inner core of the personality by a detailed description of its social roles. No matter how rigorous the effort is in such a pursuit, it can only lead to a partial, fragmented view, never to full, holistic experiential understanding. Centeredness, so conceived, can be taken as an optimal way to attain holism. The image of the archer who can hit the center of the target only by a combination of sufficient strength and perfect timing and who must examine himself and rectify the procedure from within if he fails to do so is relevant here.[46] The delicate interplay between the knowing subject and the subject of knowing necessitates not only a constant critical self-awareness but also the acumen of letting

[46] For the concept of combining sufficient strength and perfect timing, as the way of the archer, see *Mencius*, 5B: 1. Although the *locus classicus* for this reference is Mencian, the idea can strike a sympathetic chord in either Taoism or Buddhism.

oneself go in the art of self-forgetfulness 忘我.[47] To know a person holistically implies that he will neither be abstracted to a general type nor reduced to a common denominator; indeed, his integrity as a unique personality will be respected. Moreover, as a concrete person, his center is never static. Unless we can open ourselves up to the full range of activities in which he is engaged, there is little hope for us to apprehend his dynamic center, not to mention the possibility of comprehending the total personality from within.

It is, therefore, necessary to mention that, in addition to holism and centeredness, personal knowledge of the kind we are concerned with also possesses the characteristic of dynamism. Unlike the science of knowing bare facts or raw data, the art of knowing persons cannot assume a totally neutral, disinterested, and value-free position as a point of departure. We do not have privileged access to a static and thus secured objective vantage point. Instead, the ground, or more appropriately the floating island, on which we stand is unstable, if not always changing. The confluence of numerous currents of sentiment and thought constantly disturbs our effort to negotiate between the desirability of maintaining the posture of an outside observer and the necessity of becoming an inside participant. In other words, as the knowing subject through the act of apprehending is itself undergoing a transformation, the subject of knowing must be apprehended by empathetic understanding as well as by critical analysis. The dialectic interplay between these two dimensions of apprehension is a salient feature of personal knowledge. The character *t'i* 體 which forms compounds with a host of what may be called cognitive terms to indicate the profundity of the personal commitment involved in this mode of knowing is an outstanding example of personal knowledge in operation: examination 體察, taste 體味, comprehension 體認, understanding 體會, confirmation 體證, and verification 體驗.[48]

However, it is vitally important to note that a concrete person must exhibit recognizable cultural qualities that are shared by other

[47] *Chuang Tzu yin-te*, 19/6/92 (ch. 6).

[48] For a brief discussion on this, see Tu Wei-ming, "'Inner Experience': The Basis of Creativity in Neo-Confucian Thinking," in *Artists and Traditions: Uses of the Past in Chinese Culture*, ed. Christian F. Murck (Princeton: The Art Museum, Princeton University, 1976), pp. 9–11.

human beings, for he comes into existence through symbolic interchange. Unlike the Tao, he is not soundless, colorless, or odorless. After all, we are created in the process of communal participation: sharing thoughts, meanings, feelings; in fact the network of human relationships in which we are reared and nourished provides the common basis, the social reality, for our dialogues, conversations, and discussions. There is no reason to suspect that since the Wei-Chin thinkers were "individualistic," they were not part of a symbolic interchange. Actually, the characters in *A New Account of Tales of the World* often impress us as a group of rarefied aristocrats. Their life-styles, tastes, wishes, ideas, and values show a remarkable underlying compatibility and commonality. Otherwise, it would be difficult to imagine how they managed to converse in the first place. Liu I-ch'ing's 劉義慶 (403–444) persuasive defense of the meaningfulness of the way the Wei-Chin literati naturally, delightfully, and inescapably interacted with each other was certainly nostalgic reflection.[49] But, undoubtedly, he is correct in showing that the Wei-Chin literati did provide a new path for creative minds to follow. In this new epistemic era, the horizon of human sensitivity and the human intellect was widened wonderfully. As a result, a new poetic vision emerged.

It is often believed that the emergence of the distinctively Wei-Chin style of poetics, with particular emphasis on mountains, waters, and pastoral scenes, was due mainly to a naturalistic turn in the literary circle. The discovery of nature for its own sake was symptomatic of this newly developed mental attitude. With the exception of J. D. Frodsham's attempt to locate the "origins of Chinese natural poetry" in the so-called metaphysical verses 玄言詩,[50] there is little effort to explore the possible links between this particular poetic vision and the distinctively Wei-Chin styles of thought, namely profound learning, pure conversation, and personality appraisal. Before we explore the points of convergence

[49] It should be noted that Liu I-ch'ing's account of the "new tales" covered a period from the late Han to the time of Hsieh Ling-yün 謝靈運 (385–433), who was contemporary with T'ao Ch'ien. For a discussion of the world of the *Shih-shuo hsin-yü*, see Mather, *New Account of Tales of the World*, pp. xiii-xxxvi.

[50] J. D. Frodsham, "The Origin of Chinese Nature Poetry," *Asia Major*, new series, vol. 8, pt. 1 (1960), 68–103.

between poetic vision and styles of thought in the Wei-Chin period, it is vitally important to note that my emphasis on the synchronic resonance of seemingly discrete patterns of mental activities must not be construed as an implicit critique of the diachronic mode of analysis. Actually it is historically significant and intellectually fruitful to study the social, cultural, and ethico-religious continuity between the unified Han kingdom and the period of the disunity. In the history of poetry, for instance, the tradition of the so-called "Nineteen Ancient Poems" 古詩十九首 of the late Han, an artistic expression remarkably different from the constructive outlook of the *fu* 賦, may have provided impetus for the development of the *shih* in the Wei-Chin. A similar observation can also be made of *yüeh-fu* 樂府, the poetic genre of folk songs and ballads in the Han style.

With this caveat in mind, let us explore the salient features of the shared ground between the disposition of philosophical inquiry and procedures of poetic knowing. Having established a linkage between ontological reflection of the Tao and the conceptual apparatus underlying the art of personality appraisal at the epistemological level, we may find it fruitful to ask the following question: given that the ontological turn was a defining characteristic of the Wei-Chin style of thought, what kind of poetic vision would be considered most appropriate? The question is deliberately arbitrary, for there is no reason to assume that ontology and poetry in the same era must be subsumed under the same epistemological system. However, it seems likely that a question so posed can yield a more definitive answer, which hopefully will be of some significance for scholars of Chinese poetry. My observations, then, consist of a series of assumptions.

(1) *Reality and Actuality*. The shift of overall philosophical focus from cosmology to ontology must have exerted considerable influence on the form and nature of the emerging poetic vision. If we assume that the poet, in the same discourse as the philosopher, takes an active interest in probing the dimensions of a thing which constitute, as it were, its reality, it is unlikely that he will be satisfied with mere description. Surely, a sensitive poet, skilled in the art of depiction, is impelled to note, often in vivid detail, what the thing actually is. However, if he is at all mindful of the depth of his

aesthetic insight, he is also impelled to fathom what a thing is in itself, not only what a thing appears to be. The famous anecdote about the great painter Ku K'ai-chih 顧愷之 (341–402) is revealing in this connection. The reason he was so apprehensive about putting the final touches on his subject's eyes after the portraiture had been otherwise perfectly executed was his deep concern for the spirit of the person. Since the eyes were thought to "communicate the spirit" 傳神, they had to be approached with utter seriousness.[51] The idea of breathing vitality into a physical form, as in the proverb of bringing the painted dragon to life by putting in the pupils of its eyes, 畫龍點睛 is a variation on the theme.[52] Of course the poet can put the dichotomy of form and spirit into practice without being critically aware that he is doing so. However, if this quest for the real as well as the actual is taken for granted, then the inner psychic push of the poet himself and the perceived gravitational pull from the center of the thing will enable him to realize certain authentic possibilities and, at the same time, will compel him to give up several other, attractive alternatives.

(2) *Unearthing and Constructing*. One rejected alternative, which is well developed in some other poetic traditions and seems to have been in vogue at the time Han cosmological thinking was dominant, is the constructing mode. An outstanding example of this mode is the fully matured *fu* style with descriptions of hunting parks, national capitals, and the imaginary marvels with which grandiose scenes are embroidered.[53] To be sure, *fu* continued to develop in the Wei-Chin, but another poetic undercurrent emerged and gradually became the main stream of literary sensitivity: the *shih* 詩, especially the five-character version of it. It would be far-fetched to suggest that the ontological turn actually prompted the germination and eventual fruition of this particular

[51] For this fascinating account in Ku K'ai-chih's biography, see *Chin-shu* 晉書, in *Erh-shih-ssu shih* 二十四史 (Chin-ling shu-chü, 1866–1870), biography 62, 92:25a.

[52] For the historical reference to this widely known proverb, see the story of the famed painter in the Liang 梁 dynasty (502–557) legend, Chang Seng-yu 張僧繇, in Morahashi Tetsuiji 諸橋轍次, *Dai Kan-Wa jiten* 大漢和字典 (Tokyo: Taishukan shoden, 1955–1960), vol. 7, p. 1117.

[53] See Liu Ta-chieh 劉大杰, *Chung-kuo wen-hsüeh fa-chan shih* 中國文學發展史 (rpt. Taipei: Chung-hua shu-chü, 1957), pp. 110–116.

style. However, it is important to note that in the atmosphere of profound learning, "the literary form best adapted to descriptive word painting"[54] of the *fu* was no longer adequate. The communal effort to bring from concealment the deep truth of life, to uncover the hidden reality of things, and to recover the naturalness and spontaneity of the human mind required a lyric mode of self-disclosure. The need to build a gigantic structure so that men can communicate with gods was replaced by a desire to listen to one's inner voice, the rhythm of nature, indeed the music of Heaven. It was probably not accidental that the lute, like the five-character verse, became a felicitous instrument for expressing Wei-Chin lyricism. As Hsi K'ang testifies, "In truth those people who are not of a free and detached disposition cannot find enjoyment in lute music. Those who are not profound and serene cannot dwell with it. Those who are not broad-minded cannot ungrudgingly give themselves over to it. Those who are not of the utmost refinement cannot understand its deep significance."[55]

(3) *Self and Other*. It is remarkable that the communal effort to bring to light the profound meaning of the ineffable Tao in the Wei-Chin era actually took the form of commentaries on the *Book of Changes*, the *Lao Tzu*, and the *Chuang Tzu*. These thinkers who were instrumental in creating a new style of philosophizing after the collapse of the Han dynasty have often been characterized as iconoclastic. The common impression is that they, in response to Eastern Han moralism and scholasticism, rejected the mundane world of tradition, government, family, and ritual in order to express themselves as unrestrained, independent, and autonomous "free thinkers."[56] The very fact that they chose commentary as their style of philosophizing indicates that their inconoclasm was a complex one. Indeed, the disclosure of the Tao through the interpretation of ancient texts with a view to recovering the lost wisdom of the sages involves a sophisticated hermeneutic procedure, of which a salient feature is its non-individualistic orientation. The Wei-Chin thinkers were not engaged in thinking isolated private

[54] Frodsham, "Chinese Nature Poetry," p. 77.

[55] Van Gulik, *Hsi K'ang and His Poetical Essay on the Lute* (Tokyo: Sophia University, 1969), p. 112.

[56] Liu Ta-chieh, *Chung-kuo wen-hsüeh*, pp. 162–178.

thoughts. To quote Kuo Hsiang again, "The 'I' cannot produce things and things cannot produce the 'I.' The 'I' is self-existent. Because it is so by itself, we call it natural." The naturalness and spontaneity of their thought, strictly speaking, did not come from an imitation of nature. Actually the mimetic approach was alien to their world view. The strength of their imaginative power came from an inner source. And, as the three sacred texts make clear, the source is an intrinsic consequence of purifying the mind. Lest this be construed as an extreme form of asceticism, the purification of the mind here presupposes the value of communal participation. The literary writers gathered around the Ts'ao family,[57] the Seven Worthies of the Bamboo Grove,[58] and the coterie of poets in the Orchid Pavilion recorded by Wang Hsi-chih 王羲之 (321–379)[59] all suggest the centrality of dialogue, conversation, and discussion, not to mention wine, food, and music, in the cultivation of a Wei-Chin personality. It was through symbolic interchange that the thinker experienced his inner self and the meaningfulness of the other. It is difficult to imagine that the Wei-Chin poet was not part of the same rhetorical situation.

(4) *Word and Meaning*. If the poet is motivated to capture the real rather than simply the actual, to fathom the internal structure instead of the external manifestation, and to disclose his selfhood through an experiential encounter with the other, he cannot accomplish his purpose by assuming the role of an outside observer or a disinterested narrator. He can, of course, cultivate his "free and detached disposition" so that he can appreciate empathetically the order of things as it is. However, unlike the philosopher who explains, the poet expresses. The act of imaginative recreation of the poet is inevitably expressive. Thus, the poet uses his precious diction not simply to depict but to suggest, to direct, to inspire, and, if he deems fit, to shock. He appeals not to persuasive argumentation but to the internal resonance of like-minded people. The words he uses are intended to produce a compelling impression of reality, not the reality that is grasped by the ontologists as the all-

[57] See Hu Kuo-jui 胡國瑞, *Wei-Chin Nan-Pei Ch'ao wen-hsüeh-shih* 魏晉南北朝文學史 (Shanghai: Wen-i ch'u-pan-she, 1980), pp. 1–28.

[58] Ho Ch'i-min, *Chu-lin ch'i-hsien yen-chiu*, pp. 1–15.

[59] *Chin-shu*, biography 50, 80: 5a–b.

embracing fullness of the Tao, but its disclosure in a certain mood, time, place, or personality. This reminds us of the dictionary meaning of poetry as evocation.[60] What the poet evokes, in the Wei-Chin sense of lyricism, far from being an unrestrained enthusiasm for a passing phenomenon, is a penetrating insight into the enduring pattern of things. The words, so long as they are pointers to the poetic vision of such a pattern, are a necessary instrument for disclosing the Tao. As soon as the Tao is revealed and the meaning understood, they must fade away so that the ineffable Tao can be experienced directly.

(5) *Whole and Part.* The paradox that the Tao is ineffable but can be experienced directly is predicated on the belief that there is always an internal resonance between human beings and the natural order of things. The idea of an ontological alienation of humanity from the Creator, on the one hand, and the rest of the world, on the other, is totally absent; indeed, it is not even a rejected possibility. The Wei-Chin poet, accordingly, may have felt alienated from political power and influence as many of them did because of the precariousness of official life in a period of disunity, but he was never a stranger on earth amidst mountains, rivers, pastoral scenes, relatives, and friends. There was a niche in this world for him to exist, to live, to experience, and to explore. He had a home that he could return to and call his own. From such a base, he cultivated a panoramic view of his surrounding landscape. He did not suffer from the tunnel vision of an isolated, often frustrated, selfish hedonist. The wine and music that he enjoyed were certainly sensuous pleasures, but they also helped him to taste and hear the Tao in a manner that the vulgar scholar-officials, obsessed with the pursuit of fame, wealth, or power, could not at all experience. He was thus conscious of his intrinsic worth as a connoisseur of the higher and deeper truth of life. Yet, his sense of personal dignity was not simply built upon his contempt for those who failed to transcend "the wind and dust" of politics. It was rather a real commitment to a style of spiritual self-cultivation that prompted him to see a wider

[60] In the sense that the word "poetry" can be taken to mean: "a quality that stirs the imagination or gives a sense of heightened and more meaningful existence," *Webster's Third New International Dictionary*, p. 1749.

horizon beyond the imperial court and bureaucracy.[61] What the Wei-Chin poet symbolizes is not escape from politics but the courage to reject the fragmented and sometimes humiliating world of partial existence in order to live fully as a whole person.

(6) *Center and Periphery*. It is true that the poet, unlike the sage, cannot embody the Tao in its all-embracing fullness. However, even though he cannot experience the Tao in the same profundity as the sage can, he articulates the subtlety of the Tao holistically through concrete symbolization. The ability of the poet to do so, like the sage in this case, emanates from a penetrating insight into the inner structure of a thing, be it natural scenery, social condition, or human feeling. The procedure, comparable to the idea of hitting the target on mark, mentioned above, is to embrace the whole by first grasping what the heart of the matter is. To emerge from the core, as it were, involves total immersion radically different from detached observation. The detached observer may choose to move cautiously from the periphery to the center, whereas the lyric poet of the Wei-Chin style must live through the center before he can make sense out of the whole thing, for the relevance and the meaningfulness of the periphery depends on the experiential encounter. Thomé H. Fang 方東美, in his *Creativity in Man and Nature*, characterizes Ts'ao Chih 曹植 (192–232) and Juan Chi 阮籍 (210–263), together with the earlier Ch'ü Yüan 屈原 (343–277 B.C.) and the later Li Po 李白 (701–762), as fellow poets in the Taoist chorus: "Situated at the acme of the Celestial, they could gaze distinterestedly upon the stratified world below in which the tragi-comic figures are involved in the repressive lapse into folly and wit, illusion and truth, appearance and reality, all falling off from the consumate Perfection, Truth and Reality."[62] However, it seems that the "acme of the Celestial" at which they are situated is not out there in the sky, but, like the "music of Heaven," exists here and now at the center of our lived experience.

(7) *Time and Space*. Despite the seemingly exalted mood in which

[61] See Hsü Fu-kuan, "Wei-Chin hsüan-hsüeh yü shan-shui-hua te hsing-ch'i" 魏晉玄學與山水畫的興起, in his *Chung-kuo i-shu ching-shen* 中國藝術精神 (Taichung: Tunghai University, 1966), pp. 225–236.

[62] Thomé H. Fang, *Creativity in Man and Nature* (Taipei: Linking Publishing Co., 1980), p. 131.

the Wei-Chin poetic personages observed the boisterous world around, they were very much an integral part of the social scene. Ch'en Yin-k'o's 陳寅恪 brilliant study of the spiritual orientation of T'ao Ch'ien 陶潛 (365–?427) is a case in point.[63] We need not subscribe to Ch'en's distinction between old and new theories of naturalness in his discussion of the philosophical transition from the Seven Worthies to T'ao Ch'ien, but his analysis of the tripartite division of form 形, shadow 影, and spirit 神 in T'ao's thought is most instructive. According to Ch'en, what T'ao envisions in this threefold conversation is a double negation with a view to a new poetic vision of reality.[64] The spirit so conceived offers a transcending perspective going beyond the longevity of the body as symbolized by the form, and the immortality of the soul as symbolized by the shadow. Since the spirit is totally fused with the Tao, it is no longer attached to a spatial form or to a temporal soul. Rather, it fully participates in the "great transformation" 大化:

> Too much thinking harms my life;
> Just surrender to the cycle of things,
> Give yourself to the waves of the Great
>   Change
> Neither happy nor yet afraid.
> And when it is time to go, then simply go
> Without any unnecessary fuss.[65]

> 甚念傷吾生
> 正宜委運去
> 縱浪大化中
> 不喜亦不懼
> 應盡便須盡
> 無復獨多慮

Commenting on this poem, Richard Mather notes that this kind of naturalness created for T'ao Ch'ien "a heightened awareness of the transiency of life" and that "this is the price man pays for his transcendence over his own naturalness."[66] Indeed, what T'ao the poet symbolizes is more than "a stoical acceptance of life and death";[67] it is also the silent appreciation of the way we are:

[63] Ch'en Yin-k'o 陳寅恪, "T'ao Yüan-ming chih ssu-hsiang yü ch'ing-t'an chih kuan-hsi" 陶淵明之思想與淸談之關係, in *Ch'en Yin-k'o hsien-sheng lun-wen chi* 陳寅恪先生論文集, 2 vols. (Taipei: San-jen hsing, 1974), vol. 1, pp. 309–333.

[64] *Ibid.*, pp. 326–330.

[65] For this translation, see James R. Hightower, *The Poetry of T'ao Ch'ien* (Oxford: Clarendon Press, 1970), p. 44.

[66] Richard B. Mather, "The Controversy over Conformity and Naturalism during the Six Dynasties," *History of Religions* o, nos. 2–3 (1969–1970), 180.

[67] James R. Hightower, *The Poetry of T'ao Ch'ien*, p. 45.

So I manage to accept my lot until the ultimate beginning. 聊乘化以歸盡
Rejoicing in Heaven's command, what is there to doubt?[68] 樂夫天命復奚疑

In light of the seven points above, we may propose that the paradigmatic Wei-Chin poet prefers an ontological unearthing to a cosmological constructing, for his sense of reality prompts him to try to understand what a thing is in itself rather than what a thing merely appears to be. In other words, he is not satisfied with a neutral description of the perceived object, no matter how igenious it may turn out to be; he needs to "embody the thing" 體物[69] through total participation. The value he cherishes, then, is not descriptive naturalism, if it is understood to be a detailed portrayal of a natural object. Indeed, it is not the art of portraiture but the art of metaphor and metonymy that inspires the poet to articulate his inner feelings. He responds to an object only after he has been deeply "moved by the thing" 感物. He is moved by things often because of an overflow of emotion and meaning, resulting from a concern about his existential situation, a thought about a friend far away, or a longing for a different mode of life. The perennial human dilemma of affective surplus and cognitive deficit is particularly pronounced in the Wei-Chin poet. His heightened self-identity and penetrating insight into the flux and reflux of the world around him make him critically aware of the inadequacy of the conceptual apparatus to give an account of what he really feels and means. At the same time, he also comes to the realization that to optimize the power of precious diction is, next to silent appreciation, the second best way of experiencing the Tao from within. For him, to write poetry is not to give new reality to things but to evoke a common sense of sympathetic vibration among like-minded people. There is no ultimate reason for him to write; nor is there any social pressure that urges him to write. Indeed, he may choose not to, but he does.

[68] *Ibid.*, p. 270.

[69] The *locus classicus* for this seems to be the fifteenth chapter of the *Chung-yung* 中庸: "They form the substance of all things and nothing can be without them" 體物而不可遺. See Wing-tsit Chan, *Source Book*, p. 102. It should be noted that Chan's translation quoted above is based on Chu Hsi's interpretation.

François Cheng

Some Reflections on Chinese Poetic Language and Its Relation to Chinese Cosmology

Translated from French by Stephen Owen

It is our habit in the West, when we study Chinese poetry, to put the emphasis on its content (themes, genres, historical and philosophical references, etc.). Should we happen to approach the question of forms, we are usually content to enumerate the complement of prosodic rules fixed by tradition. It seems to me that the time has come to consider this poetry as a language in its own right and to ask the significance implicit in its basic structure. Using the assumptions of modern semiology, according to which all formal elements of a language are significant, we find that those formal elements reveal hidden significations not always shown by their explicit content.

We know that, following several centuries of intense creativity, Chinese poetry, as a mature language, attained under the T'ang a high degree of complexity and freedom. Exploring all the possibilities of an ideographic writing system, which offered astonishing possibilities of combination, T'ang poets uncovered in their language important deviations from ordinary language (deviations of a kind rarely attained in other languages). In spite of this freedom, their language was never given up entirely to arbitrariness or to fantasy: it operated through highly determined intentions. It goes without saying that a thorough knowledge of the structures of this language comes only from a systematic study of the full complement of critical and lexicographical works. Nevertheless, certain observations permit me to assert that these structures are based on fundamental laws of Chinese thought. Moreover, there is nothing at all astonishing in this fact: poetic language is the semiotic order par excellence, serving as the model for other methods of signification. Thus it is quite natural that the poetic language take responsibility for the most essential elements of the thought from which it issues.

As an initial approach and as a possible framework for reflection, I propose to take up certain components common to both Chinese poetic language and to Chinese cosmology (or world view) and to briefly indicate the conditions through which they function. We will see that one of the most striking traits of Chinese thought lies in the unfailing correspondence between the material universe and the universe of signs.

I should like to indicate at the outset that Chinese cosmology is not the subject of this short essay. From the ancient *I ching* 易經 or the *Book of Changes* to the works of Neo-Confucian thinkers in later imperial history, reflections on cosmology constitute an immense domain in itself. To discuss so vast a subject in any depth is obviously beyond the scope and capability of the present study.[1] I wish only to make use of the following three sets of general concepts that are important in traditional Chinese cosmological thinking: Emptiness-Fullness (*hsü-shih* 虛實), Yin-Yang (陰陽), and Heaven-Earth-Man (*t'ien-ti-jen* 天地人). My attempt is to examine the organic relations among these well-known ideas in order to illuminate some distinctive features of the language of classical Chinese poetry. Having thus stated my limited purpose, I shall now begin with a passage from the famous forty-second chapter of the *Tao te ching* 道德經 which well summarizes a concept generally accepted by the Chinese:

The Primordial Way engendered the One;
One engendered the Two;
Two engendered the Three;
Three engendered the ten thousand beings.
The ten thousand beings left Yin on their backs

[1] A concise discussion of the distinctive Chinese world view can be found in Frederick W. Mote, "The Cosmological Gulf between China and the West," in *Transition and Permanence: Chinese History and Culture*, ed. David C. Buxbaum and Frederick W. Mote (Festschrift Hsiao Kung-ch'üan, Hong Kong: Cathay Press, 1972), pp. 3–21.

And embrace Yang to their bosoms.
Harmony is born in the Emptiness of mediating Breath. . . .[2]

To simplify this greatly: the Primordial Way (Tao) is conceived as Supreme Emptiness; from this emanates the One, which is nothing less than the primal Breath (*yüan-ch'i* 元氣). This in turn engenders Two, embodied in the two vital Breaths, Yin and Yang. By their interaction, Yin and Yang govern and animate the ten thousand beings. But between the Two and the ten thousand beings we always find the Three.

According to the Taoist tradition, the Three represents the combination of the vital Breaths, Yin and Yang, and the *ch'ung-ch'i* 冲氣, the "mediating Breath" or "mediating Emptiness." This "mediating Emptiness," which comes from Supreme Emptiness, whence it derives all its power, is necessary to the functioning of the Yin-Yang pairing. It is this which draws and wins over the two vital Breaths in the reciprocal process of Becoming; without it, Yin and Yang would remain formless substances. This tripartite relation gives birth to and serves as the model for the ten thousand beings. This mediating Emptiness, which resides in the Yin-Yang pairing, resides equally in the heart of all things: as it breathes the Breaths and life into all things, it maintains them in relation to Supreme Emptiness, thereby permitting them access to Becoming, to transformation, and to unity.[3] Thus Chinese thought finds itself dominated by a double and crossing movement, which can be

[2] Cf. D. C. Lau, *Lao Tzu: Tao Te Ching* (Baltimore: Penguin Books, 1963), p. 103. A text of the Chinese original can be found in Ma Hsü-lun 馬叙倫, *Lao Tzu chiao-ku* 老子校詁 (Hong Kong: T'ai-p'ing shu-chü, 1965), pp. 128–129.

[3] In regard to the interpretation of the Three in the Taoist tradition, beyond the explanation of Huai-nan Tzu 淮南子 and Wang Pi 王弼, which both have roughly the same sense, let me cite the following three comments, taken respectively from Ssu-ma Kuang's 司馬光 *Tao-te-lun shu-yao* 道德論述要, quoted in *Pai-ta-chia p'ing-chu Lao Tzu Tao te ching* 百大家評注老子道德經, ed. Hsiang-i Lao-jen 湘綺老人 (N.p.: Te-chi shu-chü, 1924), vol. 2, p. 4a; from Fan Ying-yüan's 范應元 *Lao Tzu Tao-te-ching ku-pen chi-chu* 老子道德經古本集注, in *Lao Tzu chi-ch'eng ch'u-pien* 老子集成初編, ed. Yen Ling-feng 嚴靈峯 (Taipei: I-wen yin-shu-kuan, 1965), vol. 60, p. 11b; and from Wei Yüan's 魏源 *Lao Tzu pen-i* 老子本義, in *Lao Tzu chi ch'eng hsü-pien* 老子集成續編, ed. Yen Ling-feng (Taipei: I-wen yin-shu-kuan, 1970), vol. 62, p. 11b.

Ssu-ma Kuang: "道生一, 自無而有; 一生二, 分陰分陽; 二生三, 陰陽交而生和; 三生萬物, 和氣合而生物."

represented on two axes: a vertical axis symbolizing the coming and going between Emptiness and Fullness; and a horizontal axis, the place of interaction in the very heart of fullness, of the two complementary poles which are Yin and Yang, and likewise the place from which all things come, including Man, the microcosm par excellence which incorporates all.

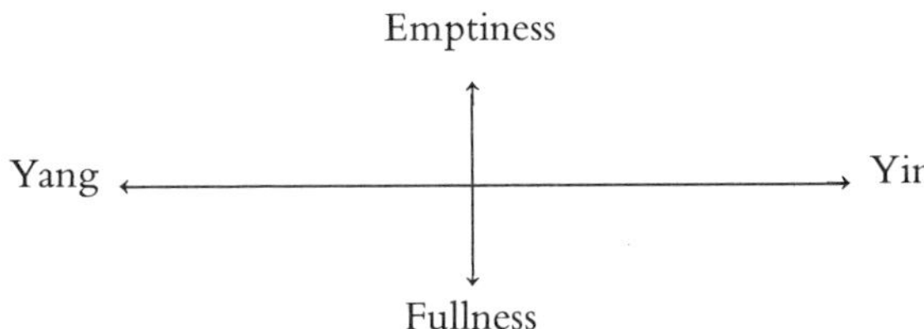

Related to the concept of Three and the position of Man is another idea fundamental to Chinese cosmology: the *San-ts'ai* 三才, the Three Entities of Heaven, Earth, and Man. This idea essentially came from the Confucian tradition. It first appeared in the "Shuo-kua" 說卦 or "Discussion of the Trigrams" in the *I ching*. Later in the Han dynasty (206 B.C. to A.D. 220), it received further development by the thinker Tung Chung-shu 董仲舒 (ca. 179 to ca. 104 B.C.) and became a very important idea in Chinese thought. It should be noted that this concept and the Taoist idea of Three (Emptiness-Yin-Yang) are intimately related. Heaven represents Yang and Earth Yin. As to Man, he possesses in spirit the virtues of Heaven and Earth and embraces in his heart the quality of Emptiness. Here Man is raised to an exceptional dignity, for he participates as a third member in the creative process of the Cosmos. In no way is his role a passive one: if Heaven and Earth are endowed with intentionality, with a will, Man—through his spirit (*hsin* 心), his feelings (*ch'ing* 情), and his desires (*yü* 欲 or *i* 意)—makes his contribution to the process of Becoming, which never

---

Fan Ying-yüan: "道一而已; 故曰: 道生一也; 猶言易有太極也. 一之中便有動靜, 動曰陽, 靜曰陰, 故曰: 一生二也... 一與二便是三, 故曰: 二生三也, 其實一也... 自三以往, 生生不窮, 故曰: 三生萬物也."

Wei Yüan: "一謂氣, 二謂陰與陽, 三謂陰與陽會合之氣, 即所謂冲氣也, 萬物負陰而抱陽, 冲氣以爲和, 即申說三生萬物也."

ceases to move toward Divine Essence (*shen* 神), for which Supreme Emptiness is the guarantor or trustee.

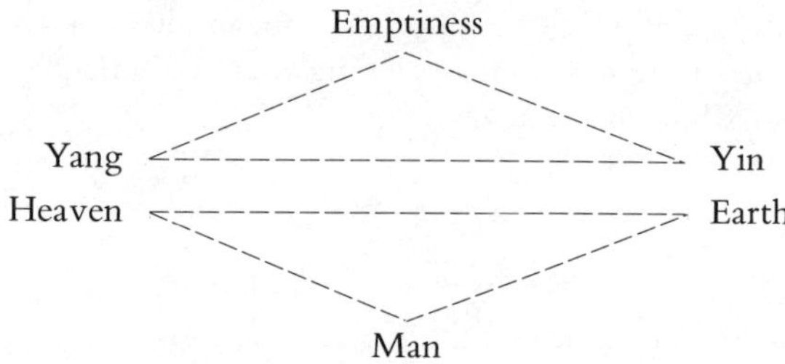

Emptiness-Fullness, Yin-Yang, and Heaven-Earth-Man thus constitute the three relational and hierarchical axes around which Chinese cosmology is organized. It is interesting to show that Chinese poetic language, in exploring the mystery of the universe of signs, does not fail to structure itself, in its three constituent levels, along these axes. The lexical level is governed by the Emptiness-Fullness pairing, just as the syntactic level is governed by the Yin-Yang pairing; and, finally, for the symbolic level, the combination of images rests on the triad Heaven-Earth-Man.

Although the limitations of space permit us to give only a summary treatment of each level, we will observe, level by level, the functioning of this language. Let me point out that in my work *Chinese Poetic Writing* I have studied this problem in a more complete way.[4] I would also like to take note of other important works which approach the same question, notably those of Yu-kung Kao.

I. The Lexical Level (Emptiness-Fullness)

On this level the notion of Emptiness-Fullness is rendered by the division of all Chinese words into those words called "full" (or "solid") and those words called "empty"; this division lies at the

[4] François Cheng, *Chinese Poetic Writing*, trans. Donald A. Riggs and Jerome P. Seaton (Bloomington: Indiana University Press, 1982), pp. 3–95.

center of traditional Chinese grammatical thought.[5] Indeed, we know that Chinese grammar, as it was conceived in ancient China, was of an essentially lexicographical order. It was through a highly refined lexicography that syntactic and modal rules were determined. This lexicography was based on the distinction between two grand categories of words: *hsü-tzu* 虛字, "empty" words, and *shih-tzu* 實字, "full" words. Later, other categories were proposed. Thus from the Sung there was the opposition of *ssu-tzu* 死字, "dead" words, and *huo-tzu* 活字, "living" words. And in the Ch'ing there was the distinction between *ching-tzu* 靜字, "words of stasis," and *tung-tzu* 動字, "dynamic words." These later distinctions actually constitute subcategories in relation to the two larger categories (empty and full words).[6]

It is no easy matter to give a precise definition to each of these categories. We observe differences in the ways in which lexicographers have delimited these classes of words over the centuries. However, it is possible to propose conditionally the following

[5] Concerning the relationship between the notion of Emptiness-Fullness in language and in philosophy, the Ch'ing scholar Yüan Jen-lin 袁仁林 (fl. late seventeenth-eighteenth century) wrote an important work entitled *Hsü-tzu shuo* 虛字說 (Interpretations of Empty Words), which attempted to integrate the theories of previous scholars with his own reflections on the nature of "empty words." The following remark may serve as an illustration of Yüan Jen-lin's reflections on the subject: "The art of using 'empty words' is not the invention of rhetoricians. It is a known fact that within the universe, Emptiness and Fullness are always interdependent, Substance and Function are inseparable, and the most dynamic movement usually takes place within supreme stillness" (虛用活用, 亦非修辭者勉强杜撰如此, 蓋天地間虛實恒相倚, 體用不相離, 至靜之中而有至動之理). See Yen I-p'ing 嚴一萍, *Hsü-tzu shuo*, in *Pai-pu ts'ung-shu chi-ch'eng* 百部叢書集成 (rpt. Taipei: I-wen yin-shu-kuan, 1967), pp. 33a and 33b.

[6] It is neither possible to recall here the history of Chinese lexicography nor feasible to cite all the lexicographical works, which would come to at least forty titles. Even if we restrict ourselves to works on *shih-tzu* and *hsü-tzu*, we have to include many commentaries on the classics, annotations on literary texts, works of criticism, as well as specialized studies on these two categories of words. Let me just point out that several modern Chinese linguists have studied the subject, notably Wang Li-ta 王立達 in his *Chung-kuo yü-fa-hsüeh hsiao-shih* 中國語法學小史 (Peking: Shang-wu yin-shu-kuan, 1963); Cheng Tien 鄭奠 and Mai Mei-ch'iao 麥梅翹 in their *Chung-kuo yü-fa-hsüeh tzu-liao hui-pien* 中國語法學資料彙編 (Peking: Chung-hua shu-chü, 1965); and Wang Li 王力 in his *Han-yü shih-kao* 漢語史稿 (Peking: K'o-hsüeh ch'u-pan-she, 1958).

definitions, which constitute a kind of generally accepted consensus:

Full words: nouns and eventually certain verbs.
Empty words: personal pronouns, prepositions, conjunctions, most verbs, adverbs, and modal particles.

Living words and dead words belong principally to the class of empty words: the former are comprised of verbs of action, while the latter unite verbs of quality, prepositions, conjunctions, and particles. As for words of stasis and dynamic words, they are situated astride full words and empty words; the opposition between them is simply that which separates nouns and verbs.

One may say in an inclusive way that Chinese lexicographers distinguished two kinds of words: some designated beings and the things themselves (nouns), while the others expressed the actions of the former (verbs, adverbs) or indicated their internal relations (pronouns, prepositions, conjunctions, and particles). The latter, restricted in number but whose use involved great subtlety, held the larger part of lexicographers' attention.

For the purposes here, our attention is naturally directed to the implications of empty words in poetry, implications largely analyzed in the innumerable *shih-hua* 詩話 ("Remarks on Poetry") or in other critical works. That which most interested the writers of *shih-hua* was the link between empty words and the quality of style. In the Chinese rhetorical tradition, good sentence style ought to take into account an equilibrium between full words and empty words. Only such an equilibrium assured the perfect operation of *ch'i-yün* 氣韻, "rhythmic breath," which was supposed to animate sentences. Let us make clear, above all, that this did not involve seeking a mechanical equilibrium between the two types of words. According to the nature of their content, certain sentences might be more heavily charged with full words (sentences which were more compact, more imagistic, or more affirmative), while others might be more heavily charged with empty words (sentences which were more wandering, more allusive, or more tentative). In poetry these studies attained an extreme refinement, especially in regard to the subject of *tzu-yen* 字眼, the "eye word" of a verse, in which the use of a full word or an empty word was never a matter of indifference.

It also happened that poets would replace a full word with an empty word in order to vary the play of Fullness and Emptiness and, above all, to introduce a dimension of depth which might shake ever so slightly the too confident certainty of the language.

But, beyond stylistic concerns, other aspects held the attention of poets. The form of Chinese poetry is extremely concise, and it often happened that the poet would omit the empty words in a verse, leaving the "true emptiness" in between the words; cadence assured the linking between words and permitted the reader, as he recited the verse, to reestablish the unrepresented empty words. In this regard we may cite a passage of the *Hsü-tzu-shuo* 虛字說 or *Interpretations of "Empty Words"* by Yüan Jen-lin 袁仁林 (fl. late seventeenth to early eighteenth century) of the Ch'ing dynasty, which describes this practice quite well:

> In its economy of form, poetry is called upon to dispense with empty words. But in context it is not necessary that they actually appear. Without being present, they are nevertheless there; one may articulate them or not articulate them, and it is precisely this which makes for the mysterious charm of a poem. The same is true for a very concise prose text. Formerly Master Ch'eng [Ch'eng I 程頤 (1033–1107) of the Sung] pleased himself by adding one or two empty words when he recited a poem, and the whole poem came alive, suddenly articulated and charged with internal transformations. Master Chu [Chu Hsi 朱熹 (1130–1200) of the Sung] proceeded in the same manner when he explained a poem. Thus the [ancient] poet was thrifty with empty words in his poems; it was for the reader to restore them, in punctuating them for chanting. The art of empty words in poetry is not so much in their actual use as in their absence, which preserves all their vital power.[7]

Thus there exists in Chinese poetry differing degrees of emptiness: a lesser degree which manifests itself in the judicious use of empty words in the heart of a sentence, and a more profund degree which reveals itself in the very absence of empty words. To be sure,

[7] Yüan Jen-lin, *Hsü-tzu shuo*, p. 32a.

this absence has the effect of giving rise to ambiguities, but these serve the designs of poets. For these ambiguities not only act to shatter the narrow sense of the words; they establish another relation between the words. Breaking the linearity of unitary meaning in the sentence, they introduce a process of reversibility or of reciprocal becoming between the subject and object, between here and elsewhere, and, finally, between what is said and what is unsaid. Here are some examples (necessarily superficial) of the omission of empty words:

(a) *Omission of personal pronoun.* This is systematic in regulated verse. It is this which creates a language of two simultaneously present dimensions, one in which the poet describes the external world, and the other in which he evokes his interior world. As an example, let us cite two lines by Tu Fu 杜甫 (712–770):

Expanded breast where are born clouds in layers;	盪胸生層雲
Eyes wide open where penetrate the returning birds.[8]	決眥入歸鳥

Thanks to the absence of personal pronouns, the poet speaks of the mountain, all the while giving the impression of speaking of himself. These two lines marvellously evoke a state of fusion in which the man and the mountain become one.

(b) *Omission of conjunction or term of comparison.* The following lines from Li Po's 李白 (701–762) "Farewell to a Friend" 送友人 illustrate this form of poetic omission:

Drifting clouds mood of the wanderer;	浮雲遊子意
Setting sun feelings of an old friend.[9]	落日故人情

In these two lines, we see that the absence of terms of comparison, such as "like" or "as," permits the poet to avoid rigidly distinguishing the things compared ("mood of the wanderer" and "feelings of an old friend") and the things to which they are compared ("drifting clouds" and "setting sun"). The result is that each of the two

[8] Kao Pu-ying 高步瀛, *T'ang Sung shih chü-yao* 唐宋詩舉要, 2 vols. (rpt. Taipei: I-wen yin-shu-kuan, 1960), vol. 1, p. 41.

[9] *Ibid.*, vol. 2, p. 446.

lines allows two simultaneous interpretations. Thus the first line might be interpreted as the "mood of the wanderer is like the drifting clouds" or "the drifting clouds have the mood of the wanderer." Similarly, the second line can be rendered as either "feelings of an old friend are in the image of the setting sun," or "the setting sun has the feelings of an old friend." In reality, through these lines so clearly marked by circularity, the poet doubtlessly intends to reconstitute the scene of parting, in which the elements of nature are not perceived simply as external decorations (or as terms of comparison) but as participating intimately in the human drama.

(c) *Omission of preposition.* These two lines, taken from a famous poem "Night, Flowers, and Moon on the River in Spring" 春江花月夜 by Chang Jo-hsü 張若虛 (fl. late seventh-early eighth century), show how the author used poetic omission to tell the story of the separation of two lovers on a moonlit night.

Who then this lonely night in his boat?	誰家今夜扁舟子
Where then longing, the pavilion in moonlight?[10]	何處相思明月樓

In this poem, while the man in his boat gets ever farther away on the river, the woman remains in her pavilion in the moonlight. In the second line the poet has taken advantage of the formal concision to avoid using a preposition ("for" or "in") after the verb "longing." This omission gives grounds for the different translations on the part of western translators. It may be "Where is the man who longs for the pavilion in the moonlight?" or "Where is the woman who longs in her pavilion in the moonlight?" We know that in reality the two lovers are thinking of one another. Thus, without the poet's giving precise external definition to the "mediating Emptiness," it rises up in the middle of the sentence, once again drawing the two principal components into a relation of reciprocity and union.

Of course, it is not a question here of omitting empty words in any way possible: one would risk falling into a contrary excess,

[10] Shen Te-ch'ien 沈德潛, *T'ang-shih pieh-ts'ai-chi* 唐詩別裁集, 2 vols. (Peking: Chung-hua shu-chü, 1975), vol. 1, *chüan* 5, pp. 158–159.

overburdening the line with full words. It is also necessary to take rhythm into account, which, just as it separates the words, suggests the subtle rapport which the words maintain between themselves. We will cite an extreme case in a line by Li Shang-yin 李商隱 (813?–858), taken from his poem "The Goddess Ch'ang O" 嫦娥, a line composed entirely of solid words but which nevertheless gives the impression of breathing, as if pierced by empty spaces:

> Emerald sea, azure sky, night, night, heart.[11] 碧海青天夜夜心

In this line (translated here word for word), through an ingenious arrangement of words traced on an essential cadence, the poet creates a time and a space in their greatest divergence. And the final word, though nominal, embodies a living heart (the moon), whose beating seems to spread in endless echoes.

II. The Syntactic Level (Yin-Yang)

On the preceding lexical level we have already observed how the functioning of empty words reveals certain syntactic aspects within a sentence. We are now going to approach a highly original form within Chinese poetry, a form placed under the sign of the Yin-Yang pairing, which works very strongly on the syntactic structure of sentences: parallelism. This form holds such a central position that *lü-shih* 律詩, which constitutes the foundation of classical Chinese poetry, has been envisaged as a dialectic between parallel and non-parallel couplets.

Parallelism is a good illustration of our assertion that in poetry all form is significant. Constructed in a two-part mode, at once opposed and complementary, parallelism cannot be rendered by a translation that contents itself with paraphrasing the two lines. Here the place of every word is defined both within the line and between the lines, thus acquiring its own particular kind of signification. Here is an example taken from the *lü-shih* "Villa on Chung-nan Mountain" 終南別業 by Wang Wei 王維 (701–761).[12] Its theme is a mystic excursion of the poet in nature.

[11] Kao Pu-ying, *T'ang Sung shih chü-yao*, vol. 2, p. 822.

[12] *Ibid.*, vol. 2, p. 427.

行	到	水	窮	處
walk	reach	water	be exhausted	place
坐	看	雲	起	時
sit	look-at	clouds	rise	moment

In *Chinese Poetic Writing* I have translated this couplet in the following manner: "Walk to the place where the water has its source; and, seated, await the birth of the clouds." But this translation touches only the linear and temporal aspects of the lines. If one goes back to the word-for-word translation and reads the two lines simultaneously, one will see that in each case the combination of words in parallel construction gives rise to a hidden significance. Thus "walk-sit" signifies movement and rest; "reach-look" signifies action and contemplation; "water-cloud" signifies universal transformation; "exhausted-rise" signifies death and rebirth; "place-moment" signifies space and time. Rich in this series of significations, the two lines represent in fact the two essential dimensions of all life. Rather than holding exclusively to one or the other, the true manner of life suggested by these lines may be perhaps to comply with the Emptiness which is found between the two that alone permits man to avoid separating himself from action and contemplation, or from space and time, and to participate internally in the true universal transformation.

We see that parallelism, in its own way, embodies this philosophy of life based on the double axis Emptiness-Fullness and Yin-Yang. The structure of parallelism, which is at once linear and contrastive, while involving "mediating Emptiness," can be adequately represented only by the *t'ai-chi* 太極 diagram:

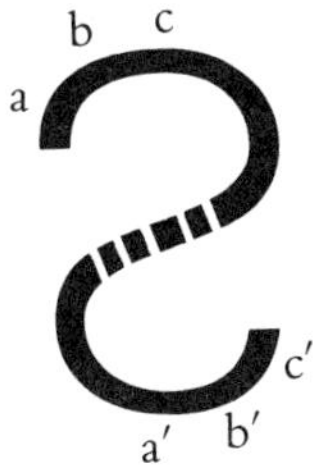

From a linguistic point of view, let me underscore that parallelism is an attempt to introduce spatial dimension into the temporal progression of language. In other words, it attempts to create an autonomous space in which the two constituent verses justify one another and are thus self-sufficient. This has important consequences for the syntactic scheme. In fact, at the heart of this autonomous space the poet invariably tries to impose a verbal order apart from that permitted by the usual rules. He can disrupt ordinary syntax, while at the same time making himself understood. When a line appears bizarre or incomprehensible, the other line, identical in structure, comes to dissipate the obscurity and show the hidden intention of the poet. In the T'ang period almost all of the lines famous for their audacious syntactic invention (notably those of Tu Fu) were written in parallel couplets. Such invention has conspicuously enriched ordinary language. Many grammatical structures created in this period still survive in contemporary usage.

III. The Symbolic Level (Heaven-Earth-Man)

Above the lexical and syntactic level is the symbolic one, which indicates the highest ambitions of the poetic language. It is truly on this level that the established language reaches its fullest signification: to manifest the human drama and, at the same time, the rapport that drama maintains with the universe. Thus this level involves the triad Heaven-Earth-Man, which poets make concrete by means of images.

We know that Chinese poets preferred a language made up almost entirely of images charged with symbolic sense to one that was direct and denotative. This of course is true of any kind of poetic language, but its use is particularly extensive in China and is further favored by the ideographic script and a long poetic history with a continuous development. These images, drawn from nature and at the same time charged with human connotations, seemed more in accord with their own vision and better able to articulate what ordinary language was unable to express. They made the concept of cosmology their own, a concept based upon a web of correspondences between human feelings and the elements of the universe. In their eyes, a unitary principle governed all beings, since everything came from the primordial Breath and complied with the interaction of the dual Breath, Yin and Yang, and with the combinations of the Five Elements. The relation between Heaven, Earth, and Man further reinforced the idea of a universal resonance (*kan-ying* 感應). Out of this context came the preeminence accorded to symbolic images, which were so many figures crystalizing the secret bond which joins all things. Through an intense and sustained creation in which all nature was, so to speak, inventoried and categorized, one participated in a general process of symbolization. Thanks to this, poets might hope to realize their dream of a total communion, excellently indicated in the expression *ch'ing-ching* 情景, a "landscape of feelings."

To describe the functioning of these images, the Chinese rhetorical tradition makes use of two figures: *pi* 比, "comparison," and *hsing* 興, "incitation." These two figures are the object of abundant commentaries too numerous to describe here. Let me simply point out that I have elsewhere devoted an essay to them, in which I have shown that, quite apart from their stylistic content, these two figures put forward the relation between subject and object, or more precisely, of man and nature. *Pi* is a process which essentially goes from man toward nature (man expresses his feelings and seeks an element of comparison in nature), while *hsing* leaves nature to return to man (nature rouses in man a latent feeling).[13] A poem or line, built on these two tropes, thus forms a dynamic circuit of nature.

In T'ang poetry, *pi* and *hsing* are used frequently. The following poems using the central image of the moon illustrate well the triadic relation of Heaven-Earth-Man. As a celestial presence, the moon transcends space and time. By watching the moon, men on earth who are separated by epochs and distances can find in it a certain unity in spirit. For this reason, it has always been considered a symbol of reunion (*t'uan-yüan* 團圓) and of perfection and supreme happiness (*yüan-man* 圓滿). The following quatrain by Chang Chiu-ling 張九齡 (678–740) can serve to illustrate the use of *pi*:

[13] François Cheng, "*Bi* et *xing*," *Cahiers de Linguistique—Asie Orientale* 6 (Paris: Centre de Recherches Linguistiques sur l'Asie Orientale, 1979), pp. 63–74.

Since my lord left me,
I have not touched my abandoned loom.
Thinking of you, I am like the full moon
Whose radiance wanes night after night.[14]

自君之出矣
不復理殘機
思君如滿月
夜夜減清輝

As for the use of *hsing*, the best example is perhaps this famous quatrain by Li Po:

Before my bed, bright moonlight—
I take it to be frost on the ground.
Raising my head I gaze at the mountain
  moon;
Bending my head I think of home.[15]

牀前明月光
疑是地上霜
舉頭望山月
低頭思故鄉

The poem by Li Po clearly shows that the image of moonlight, coming down from heaven and being associated with frost on earth, allows the poet not only to be reminded of his native country but also to feel as if he were actually there.

What I have just presented concerns simple images that relate facts directly. I would now like to examine the functioning of images by considering the two major rhetorical figures in the western tradition, metaphor and metonymy, terms generally defined as follows. Metaphor is based on analogy and consists in making use of a symbolic image to represent an idea or feeling. Therefore, metaphor can be said to be akin to *pi*, with the difference that it can be used without making the idea or feeling referred to explicit. Metonymy is based on contiguity and consists in linking up contiguous ideas or images. Thus, it can be compared to but not equated with *hsing*. For instance, metonymy starts either from the idea of reunion, moving on to separation, or from the image of the moon to that of the cloud. In Chinese poetry, especially from the T'ang period onward, these two figures are often interrelated in a metaphor-metonymy network. Thanks to the impressive corpus of existing metaphors consisting essentially of natural elements, the Chinese poet is able to remain on the metaphorical level (i.e., not having to revert to denotative language) by combining, metonymically, metaphors with other metaphors or with other elements

[14] Kao Pu-ying, *T'ang Sung shih chü-yao*, vol. 2, p. 745.

[15] *Ibid.*, p. 756.

taken from nature. As an illustration of this, I shall quote two lines from the poem "Moon Night" 月夜 by Tu Fu. In this poem, Tu Fu was separated from his wife during the An Lu-shan Rebellion. He expresses his longing for her by picturing her alone in the nocturnal mist, watching the moon:

> Fragrant mist, cloud-hair wet; 香霧雲鬟濕
> Pure brightness, jade-arm cold.[16] 清輝玉臂寒

In the first line, "cloud-hair" is a metaphor. Being an atmospheric element, the "cloud" can easily be combined by the poet with another atmospheric element, "mist," to creat a metonymic structure endowed with an intrinsic necessity. In the same way, the second line contains the "jade-arm" metaphor. By virtue of its smooth and lustrous quality, "jade" can naturally be combined with the moon's brightness. Through their ingenious combinations, these two lines intimately link human elements with the surrounding objective world. But the richness of these lines is not to be attributed to mere ingenuity. Their combined imagery strives for something that transcends the individual images. It should be recalled that, on that same night, the poet also stood alone in the moonlight, surrounded by mist. In that mist, he *actually* felt he could, through metonymy, touch the "cloud-hair," and caress the "jade-arm," of his wife. Therefore, beyond merely objective description, the poet expresses the depth of his desire to break through the fetters of time and space in order to call forth an infinitely open moment of the present.

It is appropriate here to refer again to the notion of the triad of Heaven-Earth-Man. In the optics of Chinese poets, the interchange between subject and object must lead to something else, something open. If it is true that the images are born prior to the intimate relation between Man and Earth, they nevertheless tend irresistibly toward something beyond—what Ssu-k'ung T'u 司空圖 (837–908) of the T'ang dynasty calls the "image beyond images" 象外之象 and the "meaning beyond images" 象外有意. This something beyond is properly embodied in Heaven. In its own manner, poetic practice confirms what is triadic in Chinese thought and does not

[16] *Ibid.*, p. 458.

envisage relations which are restricted to two members. In such a binary mode of thought, two entities face to face would find themselves in a situation of sterile opposition, which separates them from their roots and breaks the true circular movement. Man is not an isolated subject any more than Earth is a pure object; the link between them has no meaning except in an openness, for which Heaven is the indispensible symbol.

If we need other examples, I would gladly cite Li Po's quatrain "Stairs of Jade" 玉階怨, which I have analyzed extensively in *Chinese Poetic Writing*.

Stairs of jade give birth to white dew;	玉階生白露
Late in the night penetrates stockings of silk.	坐久侵羅襪
However, lowers shades of crystal;	却下水精簾
Through transparence contemplates moon of autumn.[17]	玲瓏望秋月

Through a sequence of shared images (stairs of jade, white dew, stockings of silk, shades of crystal, moon of autumn)—luminosity mixed with chill—images which give the impression of having generated one another, the poet restores a scene which is at once the exterior environment and the interior universe of the woman who waits. The poem ends with an image of the moon which, while reuniting in itself all the preceding images, extends the thought of the woman. For the roundness of the moon is a symbol of the reunion of lovers, and at the same time a remote and inaccessible presence. It conveys better than any word the desire of the woman stretching toward the infinite.

[17] *Ibid.*, p. 756.

James J. Y. Liu

The Paradox of Poetics and the Poetics of Paradox

The paradox of poetics and the poetics of paradox are both rooted in the paradox of language, which must therefore engage our attention first. Basically, the paradox of language may assume two forms. In the first form, the paradox lies in the seeming contradiction between the presumed necessity of language and its alleged inadequacy: we need language as a medium of human communication, yet poets, critics, and philosophers have eloquently complained that ultimate reality, or deepest emotion, or sublime beauty, cannot be conveyed in words. (The eloquence with which they complained about the inadequacy of language is of course but one illustration of the paradox.) In the second form, the paradox lies in the seeming contradiction between the assertion that ultimate reality, or deepest emotion, or sublime beauty, can be conveyed without words, and the very act of making this assertion in words. It was all very well for Sakyamuni to pick a flower and for Kasyapa to smile with instant understanding without either of them saying a word, but those who tell the story as an example of wordless communication cannot help using words.

In order to see how a realization of the paradoxical nature of language led to a realization of the paradoxical nature of poetry and of poetics, and then to a poetics of paradox, we need to consider some pre-Ch'in texts. Since the relative dates of some of these texts are matters of controversy, which we cannot go into here, I shall not follow a strictly chronological order in citing these texts.

As may be expected, the paradox of language features prominently in the *Lao Tzu* 老子 and the *Chuang Tzu* 莊子. To avoid the awkwardness of writing "The *Lao Tzu* says" or "The *Chuang Tzu* says," I shall sometimes refer to these two works by the names of their putative authors, without implying a belief in Lao Tzu's historical existence or in Chuang Chou's exclusive authorship of the book named after him. Not only do these two works contain numerous passages about the paradox of language, but their very existence constitutes an example of the paradox. The familiar words traditionally placed at the beginning of the *Lao Tzu* point out the inadequacy of language as a means of conveying ultimate reality:

The *tao* that can be "*tao*-ed" is not the constant Tao;	道可道, 非常道.
The name that can be named is not the constant Name.[1]	名可名, 非常名.

Yet in Chapter 25 (for convenience's sake, I shall refer to the traditional numbering of chapters, whether this represents the original order of the parts or not) Lao Tzu recognizes the necessity of language:

I do not know its name, but force myself to style it "*tao*;"	吾不知其名, 强字之曰道.
Force myself to name it "great."[2]	强爲之名曰大.

It seems that Lao Tzu is not advocating the total abolition of language but only warning against the danger of taking words as permanent embodiments of reality. According to Lao Tzu, words have no *fixed* meanings, but they are not meaningless. All words are makeshift devices that should be discarded as soon as understanding is reached. If we borrow the terminology of Ferdinand de Saussure, to name something "*tao*" is an act of *parole*, whereas the ideal Name

[1] The text follows Kao Heng 高亨, *Lao Tzu cheng-ku* 老子正詁 (rev. ed., Peking: Chung-hua shu-chü, 1956), p. 1. For variant readings in the manuscript copies found at Ma Wang Tui 馬王堆, see *Lao Tzu chu-shih* 老子注釋 (Shanghai: Jen-min ch'u-pan-she, 1977), p. 49. English translations of the *Lao Tzu* are too numerous to mention.

[2] Kao Heng, *Lao Tzu cheng-ku*, pp. 60–61. I have added the character for *ch'iang* 强 to the second sentence, following the Li Yüeh 李約 edition; see Yen Ling-feng 嚴靈峯, *Lao Tzu chang-chü hsin-pien* 老子章句新編 (Taipei: Chung-hua wen-hua ch'u-pan shih-yeh wei-yüan-hui, 1954), pt. 1, pp. 8–9.

would be part of a hypothetical *langue*. Lao Tzu seems to admit the necessity of individual speech acts (*parole*) but to deny the possibility of language as permanent system (*langue*).

A more radical way of presenting the paradox of language occurs in Chapter 56: "One who knows does not speak; / One who speaks does not know" (知者不言; 言者不知).[3] This prompted the poet Po Chü-i 白居易 (772–846) to ask, in his poem "On Reading the *Lao Tzu*" (讀老子) the following question:

"One who speaks does not know;
one who knows is silent."
This remark I have heard from the
Old Master.
If you say the Old Master was one
who knew,
Wherefore did he himself write his
"Five Thousand Words?"[4]

言者不知知者默
此語吾聞於老君
若道老君是知者
緣何自著五千文

Perhaps Po wrote this poem as a *jeu d'esprit* rather than as a serious refutation of Lao Tzu, as Ch'ien Chung-shu 錢鍾書 appears to take it. In his *Kuan-chui pien* 管錐編 (which may be paraphrased as "Collection of Limited Views"), Ch'ien takes Po Chü-i to task for failing to remember certain passages in the *Chuang Tzu* as well as various Buddhist sutras, all of which could offer ways out of the seeming self-contradiction.[5] Let us enter the spirit of the game and deal with the paradox without resorting to any other text than the *Lao Tzu* itself, by arguing as follows. Since Lao Tzu has spoken, he is not one who knows; therefore, his words cannot be taken as true, including the statement, "One who speaks does not know," in which case this statement cannot be taken as proof that Lao Tzu does not know! This circular argument could go on forever, but for our present purpose we had better stop here.

A variation of the paradox appears in Chapter 81: "True words are not beautiful / Beautiful words are not true" (信言不美, 美言

[3] Kao Heng, *Lao Tzu cheng-ku*, p. 119, Cf. *Lao Tzu chu-shih*, p. 29.

[4] *Po shih Ch'ang-ch'ing chi* 白氏長慶集 (SPTK ed.), *chüan* 65. For further discussion of this poem, see my note in *Chinese Literature: Essays, Articles, Reviews* 4, no. 2 (July 1982), 243–244.

[5] *Kuan-chui pien* (Peking: Chung-hua shu-chü, 1979), pp. 413, 456–458.

不信).[6] This has been explained by Liu Hsieh 劉勰 (ca. 460–532) in his *The Literary Mind: Elaborations* (Wen-hsin tiao-lung 文心雕龍) in the following manner: "Lao Tzu disliked artificiality and therefore declared, 'Beautiful words are not true'; yet his own 'Five Thousand Words' are refined and subtle, which shows that he did not really reject beauty."[7] In fact, we can deal with this paradox in the same way as we dealt with the previous one: since Lao Tzu's words are beautiful, they cannot be true; therefore, the statement "beautiful words are not true" cannot be taken as true; if so, this statement cannot be used as proof that Lao Tzu's words are not true.

Chuang Tzu deals with the paradox of language with even greater subtlety than Lao Tzu. Various passages in the *Chuang Tzu* emphasize the inadequacy of language and its necessity. In Chapter 2, after having remarked (or perhaps paraphrased an existing saying, as A. C. Graham suggested),[8] "The myriad things and I are one," Chuang Tzu adds: "Since we are already one, how can I say a word? Yet since I have already called it 'one,' how can I say that I have not said a word?"[9] The paradox is elaborated in Chapter 13:

> What the world values as speech are books.[10] Books are nothing more than words; words have something that is valued. What is valued in words is meaning; meaning is derived from something.[11] That from which meaning is derived cannot be transmitted in language. Yet the world,

[6] Kao Heng, *Lao Tzu cheng-ku*, p. 152. Cf. *Lao Tzu chu-shih*, p. 40.

[7] Wang Li-ch'i 王利器, *Wen-hsin tiao-lung hsin-shu* 文心雕龍新書 (Peking: Centre Franco-chinois d'études sinologiques, 1952; rpt. Taipei: Ch'eng-wen Publishing Co., 1968), p. 88. The translation has previously appeared in my *Chinese Theories of Literature* (Chicago: University of Chicago Press, 1975), p. 51.

[8] A. C. Graham, trans., *Chuang Tzu* (London: George Allen and Unwin, 1981), p. 56.

[9] For the text which I have translated here, see *Chuang Tzu yin-te* 莊子引得 (Peking: Harvard-Yenching Institute Sinological Index Series, 1947), 5/2/53. The translation has previously appeared in my *Chinese Theories of Literature*, p. 62.

[10] For the text of this long passage, see *Chuang Tzu yin-te*, 36/13/64 ff. In translating the word *tao* 道 as "speech" I am following Ch'eng Hsüan-ying 成玄英. See Kuo Ch'ing-fan 郭慶藩, *Chuang Tzu chi-shih* 莊子集釋 (preface by Wang Hsien-ch'ien 王先謙, dated 1894; Peking: Chung-hua shu-chü, 1961), p. 489.

[11] This translation is also based on Ch'eng Hsüan-ying's commentary, *ibid.*

> because it values language, transmits books. Although the world values them, I still think they are not worth valuing, because what it [the world] values is not valuable. Therefore, what can be seen when one looks are forms and colors; what can be heard when one listens are names and sounds. How lamentable that people of the world think forms, colors, names, and sounds are adequate to capture their natures! If indeed forms, colors, names, and sounds are in the end not adequate to capture their natures, then one who knows does not speak, and one who speaks does not know. Yet how could the world realize this![12]

To drive the point home, Chuang Tzu then tells the parable about the wheelwright who condemned books as the "dregs and lees of the ancients,"[13] yet this parable appears in a book!

The paradox of language appears in its second basic form in Chapter 24, where the fictional Confucius, having said, "I have heard wordless words,"[14] proceeds to describe them in words. Words, to Chuang Tzu, as they are to Lao Tzu, are makeshift devices, not permanent embodiments of reality. In Chapter 2 we are told, "The Tao has never had boundaries, and language has never had constancy."[15] In Chapter 25 we read, "The name 'Tao' is what we temporarily adopt to make things go."[16] In Chapter 26, after suggesting the analogies of language with the fish net and the hare trap, Chuang Tzu concludes: "The purpose of words lies in meaning. When you have got the meaning, you can forget the words. How can I get someone who has forgotten words to have a

[12] This translation is new. Cf. Burton Watson's translation in *The Complete Works of Chuang Tzu* (New York and London: Columbia University Press, 1968), p. 152.

[13] For the text, see *Chuang Tzu yin-te*, 36/13/70. Cf. Watson, *Complete Works of Chuang Tzu*, pp. 152–153.

[14] *Chuang Tzu yin-te*, 67/24/66. Cf. Watson, *Complete Works of Chuang Tzu*, p. 271.

[15] *Ibid.*, 5/2/55. Cf. Watson, *Complete Works of Chuang Tzu*, p. 43; Graham, *Chuang Tzu*, p. 57.

[16] *Ibid.*, 73/25/80. For the translation "to make things go," see Kuo Hsiang's 郭象 commentary quoted in Kuo Ch'ing-fan, *Chuang Tzu chi-shih*, p. 919. Cf. Watson, *Complete Works of Chuang Tzu*, p. 293.

word with him?"[17] The last sentence is obviously a self-conscious illustration of the paradox of language.

Not only does Chuang Tzu present the paradox of language, but he also hints at a way of resolving or transcending it, by questioning and denying distinctions that are generally taken for granted. A crucial passage occurs in Chapter 2: "Now, is speaking not blowing air? One who speaks says something; it is just that what he says has not been fixed. Has he really said something, or has he not said anything? If you think it differs from the twittering of a fledgling, is there really a distinction, or is there no distinction?"[18] In translating the first sentence as a question instead of a statement, as previous translators have done,[19] I am following Ma Ch'i-ch'ang 馬其昶 (1855–1929), who identified the particle 也 with 邪.[20] This seems to me more consistent with what follows, for it raises the question whether there is really any distinction between human speech and natural sounds, such as the wind blowing, just as the last sentence quoted raises the same question with regard to the twittering of fledglings.

In Chapter 25 an attempt is made to deny the distinction between speaking and not speaking: "Although his mouth speaks, his heart has never spoken."[21] The point is elaborated at the end of the chapter: "If speech is adequate, then one can speak all day and fully describe the Tao; if speech is not adequate, then one can speak all day and fully describe [mere] things. The ultimate of the Tao and of things cannot be adequately carried by speech or silence. Neither to speak nor to be silent is [the way to] discuss the ultimate."[22] The

[17] *Ibid.*, 75/26/48. Cf. Watson, *Complete Works of Chuang Tzu*, p. 302. I am indebted to Watson for the translation of the last sentence.

[18] *Ibid.*, 4/2/23.

[19] E.g., Watson, *Complete Works of Chuang Tzu*, p. 39; Graham, *Chuang Tzu*, p. 52.

[20] Ma Ch'i-ch'ang, *Chuang Tzu ku* 莊子故 (preface dated 1894, first published 1905; rpt. with commentary by Yen Fu 嚴復 and preface by Tseng K'e-tuan 曾克耑 dated 1953, no indication of place of publication), *chüan* 1, p. 9b.

[21] *Chuang Tzu yin-te*, 71/25/35. Cf. Watson, *Complete Works of Chuang Tzu*, p. 285.

[22] *Ibid.*, 73/25/81ff. For the last sentence I have adopted the reading "i ch'i yu chi" 議其有極 instead of "i yu so chi" 議有所極. See Kuo Ch'ing-fan, *Chuang Tzu chi-shih*, p. 919. Cf. Watson, *Complete Works of Chuang Tzu*, p. 293.

refusal to draw a distinction between speaking and not speaking appears in even stronger terms in Chapter 27: "If we do not speak, then [things] will be all the same. Sameness, because of words, becomes differentiated, yet words are the means by which we try to make the differentiated the same again. Therefore, I say 'No words!' Words are 'no words.' One who speaks all his life has never spoken, and one who does not speak all his life has never avoided speaking."[23] The translation above is based on the interpretation of Ma Ch'i-ch'ang, who identified 與 with 以.[24] This makes much better sense than taking 與 as "and," for in that case the second sentence quoted would be redundant: "Sameness and words are not the same; words and sameness are not the same," which verges on nonsense. Even if we take 齊 as "unity," as Burton Watson did, the sentence would still be a redundancy.[25] Following Ma's interpretation, we may paraphrase the passage as follows. Things in themselves are undifferentiated; it is only when we talk about them that they become differentiated. Yet when we try to persuade others not to differentiate things, we cannot help using words. That is why Chuang Tzu cries out in apparent despair, "No words!" But if "no words" are words, then words are "no words." If there is no distinction between "words" and "no words," or between "speaking" and "not speaking," then neither the question whether language is adequate nor the question whether it is necessary is relevant any more, and the paradox of language is transcended. To parody Lao Tzu's remark that "the Tao constantly does nothing yet leaves nothing undone" (道常無爲而無不爲),[26] we might say, "One constantly says nothing yet leaves nothing unsaid" (人常無言而無不言).

Even the Confucians, with their generally positivistic outlook, could not escape entirely from the paradox of language. On one occasion, Confucius, perhaps feeling discouraged, remarked, "I wish not to say anything," and when Tzu-kung 子貢 asked, "If you, Master, do not say anything, what are we, the younger

[23] *Chuang Tzu yin-te*, 75/27/6 ff.

[24] Ma Ch'i-ch'ang, *Chuang Tzu ku*, *chüan* 7, p. 7b.

[25] Watson, *Complete Works of Chuang Tzu*, p. 304; cf. Graham, *Chuang Tzu*, p. 107.

[26] Kao Heng, *Lao Tzu cheng-ku*, p. 82.

generation, to pass on?" Confucius replied, "What does Heaven say? The four seasons move on, the myriad things are born. What does Heaven say?"[27] This Confucian concept of a Heaven that says nothing but leaves nothing undone is not very different from the Taoist concept of the Tao that does nothing but leaves nothing undone. The fact that Confucius had to use words to express his wish not to say anything and to explain that words were not necessary is yet another illustration of the paradox of language in its second basic form.

Mencius illustrates the paradox of language in its first basic form. Having just said that his two strong points were that he "understood language" and that he was good at "cultivating his vast *ch'i*," he replied to the question what he meant by the word *ch'i* by saying, "It is hard to put into words."[28] Nonetheless, he launched into a fairly long description of it, just as Lao Tzu describes the Tao in various ways after having declared that it could not be named.

Perhaps the Confucian attitude to the paradox of language is best summed up in the remark attributed to Confucius in the "Appended Words" ("Hsi-tz'u" 繫辭) to the *Book of Changes* (I ching 易經): "Writing does not exhaust words; words do not exhaust meaning" (書不盡言; 言不盡意),[29] which seems to indicate a calm acceptance of both the necessity of language and its inadequacy, even though this is followed a few sentences later by the statement, "The Sage appended phrases thereto in order to exhaust its words" (聖人 . . . 繫辭焉以盡其言).[30]

Yang Hsiung 揚雄 (53 B.C. to A.D. 18) appears to be paraphrasing the remark quoted above when he writes, "when speech cannot convey [what lies in] one's heart and writing cannot convey one's speech, it is hard indeed!" But he apparently thinks that this applies only to ordinary people but not to the sage:

> Only the sage obtained the understanding of speech and the [proper] form of writing, letting the white sun shine on it and

[27] *Lun-yü* 論語, XVII, 17.

[28] *Meng-tzu yin-te* 孟子引得 (Peking: Harvard-Yenching Institute Sinological Index Series, 1930), 11/2A/6.

[29] Sun Hsing-yen, 孫星衍, *Chou I chi-chieh* 周易集解 (TSCC ed.), p. 604.

[30] *Ibid.*, p. 605.

> the great rivers wash it, so that it became vast and irresistible. When words encounter each other as people meet face to face, for drawing forth what one desires in one's innermost heart and communicating people's indignation, there is nothing better than speech. For encompassing and enwrapping the things of the world, recording what is long past to make it clear in the distant future, setting down what the eye could not see in antiquity, and transmitting across a thousand *li* what the heart cannot understand, there is nothing better than writing. Therefore, speech is the voice of the heart and writing is the picture of the heart.[31]

This passage seems to reaffirm the power of language, but in another passage the paradox of language reappears, though seen from the hearer's or reader's point of view: "The sage opened his mouth freely and formed speech; let go his brush and formed writing. [His] speech can be heard but cannot be exhausted; [his] writing can be read but cannot be exhausted."[32] Instead of asserting that one cannot fully express one's meaning in words, Yang Hsiung is asserting here that one cannot fully understand another's meaning through words, thus anticipating certain trends in contemporary western theories of literature and unwittingly providing an example of the paradox of hermeneutics.

The dictum "words do not exhaust meaning" is given a twist by Ou-yang Chien 歐陽建 (?–A.D. 300) in his essay, "Words Do Exhaust Meaning" ("Yen chin i lun" 言盡意論):

> Now, Heaven does not speak, yet the four seasons move on. The sage does not speak, yet his discernment remains. Forms do not wait for names before the square and the circle appear; colors do not wait for designations before black and white are manifest. If so, then names, with regard to things, have no use; words, with regard to principles, can do nothing. Yet both the ancients and the moderns have engaged in the rectification of names, and sages and wise men cannot abolish words. Why is

[31] *Fa-yen* 法言, "Wen shen" 問神 chapter. Rpt. in *Chung-kuo wen-hsüeh p'i-p'ing tzu-liao hui-pien* 中國文學批評資料彙編, ed. K'o Ch'ing-ming 柯慶明 and Tseng Yung-i 曾永義 (Taipei: Ch'eng-wen Publishing Co., 1978), vol. 1, p. 85.

[32] *Ibid.*, p. 87.

this so? It is truly because when principles are obtained in the mind, without words one cannot let [the intent of one's mind] flow freely, and when things are fixed by themselves, without words one cannot distinguish them. Without words to let the mind's intent flow freely, there would be no means by which we could contact each other; without names to distinguish things, our discernment would not be manifest. When discernment is manifest, then names and categories differ; when words and designations come into contact with each other, then one's feelings and intents flow freely. When we trace their origins and seek their roots, [we find that] it is not that things have their natural names, or principles their inevitable designations. If we wish to distinguish realities, then we must differentiate their names; if we wish to declare our intents, then we must establish their designations. Names shift, following things; words change, according to principles. This is just like an echo responding to the issuance of a sound, or a shadow attaching itself to the existence of a body: one cannot separate them into two. If [words and meaning] cannot be separated into two, then there is no word that does not exhaust the meaning.[33]

Ou-yang Chien's arguments do not constitute a valid refutation of the dictum "words do not exhaust meaning," since they deal with language at the level of everyday discourse, whereas the dictum probably concerns the inadequacy of language at the level of ultimate reality. Ou-yang is in fact merely reiterating Lao Tzu's idea that words do not have fixed meanings, as Ch'ien Chung-shu has pointed out.[34]

One would expect the awareness of the paradox of language to lead eventually to an awareness of the paradox (or perhaps one should say the meta-paradox) of poetics, for if poetry, often considered the most exalted and most expressive form of language,

[33] *Yi-wen lei-chü* 藝文類聚, *chüan* 19; also "Ch'üan Chin wen" 全晉文 (in *Ch'üan Shang-ku San-tai Ch'in Han San-kuo Liu-ch'ao wen* 全上古三代秦漢三國六朝文, ed. Yen K'o-chün 嚴可均, *chüan* 109; rpt. in K'o and Tseng, *Chung-kuo wen-hsüeh*, p. 209.

[34] *Kuan-chui pien*, p. 1219.

cannot escape from its paradoxical nature, how much more paradoxical is it to discuss poetry in the same medium, language? Such an awareness is indeed shown by Lu Chi 陸機 (261–303) in the preface to his "Wen-fu" 文賦 (known in English variously as "Rhymeprose on Literature," "Exposition on Literature," or simply "On Literature"). Since this preface is of crucial importance to the present discussion, I shall translate it anew and analyze it in some detail, much annotated and translated as it is.[35]

> Whenever I read the creations of talented authors, I presume to think I have obtained some insight into the way their minds worked. Now, in issuing words and dispatching phrases, there are indeed numerous variations, yet as to whether it is beautiful or ugly, good or bad, this is something one *can* speak of. Whenever I compose a literary work myself, I perceive the nature of writing even more keenly, constantly worried that my ideas may not match things or that my words may not capture my ideas, for the difficulty lies not in knowing how, but in being able to do it.
>
> Therefore I have created this "Exposition on Literature" to describe the luxuriant beauties of former authors, taking this opportunity to discuss the causes of gains or losses in writing. Someday perhaps it may be said to have subtly exhausted the wonders of literature. Although, with regard to holding a wooden-handled ax to cut down a branch [and make another wooden ax-handle], the model is not far to seek, when it comes to the changes that follow the movement of the hand [in response to the working of the mind], these are indeed difficult to capture in words. In general, what *can* be said in words is all presented here.

In the opening sentence, Lu Chi adopts the reader's point of view

[35] For the text, see *Wei Chin Nan-pei-ch'ao wen-hsüeh-shih ts'an-k'ao tzu-liao* 魏晉南北朝文學史參考資料 (Hong Kong: Hung-chih shu-chü, 1961), pp. 252–275. For translations, see Ch'en Shih-hsiang's in *Anthology of Chinese Literature*, ed. Cyril Birch (New York: Grove Press, 1965), vol. 1; and Achilles Fang's in *Harvard Journal of Asiatic Studies* 15 (1951); rpt. in *Studies in Chinese Literature*, ed. John Bishop (Cambridge: Harvard University Press, 1965).

and expresses his confidence in his ability not only to understand what former authors wrote but also to know how their minds worked when they wrote. Next he affirms the possibility of critical discrimination in spite of the infinite variety of literature. Both his self-confidence and his affirmation are based on his own experience as a writer, which enables him to identify with former writers, and this identification in turn enables Lu Chi the poet to write as Lu Chi the critic, without ceasing to be the poet at the same time, for after all the "Wen-fu" is as much a *tour de force* of elegant writing as a treatise on the art of writing. He points out that writing is not simply a matter of matching words with things (物, which refers to any external phenomenon, not strictly limited to "objects") but involves first conceiving or perceiving things and then expressing in words one's own conceptions or perceptions of things. He further points out the difference between knowing in theory how to do a thing and actually being able to do it. If we may illustrate his point with a modern analogy: it is one thing to know in theory what one should do to drive a car, but quite another to be able to drive one.

When someone tries to write an *ars poetica*, as Lu Chi does here, then to the difficulty of writing is added the difficulty of writing about the difficulty of writing. To continue our homely analogy: it is one thing to be able to drive a car, but quite another to teach someone else to drive. Anyone who writes poetry attempts the seemingly impossible task of describing the indescribable nature of reality, and anyone who writes an *ars poetica* attempts the seemingly even more impossible task (assuming, for the sake of argument, there are degrees of impossibility) of describing the indescribable nature of writing. Yet this is precisely what Lu Chi is attempting to do.

One sentence in the second paragraph quoted above presents a problem: 他日殆可謂曲盡其妙. All commentators since Li Shan 李善 (?–689) have taken 他日 to mean "someday in the future," with the exception of Ch'ien Chung-shu, who takes it as a reference to the past and the whole sentence as a reference to the works of former writers.[36] Ch'ien argues that if we take the sentence to

[36] *Kuan-chui pien*, pp. 1180–1181.

mean, "Someday this may be said to have exhausted the wonders of literature," it will contradict the statement "these are indeed difficult to capture in words," as well as the line in the main text, "This is what the wheelwright P'ien could not put into words" (是蓋輪扁所不得言). Although it is true, as Ch'ien has demonstrated, that 他日 could refer to the past rather than the future, the sentence concerned seems to be placed too far from the mention of former writers to be a reference to them. Moreover, the conjectural term 殆可 would seem inappropriate for a reference to the past. In any case, if we do take 他日 as a reference to the future, it does not necessarily contradict "these are indeed difficult to capture in words," for Lu Chi is playing on the paradox of poetics, first disclaiming the possibility of describing the secret of the art of writing, and then proceeding to do exactly that. The sentence "Someday perhaps it may be said to have subtly exhausted the wonders of literature" is consistent with the last sentence of the preface: "In general, what *can* be said in words is all presented here." The allusion to the *Book of Poetry*[37] proves that Lu Chi is perfectly aware of the paradoxical nature of poetics: in using poetic language to describe the art of poetry he is like someone using a wooden-handled ax to cut down a branch and make another wooden ax-handle. The allusion to Chuang Tzu's parable of the wheelwright who could not describe in words how his hand followed the working of his mind is but the reverse side of the coin, for the parable itself is told in words. In short, Lu Chi shows his awareness of the paradox of poetics in the preface, and then gives a brilliant demonstration of it in the *fu* itself.

Among post-Han poets who realized the paradoxical nature of poetry, if not of poetics, is T'ao Ch'ien 陶潛 (365?–427), as seen in the concluding couplet of his most famous poem:

In all this, there is a true meaning;	此中有眞意
I was about to speak, but have forgotten words.[38]	欲辯已忘言

[37] See Bernard Karlgren, *The Book of Odes* (Stockholm: Museum of Far Eastern Antiquities, 1974), p. 102 (Ode 158).

[38] *Ching-chieh hsien-sheng chi* 靖節先生集 (SPPY ed.), *chüan* 3, p. 17a.

The point is not that the poet wishes to express "The Truth" but cannot find the words, but rather that having got the "true meaning," he has followed Chuang Tzu's advice and forgotten words. The paradox is, of course, that he has to tell us this in words. It is also relevant, as J. R. Hightower reminds us, to remember another remark from the *Chuang Tzu*: "Great eloquence has no words" (大辯不言).[39] Furthermore, T'ao Ch'ien is playing on the double meaning of *pien* (written 辯 or 辨): both to "speak" or "argue" or "be eloquent" and to "distinguish" or "make distinctions." To speak eloquently is to make distinctions, but someone who has experienced reality as an undifferentiated whole and does not wish to make distinctions has no other resort than language, which involves distinctions, if he wishes to convey *in poetry* his sense of the holistic nature of reality. Thus, T'ao Ch'ien succinctly sums up Chuang Tzu's perceptions of the paradox of language as it applies to poetry.

It is now time to discuss Liu Hsieh, who is generally positivistic about the power of language and literature, and optimistic about the possibility of interpretation. Nevertheless, he is not unaware of the difficulties of writing and of poetics. In the chapter "Intuitive Thinking" ("Shen-ssu" 神思) he writes:

> At the moment when one grasps the writing brush, one's vital spirits are doubly strong before phrases are formed; by the time the piece is completed, half of what one's mind originally conceived has been frustrated. Why so? Ideas turn in the void and can easily be extraordinary, but words must bear witness to reality and can achieve artistry only with difficulty. Hence, ideas derive from thought, and words derive from ideas. If they correspond closely,there will be no discrepancy; if they are apart, one will miss by a thousand *li*.[40]

This passage echoes Lu Chi's concern that one's ideas may not

[39] This is my translation. Cf. J. R. Hightower, "T'ao Ch'ien's 'Drinking Wine' Poems," in *Wen-lin: Studies in the Chinese Humanities*, ed. Chou Ts'e-tsung (Madison: University of Wisconsin Press, 1968), p. 14, and A. C. Graham, *Chuang Tzu*, p. 156.

[40] For text, see Wang Li-ch'i, *Wen-hsin tiao-lung*, p. 80. New translation. Cf. Vincent Yu-chung Shih, trans., *The Literary Mind and the Carving of Dragons* (New York: Columbia University Press, 1959), p. 156.

match things or one's words may not capture one's ideas. In the same chapter, Liu Hsieh further remarks:

> As for subtle intentions beyond thought and oblique moods beyond writing, these are what words cannot pursue and what the brush knows it should stop to write about. To reach the ultimate of subtleties and then expound their wonders, to reach the ultimate of changes and then communicate their working: even I Chih could not speak of the cooking cauldron, nor could the wheelwright P'ien talk about the ax. Is it not abstruse indeed?[41]

It is obvious that Liu Hsieh was aware of the seeming impossibility of writing about the secret of the art of writing, yet he was undeterred from writing his *magnum opus*, perhaps in the spirit of Confucius, who knew it could not be done but tried to do it (知其不可而爲之).[42]

The awareness of the paradox of poetics is also perceptible in the postface ("Hsü-chih" 序志 or "Relating My Intention"), where, after congratulating himself on the comprehensiveness of his work, Liu Hsieh adds with uncharacteristic modesty: "However, 'Words do not exhaust meaning': even the Sage found difficulties therein. My knowledge being limited to the capacity of a pitcher or the view from a tube,[43] how can I lay down laws with squares and rulers? Now that the remote ages of the past have purified my hearing, perhaps the distant generations of the future may pollute their sight with my work."[44] From the author of the greatest *ars poetica* ever written in Chinese, this must be considered a handsome admission of the paradox of poetics.

The realization of the paradoxical nature of language, poetry, and poetics did not lead, as it logically might have, to the abandonment of all language, poetry, and poetics, but, on the contrary, it

[41] Wang Li-ch'i, *Wen-hsin tiao-lung*, p. 81. New translation. Cf. Vincent Yu-chung Shih, trans., *The Literary Mind*, pp. 157–58.

[42] *Lun-yü*, XIV, 38.

[43] Allusions to *Tso-chuan* 左傳, seventh year of Duke Chao 昭公, and to *Chuang Tzu*, 45/17/78.

[44] Wang Li-ch'i, *Wen-hsin tiao-lung*, p. 130. New translation. Cf. Vincent Yu-chung Shih, trans., *The Literary Mind*, pp. 7–8.

led to the development of a poetics of paradox, by which I do not mean a poetics exclusively concerned with the use of paradoxes, or one based on the theory that all poetic language is paradoxical (as Cleanth Brooks claimed), but one based on an awareness of the paradoxical nature of language and poetry. This poetics of paradox may be summarized as the principle of saying more by saying less, or, in its extreme form, the principle of saying all by saying nothing. In the writings of some T'ang poets and critics we can discern the emergence of such a poetics.

The principle of saying more by saying less underlies the preference shown by many T'ang poets and critics for conciseness over verbosity, implicitness over explicitness, and suggestion over description. For example, Wang Ch'ang-ling 王昌齡 (689–757?) evinces preference for conciseness when he esteems the most ancient poetry because "the meaning can be seen in one line" (一句見意),[45] whereas in later poetry it requires two or even four lines to reveal the meaning. His advocation of suggestiveness can be seen in the following passages: "In general, poetry that combines description of objects with meaning is good. If there is description of objects but no meaning or inspired mood, then even if it is skillful, there is no place for it."[46] And, "The concluding line must make one feel as if the thought had never ended; only then is it good."[47] This remark foreshadows Yen Yü's 嚴羽 (fl. 1180–1235) assertion that in good poetry "the words come to an end but the meaning is endless" (言有盡而意無窮).[48]

[45] Quoted in Kukai 空海 (also known as Kobo Daishi 弘法大師 and Henso Kinko 遍照金剛, 773–834) in *Bunkyō hifuron* or *Wen-ching mi-fu-lun* 文鏡秘府論 (rpt. Peking: Jen-min wen-hsüeh ch'u-pan-she, 1975), p. 128. (Since the work is entirely in Chinese, there seems no reason not to refer to the title in its Chinese rather than Japanese pronunciation.) Also in *Chung-kuo wen-hsüeh p'i-p'ing tzu-liao hui-pien*, ed. Lo Lien-t'ien 羅聯添, vol. 2, p. 57. Cf. Richard W. Bodman, "Poetics and Prosody in Medieval China: a Study and Translation of Kukai's 'Bunkyō hifuron'" (Ph.D. dissertation, Cornell University, 1978), p. 368.

[46] *Wen-ching mi-fu-lun*, p. 133; Lo Lien-t'ien, *Chung-kuo wen-hsüeh*, p. 60. Cf. Bodman, "Poetics and Prosody," p. 382.

[47] *Wen-ching mi-fu-lun*, p. 139; Lo Lien-t'ien, *Chung-kuo wen-hsüeh*, p. 63. Cf. Bodman, "Poetry and Prosody," p. 398.

[48] *Ts'ang-lang shih-hua* 滄浪詩話, in *Li-tai shih-hua* 歷代詩話, ed. Ho Wen-huan 何文煥 (Taipei: I-wen yin-shu-kuan), p. 4a.

In practice, the principle of saying more by saying less is well exemplified by the poetry of Wang Wei 王維 (701?–761?) at its best and most typical, characterized by conciseness, implicitness, and suggestiveness. These qualities are particularly noticeable in some of his most famous concluding couplets, such as:

You ask for reasons for adversity or success—	君問窮通理
The fisherman's song enters deeply into the shore.[49]	漁歌入浦深

The apparent non-answer is more effective than any explicit answer would be.[50] That Wang Wei was conscious of the paradox of poetry can be seen in his "Preface to *Poems on Flowers and Medicinal Herbs* by the Reverend Master Kuang of Chien-fu Monastery" (薦福寺光師房花藥詩序), where he turned the principle of saying more by saying less upside down: "There is nothing in which the Tao does not reside; so how can things be worth forgetting? Hence, the more he sings and chants of these things, the more I perceive his silence."[51] Behind this statement is Chuang Tzu's paradox that to speak is not to speak. If this is accepted, then it provides an excuse for writing poetry, even when one admits the futility of language.

The paradox of answering a question by not answering is also present in the familiar quatrain by Li Po 李白 (701–762):

Question and Answer in the Mountains	山中問答
You ask me why I nestle among the green mountains;	問余何事棲碧山
I smile without answering, my mind, all by itself, at ease.	笑而不答心自閒
Peach blossoms on flowing water are going far away:	桃花流水杳然去
There is another cosmos, not the human world.[52]	別有天地非人間

[49] Chao Tien-ch'eng 趙殿成, ed., *Wang Yu-ch'eng chi chu* 王右丞集注 (SPPY ed.), *chüan* 7, p. 4b.

[50] For further discussion, see Pauline Yu, *The Poetry of Wang Wei* (Bloomington: Indiana University Press, 1980), pp. 163–164.

[51] *Wang Yu-ch'eng chi chu, chüan* 19, p. 15a. Quoted in *Kuan-chui pien*, p. 457.

[52] *Li T'ai-po shih-chi* 李太白詩集 (SPPY ed.), *chüan* 19, p. 2b.

More explicit evidence of the poetics of paradox can be found in the writings of Monk Chiao-jan 皎然, such as in his *Models of Poetry* (Shih-shih 詩式): "As for spontaneously outstanding lines, they compete with Creation; they may be groped into by the imagination, but are hard to describe in words. Unless one is a true writer, one cannot know this."[53] This awareness of the paradox of poetics did not stop him from prescribing rules for writing poetry. However, under the heading, "There are two things to be rejected in poetry" (詩有二廢), he writes: "Although one would wish to reject skill and advocate straightforwardness, natural order of [intuitive] thought cannot be left aside. Although one would wish to reject words and advocate meaning, classical beauty cannot be omitted."[54] It seems that he saw wordless poetry as an *ideal*, but realized that in practice one could not do without words. Nonetheless, he advocated "meaning beyond words," even though he disagreed with Wang Ch'ang-ling that the most ancient poetry should be esteemed highest because the meaning could be seen in one line.[55] In the section labeled "Examples of poetry with multiple meanings" (重意詩例) he writes: "All [poetry] that has twofold meanings or more expresses intentions beyond words. If one encounters a superior master like the Duke of K'ang-lo [Hsieh Ling-yün] and observes [his poetry], one will see only his emotion and nature but will not see any words. This is because he has reached the ultimate of the Tao."[56] To our disappointment, Chiao-jan does not explain what he means by "twofold meaning," "threefold meaning," or "fourfold meaning," and the lines he quotes do not make his point clear. All we can say is that he sees a link between the ideal of wordless poetry and the practice of using language in such a way as to suggest multiple levels of meaning, or "meaning beyond words." In this way, he seems to have anticipated some modern western critics who emphasize "ambiguity" or "plurisignation" in poetry.

[53] Lo Lien-t'ien, *Chung-kuo wen-hsüeh*, p. 83. See also Maureen Robertson, ". . . To Carve What Is Precious . . . ," in *Transition and Permanence: Chinese History and Culture*, ed. David C. Buxbaum and Frederick W. Mote (Festschrift Hsiao Kung-ch'üan, Hong Kong: Cathay Press, 1972), pp. 338–339.

[54] Lo Lien-t'ien, *Chung-kuo wen-hsüeh*, p. 85.

[55] *Ibid.*, p. 97.

[56] *Ibid.*, p. 89.

The poetics of paradox found its most elegant expression in *The Twenty-four Moods of Poetry* (Erh-shih-ssu shih-p'in 二十四詩品) of Ssu-k'ung T'u 司空圖 (837–908), especially in the poem entitled "Han-hsü" 含蓄, which has been translated as "Conservation" by H. A. Giles,[57] "Contenir une masse (d'éléments étrangers)" by Bruno Belpaire,[58] "The Pregnant Mode" by Yang Hsien-yi and Gladys Yang,[59] "Reserve" by Wai-lim Yip,[60] and "Potentiality" by Pauline Yu.[61] I think that "Reserve" is the best translation, since it means both "holding back" (*han*) and "storing up" (*hsü*). To elaborate: by being "reserved" in words one could build up a "reserve" of meaning. So much for the title. Here is the text of the poem itself, with my translation:

Without putting down a single word,
Fully capture the air's flow.
Words that do not touch distress
Already carry unbearable grief.
Herein is something that truly controls:
With it sink or swim!
Like straining wine till the cup is full,
Or turning back the blossoming season to
  autumn.
Far-reaching: dust in the air,
Sudden and transient: foam on the sea.
Shallow or deep, gathering or scattering:
Take ten thousand, come to one close.[62]

不著一字
盡得風流
語不涉難
已不堪憂
是有眞宰
與之沈浮
如淥滿酒
花時返秋
悠悠空塵
忽忽海漚
淺深聚散
萬取一收

[57] H. A. Giles, *A History of Chinese Literature* (New York and London: D. Appleton and Co., 1923), p. 183.

[58] Bruno Belpaire, *T'ang Kien Wen Tse* (Paris: Editions Universitaires, 1957), p. 73.

[59] Yang Hsien-yi and Gladys Yang, trans., "The Twenty-four Modes of Poetry," *Chinese Literature*, no. 7 (1963) 70.

[60] Wai-lim Yip, trans., "Selections from the 'Twenty-four Orders of Poetry,'" *Stony Brook* 3–4 (1969) 280–281.

[61] Pauline Yu, "Ssu-k'ung T'u's *Shih-p'in*: Poetic Theory in Poetic Form," in *Chinese Poetry and Poetics*, ed. Ronald C. Miao (San Francisco: Chinese Materials Center, 1978), vol. 1, p. 99.

[62] Kuo Shao-yü 郭紹虞, *Shih-p'in chi-chieh* 詩品集解 (Hong Kong: Shang-wu yin-shu-kuan, 1965), p. 21; Tsu Pao-ch'üan 祖保泉 *Ssu-k'ung T'u Shih-p'in chu-shih chi i-wen* 司空圖詩品注釋及譯文 (Hong Kong: Shang-wu yin-shu-kuan, 1966), p. 42.

The first two lines epitomize the poetics of paradox, even though they represent only one aspect of Ssu-k'ung T'u's theory of poetry.[63] The message contained in these oft-quoted lines is perhaps not as impossible as it sounds, for the character 著 (pronounced *chu* or *chuo*) means "manifest" as well as "attach to," and the first line, apart from meaning "without putting down a single word on paper," may also mean, "without attaching a single word to any particular object."[64] In the second line, the expression *feng-liu* 風流 is admittedly untranslatable, as Wai-lim Yip remarked, but we can still discuss its possible meaning in this context. Here, I think, the term does not mean "wit" (Giles), or "beauty" (Yang and Yang), or "flowing grace" (Yip, who adds a note that it refers to "Taoist-tinctured way of living"), or "elegant style" (Yu), but means something like the "moving spirit" or "life rhythm" of Nature. As the *Tz'u Hai* 辭海 puts it, "This refers to the quintessential spirit, the tone or flavor, which cannot be sought from traces or appearances" (此謂精神韻味不可以迹象求者). The first two lines together, then, suggest that without describing any particular object, one may fully capture the essence or spirit of Nature, as shown, for instance, in the movement of the air. Belpaire's translation, "[la force] de dispersion du vent," by being literal, comes closer to the original meaning than the various English versions mentioned.[65]

This interpretation can be corroborated by lines from another poem in the series, "Embodying" ("Hsing-jung" 形容):

[63] For other aspects of Ssu-k'ung T'u's theory of poetry, see Wong Yoon-wah, "Ssu-k'ung T'u: The Man and His Theory of Poetry" (Ph.D. dissertation, University of Wisconsin, 1972). (The published version, *Ssu-k'ung T'u: A Poet-Critic of the T'ang* [Hong Kong: The Chinese University, 1976] omits the chapter on poetic theory and is limited to biography.) See also Maureen Robertson's article mentioned in n. 53 and Pauline Yu's mentioned in n. 61.

[64] Hsiao Shui-shun 蕭水順 points out that *chuo* means "attach to" but interprets the whole line as "not attaching a word to paper" or "not a word in the poem is stuck" (詩中各字未嘗有一字黏著). See his "Ssu-k'ung T'u *Shih-p'in* yen-chiu" 司空圖詩品研究 (Taipei: Shih-ta Kuo-wen Yen-chiu-so, 1972), p. 15.

[65] In his study of the poet-critic Wang Shih-chen 王士禛 (1634–1711), Richard John Lynn translates Ssu-k'ung's couplet as "Without writing down a single word, completely get the spirit of it." See his "Orthodoxy and Enlightenment: Wang Shih-chen's Theory of Poetry and its Antecedents," in *The Unfolding of Neo-Confucianism*, ed. W. T. de Bary (New York: Columbia University Press, 1975), p. 245.

The changing appearance of the wind-swept clouds,	風雲變態
The quintessential spirit of flowers and plants,	花草精神
The waves and billows of the sea,	海之波瀾
The rugged crags of the mountains—	山之嶙峋
All these resemble the great Tao:	俱似大道
Identify with them intuitively, even to the dust.	妙契同塵
Leave forms behind but catch true likeness,	離形得似
Then you will come close to being the right one.[66]	庶幾斯人

In both poems, Ssu-k'ung advises writers not to describe the outward appearances of individual objects but to attempt to capture the inner essence of Nature as a whole. By saying as little as possible about the former, one can suggest as much as possible about the latter.

For lines 3 and 4 of "Reserve," I have adopted the variant reading 語不涉難, 已不堪憂 instead of 語不涉己, 若不堪憂, since the former is more relevant to the theme of this poem: "without explicitly speaking of distress, one can suggest unbearable grief." Line 5 alludes to the *Chuang Tzu*: "There seems to be something truly in control; it is just that we do not see signs of it."[67] In the present context, "something truly in control" seems to refer to intuition, with which the writer should sink or swim. In other words, one should rely on intuition rather than mechanical artistry. Lines 7 and 8, as Kuo Shao-yü 郭紹虞 and Tsu Pao-ch'üan 祖保泉 have pointed out, are examples of "reserve:"[68] when straining wine, even when the cup is full, one still leaves something in the strainer, and when flowers are prevented from full blossoming, something is reserved. Following Kuo's commentary, we may interpret the last four lines as follows. Dust in the air stretches far, while foam on the sea appears for a brief moment. Although phenomena such as these may differ from each other in being shallow or deep, gathering or scattering, they all follow the

[66] See n. 62. The translation has previously appeared in my *Chinese Theories of Literature*, p. 35, where reasons are given for the way I translated certain lines.

[67] *Chuang Tzu yin-te*, 4/2/15. Cf. A. C. Graham, *Chuang Tzu*, p. 151.

[68] See n. 62.

same principle. One may take a thousand things, but they all come to rest in one thing, "reserve."

Since this conference is concerned with the evolution of Chinese poetry and poetics from the Han through the T'ang, I shall stop here and leave the discussion of later developments of the poetics of paradox to some other occasion.

Stephen Owen

The Self's Perfect Mirror: Poetry as Autobiography

> So writers of ancient times trusted their persons to ink and the brush, let their thoughts be seen in their compositions; depending neither on a good historian nor on patronage of the powerful, their reputations were handed down to posterity on their own force.
> *Ts'ao P'i (187–226), "On Literature"* [1]

The ancients tell us that there are three kinds of achievement by which a person may hope to endure: moral power, deeds, and words (立德, 立功, 立言).[2] The promise that these forms of achievement do endure contains no clue as to the pragmatic means of their preservation. The later-born Ts'ao P'i 曹丕 looks to precisely that question—to *how* a reputation may be conserved, not to the accomplishment that makes it worthy of survival. Three possibilities are raised: trust a historian; struggle for political power; or give your energies to writing. These means to immortality swerve in interesting ways from the ancient "three immortalities" (三不朽): "moral power" (德) passes unmentioned; office achieved by patronage takes the place of "deeds" (功); and Ts'ao P'i emphatically arrogates to a person's own capacity the hope of immortality through the word—the most trustworthy way to reach posterity.

Ts'ao P'i's relative evaluation of the means assumes a desire common to all three, the desire for a cultural immortality which,

[1] Ts'ao P'i 曹丕, "On Literature" ("Lun-wen" 論文), in the *Wen-hsüan* 文選, ed. Hsiao T'ung 蕭統 (501–531) (Taipei: Shang-wu yin-shu-kuan, 1960), p. 1128.

[2] *Tso chuan* 左傳, "Hsiang kung" 襄公 24, 1.

though it promises a less tangible futurity than techniques of refining and ingesting cinnabar, nevertheless admits a more sure and public validation of its efficacy. The intensity of the desire makes one wary of the means to accomplish it. Office and the fame that comes with state service are, at best, risky enterprises; and even the finest historians may neglect some complex and less obvious worthiness, may foolishly trust unreliable sources, may fail to account for the fullness of the self as the person commemorated would wish it to be known.

We wish to be remembered—not simply our names, which may be passed down to the dullest of descendants, but some sense of who we were. In a few generations the ancestral sacrifices will cease, and thereafter a literary text may be the most trustworthy posterity, ever mindful of its filial duties, always honoring the human who was its parent and author.[3]

The traditional biographer's responsibility to record the facts of a person's history is subordinate to a greater responsibility to transmit a moral truth about the subject—"what kind of person he was." One who undertakes to transmit such truths on his own behalf is the autobiographer. Thus autobiography is not an easily recognizable literary form, but an intention, and for the reader, the intuition or the presumption of such an intention. It was Ts'ao P'i's suggestion that a literary text may take the place of the historian's task to more surely transmit that sense of "what kind of person he was."

In the western tradition narrative is the center of biography and autobiography; it is the literary construction of a Life out of life's infinite detail. This narrative core of the autobiographical mode sets the autobiographer in a paradoxical and uncomfortable position, asking a summation that can be perfectly given only posthumously. The Augustinean tradition of confessional autobiography is one solution to the problem posed—the narration of a conversion after

[3] The theme of poem as progeny is an interesting and minor stream in the tradition, explicit (obsessively so) only in the poetry of Meng Chiao, none of whose male children reached maturity. It is closely related to the idea of poem as *somaton*, "little body," common in western literary theory as well as in Chinese. A poem has a complete physiology with "bones," "veins," "*ch'i*," "head," and "tail," etc.

which there is life but no change, a long epilogue of beatific reflection whose constancy is a foretaste of an eternal constancy to come. Out of the Augustinean tradition, western narrative autobiography becomes possible: it recounts the essential changes of life between youth and maturity, a *Bildung* after which human nature grows steady. But such autobiography can have no place in the Chinese tradition: one may "set one's mind on study at fifteen and be established at thirty," but all the most interesting stages of sagely development occur from the age of forty on.[4] Given this Confucian *Bildung* of late-flowering, it is hard to anticipate a final stasis from which to look back and write one's Life as a whole.

In traditional Chinese literature, narrative, in itself, plays a less important role in the presentation of a human life. The life-narrative is often no more than a sequence of mere contingencies, mere happenings, through which a person has an opportunity to show himself. The perfect form of this non-narrative autobiography may be the individual's "collected works" (*pieh-chi* 別集), which, from the early ninth century on, increasingly came to be edited by the authors themselves, works arranged in chronological order (often within a generic framework), contextualized by prefaces and notes. Here editorial exclusions, arrangement, and juxtapositions created a species of interior history, not narrating a life story, but letting a life story unfold in the author's sequence of responses. In more recent times editors have refined this still further in the late classical (and modern) form of a collection, with prose biographies and circumstantial documents by others (e.g., eulogies, letters, answering poems), with multiple prefaces, perhaps with a *nien-p'u* 年譜 (chronology), and interpretive commentary mixed with notes on the historical circumstances surrounding the composition of a particular text. In the more purely autobiographical domain of constructing a collection, there are *pieh-chi* like that of Yang Wan-li 楊萬里, divided into numerous subcollections, each with a preface announcing the author's external circumstances and interior disposition at that stage of his life. In this we find the initial movement

[4] *Hung-lou-meng* 紅樓夢 or *Dream of the Red Chamber* would seem to be an interesting exception, but in its autobiographical dimensions it is less a true *Bildung* than a case in which the world changes around the protagonist.

toward a documentary *Bildung*, tracing the formation and development of a poet.

Let us leave aside the combinatory, complete form and look to the autobiographical document of which a *pieh-chi* is made—the literary text, especially the poem. The poem (here only *shih* 詩) was a privileged document of inner life, a presentation of self that potentially carried strong autobiographical dimensions. By its very definition, *shih* was the stuff of inner life, the person's *chih* 志, "intent," and *ch'ing* 情, "emotions" or "subjective disposition." Here, rather than in narrative, was the center of interest for traditional theorists—not how a person changed over time, but how a person could be known at all or make himself known.

Abraham Cowley wrote, "It is a hard and nice subject for a man to write of himself, it grates his own heart to say anything of disparagement, and the reader's ears to hear anything of praise from him." [5] The autobiographer's powers are the inverse of the powers claimed by the biographer. The biographer's strength and weakness is his distance from his subject; proximity is the weakness and strength of the autobiographer. The autobiographer may hope to emulate the biographer's distance by the ruthlessness of the confessional mode or by reflection on a past self (impossible in the immediacy of the *shih*, which, even when telling of the poet's past, focuses on the present of the remembering self rather than on the self remembered). The autobiographer strives to establish such distances against the suspicion of self-interest that surrounds the act of autobiography. Authenticity must be autobiography's first concern.

A second and related problem attends all autobiographical discourse: what it means to "know oneself." To "know oneself" is to know oneself as other, a disjunction between the knower and the known which calls into question, even as it proclaims, the autobiographer's unique intimacy with his subject. The act of autobiography irrevocably divides and subdivides the assumed unity of the self. And if the Chinese tradition lacks the promise of the possibility of self-knowledge, assumed in the Delphic *gnothi seauton*, it still

[5] Abraham Cowley, "Several Discourses by Way of Essays, in Verse and Prose," in *The Works of Mr. Abraham Cowley* (9th ed., London: J. Tonson, 1700).

exhorts a more indeterminate "self examination," *tzu-hsing* 自省, which assumes that something of the self and its motives are accessible through conscious effort.

The most common poetic promise of authenticity and defense against the division of the self is the assertion of spontaneity. Such is the Confucian entelechy of learning in the sage—not to "know the good" or "do the good," but instinctively to "be good"—"at seventy I followed what my heart desired without transgressing." [6]

Considering poetic autobiography in its Chinese context, we must attend to the Chinese formulations of the nature and problems of autobiography: how it is possible to speak of the self without falsifying it; how the structure of the self changes under such discourse; how identity is won out of categorical role. In the past I have emphasized the assumed involuntarism of the *shih*, that an organic bond is posited between inner life and exterior poem.[7] Here I would like to consider the dangers that beset such an assumption—elements of motivated and voluntary self-presentation in which the poet, aware that he will be known through the poem, struggles to be authentic or to authenticate his self-presentation.

A Double Self

Let us say that poetic autobiography begins in apology, in the need to "explain oneself." Such a need arises only under certain conditions: the poet feels that the self and its motives are more interesting, more complicated, or simply different from what they appear to be; he is pained at the discrepancy, seeks to rectify it, show what is truer and more worthy. Poetic autobiography arises from the fear of being misprized. The human ceases to be an innocent unity of nature and action; he is now a doubleness, an outward appearance concealing, dimming, or distorting some true and hidden nature.

[6] *Lun-yü* 論語 or *The Analects*, II, 4.

[7] Stephen Owen, *Traditional Chinese Poetry and Poetics: An Omen of the World* (Madison: University of Wisconsin Press, 1985).

Suppose, for example, we were to observe some Chin 晉 dynasty (265–419) farmer at his task and believe, according to the biases of the age, that this was some mere peasant dullness, some routine and unreflective performance of a primordial labor whose sole purpose was to sustain his uninteresting life. The farmer turns to us and explains that, in fact, his is the natural human condition, that all human contentment depends on living a life like his. He continues: for a while he had been forced to serve as an official, but he has managed to escape that odious bondage and return to these tasks that are spiritually less fettering. He shows us his poems. We are astounded. The man is not at all what he seemed.

But when we reflect further on our encounter with this eloquent peasant, we wonder why he felt the need to explain himself to us by word and poem, why he was not content to let himself be seen as "mere peasant." When Confucius and Tzu-lu encountered a pair of philosophical plowmen and "asked about the ford," the plowmen gave both master and disciple wise advice: they did not, like this farmer-poet, try to explain their "true nature" or seek to justify why they did what they did.[8]

When working at humdrum office tasks, this Chin farmer felt a deep conflict between his nature and the role he was playing: he gave up his post and "returned to his fields and gardens." But once he admitted the possibility of a "true nature," distinct from his appearance through outer acts, the unity of the self was not so easy to restore. A doubleness now haunts his life and his poems: nature and behavior, the inner and outer man, no longer *are* a unity; they must actively be brought together, and their unity must be actively asserted, a bond forged by the force of will. Our farmer is T'ao Ch'ien 陶潛 (365–427), who turns out to be the greatest of the pre-T'ang poets. It is not that T'ao Ch'ien simply "is" a Chin farmer; he *wants* to be a Chin farmer. Yet one of the characteristics of a true Chin farmer may be to inhabit his role without reflection, choice, or desire. The capacity to reflect on one's nature—at first necessary to articulate T'ao's discomfort in his role as official—endures in this voluntary peasant and becomes the autobiographical impulse, the continuous exposition of "who I *really* am," "what I *really* am like." T'ao Ch'ien is an immensely attractive figure, but what

[8] *Lun-yü*, XVIII, 6.

attracts us may be a complex desire for simplicity rather than simplicity itself.

We are perplexed at this simplicity that is not so simple. We look at those poems again:

Returning to Dwell in My Fields and Gardens (I)
When young, nothing in me chimed with
  the common:
In its roots, my nature loved mountains and
  hills.
I erred, fell into the world's net of dust
In all for some thirty years.
The captive bird yearns for its former groves;
A fish in a pond broods on depths it once
  knew.
I clear away undergrowth at the edge of the
  southern wilds,
Preserve my simplicity, return to my gardens
  and fields.
My holding is only ten acres or so
With a thatch cottage of just a few rooms.[9]
Willow and elm shade my back eaves;
Peach and plum are ranged before my hall.
Dim in my eyes are distant villages;
Hamlets from which the smoke winds
  upward.
Dogs bark deep in the lanes;
A cock crows in the tip of a mulberry.
My door and yard have no mixture of dust;
Empty chambers give ample leisure
Long I was caught in a cage—
Now again I revert to Nature.[10]

歸園田居
少無適俗韻
性本愛邱山
誤落塵網中
一去三十年
羈鳥戀舊林
池魚思故淵
開荒南野際
守拙歸園田
方宅十餘畝
草屋八九間
楡柳蔭後簷
桃李羅堂前
曖曖遠人村
依依墟里煙
狗吠深巷中
鷄鳴桑樹顚
戶庭無塵雜
虛室有餘閒
久在樊籠裏
復得返自然

When we saw this man "clearing away undergrowth" by the

[9] *Mu* 畝, translated as "acre," is in fact considerably less than an acre; T'ao's holdings are thus more modest than the translation suggests. *Chien* 間 is a square measure of house space; the smallness of T'ao's "eight or nine *chien*" has been Englished as a few rooms.

[10] T'ao Ch'ien 陶潛, *T'ao Yüan-ming chi* 陶淵明集 (Peking: Chung-hua shu-chü, 1982), pp. 40–41.

fields, we took him to be a farmer like all others; and if we may not think of a farmer as *su* 俗, "common," "uncouth," whom can we think of as *su*? But in the very first line of his poem, this farmer informs us that he has always had an instinctive antipathy to the "common"—suddenly we realize, to our surprise, that this would-be peasant is not defining himself in relation to farmers, but in relation to us, the people who read poetry! It is we who are being called *su*, "common" on account of the very learning, ambitions, refinement (*ya* 雅), and occupations which we had always believed to be eminently un-*su*, "un-common." [11]

In the second line he expands his rejection of us and our world: his being "un-common" comes from an unalterable disposition of his nature that loves "mountains and hills"—setting himself apart from our "common" fondness for wealth, honor, and position. We are still secretly convinced (though we will never again hazard our conviction on a further inquiry) that the average farmer would, like us, prefer wealth, honor, and position. Then, as if to prove that his revulsion at our values is no rustic "sour grapes," he tells the story of a public career and flight from it, as if from a cage, back to this hard and satisfying labor of clearing farmland. Indeed, he evokes such a picture of georgic bliss that we can—just for a moment—stand with him and see why he so despises our life. We were in error: he is not "a farmer:" he is T'ao Ch'ien being himself, a condition that happens to involve being a farmer.

T'ao Ch'ien, the first great poetic autobiographer, teaches us much about autobiography: the very act of "explaining oneself" is predicated on a doubleness—a true self and a surface role.[12] The

[11] *Su* 俗 originally meant something like "common usage," "custom," "having to do with the lowborn populace." Under the force of usages such as in this poem (including usages by T'ao's predecessors) and with the idealization of the peasantry, *su* came to describe a "worldliness" or "vulgarity" manifest in the upper classes. My whimsical Chin persona, the sophisticated office-holder who meets T'ao Ch'ien in the fields, is being shocked at the altered significance of the term in T'ao's poem.

[12] Many might claim the distinction of being the first poetic biographer for the fourth century B.C. poet Ch'ü Yüan 屈原. There are serious questions about the relation between the historical figure and the poems attached to his name. But, beyond the question of attribution, an autobiographical interpretation of Ch'ü Yüan's work depends on a complex exegetical reconciliation between the text and a biography known from external sources. T'ao Ch'ien is the true autobiographer, both mytholographer and exegete, of his own life.

surface role may turn out to be a lie (T'ao as we might have seen him some years before, performing the routine functions of a magistrate). More remarkably, the surface role may be genuine, but still not sufficient to understand the true self (the farmer who turned out not to be merely "a farmer," but rather T'ao Ch'ien being himself). Doubleness is inevitable: the surface role must be distinct, to be chosen or rejected by the "true self." And in that very act of distinguishing self from role, we have the first assertion of the uniqueness of the self: it must involve a willful individuation from some category in which others find themselves—farmers and readers of poetry. We made a mistake: we thought this was a farmer, and it turned out to be T'ao Ch'ien. For us to understand the distinction, T'ao Ch'ien had to explain himself; and, as he did so, we discovered that he was speaking to us, articulating his nature not in relation to farmers, but in relation to our kind.

T'ao Ch'ien's poetry constantly tells us of the unity of self and role, but it does not embody such unity: it betrays its doubleness, a self-consciously assumed role preceded by judgment and choices made by a "true nature." Both we and the poet learn to distrust surfaces; we now require some assurance that what emerges on the surface, as in a poem, is indeed "true nature." And we come to wonder how inner and outer can ever be brought together again.

Secret Motives

There is an innocent poetry, addressed to one's own pleasure and to the pleasure of one's friends. In the Chin such poetry seems supremely sophisticated, filled with allusions, ornament, gracious sentiments; indeed, this poetry revels in its sophistication, giving no thought to the possibility that later readers might distrust it for its artfulness (or perhaps, on a deeper level, be bored with its innocence). But once the poet becomes the poet-autobiographer, that innocent sophistication disappears: now the poet must always look cautiously ahead to how he will appear in his poems. His greatest fear is that others, reading his work, will catch a whiff of secret motives. If the outer poem, like the outer role, is a voluntary, motivated construct, then there is always the possibility of manipulation and distortion. As a youth T'ao Ch'ien, our Chin farmer, fooled others and himself into believing he was suited for public office; just now we were deceived in thinking he was simply a farmer. All we know about him is what we perceive on the outside, what he tells us and shows us about his inner nature. We must wonder if he is telling the truth about himself now and, more seriously, if he does or can know such a truth.

The poet-autobiographer must offer a defense against the suspicions he has raised. He tells us that these poems are spontaneous, offhand, casual, trivial productions of so little importance to the poet that the reader need have no suspicions of secret motives. But we have grown wary: such assertions of casualness and unconcern seem to be a sure mark of a fall from innocent sophistication. Such assertions are meta-apology and arise from the anxiety that the text might seem to be the product of hidden motives. The first meta-apologist, casually inserting a note to remind us of the offhand nature of his compositions, turns out to be the first great autobiographical apologist, endlessly justifying to us his values and his acts:

> I live at ease and with few delights. Moreover, as nights have been growing longer recently, I happen to have some fine wine. Not an evening passes but I drink, finish it all by myself, my eyes watching my shadow. All at once I'll find myself drunk, and in this condition jot down a few lines for my own amusement. I have accumulated a great deal of paper with writing on it, with no order at all in the language. So I happened to have an old friend copy them out for his pleasure.[13]

We wondered about that when we read his poems—how we happened to find them all written neatly out before us—strange, coming from a person who cares so little for us. In this preface to "Drinking Wine" 飲酒, T'ao Ch'ien documents the circumstances of composition and preparation of a manuscript of poems; he notes the stages of the process more fully than any of his contemporaries, taking care to emphasize the dominance of whim and accident at every stage of the complicated procedure. We might concede that the natural, spontaneous human could compose poems for his own

[13] T'ao Ch'ien, *T'ao Yüan-ming chi*, pp. 86–87.

amusement, but to copy them out and circulate them smells of "fishing for fame in the world"; hence we have an *amicus ex machina* to perform this disreputable task. The preface is necessary: T'ao cannot let these poems go without assuring us that their "publication" is none of his doing; he fears that others might believe that *he* had them circulated. He wants no one to suspect, even for a moment, that he knew what he was doing or cared in the "Drinking Wine" poems: all is drunkenness, accident, whim—all the proofs of spontaneity, which later poets were to wear as talismans against the suspicion that a poet reveals himself not as he is, but as he wishes himself to be seen. This is not a poet who simply drinks; this is a poet who drinks and watches his own shadow, observing himself, his solitude, and his movements as he drinks.

It should be said, once and for all, that T'ao Ch'ien is not the naive and straightforward poet he claims to be. T'ao is the patron-ancestor of hundreds of T'ang, Sung, and late classical poets—obsessively self-conscious, defensive about his values and acts, trying desperately to win a naiveté out of a conflict of inner values. It was for these complications that later ages loved him. T'ao Ch'ien is *not* a poet of "fields and gardens" 田園 (in contrast to Hsieh Ling-yün [385–433], who *is* a poet of "landscapes" 山水); T'ao's "fields and gardens" are no more than a setting in which this image of the naive self can be at rest. The outer world falls away; the self becomes the topic of the poem; self-knowledge and authenticity become a problem. These complications accompany T'ao's status as the first great autobiographer, in his prose as well as in his poetry—the "Return" 歸去來辭,[14] the "Biography of Five Willows" 五柳先生傳,[15] and even in "An Elegy for Myself" 自祭文.[16]

Coming to T'ao Ch'ien's poetry from the work of his contemporaries and immediate predecessors, we notice the number of non-social occasional poems in his collection; i.e., poems that grow out of and address particular life circumstances, but which are not addressed to anyone (though T'ao did write many social occasional

[14] *Ibid.*, pp. 159–163.
[15] *Ibid.*, pp. 175–176.
[16] *Ibid.*, pp. 196–199.

poems). Such non-social occasional poems include the majority of T'ao's most famous works: "Returning To Dwell in My Fields and Gardens," "Moving" 移居,[17] "Drinking Wine," "Giving Up Wine" 止酒,[18] "Begging" 乞食.[19] We must ask to whom and for whom such poems were written. The English term for readership, "audience," betrays its origins in drama; it is that large, faceless crowd of onlookers which remains the secret object of even western lyric poetry's address. But this assumption of a large, anonymous readership is the accident of a particular history; it cannot be taken for granted as necessary and inevitable for all poetry. A similar (though still distinct) notion of "audience" does develop in Chinese poetry, not out of the quality of address necessary in drama, but out of the autobiographical mode.

The nature of a poetic voice and the nature of its address to others are largely a function of genre. T'ao Ch'ien, the poet-autobiographer, perfected a new genre, apparent in his titles: he speaks of himself, as a particular historical being, to no one in particular and hence to anyone at any time. Here is the address to futurity implicit in the Ts'ao P'i passage; and this genre, this new kind of title, was taken up extensively by T'ao's admirers among T'ang and later poets.

We must set T'ao Ch'ien's poetry in its contemporary generic context. In the fourth and early fifth centuries there were fictional genres with impersonal voices—*yu-hsien shih* 遊仙詩 (poems on immortals), *yung-wu* 詠物 (poems on things, often allegorical in this period), and some *yüeh-fu* 樂府. There was another group of genres which provide the close antecedents of T'ao Ch'ien's new voice, genres in which the poet spoke intensely of himself, but with a generalized lyric "I," an "I" that links the self with common human experience: in this grouping fall *yung-huai* 詠懷 and "unclassified poems" 雜詩. Such poems, by their titles and in their texts, tend to avoid reference to specific site and occasion. T'ao Ch'ien's poems in this mode are quite distinct from his non-social

[17] *Ibid.*, pp. 56–57.

[18] *Ibid.*, pp. 100–101.

[19] *Ibid.*, p. 48.

occasional poems. The third group of contemporary genres are the occasional genres. When a poet spoke of himself as a particular historical being, at a particular location and particular time—his specific experiences, responses to occasion, and attitudes—then he was usually addressing someone in particular, someone he knew.

In his non-social occasional poems T'ao Ch'ien speaks of himself in detail to everyone and to no one in particular. In later poetry we become accustomed to such a mode of address, but in the Chin we must marvel at this voice. Why a person would speak thus, speak to no one, requires some explanation: T'ao offers such an explanation in the preface to "Drinking Wine"—"I just happened to scribble these poems out, dear reader; don't believe I was writing them for you." Yet as he excuses himself in the preface, he lets us know that he knows these poems are coming to us, the nameless, future readers of poetry of other places and other times.

It is to such a vast future audience that the poet-autobiographer must speak: he offers them interior history, just as the common historian offers them outer history. The poet-autobiographer is not merely addressing Lord So-and-So, showing his virtues in hopes of a position (though later poets may, for the sake of economy, address Lord So-and-So and eternity simultaneously). His first address to us must convince us that he does not want to convince us of anything, assure us there is no motive in his writing: he speaks to us, telling us he has no intention of speaking to us at all.

T'ao Ch'ien's poetry is filled with contradictions, the contradictions that come from a sophisticated, self-conscious man who yearns to be unsophisticated and unself-conscious. Our pleasure in his poetry is equally contradictory: *his* naiveté we can love, though we would probably be bored by a truly unsophisticated and unself-conscious poet. Whether we acknowledge it or not, our pleasure in T'ao Ch'ien lies in the uncomfortable complexity of the person.

Returning to Dwell in My Fields and Gardens (II)

In the wilderness, few human affairs;
To poor lanes wheels and bridles rarely come.
I close my wicker gate in broad daylight—

野外罕人事
窮巷寡輪鞅
白日掩荊扉

No worldly fantasies in my empty chambers.
Now and again at the bends of the village
Pushing back brush we come and go;
And when we meet, our talk is not mixed
With anything but how tall hemp and
  mulberry grow.
Daily the mulberry and hemp grow taller;
Daily my lands grow more broad.
Yet always I fear that the frosts will come,
That there will be ruin, as with the grass and
  weeds.[20]

虛室絕塵想
時復墟曲中
披草共來往
相見無雜言
但道桑麻長
桑麻日已長
我土日已廣
常恐霜霰至
零落同草莽

He would put us to shame for our worldliness, but we (the readers of poetry to whom he speaks) should not let our shame lull us into ignoring the rich complexity in his vision of simplicity. "In the wilderness, few human affairs"—the line here is no more than the mark of an attitude and a relation: it might be literally true for a misanthropic hermit, but it is *not* literally true for T'ao Ch'ien. The fields he tends and so proudly extends are not *yeh* 野, "wilderness," or in T'ao's phrasing, *yeh-wai* 野外, "beyond [in] the wilderness," "deep in wilderness," often suggesting an immortal world.[21] *Yeh-wai* is a special structure of space—a cultivated, civilized world, beyond which is wilderness, and beyond that, something otherworldly, at the farthest extreme from human civilization. In such a remote place there would, of course, be "few human affairs" 罕人事, the acts of civilization and its "problems" (also *jen-shih* 人事). But as we read the poem, we find it is filled with what we might ordinarily have called *jen-shih*, "human affairs and problems"—this agrarian society where men come and go from their labors, talking only of vital concerns, the success of crops, extending fields into the wilderness, worry about an early frost. We must suppose that T'ao does not count these as "human affairs/problems"; rather "human affairs/problems" refer us to a political domain quite distinct from this agrarian society. Implicitly

[20] *Ibid.*, pp. 41–42.

[21] It would be tempting to take *yeh-wai*, "beyond the wilderness," as "at the edge of wilderness"; i.e., where clearing land occurs. But this interpretation would be untrue to the common use of the phrase and parallel phrases as "beyond this world."

T'ao is addressing readers to whom "human affairs/problems" mean their own, readers from the civilized domain at the opposite extreme from *yeh-wai*.

Our grand carriages cannot penetrate the narrow lanes of his village; he tells us he speaks only to villagers and only about crops. We, the snubbed readers, are sincerely uninterested in the state of T'ao's crops or of the crops of his fellow villagers; but we find that we *are* interested in someone who tells us, in our written poetic language, that *he* is interested only in his crops. Though rejected, we note with some approval that it is only our affairs that merit the characterization "human," as opposed to farmers' problems, presumably not "human." *We* know that T'ao has given us simply another token of his rejection of our world, like the aloofness of the misanthropic recluse in the first line; but we suspect that T'ao's fellow villagers would not feel pleased to be so lightly excluded from the species. We know that in poetry the terms for an immortal's world, the terms for the world of the solitary recluse, and the terms for a farmer's world can be used *interchangeably*; such easy interchanges occur only when each of these worlds has no subsistence in its own right, but is only a negation of the public, political world, the world of the people who read poetry. T'ao Ch'ien's poetry really cares little for farmers: it speaks to and for our flurried world of carriage-riders and poetry readers.

The last lines speak of a fear of early frost, that his crops will be ruined. But the line is phrased with deliberate ambiguity to encompass anxiety about the poet's own mortality, that he may fall to earth like "common plants" and ordinary mortals. Against just such an anxiety about our mortality, Ts'ao P'i enjoined us to "trust our persons to ink and the brush," to write poems that will perpetuate our identity and memory of us. To write poems is to communicate, *t'ung* 通, one's nature to others, to those who read poetry and cherish the memory of poets. But this poem communicates only blockages and closings, *se* 塞, a world closed off to the very people to whom a poem tries to speak. His lane is too narrow, his gate is closed, he will not speak to us; he tells us this again and again. And he passionately desires that we recognize and always remember the calm dispassion of his mind, that he has no concern for us at all. He has nothing to say to our kind.

Roles and Sages

The vision of the self which the poet wishes to present is his "role"; and yet the self which the poet-autobiographer actually reveals to us is often a much more contradictory and unsteady being. Traditional commentary tends to honor the desires of poets and takes note only of the uncomplicated surfaces. But still we suspect that the true allure of the autobiographical text may lie in the complications which agitate the surface. It may not be T'ao Ch'ien, the self-satisfied farmer-recluse, that we love, but another T'ao Ch'ien, painfully self-conscious, unsure of who he is, warring against the inner claims of his own class to win for himself satisfaction in being the farmer-recluse. Our affection for Wang Wei may not look to his dispassionate calm, but to some fierce and active mastery of self, a passionate austerity. It may not be expansive wildness that engages us in Li Po's poetry, but a frenzy of posing—sometimes aggressively, sometimes playfully—in which his rich imagination is harnassed and whipped on by some darker need.

The roles which such poets play, the roles in which such poets would have themselves seen by others, are not the mere typology of personality, a hollow form of definition received from the community, but a particular confluence of innate disposition and desire. The term "role" is the unfortunate legacy of a poetics (and following the poetics, a psychology and sociology) which is grounded in drama; and thus "role" assumes an absolute disjunction between itself and "true nature." Unlike the doubleness we spoke of earlier, this lineage of the concept of role assumes the complete separation of person from role (allowing relations of affinity, mutual influence, etc.). Out of Greek drama, the enactment of a "role" often involves the use of a "mask," through which (as Oscar Wilde says) the truth may be told, but which purposefully conceals the being who is telling the truth. We use the term "role" in a different sense here: it is not independent of the self, but an organic dimension of it; role is desire, the surface of the self as it wishes to be known; role is the entelechy of a process of self-definition. Thus we see T'ao, the farmer-recluse, *not* as the complete definition of T'ao Ch'ien and *not* as a false mask: it is the T'ao Ch'ien that he himself would wish to be.

Some embodiments of role are grander than others, and it may be that such grandeur is a function of the complexity and intensity of desire to "become" the role. But desire always reveals some lack, some dissatisfaction and unsureness which are visible in direct proportion to the intensity of the desire: "when things do not achieve their equilibrium, they sing out" 物不得其平則鳴.[22] When such desire is strongly imprinted in the enactment of the role—as in T'ao Ch'ien's constant need to say to us that he has nothing to say to our kind—then the enactment of the role has an allure and cutting edge which less passionate inhabitants of a role can never achieve. Ch'ien Ch'i and a dozen other poets sought a role similar to that of the High Tang poet Wang Wei 王維 of the second half of the eighth century; but the genius that distinguishes Wang Wei's work may be the fierceness of his desire to be such a person—a peculiar violence against self that refuses to permit the common human response. The genius in Wang Wei's poetry is not a distinction of craft or even of art, but of a powerful and complicated human identity. This is heresy in western literary theory; it need not be heresy here.

A poet inscribes his identity in a poem just as all humans inscribe identity in their lives. This identity is role surrounded by rich echoes of complication, contradiction, and desire, echoes which always remind us that the self is more than its role. When those echoes are loud, we are reminded of the indeterminancy of human nature; we intuit layers upon layers of hiddenness; we wonder what a particular person's nature really is. A grand role like T'ao Ch'ien's recalls its negations; and, in doing so, it transcends mere role to enact the relations between humans and roles. We read not of a farmer-recluse named T'ao Ch'ien, but of T'ao Ch'ien, presenting himself as farmer-recluse, with all the complications that attend such an act. Apart from his role(s), a human is plastic, indeterminate, a mere history of accidents, occasions, and changes, unknowable either to self or to others; a role is determinate and communicable, a form through which the indeterminate self can be known.

[22] Han Yü 韓愈, "Preface on Sending Off Meng Chiao" 送孟東野序, in *Han Ch'ang-li chi* 韓昌黎集 (rpt. Hong Kong: Shang-wu yin-shu-kuan, 1964), *chüan* 19, p. 7.

And the greatest poets enact the relations between the two—between self and role—the process by which the two seek perfect correspondence.

The obsession with authenticity, the vision of Confucius at seventy, grows from the hope of some consummate union of self and role: such a condition is called "sagehood" (in its Mencian version, the sage being the only role in which the innate goodness of the human can be fulfilled). In his unity of being, the sage sees through the surface roles of others: he sees the complications, the hidden motives, all tensions between surfaces and the inner self. "The Master said, 'Look to *how* it is; observe from what it comes; examine in what he finds rest. How can a person remain hidden, how can he remain hidden?!' "[23] We are enjoined to scrutinize not only the quality of act and behavior, but also their motives and, beyond that, the kind of condition in which the person is "at rest." The sage sees through surfaces to the true nature of the creature.

Exercising the wise vision of the sage, virtue may be discovered as well as evil: we may honor the person no longer hidden, or we may condemn him. But if there is a disjunction between the inner person and the role, between tone of voice and statement, then no matter how great the virtue we discover, the person is no sage. At seventy Confucius' acts and his heart's desires were the same: he *is* the sage. But we have "seen through" T'ao Ch'ien, and, however much we honor this person and his desires, we recognize an anxiety and unsureness that cannot belong to the sage.

Then suppose we found a poet who, writing of himself, confidently exposes the tension between person and role—someone who does not merely present his desired vision of the self, but, with the sharp eyes of the sage, sees through it. On one level such a person would be the quotidian human with ordinary hopes and illusions—perhaps poetically more interesting than the sage, but less grand. On another level such a person would *be* the sage, seeing through a role to its secret motives and desires, revealing a person (who happens to be himself) as other than that person might wish himself to be seen. It is, admittedly, a paradoxical stance, but the governing voice has the honesty and clear assurance of the sage. We

[23] *Lun-yü*, II, 10.

might look for such a voice in the work of "the sage of poetry" 詩聖, Tu Fu 杜甫 (712–770).

Empty Purse	空囊
Azure cypress, bitter but still to be eaten;	翠柏苦猶食
Morning's rose clouds can be my morning meal.	晨霞朝可餐
People of the age have all sown recklessly,	世人共鹵莽
And my way finds itself among hardships.	吾道屬艱難
No cooking fire; the well, frozen at dawn;	不爨井晨凍
No greatcoat for covers; my bed, cold at night.	無衣牀夜寒
Yet I fear the embarrassment of an empty purse	空囊恐羞澀
And leave there one coin, watched over, to be seen.[24]	留得一錢看

"The Master said, 'Look to *how* it is; observe from what it comes; examine in what he finds rest. How can a person remain hidden, how can he remain hidden?!'" "Look to *how* it is"—in the title he implies an untruth, that his purse is empty, but he tells us the truth in the end. The untruth is not a great lie—it is a figurative truth, a purse not empty but virtually empty. He could have, without guilt, left this merely figurative truth standing; and even if he felt uncomfortable with its literal untruth, he knows that we, the readers of the poem, would never have known the untruth unless he confessed it to us. Yet others, seeing the weight in his purse, would never have known that this coin was not ready cash, only pride—this too he confesses.

Observe from what it comes—he tells us a literal untruth not to deceive us, but so that we will not be deceived as others are deceived, misunderstanding the coin in his purse. Then he tells us the literal truth because he cannot bear to leave us with a partial truth—he exposes his acts and motives to us. He exposes the motive for his deceptive coin—the fear of embarrassment. Yet in exposing the motive, he reveals that he is not so fearful of embarrassment after all.

[24] Ch'iu Chao-ao 仇兆鰲, *Tu-shih hsiang-chu* 杜詩詳注, 5 vols. (Peking: Chung-hua shu-chü, 1979), vol. 2, *chüan* 8, pp. 620–621.

Examine in what he rests—we see much in which Tu Fu finds no rest. Cypress cone and roseate clouds are the foods of immortals, foods of purity and otherworldliness, and they are to be Tu Fu's food; they are exposed, the bitter and insubstantial food of hungry necessity. He can find no contentment in them, nor can he pretend to contentment. In hardship, hunger, and cold there is no physical rest. Yet he could purchase a brief respite if he spent that single coin of pride: he keeps the coin, and we learn that he finds greater comfort in avoiding the shame of poverty than in some minor alleviation of his condition. We approve. But he does not simply point to his coin and tell us he is not destitute; he confesses he has it and why he keeps it. And we look beyond "finding rest" in the avoidance of shame to a still more basic "rest" in telling the truth about oneself, making the inner person and the outer person of the poem the same.

There is a wondrous complexity of the human in Tu Fu's poetry: strangely, an honest and authentic voice emerges out of a double untruth—an untruth in telling us his purse was empty and an untruth in telling others his purse is not empty. Tu Fu is the sage-autobiographer, penetrating all the deceptive surface roles that belong to his unsagely, merely human self. "How can a person remain hidden, how can he remain hidden?!"

The voice is not that of the accomplished sage; it is the voice of the fallible human becoming sage, driven by a restless honesty and fidelity to life's circumstances. Yet this movement from ordinary human toward sage is all the more powerful because it is not the perfect transparency of the sage, but the self being laid bare, breaking through those illusions and poses that would comfort lesser men.

He begins with an "Empty Purse": he plans to tell us of his destitution. Yet he begins not with a statement of want but of possession—having cypress cones and rose clouds to eat. These are foods of immortals, chosen for their purity by those who would live forever; in Tu Fu's poem they threaten death by starvation. He boasts of having these, but with an easy irony that exposes his boast as hollow—a provision that is no provision, just like an empty purse that is not empty.

He blames his destitution on the age—"reckless sowing," *lu-*

mang 鹵莽, a dead metaphor for careless action, a metaphor that is made alive again in Tu Fu's hunger.[25] Bad husbandry and bad government are blamed on the "people of the age" 世人, also mere "mortals" in opposition to the sort of being who dines on cypress cones and rose clouds. He, destitute gourmand of immortal fare, claims distinction from worldlings, only to admit later that he keeps his coin of pride for the sake of *their* good opinion.

In the third couplet he confesses his destitution, says straightforwardly what he had said in the first couplet through the negations of irony; he confesses his utter destitution only to unconfess it in the final couplet. And he confesses his destitution only to admit that there is something worse than that destitution—shame. In the end all is revealed, and in his honesty beyond honor there is an unmistakeable humor, a distance from which he laughs at himself. It is Tu Fu's genius—perhaps the genius of the sage—to be both sincere and wry, to both inhabit and indulgently observe the foolishness of the human creature.

There is another, less profound, kind of poetic autobiographer, the autobiographer of his own deeds. Such an autobiographer never needs to wonder who or what he is because he lives through his deeds; they are sufficient excuse for the self, and the self is sanctioned to disappear into the deeds. Such a person endures as a mere instrumentality—that by which certain important things were done. The great poetic autobiographers of China are rarely of this sort; but even in China there seems to be some law of proportion in this, that the fewer one's deeds on behalf of the civilization, the more one must enquire whether there might be some worth in the self that transcends acts and can exist without them. Tu Fu has accomplished nothing, or, more important, feels that he has accomplished nothing. And if he seeks to tell us of himself, if he would

[25] *Lu-mang* 鹵莽 is, in fact, a compound simply meaning "careless." However, a famous usage in the *Chuang Tzu* 莊子 (*Chuang Tzu yin-te* 莊子引得, 71/25/38–39) was erroneously explained by an early commentator, Ssu-ma Piao 司馬彪, as "plowing shallow and sowing sparsely" 淺耕稀種, with careless husbandry used as a metaphor for careless government. The implications of careless government are primary in Tu Fu's poem (though intended critically rather than positively as in the *Chuang Tzu*); but the implication of careless husbandry seems to be evoked in the paradigm of starvation, established in the first lines.

claim that his life has interest and value to the later-born, then it must be for what he *is*, rather than for what he has done.

Tu Fu is the meticulous exegete of his inner life, ever watchful against the delusory simplicity of a comfortable role. But "role" is the determinate, communicable aspect of the self; and to explicate the self requires that one not only know the self, but know it in communicable terms. The autobiographer of "being" rather than "deeds" is doomed to speak through role, even though role will always fail the contradictory and indeterminate complexity of the self. Tu Fu, with an intuitive distrust of role's limitations, gives the fuller, more contradictory self an animate presentation by continuously negating his roles and undermining them.

"Empty Purse" is not an isolated example of Tu Fu's movement through role to a presentation of the more complex self beyond role: such poems appear from his early work, on through the poetry of the K'uei-chou 夔州 period. In "Written on the Hermitage of Mr. Chang" (first of two) 題張氏隱居二首之一, Tu Fu sets out seeking the companionship of the recluse and ends up with a distrust of "seeking companionship."[26] In "Going from the Capital to Feng-hsien" 自京赴奉先縣五百字,[27] the long opening is a remarkable piece of self-analysis, laughing at his various self-images, which hover between the grand and grandiose: he "secretly compares himself" to the great ministers of antiquity, as Confucius "secretly compared himself" to old P'eng;[28] the proposition is admirable, but not only does Tu Fu fail the greatness of his ancient exemplars, he also fails the ancient maker of "secret comparisons," Confucius.

Mockery of his failed ambitions occurs throughout the great poem sequences of the K'uei-chou period, such as "Autumn Meditations" 秋興八首[29] and "Autumn Wastes" 秋野五首.[30] But this process of self-exposure occurs on more profound levels: if he speaks with too much assurance, Tu Fu may turn on that confident

[26] Ch'iu Chao-ao, *Tu-shih hsiang-chu*, vol. 1, *chüan* 1, pp. 8–11.

[27] *Ibid.*, vol. 1, *chüan* 4, pp. 264–275.

[28] *Lun-yü*, VIII, 1.

[29] Ch'iu Chao-ao, *Tu-shih hsiang-chu*, vol. 4, *chüan* 17, pp. 1484–1499.

[30] *Ibid.*, vol. 4, *chüan* 20, pp. 1732–1735.

voice and expose its weakness. In the "Barren Palms" 枯椶[31] from his Szechwan years, Tu Fu laments the palms as an allegorical emblem of the suffering people—a pious, proto-"new *yüeh-fu*" stance. But in the closing of this poem, he turns on himself: an oriole, pecking for grubs in the dying trees with the self-preserving pitilessness of the Taoist sage, turns and sees a passing tumbleweed (the conventional emblem of the poet wanderer); the oriole comments that in its own miserable state it has no right to lament others. The pious voice of the poem suddenly loses its authority: it is both mocked and pitied. In large ways and small, Tu Fu continually steps out of roles he has assumed to show us their fragility, their motives, and their failures.

Metamorphosis

The poet-autobiographer, exegete of the inner self, hopes to tell futurity who he is, who he was. But in that very process the self becomes somehow doubled, fragmented, recedes into indeterminacy and uncertainty: voice and statement contradict one another. Out of this loss of intelligibility and unity there grows the strong desire to restore coherence to the self. Perhaps the most common way in which this desire was fulfilled in the course of Chinese literary history (and the least satisfying way) was the direct assertion of casualness and spontaneity in composition. From T'ao Ch'ien's self-conscious disclaimer of self-consciousness in the preface to "Drinking Wine," to Po Chü-i's 白居易 (772–846) studied ease, to the eleventh-century philosopher-poet Shao Yung's 邵雍 (1011–1077) hundred poems, each beginning and closing with the line "It's not that I, Shao Yung, really love poetry" (堯夫非是愛吟詩), to the Kung-an poets of the Ming and their successors in the *hsing-ling* 性靈 poets of the Ch'ing—for fifteen hundred years we hear a constant stream of voices promising authentic and spontaneous revelation of the self. Almost all contain implicit or explicit commentary on their own spontaneity, and they all belong firmly

[31] *Ibid.*, vol. 2, *chüan* 10, p. 855.

in the condition which Schiller called "the sentimental" (not to be confused with the popular sense of the term).

Tu Fu goes beyond the cultivated stance of spontaneity to turn on his own self-image those sage eyes that see through the limitations of role. His legacy to later poets was the capacity to laugh at oneself. But it was Tu Fu's particular gift that even as he engaged in these acts of irony, he never lost sympathy for that aspect of the self trapped in mere role. Yet among his successors, particularly among the Sung poets, that self-directed irony too often becomes cruel: masks of playfulness poorly disguise a self-mockery whose harshness exposes not self-knowledge but a profound inner discord. The gift of irony, in itself, no better healed the divided self than the delusory hope of spontaneity.

A unified self can never exist so long as knower and known are presented as the same person. But suppose the self were to be recognized in another being: instead of making the self other in self-consciousness, here the poet would see an other as the self. The being out there is unified—not divided against itself in self-consciousness—yet there is a bond of affinity to validate the identification. To see oneself in another being is a capacity of distance. Tu Fu, who "sees through" his roles as if observing himself from the outside, moves on to look in the world for such an "other self." The first stage of the process is simile:

Wind-tossed, fluttering—what is my likeness?—	飄飄何所似
Between Heaven and Earth, a single gull of the sands.[32]	天地一沙鷗

In the Chinese poetic tradition Tu Fu's is the most perfect and most difficult autobiographical voice. Its perfection resides in its triumph over the reflective division of the self, in a triumph of coherence and intimacy which arises, paradoxically, from a growing distance—at first the distance of irony, then a greater distance in which he sees himself in another. The "single gull of the sands," "Lakes and rivers fill the earth—one old fisherman"—such images of the "other self," observed from a distance, are familiar to readers of Tu Fu.

[32] *Ibid.*, vol. 3, *chüan* 14, pp. 1228–1230.

Consonant with the autobiographer's unchanging concern, such images are often the centers of an otherwise empty world. The voice in the poem no longer attempts to explain the self's secret nature to *us*; the poet turns away from us, looks into the world to discover there the means for his own understanding. The voice achieves authenticity; we no longer suspect its motives; the poet no longer claims to "know" who he is, but seeks images in the mind and in the outer world to answer the question "what is my likeness."

Yangtze and Han	江漢
At Yangtze and the Han, a wanderer longing to return;	江漢思歸客
Of Ch'ien and K'un, one worn-out man of learning.	乾坤一腐儒
A wisp of cloud, Heaven shares such distance;	片雲天共遠
The long night—moon, the same in solitude.	永夜月同孤
In sinking sunlight a mind with vigor still,	落日心猶壯
In autumn's wind this sickness almost cured.	秋風病欲蘇
Since ancient days they've kept old horses	古來存老馬
Which did not need to take to the far-faring road.[33]	不必取長途

It is a famous poem and a strange one, a poem animated by Tu Fu's unique combination of distance and intimacy. Neither an image of the self nor a parallel couplet belong properly in the opening of a regulated verse; here we have both, a formal displacement to match the theme of displacement. Tu Fu's need to get to the central business of "who I am" brushes aside the more stately ceremonies of regulated verse structure. He gives us two figures for the self; the self can be and is both figures at once, but their serial presentation reminds us of this poet's latitude to see himself as many things—even a true role has no power to stabilize and define this poet—it is only a name he has in passing.

From the very beginning Tu Fu sees himself as if from the outside, alone in a magnitude. He is *k'o* 客, a "wanderer," the

[33] *Ibid.*, vol. 5, *chüan* 22, pp. 2029–2030.

human known in relation to a subjective topography, a physical displacement of journeys and returns in which all locations but one remind him he is not "at home." Immediately he dresses in another role, another mode of displacement, a "worn-out man of [Confucian] learning," this also a falling away, but a falling away in time and quality which seems to promise no hope of return. Here the location is not "Yangtze and Han" but Ch'ien and K'un, Heaven and Earth in their cosmic sense, a location that is no location and that, unlike the location of the first line, gives no directions. Between the two lines perspective is enlarged, diminishing the solitary figure in the scene, but enlarging the scope and magnitude of the observing eyes. The two selves, viewer and viewed, vary inversely in their proportions: here is the largest being and the tiniest.

The grammar of the second couplet has all the indeterminacy of Tu Fu's later style. On one level the "wisp of cloud" is as far as the sky (*t'ien*/天, the vault of Heaven that lies beyond the empty air, *k'ung* 空); the "long night" is as solitary as the moon (for *ku* 孤, "solitude," commonly modifies nights as well as moons). But we know that the poet too "shares" the quality of distance with the heavens and cloud, that he is the "same" as night and moon in solitude.

The observer's remote eyes see the self at a distance, see a cloud at the "sky's edge" (*t'ien-ya* 天涯, the "horizon," the "ends of the earth"), a cloud whose rootless wanderings are the "other self" of the human wanderer: the observer discovers himself there, at the "sky's edge," at the "ends of the earth." And in the blur of distance, the diminutive self easily becomes/becomes-confused-with the "other." Then looking up, also as far as heaven (*t'ien*) beyond the empty air, is another version of that remote, solitary shape—the moon, another transformation of the self after "wanderer," "man of learning," "wisp of cloud." There is almost a reciprocity here, of seeing and being seen—the opening lines with the person as if seen from far above, now the person looking at shapes far from him and above him, other selves that might likewise see him. Like Li Po before him, Tu Fu called the moon a mirror (江邊星月二首之一).[34] There are so many solitudes in this immensity that it

[34] *Ibid.*, vol. 4, *chüan* 21, p. 1899.

seems there should be something like a companionship of solitudes: but these prove no more than solitary mirrors that look on him from afar as he looks on them. The mirror is the autobiographer's device; yet these mirrors are set afar and reveal a metamorph passing from shape to shape.

The third couplet "turns," 轉, turns from outer self to inner, turns from wearing away to regeneration. In the cyclical movement of Ch'ien and K'un (the third couplet often takes up the second line, as the second couplet takes up the first line) what reaches an extreme may revert to its opposite—物極必反. The worn-out may be new again. Displacement in the landscape, being "not at home," generates other displacements—youthful "vigor" in evening and old age, healing amid autumn's destructive powers. Ultimately, his solitude means uniqueness and difference from the common movements of the universe.

His final metamorphosis is into the old horse, the mind's emblem of the self, not in the scene. Here too he is displaced and unique, an old horse whose circumstances are inappropriate for the average old horse. He, unlike them, must take to the long-faring road. Yet here is his uniqueness; the difference that comes of displacement and isolation regenerates him while others die in the comfort of their stables in this time of endings.

This autobiographer reflects on his singularity—that is the stuff of autobiography—in a poem generated around a constant interplay of singularities and multiplicities, a self distinct from others that retains its identity in passing through many shapes. He sees this singularity reflected all around him, and out of the multiplicity of his variations he wins a victory of coherence. He unifies antitheses: he is the farthest and the nearest, the fading and the rejuvenating, the most diminutive and the most immense.

"Yangtze and Han" comes from what Tu Fu called his "journey south," *nan-cheng* 南征. In 768 Tu Fu left K'uei-chou and travelled down the Yangtze, turning south along the eastern edge of Lake Tung-t'ing, past Yüeh-yang and White Sands Post Station, on south along the Hsiang River deep into southern Hunan (he turned back there and started north again, dying in 770 before reaching the Yangtze). It was his final journey—he seems often to have sensed this—and it was a perplexing journey, going south into regions where no one went unless sent there in administrative exile. He offered many reasons for the journey—to flee war and rebellion, to see friends and patrons—but beyond these too easy explanations, there was to him something mysterious and portentous about the journey, as if he were bound in some mythic itinerary whose significance was to be revealed to him in transit. This sense of enacting some mythic narrative is apparent in the "other selves" he generates for himself in these final poems; they are figures of myth and legend, each of which offers an explanation of who he is, where he is going, why he is going there: he is going off to be the "old man star" 老人星 in the southern constellations; he is Chia I, going to exile in Ch'ang-sha; he is the wandering soul of Ch'ü Yüan, beyond the "Summons," too deep in the southern wilderness; he is the "wandering star" 客星, the raft that carried a man down the Yangtze, out into the oceans, and up into the heavens; he is the stormbird, whose coming presages the tempest.[35] He is a self in search of a role to tell him who he is, to surround his goings with a significant and preordained narrative.

The most powerful of these mythic roles for the self is that of the great P'eng, from the parable of magnitude and metamorphosis told in the first chapter of the *Chuang Tzu* 莊子. Leviathan K'un 鯤 (whose name means "roe," the most immense and the tiniest), a creature of waters like Tu Fu, undergoes a metamorphosis into a creature of air, the mighty P'eng, whose wingspan stretches from horizon to horizon. The transformed P'eng awaits the storm whose name is *fu-yao* 扶搖, "Whirlwind," to carry it up ninety thousand *li*, where it "plans to go south," to set off for the "southern deeps," *nan-ming* 南溟. This is the grandest "journey south," a myth that draws together many major themes of Tu fu's last poetry—a singular creature heading southward, a grandeur whose magnitude eludes common recognition (see the *Chuang Tzu* parable and the closing of "Ballad of the Old Cypress" 古柏行),[36] the bird moving with the storm (see "Ballad of the White Duck" 白鳧行),[37] meta-

[35] Of course, several of these figures—the "unsummoned soul" and the "wandering star"—appear commonly in Tu Fu's K'uei-chou poetry: in that work we can see the beginnings of Tu Fu's fascination with filling portentous roles of history and myth.

[36] Ch'iu Chao-ao, *Tu-shih hsiang-chu*, vol. 3, *chüan* 15, pp. 1357–1362.

morphosis and regeneration, all on the way to the "southern deeps."

Mooring Beneath Yüeh-yang
Through river lands I've passed a thousand
  miles,
Draw near to city of mountain rising,
  upward a hundred tiers.
A wind from the shore topples the evening
  waves;
Snow on the boat spatters in the cold
  lamplight.
Delayed here, my talent does not end;
In trouble and hardship my spirits grow and
  swell.
"Plans to go south"—not yet to be
  considered:
In metamorphosis still, Leviathan and
  P'eng.[38]

泊岳陽城下
江國踰千里
山城近百層
岸風翻夕浪
舟雪灑寒燈
留滯才難盡
艱危氣益增
圖南未可料
變化有鯤鵬

He journeys far and comes to a place where a storm holds him up, forces him to linger, impatiently. There his eyes follow the mountain city upward, rising ever higher above him as he draws nearer in his boat. From waters to the heights of city and sky, his thoughts on horizontal travels are directed to the vertical, the shore-slope from which the storm winds topple darkening waves and send snow spattering over his boat. This poet, who so often sees mythic landscapes embedded in sublunary scenes, may find a secret form in the mooring—the edge of the vertical stormwind that will carry the metamorphosed P'eng high into the upper air. Once aloft, it can "plan to go south"—not yet. This creature of waters awaits his metamorphosis at the vertiginous edge.

As in "Yangtze and Han" regeneration accompaines metamorphosis: the third, "turning couplets" of both poems are very close—a weariness of hardships and growing lateness in which the

[37] *Ibid.*, vol. 5, *chüan* 23, p. 2037.

[38] *Ibid.*, *chüan* 22, p. 1945. In line 5 I am following the Ch'iu Chao-ao text rather than the *Chiu-chia* 九家. The essential variant in the Ch'iu text is the 難 of line five; *Chiu-chia* reads 雖, which gives a very different and, I believe, incorrect interpretation. The reading *nan* is supported by at least one of the early editions, the *Fen-men chi-chu Tu kung-pu shih* 分門集註杜工部詩 (SPTK ed.), *chüan* 12.

singular creature is renewed, some powers enduring, some healing or increasing. But unlike "Yangtze and Han," here the self's metamorphosis is openly acknowledged, and acknowledged in the grandest terms.

Somewhat farther down the coast of the lake, on the north shore of the large bay called "Green Grass Lake" 青草湖, the metamorphosis is complete: Tu Fu no longer speaks of the P'eng as object, setting it outside the self in the act of naming it; he *is* the P'eng in doing what the P'eng does, embarking for the "southern deeps."

Spending the Night at White Sands Post Station
Spend night on the water, now still in last shining,
The smoke from men's dwellings, then this pavilion.
Here by the station, the sands white as ever;
Beyond the lake, grasses, recently green.
The million images of things—all springtime vapor;
On that lone raft still, I am the wandering star.
Following the waves, moonlight infinite,
And on its sparkling I draw near to the southern deeps.[39]

宿白沙驛
水宿仍餘照
人煙復此亭
驛邊沙舊白
湖外草新青
萬象皆春氣
孤槎自客星
隨波無限月
的的近南溟

In metamorphosis a thing may become its opposite: an aging man may grow more vigorous; a tiny being on a vast lake may become the mighty P'eng; the fall of night may make the lake brilliantly white. Strangely, this condition in which the poet finds himself is one of "true names" 正名: green grasses by Green Grass Lake, white sands by White Sands Station. Again the poet is on a margin, an edge—by the shore, at the juncture between day and night. But as night grows, the margin dissolves and he has embarked: white sands in moonlight merge with the sparkling of the moonlit lake—a dark, glittering expanse that seems to be, and may in fact be the "river of stars," the heavens through which the "wandering star" and great P'eng pass. What seemed to be a solid earthly world was

[39] *Ibid.*, p. 1954.

illusory: the spring scene, with its distant burgeoning of green vegetation, is no more than a complex configuration of *ch'i*, hazy, insubstantial. And this place that seemed to be earth and water may be the magnitude of blue heavens necessary to bear the poet/P'eng on his journey to the "southern deeps."

Epilogue

We hope to be remembered, and for that hope we may "trust our persons to ink and the brush." But in this initial autobiographical impulse we discover an unknown complexity in the self—false roles and partial roles, unsuspected motives, and a growing distrust of surfaces. To our astonishment we discover that, apart from its roles, the self eludes us. Once that lesson is learned, when we write of the "true self," we make distrust of roles and surfaces the subject of the poem. It is an unsatisfying compromise: within all the anxiety and contradiction, we still presume there is some hidden unity that can be called the "self."

Out of the need to explain "who I am," we generate the question "who am I?" The surprise and magnitude of that question—for this question is one of the oddest fruits of high civilization—overwhelms the old autobiographical mode of discourse. The poet-autobiographer turns his attention away from that future audience to which he once looked so intensely. He wonders now, seeks an image of who he "is," the self's perfect mirror that strips away all illusion. He may discover he is not at all the person he thought he was, as when Po Chü-i encounters with surprise "His Own Portrait" 自題寫眞:

I didn't recognize my own face,	我貌不自識
But Li Fang painted my true portrait.	李放寫我眞
Calmly I observe the spirit and the bones—	靜觀神與骨
This must be some man of the mountains!	合是山中人
The wood of reed-willow easily rots;	蒲柳質易朽
The heart of the wild deer is hard to tame.	麋鹿心難馴
So why on the red stairs of the palace	何事赤墀上
Have I served in attendance these five years?	五年爲侍臣

Worse still, this stiff, uncompromising nature	况多剛狷性
Must find it hard to share the world's dust.	難與世同塵
Not a nobleman's physiognomy, this! What's more	不惟非貴相
I fear I see cause for ruin here.	但恐生禍因
Quit and flee as soon as I can—that's what I must do—	宜當早罷去
Preserve this body of clouds and streams.[40]	收取雲泉身

[40] Po Chü-i 白居易, *Po Chü-i chi* 白居易集, ed. Ku Hsüeh-chieh 顧學頡 2 vols. (Peking: Chung-hua shu-chü, 1979), vol. 1, *chüan* 6, p. 109.

II. Concepts and Contexts

Kang-i Sun Chang

Description of Landscape in Early Six Dynasties Poetry

Every important age in literature designates a particular kind of aesthetic judgment. In literary criticism, we call such a judgment "taste." Although taste often seems rather subjective (e.g., "Everyone to his own taste"), one of the functions of criticism is precisely to provide a set of criteria for judging what is beautiful and appropriate in literature. As such, certain critical standards and concepts may become popular at a particular age, and then gradually fall from favor.

During the Six Dynasties in China, it was the idea of "description" that came to dominate the aesthetic taste in poetry. The basic tenet was that good poetry should be characterized primarily by skillful and detailed descriptions of the natural world. As the critic Liu Hsieh 劉勰 (ca. 456–ca. 522) said in his chapter on "The Physical World" ("Wu-se" 物色):

> Recently, literature has been prized for descriptive similitude [*hsing-ssu* 形似]. Writers pierce through to the inner structure of a landscape and penetrate the appearances of plants. . . . The ability to achieve perfection in the description of things depends on an intimate knowledge of the fitness of terms for certain specific descriptive purposes. Thus, skillful expressions and precise descriptions [*ch'iao-yen ch'ieh-chuang* 巧言切狀] are like the stamping of a seal into the seal ink paste, for the impression so made will reproduce the seal to its minutest detail without further carving and cutting. Because of such a skill, we are able to see the appearances of things through the descriptive language, and to experience the seasons through words.[1]

The idea that writers should "pierce through to the inner structure of a landscape and penetrate the appearances of plants" is indeed very different from that longstanding orthodox view of poetry as stated in the "Great Preface" to the *Book of Songs*: "Poetry is that which expresses the heart's intent. What is cherished in the heart is intent. When expressed in words, it is poetry."[2] This classic statement does not talk about description; perhaps that implies that description, if it can be regarded as a defining element of poetry at all, should only be subordinate to the expressive component of poetry.

At the time of Liu Hsieh, however, the shift from "expression" to "description" in poetry was so compelling, and the systematic importance given to the new aesthetic attitude was so overwhelming, that P'ei Tzu-yeh 裴子野 (467–528) harshly attacked this great burst of descriptive artifice in his "Tiao-ch'ung lun" 雕蟲論 (Discourse on the Carving of Insects). He criticized his contemporary poets for devoting themselves to the description of such "insignificant" things as plants, trees, the wind, and clouds. In P'ei's view, "the aspirations of these poets were superficial, and their ambitions were low."[3]

Did P'ei Tzu-yeh overstate the difference of "description" and "expression" in literature? Obviously lyric poetry must always be expressive, and it is hard to believe that poetry can have very meaningful effects without some expressive values. By the same token, all poetry is to a certain extent "descriptive." We can therefore assume that it was the excessive emphasis on descriptive details in poetry and the supreme significance which the critics

---

[1] "Wu-se" 物色, in *Wen-hsin tiao-lung* 文心雕龍. See Vincent Yu-chung Shih, trans., *The Literary Mind and the Carving of Dragons* (Taipei: Chung-hua shu-chü, 1975), pp. 350–351, with modifications.

[2] See also James J. Y. Liu, "The Individualist View: Poetry as Self-Expression," in his *The Art of Chinese Poetry* (Chicago: The University of Chicago Press, 1962), pp. 70–76.

[3] Li Fang 李昉, ed., *Wen-yüan ying-hua* 文苑英華 (rpt. Taipei: Hsin-wen-feng ch'u-pan kung-ssu, 1979), vol. 5, *chüan* 742, pp. 3873–3874. See also Chu Tzu-ch'ing 朱自清, *Shih-yen-chih pien* 詩言志辨 (rpt. Taipei: K'ai-ming shu-chü, 1964), pp. 38–39; and David R. Knechtges, trans., "Introduction," *Wen xuan or Selections of Refined Literature* (Princeton: Princeton University Press, 1982), vol. 1, pp. 13–14.

concurrently assigned to "description" that provoked P'ei Tzu-yeh into the condemnation of his contemporaries.

In fact, the term "description" in western literature is equally characterized by a vague and questionable status.[4] The fact that "description" has no genuine status leads us to distrust its true value. Even the sole pleasure of describing for its own sake may not be regarded as "legitimate" in literature.[5] More specifically, "description" often carries a pejorative meaning that suggests mere artificial ornament and useless details. Phillipe Hamon, the renowned teacher of stylistics, sums up this general view of description in the following words: "The theoretical discussions *a propos* of the descriptive often evolve around the notion of the 'detail.' . . . Now, classical theoreticians seem to have seen in description only a risky 'drift' from detail to detail—a process which, above all else, threatens the homogeneity, the cohesion, and the dignity of the work."[6]

What was unusual about the Six Dynasties literary scene in China was not simply that "description" had formed an important element in *shih* poetry, but rather that it became one of the touchstones of the poet's talents. The *Shih-p'in* 詩品 by Chung Hung 鍾嶸 (fl. 502–509) can readily serve as a good document of this unique promotion of the descriptive mode in Six Dynasties poetry. Chung Hung's approach was characteristically judgmental; he believed that one of the principal duties of a critic was to rank his contemporary poets according to a set of criteria commonly agreed upon. Most strikingly he gave high rankings to Chang Hsieh 張協 (?–307), Hsieh Ling-yün 謝靈運 (385–433), Yen Yen-chih 顏延之 (384–456), and Pao Chao 鮑照 (405–466) mainly because of their outstanding art of description. The comments which Chung Hung made in his evaluation of the four poets are most illuminating:[7]

[4] Philippe Hamon, "Rhetorical Status of the Descriptive," in *Toward a Theory of Description,* ed. Jeffrey Kittay. *Yale French Studies*, no. 61 (New Haven: Yale French Studies, 1981), pp. 1–26.

[5] Hamon, "Rhetorical Status," p. 8.

[6] *Ibid.*, p. 11.

[7] For the following quotations, see *Shih-p'in chu* 詩品注, commentary by Ch'en Yen-chieh 陳延傑 (Hong Kong: Shang-wu yin-shu-kuan, 1959), pp. 17f.

(1) Chang Hsieh in the first rank (*shang-p'in* 上品):
"His literary style was flowery yet lucid, with very little blemish and verbosity. In addition, he was skillful at creating descriptive similitude [*ch'iao-kou hsing-ssu chih yen*]."
"...文體華淨, 少病累, 又巧構形似之言..."

(2) Hsieh Ling-yün in the first rank:
"His style somewhat resembled Chang Hsieh's, and so he also favored the device of artful structure and descriptive similitude [*ch'iao-ssu*]."
"...雜有景陽[張協]之體, 故尙巧似..."

(3) Yen Yen-chih in the second rank (*chung-p'in* 中品):
"He was fond of artful structure and descriptive similitude [*ch'iao-ssu*]; his style was refined and dense."
"尙巧似, 體裁綺密..."

(4) Pao Chao in the second rank:
"He was skillful at creating descriptive expressions; his poetry had inherited Chang Hsieh's beautiful and crafty style.... He preferred artful structure and descriptive similitude [*ch'iao-ssu*]."
"善製形狀寫物之詞, 得景陽之淑詭...貴尙巧似..."

It is worth noting that Chung Hung consistently used a compound *ch'iao-ssu* 巧似 to describe good descriptive skills. The term may be seen as an abbreviated form of *ch'iao-kou hsing-ssu* 巧構形似, which literally means "artful structure and descriptive similitude." "*Hsing-ssu*" seems easy to understand; it clearly points to the general proclivity of the Six Dynasties poets to portray landscapes and things according to the principle of verisimilitude. The meaning of *ch'iao-kou* is more vague, which may change according to the particular context in which it occurs.[8] I believe

[8] In Chung Hung's evaluation of Chang Hsieh, the compound was meant to serve as a verb. But modern scholars tend to see *ch'iao-kou* as an adjective or a noun. For example, see Liao Wei-ch'ing 廖蔚卿, "Ts'ung wen-hsüeh hsien-hsiang yü wen-hsüeh ssu-hsiang te kuan-hsi t'an Liu-ch'ao ch'iao-kou hsing-ssu chih yen te shih" 從文學現象與文學思想的關係談六朝巧構形似之言的詩, in *Chung-Kuo ku-tien wen-hsüeh lun-ts'ung* 中國古典文學論叢 (Taipei: Chung-wai wen-hsüeh yüeh-k'an-she, 1976), vol. 1, pp. 39–70, and Lin Wen-yüeh 林文月, *Shan-shui yü ku-tien* 山水與古典 (Taipei: Ch'un-wen-hsüeh ch'u-pan-she, 1976), pp. 126–128.

that, when viewed as a noun or an adjective, *ch'iao-kou* refers largely, though not exclusively, to the art of parallelism (*tui-chang* 對仗) prevalent during the Six Dynasties. Parallelism was apparently a skill acquired by laborious effort and practice, but to the poets and critics at the time it was essentially a device for imitating nature itself, as Liu Hsieh put it in his *Wen-hsin tiao-lung*: "Nature, creating living beings, endows them always with limbs in pairs. The divine reason operates in such a way that nothing stands alone. The mind creates literary expressions, and organizes and shapes one hundred different thoughts, making what is high complement what is low, and spontaneously producing linguistic parallelism."[9]

Evidently parallelism went hand in hand with the basic emphasis on descriptive realism in Six Dynasties poetry. For if parallelism was considered a reflection of natural phenomena, it was only natural that it would become a convenient device for producing *hsing-ssu* in poetry. Herein lies a very basic difference between the Chinese and the western sense of "description" as pointed out by Stephen Owen: "'Description' in the western sense is creating again in words the created world.... Description, in a Chinese sense, would be that art of noticing pattern incarnate in the sensible world."[10] Thus, *ch'iao-ssu* as a literary concept may well refer to that descriptive art (i.e., parallelism) designed to capture the "pattern incarnate in the sensible world." That the term was not mere jargon in contemporary criticism was quite obvious. *Ch'iao-ssu* appears in several variant forms, but, whichever form it takes, it always points to the same area of meaning that seems to suggest both skillful parallelism and descriptive realism. And it is in this particular sense that the word "description" is used in this essay.

Another interesting phenomenon during the Six Dynasties period was that critics and poets alike often employed the same critical terms to evaluate the descriptive techniques in *fu* 賦 as they did for *shih* 詩. For example, Shen Yüeh 沈約 (441–513) praised Ssu-ma Hsiang-ju 司馬相如 (ca. 179–117 B.C.), the master of Han *fu*, for "his skill in producing descriptive phrases" (巧爲

[9] From "Li-tz'u p'ien" 麗辭篇. See Vincent Yu-chung Shih, trans., *The Literary Mind*, pp. 270 and 274, with modification.

[10] Stephen Owen, "A Monologue of the Senses," in *Toward a Theory of Description*, ed. Kittay, p. 252 and p. 257.

形似之言),[11] in the same way that Chung Hung and Liu Hsieh would describe some *shih* poets. This gives us the impression that *shih* and *fu* might begin to share very similar aesthetic values at the time. And such an assumption is quite justified, for as *shih* became more descriptive than before, *fu* also acquired more expressive elements. The rise of the "shorter *fu*" (*hsiao-fu* 小賦) during the Six Dynasties seemed to be a reflection of the mutual influences and intermingling of the two genres. That classic distinction between *shih* and *fu* first made by Lu Chi 陸機 (261–303) in his "Wen fu" 文賦—"*Shih* traces emotions daintily; *Fu* embodies objects brightly"[12]—no longer seemed as potent two hundred years later in Liu Hsieh's time. To a critic like Liu Hsieh, both *shih* and *fu* must be *t'i-wu* 體物 or "descriptive of things."[13]

The rise of the descriptive mode in Six Dynasties *shih* poetry was bound to be influenced by the aesthetic principles of *fu*. The poet, living under the pressure of new aesthetic requirements, felt invoked not only to devise new descriptive methods in *shih* poetry, but to search for inspiration from other genres. And *fu*, a literary form traditionally rooted in the art of description, naturally served as a convenient source of imitation. As Liu Hsieh put it in his *Wen-hsin tiao-lung*: "In describing and picturing appearances/The richness [of *fu*'s patterns] is like that of carving and painting" (寫物圖貌蔚以雕畫).[14] In the main, the *shih* poet began to add to his private poetic world the depiction of a larger natural world similar to that of *fu*. It was as though a thousand new variations, distinctions, and similarities of things all lay open before the poet's eye.

The pivotal position of description in *shih* poetry and the commanding impact of *fu* on it was not fully realized until the early part of the Southern Dynasties (420–589) when "landscape poetry"

[11] See Shen Yüeh 沈約, "Hsieh Ling-yün chuan" 謝靈運傳, in *Sung shu* 宋書, ed. Editorial Board of Chung-hua shu-chü (Peking: Chung-hua shu-chü, 1974), vol. 6, *chüan* 67, p. 1778.

[12] Achilles Fang, trans., "Rhymeprose on Literature," in *Studies in Chinese Literature*, ed. John L. Bishop (Cambridge: Harvard University Press, 1966), p. 12.

[13] "T'i-wu" means literally "to embody things," but in poetry it refers rather to the technique of description. See Chu Tzu-ch'ing, *Shih-yen-chih pien*, p. 38.

[14] "Ch'üan-fu" 詮賦, in *Wen-hsin tiao-lung*. See Vincent Yu-chung Shih, trans., *The Literary Mind*, pp. 66–67.

(*shan-shui shih* 山水詩) began to develop.[15] *Shan-shui shih* means literally "poetry of mountains and waters," and it is in this new subgenre of *shih* that we see a great leap forward in establishing a systematic mode in the art of description. More specifically, "mountains" and "waters," the two primary components of *shan-shui* poetry, began to serve as the basis for parallelism that was believed to reflect the symmetry perceived in nature. Of all his contemporaries, Hsieh Ling-yün was the one most credited with promoting *shan-shui* poetry. Yen Yen-chih and Pao Chao were the two other poets also known for their *shan-shui* poems during the Liu-Sung period (420–479), and, as we have seen, they were also among those four who were thought to be skillful at creating *hsing-ssu* in poetry. It is apparent that it was in landscape poetry that descriptive realism finally reached its peak. Yet the evolution of this descriptive mode was gradual, and the intention of this essay is not to chronicle the process of its development. I shall choose Hsieh Ling-yün and an earlier poet, Chang Hsieh, as the focus of discussion, for they were the two "first-rank" poets singled out by Chung Hung for their outstanding descriptive techniques.

I. Chang Hsieh (?–307)

Chang Hsieh represented a large number of intellectuals who retreated to the mountains at a time of social and political unrest during the Western Chin (Hsi-chin 西晉). The Wei-Chin period had been noted for "poetry of wandering immortals" (*yu-hsien shih* 遊仙詩), a literature dedicated to the creation of an ideal world in which the poet imagines that he is wandering like the immortals. The specific function of *yu-hsien* poetry maintained that "nature" so portrayed belonged to another world, and was therefore ap-

[15] Of course, the term "landscape poetry" may be misleading here. See J. D. Frodsham, *The Murmuring Stream: The Life and Works of the Chinese Nature Poet Hsieh Ling-yün (385–433), Duke of K'ang-lo* (Kuala Lumpur: University of Malaya Press, 1967), vol. 1, p. 88. In the western sense, "landscape" often refers to general scenery, while the Chinese *shan-shui* is characterized by the binary structure of mountain and water scenes; see Stephen Owen, *Traditional Chinese Poetry and Poetics: An Omen of the World* (Madison: University of Wisconsin Press, 1985).

proachable only by way of imagination. The emphasis was placed on the eye of the mind, rather than on sense perception itself. However, *yu-hsien* poetry did exercise an important influence on the descriptive techniques in the *shih* poetry in general. This was because the description of this ideal world was often modeled after the actual scenery of the remote mountains where the hermits lived.[16] More importantly, it helped to develop the sense of a vast poetic world, in which the poet's eye incessantly traverses the cosmos, presenting to us large images of the sun, skies, and mountains.

Chang Hsieh was only one of the poets during his time to be influenced by *yu-hsien* poetry, but he went further to develop a distinct descriptive orientation. Some years later, the great master of *yu-hsien* poetry Kuo P'u 郭璞 (276–324) also replaced the landscape of the immortal world with that of the hermit's world, but the primary focus of his poetic world was on the constant search for immortality.[17] Chang Hsieh, however, had a taste for the realistic description of the natural world. His series of "Miscellaneous Poems" (*tsa-shih* 雜詩) gives us a vivid picture of the natural landscape as seen by a hermit. For example, Poem No. 3 reads:

The autumn wind fans the white season;[18]	金風扇素節
Rosy clouds usher in the gloomy period.	丹霞啓陰期
Soaring clouds resemble a rising mist;	騰雲似涌煙
The dense rain is like loosened silk threads.	密雨如散絲
Cold flowers bloom in yellow hues;	寒花發黃采
The autumn grass bears emerald dew.	秋草含綠滋

[16] See also Lin Wen-yüeh, *Shan-shui yü ku-tien*, pp. 1–12; Koichi Obi 小尾郊一, *Chūgoku bungaku ni arawareta shizen to shizenkan* 中国文学に現われた自然と自然観 (Tokyo: Iwanami, 1962), pp. 259–271; and Richard B. Mather, "The Landscape Buddhism of the Fifth Century Poet Hsieh Ling-yün," *Journal of Asian Studies* 18, no. 1 (1958), 67–79.

[17] Although in Poem No. 1 of his *yu-hsien* series Kuo P'u describes the mountains and forests where the hermits reside, without a single mention of the immortals. See *Ch'üan Han San-kuo Chin Nan-pei-ch'ao shih* 全漢三國晉南北朝詩, ed. Ting Fu-pao 丁福保 (rpt. Taipei: Shih-chieh shu-chü, 1969), vol. 1, p. 423. Henceforth referred to as CHSK in the text.

[18] The "autumn wind" reads "metal wind" in the Chinese original. "Metal," being one of the five elements, is traditionally used to symbolize autumn. "The white season" also refers to the fall season.

Living in leisure, I savor a million things;
8 Away from the crowd, I dwell lovingly on my own thoughts.
On my desk there is no message from Master Hsiao;
In my courtyard, no footprints of Master Kung.[19]
My high ideals made me depart from princes and nobles;
12 My merits in Tao, once accumulated, will surely form a firm base.
A man of virtue is never bothered by things;
The influence he leaves behind is enough to affect his age.
(CHSK, I, 393)

閑居玩萬物
離羣戀所思
案無蕭氏牘
庭無貢公綦
高尚遺王侯
道積自成基
至人不嬰物
餘風足染時

The first striking feature of the poem which catches our attention is the pervasive weight of parallelism. The poem presents an orderly arrangement of the scenery in which things corresponding by nature are brought together to stand side by side. Thus, the wind parallels the clouds (lines 1–2); the clouds parallel the rain (lines 3–4); the flowers go together with the grass (lines 5–6). The overwhelming presence of parallelism creates the illusion that the poetic self is replaced temporarily by the scenery; it culminates in a transcendence of time where the sky, the elements, and the earth exist in harmony. I believe that it was largely due to his distinguished skill in this kind of parallelism that Chang Hsieh was regarded so highly by Chung Hung.

The poem's unusual emphasis on the descriptive details of a natural scene seems to contrast sharply with poems prior to this period. For example, the description of nature in the "Nineteen

[19] Upon hearing the news that Mr. Hsiao and his good friend Mr. Chu were given office, Mr. Kung and Mr. Wang, the two Han recluses, ran away immediately, lest they should be offered official posts as well. These two lines suggest that Chang Hsieh had resigned himself completely to living in the mountains like the Han hermits. For the source of this allusion, see *Han shu* 漢書, *chüan* 78 (Peking: Chunghua shu-chü, 1962), vol. 10, p. 3290.

Old Poems" (古詩十九首) usually serves only as a background for the expressive elements of poetry. The natural scenes described in these earlier poems are often limited to one dominant natural object, be it the bright moon or a flourishing willow. The poet rarely found it necessary to elaborate on the various aspects of a scene, for to him the chief function of poetry was to express feelings. The images of nature in these earlier poems generally function on the principle of association—what Liu Hsieh called *i shao tsung to* 以少總多 ("using a part to sum up the whole") in his *Wen-hsin tiao-lung*.[20] In other words, the orientation then was toward a primary concern with typicality rather than with particularity and comprehensive details.

With Chang Hsieh, however, the description of nature has ceased to be the mere background for the poetic world. It is the principle of the "details," rather than that of the association of images, which is at work. When the poet's purpose is to portray things according to the principle of verisimilitude, detailed description becomes his best artistic device. And the reader's attention is consequently guided from the general to the particular. As in the poem cited above, Chang Hsieh has explored many different aspects of the scenery. In presenting an autumn scene, the poem does not just give us a single line or couplet on the autumn wind as the "Nineteen Old Poems" might have done; rather, it carefully describes the scenery of an autumn day consisting of the wind, the clouds, the rain, the flowers, and the grass. It is only after the scene is described point by point (lines 1–6) that the poet starts to talk about his feelings. The impression created is that the expressive component of the poem evolves from the descriptive passages. At least we can say that in the first half of the poem the principle at work is one of description for description's sake.

This, of course, is not to deny the importance of the expressive elements in Chang Hsieh's poem. In fact, Chang Hsieh's *tsa-shih* as a whole belonged distinctively to the "expressive" tradition. *Tsa-shih* was a sub-genre of the *yung-huai* 詠懷 ("expressive") poetry, and the *tsa-shih* poems by Chang Hua 張華 (232–300), Lu Chi

[20] "Wu-se" 物色, *Wen-hsin tiao-lung*. See Vincent Yu-chung Shih, trans., *The Literary Mind*, pp. 349–350.

(261–303), and Tso Ssu 左思 (?–ca. 308) were all noted for their expressive qualities.[21] Yet as time went by this type of poetry became more descriptive of seasonal changes and man's reactions to them. Critics in the Six Dynasties called this new tendency in poetry *kan-wu* 感物, meaning "to be moved by nature."[22] According to this view, seasonal changes were the vital mediator between the poet and his poetry. In his "Wen-fu" 文賦 Lu Chi describes the special nature of *kan-wu* in a tone that recalls the underlying feelings in the *tsa-shih* poetry:

Moving along with the four seasons, he sighs at the passing of time;	遵四時以歎逝
Gazing at the myriad objects, he thinks of the complexity of the world.	瞻萬物而思紛
He sorrows over the falling leaves in sinewy autumn;	悲落葉於勁秋
He takes joy in the delicate bud of fragrant spring.[23]	喜柔條於芳春

Indeed, many of the *tsa-shih* poems in the Western Chin open with seasonal images:

The autumn wind blows up on the heels of evening;	秋風乘夕起
The bright moon shines in tall trees. . . .	明月照高林
(WH, *chüan* 29, I, 648)	

How piercingly cold the autumn wind is;	秋風何冽冽
The white dew turns into the morning frost. . . .	白露爲朝霜
(WH, *chüan* 29, I, 650)	

To the late spring, the gentle air comes responding;	暮春和氣應
	白日照園林

[21] See the *tsa-shih* 雜詩 category in *Wen hsüan* 文選, commentary by Li Shan 李善, 2 vols. (rpt. Taipei: Ho-lo t'u-shu ch'u-pan-she, 1975), vol. 1, pp. 643–655. Henceforth referred to as WH in the text.

[22] "Wu-se," in *Wen-hsin tiao-lung*. See Vincent Yu-chung Shih, trans., *The Literary Mind*, p. 349. See also the opening lines in *Shih-p'in chu*.

[23] From Fang, trans., "Rhymeprose on Literature," p. 7. I have changed "virile autumn" to "sinewy autumn" here in order to give a more literal rendering of *chin-ch'iu*.

The bright sunlight shines upon the wooded
park.
(WH, *chüan* 29, I, 650)

In like manner, three of the ten extant *tsa-shih* by Chang Hsieh begin with seasonal descriptions:

In the autumn night a cool wind rises; 秋夜涼風起
Its pure air disperses the confused noise and filthy current.... 淸氣蕩喧濁
(WH, *chüan* 29, I, 650)

The Fire recedes into the autumn quarter; 大火流坤維
The bright sun hastens to the West. 白日馳西陸
(WH, *chüan* 29, I, 651)

The autumn wind fans the white season; 金風扇素節
Rosy clouds usher in the gloomy period. 丹霞啓陰期
(WH, *chüan* 29, I, 651)

Upon closer scrutiny, however, one finds that Chang Hsieh's poetry has a tendency to break away from the traditional mold of *tsa-shih*. A typical *tsa-shih* usually focuses on a moonlit scene in which the persona of the poet, lonely and sleepless, walks out to the courtyard, or goes for a short outing in the autumn breeze, in search of temporary release from the troubled world. The persona looks around and enjoys the beautiful scenery, but at the end of the poem would almost always feel sorry for his own lonely state.[24] In Chang Hsieh we feel that the perspective is beyond the autumn moon and evening breeze, for it is the scenery of mountains, valleys, and forests which becomes the vital content of poetry, making nature seem larger in scope.

The description of a sleepless person facing the moonlight so characteristic of the *tsa-shih* poetry had a long history in Chinese poetics, which could be traced back to the "Nineteen Old Poems No. 19":

The bright moon, how white and snowy; 明月何皎皎
It shines upon my bed screens of thin silk. 照我羅床幃

[24] See, for example, WH, I, 644, 645, 648, 650.

Worried and grieved, I cannot sleep; 憂愁不能寐
Gathering up my robes, I rise and walk to and fro. . . . 攬衣起徘徊
(CHSK, I, 25)

This image of the bright moon was later extended to include that of the autumn breeze in the Wei-Chin *shih* poetry, but the basic poetic world remained unchanged for some time. This is because natural objects were still viewed mostly from the inner chamber. The opening lines of Juan Chi's 阮籍 (223–262) series of eighty-one poems entitled "Yung-huai" ("Expressing My Feelings") serve as a typical example:

In the middle of the night, I cannot sleep; 夜中不能寐
I rise, take a seat, and begin to play my singing lute. 起坐彈鳴琴
On the thin curtain the bright moon shimmers; 薄帷鑒明月
A clear breeze blows in the collar of my garment. . . . 清風吹我襟
(CHSK, I, 215)

The theme of the inner chamber lays the artistic groundwork for the practice of many *shih* poets in the early five-character line poetry (*wu-yen shih* 五言詩). The degree of importance given to this particular orientation in Wei-Chin poetry was such that even *shih* poems written on a completely different subject would often employ this very motif. For example, Lu Chi's poem "On the Road to Lo-yang" (赴洛道中作) is primarily about a journey—the traveler "crosses over mountains and streams," "climbs up towering hills," and "travels through level grasslands" (lines 1–4). Yet the poem ends with the description of an evening scene similar to that of Juan Chi's poem:

The clear dew drops glittering in white; 淸露墜素輝
The bright moon, how brilliantly it shines. 明月一何朗
I rest my head on the table, but cannot sleep; 撫几不能寐
Pulling up my clothes, I ponder over things in loneliness. 振衣獨長想
(WH, I, 574)

In general terms, the *tsa-shih* poetry during the Western Chin period has a tendency to substitute the inner-chamber motif with an emphasis on the natural scenery outside, however brief the descriptions may be. As has been mentioned, the lonely and sleepless persona in a *tsa-shih* poem often walks out to the courtyard or goes for an outing instead of staying indoors. Compared to his contemporaries, Chang Hsieh was even more conscientious in depicting the particularity and uniqueness of the scenery "outside." All the sensible objects in the mountains seemed to Chang Hsieh a stimulus for his contemplation. The many ramifications of the symmetrical world were the embodied symbol of his harmonious spiritual state. Thus, the description of landscape has now become an act of externalizing internal feelings, thoughts, and perceptions. All of Chang Hsieh's *tsa-shih* poems, with the single exception of Poem No. 1, are characterized by detailed descriptions of mountain scenes, and concluded with statements of his spiritual realization. Such a power of creating scenery can be said to be a good example of *kan-wu*, as Chang Hsieh wrote in his *Tsa-shih* No. 6, line 9, "Moved by things [*kan-wu*], my feelings fill my heart" (感物多思情). Viewed in this perspective, the important role which the description of "mountains" and "waters" played in the later "landscape poetry" was merely a step beyond this *kan-wu* idea. The progression is significant; the art of descriptive similitude cannot be evolved overnight. What Liu Hsieh referred to as "the inner structure of scenery" and "the appearance of plants" could not be portrayed with living resemblances unless the poets themselves had already accepted the necessary link between the external scenery and their inner state of mind. It is in this sense that Chang Hsieh should be considered an important poet in the development of the description of landscapes in the Six Dynasties *shih* poetry.

II. Hsieh Ling-yün (385–433)

The beginning of the Eastern Chin marked a changing perspective of landscape for the prevailing literati culture in China. The government moved to south of Yangtze, and the rich aristocrats who went along to the south were struck by the newness of the southern scenery.[25] Places such as Yung-chia (i.e., Wenchow) and K'uai-chi in Chekiang Province were particulary noted for their beautiful mountains and rivers. Touring the scenic sights suddenly became a vogue for upper-class people.[26] And gradually the dazzling scenery of the south emerged as a primary topic for *shih* poetry, *fu*, prose literature, and painting. The theme of "mountains and waters" (*shan-shui*) began to flourish in *shih* poetry during the Liu Sung dynasty (420–479). And Hsieh Ling-yün, more than any poet of the time, seemed to embody the forces that inspired the genuine love for southern landscape. A grandson of the famous general Hsieh Hsüan 謝玄 (343–388), Hsieh Ling-yün had the fortune of growing up in a distinguished household surrounded by the most alluring scenery and luxurious settings. The family estate at Shih-ning (in modern Chekiang Province), first built by his grandfather, was carefully situated near beautiful hills and streams. Later, when Hsieh was demoted to the prefecture of Yung-chia in 422, he began to spend days traveling around the beautiful mountains and awe-inspiring rivers.[27] It is hardly surprising that Hsieh Ling-yün has been traditionally regarded as the forefather of both the *shan-shui* poetry and prose essays on travel, the so-called "*yu-chi*" 遊記.[28]

What Hsieh Ling-yün brought to the *shih* genre was a new attitude toward nature and a new set of techniques that attempted to present nature with a force of descriptive realism not to be surpassed by anything but nature itself. No less inspiring was his adventurer's point of view. With Chang Hsieh the hermit, nature was usually defined by the poet's immediate surroundings. With Hsieh Ling-yün, the poet became a tireless traveler, constantly

[25] See Liu I-ch'ing, in Richard B. Mather, trans., *Shih-Shuo Hsin-yü: A New Account of Tales of the World* (Minneapolis: University of Minnesota Press, 1976), p. 45.

[26] See Lin Wen-yüeh, *Shan-shui yü ku-tien*, p. 14; and Yeh Hsiao-hsüeh 葉笑雪, "Preface" to his *Hsieh Ling-yün shih-hsüan* 謝靈運詩選 (Hong Kong: Hsin-yüeh ch'u-pan-she, 1962), pp. 1–2

[27] H. C. Chang, *Chinese Literature II: Nature Poetry* (New York: Columbia University Press, 1977), pp. 40–43; and Lin Wen-yüeh, *Shan-shui yü ku-tien*, pp. 83–84.

[28] Hsieh Ling-yün wrote *Yu ming-shan chih* 遊名山志 [An account of travels to famous mountains], the first piece of *yu-chi* literature known to have existed.

climbing mountains and crossing rivers in a vigorous search for unusual sights and spectacular scenes. Nature to him was not just ordinary and familiar; it was full of unexpected wonders. Nature was something to discover, to enjoy, and to conquer. If Chang Hsieh's poetic world is one of peace and calm, then Hsieh's would be best described as one of activity and exploration. And this underlies the essential difference between earlier nature poetry and the *shan-shui* poetry.

In sharp contrast to the "farmland" (*t'ien-yüan* 田園) poet T'ao Ch'ien 陶潛 (365–427), who generally wrote about less dramatic scenery in his poetry, Hsieh favored the description of scenery viewed from a mountain summit or the top of a tower. To Hsieh Ling-yün, and to his successors in landscape poetry Pao Chao and Hsieh T'iao 謝朓 (464–499), mountain climbing was the ultimate means to spiritual salvation.[29] This particular theme recalls that of a *fu* by Sun Ch'o 孫綽 (314–371), "Wandering on Mount T'ien-t'ai" (遊天台山賦); Sun's elaborate description of his mountain journey and the reference to Taoist ideas seem to point in the direction of the *shan-shui* aesthetics.[30] In fact, the idea of "ascending heights" (登高) had been essential to the *fu* tradition since early times, as Liu Hsieh pointed out in his chapter entitled "Elucidation of *Fu*" (詮賦).[31] Yet Hsieh Ling-yün was the first poet in *shih* poetry to give prominent significance to the theme of journeying to a mountain top. Some of Hsieh's most celebrated poems open with parallel couplets on mountain climbing:

At dawn with staff in hand I searched for sheer cliffs;	晨策尋絕壁
At dusk I stopped to rest among the mountains.	夕息在山棲

(CHSK, II, 643)

[29] For poems on mountain climbing by Pao Chao and Hsieh T'iao, see, for example, CHSK, II, 683–685; II, 806.

[30] See Ch'ü T'ui-yüan 瞿蛻園, ed., *Han Wei Liu-ch'ao fu hsüan* 漢魏六朝賦選 (rev. ed., Shanghai: Ku-chi ch'u-pan-she, 1979), pp. 162–171. For English translation, see "Wandering on Mount T'ien-T'ai," in Burton Watson, trans., *Chinese Rhyme-Prose* (New York: Columbia University Press, 1971), pp. 80–85.

[31] See Vincent Yu-chung Shih, trans., *The Literary Mind*, pp. 62 and 66. See also Hans. H. Frankel, *The Flowering Plum and the Palace Lady: Interpretations of Chinese Poetry* (New Haven: Yale University Press, 1976), p. 113.

At dawn I set out from the sunlit cliffs;
At sunset I rested by the shaded peaks.
(CHSK, II, 643)

朝旦發陽崖
景落憩陰峯

Hsieh Ling-yün's greatest innovation lies yet in his impressive account of journeys by water, in which the southern landscape shows its greatest charms. In Chang Hsieh's *tsa-shih* we see only the northern landscape as perceived by a poet-recluse. Descriptions of water scenery in Chang's poetry are often limited to the visual impressions of far-away waterfalls. Moreover, Chang tends to use cosmological images. The effect created is therefore one of static harmony, devoid of any hurried rush of action. By contrast, Hsieh Ling-yün's descriptions of journeys by boat often produce a headlong effect, with the persona, as he presses forward seeking unusual sights, always feeling that "time is short."[32]

In order to see how Hsieh Ling-yün's method of description differs from that of the earlier poets, it may be useful for us to examine one of his poems which includes both mountain climbing and river crossing in the same poem. The following poem entitled "I Follow Chin-chu River, Cross the Mountain, and Go Along by the Stream" (從斤竹澗越嶺西行) is a good example:

When the apes howl, one is sure the dawn
  has broken;
Though here in this deep valley no sunlight
  can be seen.
Under the cliffs the clouds just begin to
  gather;
While on the flowers the dew is still
  glistening.
I keep to the winding path that curves
  around the mountain side;
I labor up treacherous slopes and hills.
Crossing the streams, I wade through
  rapids;
Scaling cliff-ladders, I climb afar.

猿鳴誠知曙
谷幽光未顯
巖下雲方合
花上露猶泫
逶迤傍隈隩
迢遞陟陘峴
過澗既厲急
登棧亦陵緬

[32] See also Frankel, *ibid.*, p. 14.

The riverbank keeps on twisting and
turning;
I enjoy following the meandering stream.
Pepperworts and duckweeds float upon
hidden depths;
Reeds and rushes overspread the clear
shallows.
I stand on a rock to fill my cup from a
waterfall;
And pull down branches to pluck young
leaves.
I imagine seeing a mountain-hermit;
His "fig-leaf jacket and rabbit-floss belt" as
if before my eyes.
I gather a handful of orchids, but my effort
in tying them is in vain;
I pluck the hemp, yet there is no one for me
to open my heart to.
To appreciate this with a sensitive heart is
pleasure;
But the hidden truth who can ever discern
it?
Looking at this scenery I can cast off my
material concerns;
Once enlightened, I let everything go its
own way.[33]
(CHSK, II, 644)

川渚屢逕復
乘流翫迴轉
蘋萍泛沈深
菰蒲冒淸淺
企石挹飛泉
攀林摘葉卷
想見山阿人
薜蘿若在眼
握蘭勤徒結
折麻心莫展
情用賞爲美
事昧竟誰辨
觀此遺物慮
一悟得所遣

The usual procedure of Hsieh Ling-yün's poetry is to separate the highly descriptive couplets in the first half of the poem from the rational discourse at the end. As in this poem, lines 5–8 describe the crossing of the mountain peak, and lines 9–14 detail the journey by boat. The poem then concludes with a statement on the cultivation of the Taoist ideal, which gives one the impression that the physical

[33] The line alludes to an important concept in Taoism called "wu so pu ch'ien" ("there is nothing that one cannot let go of"). See also Yeh Hsiao-hsüeh, *Hsieh Ling-yün shih-hsüan*, p. 94, n. 4.

journey is actually a spiritual journey.[34] Such a conclusion was obviously influenced by the *hsüan-yen shih* 玄言詩 (poetry of Taoist discourse) popular during the Eastern Chin. Yet, unlike the *hsüan-yen* poetry in which "there was more philosophy than poetry,"[35] Hsieh's landscape poetry was concerned mainly with the beauty of nature and the value inherent in it. Line 19 of the above poem sums up the basic attitude of a *shan-shui* poet—that "to appreciate this [scenery] with a sensitive heart is pleasure." In other words, to Hsieh Ling-yün, the contemplation of beautiful scenery was self-sufficient and eternal. And it is in this context that a discussion of Hsieh's descriptive techniques is meaningful.

As has been mentioned, Hsieh Ling-yün was praised by Chung Hung for his outstanding ability to produce parallel structure. Even to poets and critics centuries later, he was known primarily as one who excelled in the art of parallelism: "K'ang-lo [Hsieh Ling-yün] had a prodigious skill in artful composition, with no sense of the [usual] tediousness of parallelism";[36] and "Hsieh's poetry was superior precisely in its handling of parallelism. . . ."[37] Indeed, it was through parallelism that Hsieh Ling-yün displayed most effectively his all-encompassing view of nature. If we go back to the poem cited above, we shall notice that the poet has employed two distinct types of parallelism. The first kind is made up of lines which are free from an explicit reference to the poetic self:

Under the cliffs the clouds just begin to gather 巖下雲方合
[*ho*],

[34] Frankel, *The Flowering Plum*, p. 14; and Francis A. Westbrook, "Landscape Transformation in the Poetry of Hsieh Ling-yün," *Journal of the American Oriental Society* 100 (1980) 237–254. Note also Tsung Ping's 宗炳 statement in his "Hua shan-shui hsü" 畫山水序: "Mountains and waters manifest Tao through their appearances" (山水以形媚道). See Chang Yen-yüan 張彥遠, *Li-tai ming-hua chi* 歷代名畫記 (rpt. Taipei: Kuang-wen shu-chü, 1971), 6.202.

[35] From *Shih p'in* by Chung Hung, as translated by Frodsham, *The Murmuring Stream*, vol. 1, p. 87.

[36] By Lu Shih-yung 陸時雍 of the Ming dynasty. See *Shih-ching tsung-lun* 詩鏡總論, in *Hsü li-tai shih-hua* 續歷代詩話, ed. Ting Fu-pao (Taipei: I-wen yin-shu kuan, 1964), 5.4a.

[37] By Shen Teh-ch'ien 沈德潛 (1673–1769). See Kuo Shao-yü 郭紹虞, *Ch'ing shih-hua* 清詩話 (rev. ed., Shanghai: Ku-chi ch'u-pan-she, 1978), vol. 2, p. 532.

While on the flowers the dew is still glistening [*hsüan*]. 花上露猶泫
(lines 3–4)

Pepperworts and duckweeds float [*fan*] upon hidden depths; 蘋萍泛沈深
Reeds and rushes overspread [*mao*] the clear shallows. 菰蒲冒清淺
(lines 11–12)

The second type of parallel couplets, however, centers on the action of the persona:

Crossing [*kuo*] the streams, I wade through [*li*] rapids; 過澗既厲急
Scaling [*teng*] cliff-ladders, I climb [*ling*] afar. 登棧亦陵緬
(lines 7–8)

I stand [*ch'i*] on a rock to fill [*i*] my cup from a waterfall, 企石挹飛泉
And pull down [*p'an*] branches to pluck [*chai*] young leaves. 攀林摘葉卷
(lines 13–14)

The first kind of parallelism is mainly descriptive of landscapes in which the temporal dimension is essentially lacking. The cliffs, the flowers, the duckweeds, reeds, etc., are the focus of our attention, and the natural object seems to occupy a prominent place. It is this object-oriented parallelism that attempts to hold things in perfect symmetry, one which will give ultimate pleasure to the sensitive heart. By creating such parallel couplets, the poet succeeds in conveying the sense that his poetry reflects the inherent symmetric structure of nature through a "higher" order of descriptive realism. This kind of parallelism, as a means of verisimilitude, is what defines Hsieh's art of description in general.

The second type of parallelism is basically action-oriented, as it centers upon the action of the persona. These couplets emphasize change and movement, and often suggest great physical strivings on the part of the poetic self. Hsieh Ling-yün's creative manipulation of the so-called *chü-yen* 句眼 ("the eye of the line") also enhances the verb-quality of these parallel couplets. A *chü-yen* is usually a verb or an adverb which serves to connect or give vigor to the noun segments of the line.[38] In sharp contrast to the object-oriented parallelism where one *chü-yen* per line is the norm (see examples cited above), the action-oriented parallelism often contains two *chü-yen* in each line. The sheer number of *chü-yen* (i.e., *kuo, li, teng, ling, ch'i, i, p'an, chai*) introduces a poetic force that gives one the impression that the persona is constantly striving to arrest time, to hold in hand the beauty of nature, and to overcome his inner feeling of loneliness.[39]

The action-oriented parallelism, though seemingly unrelated to the description of landscapes per se, does play an important part in Hsieh's art of description. Through the use of these action-oriented couplets, the poet manages to change scenes constantly and yet at the same time maintain the self-sufficient quality of each scene. The scenery does not move; it is the poet-persona who constantly moves back and forth to "select" the particulars of nature. Thus, in each of Hsieh Ling-yün's poems we do not see just one static picture, but a series of independent scenes which are combined to give living resemblances to nature. This artistic achievement is done most effectively through the balanced structure of parallelism, although on the surface one may see only the profuse array of various parallel lines in Hsieh's poetry.

Clearly, the total power of Hsieh's poetry lies in the proper balance of his two basic types of parallelism. The combined effect of both prevents the poems from being either flatly descriptive or exhaustingly action-oriented. But since a particular aim of this essay to emphasize Hsieh Ling-yün's role in the description of landscape—what I may call "descriptive realism"—the following

[38] For the traditional discussions of the various functions of *chü-yen*, see Chou Chen-fu 周振甫, *Shih-tz'u li-hua* 詩詞例話 (Peking: Chung-kuo ch'ing-nien ch'u-pan-she, 1962), pp. 202–206. For a study of *chü-yen* in English, see Craig Fisk, "The Verse Eye and the Self-animating Landscape in Chinese Poetry," *Tamkang Review* 8 (April 1977), 123–153.

[39] For a discussion of the theme of loneliness and Hsieh's treatments of verbs, see Yeh Chia-ying 葉嘉瑩, "Ts'ung Yüan I-shan lun-shih chüeh-chü t'an Hsieh Ling-yün yü Liu Tsung-yüan te shih yü jen" 從元遺山論詩絕句談謝靈運與柳宗元的詩與人 in her *Chung-kuo ku-tien shih-ko p'ing-lun chi* 中國古典詩歌評論集 (Hong Kong: Chung-hua shu-chü, 1977), pp. 35–44.

discussion will dwell on Hsieh's first type of parallelism. Our main question will be: How does the poet organize the natural objects in a poetic scene, so that the artistic structure becomes the semblance of nature?

The basic unit of a "scene" in Hsieh's poetry is usually that of the parallel couplet. The couplet, though consisting of only two lines, has a symbolic power of encompassing the whole of nature's order. What is important is the endless coordinations among things in the universe. But these relations have to be discovered and selected by the poet himself, and in Hsieh's case the basic components in nature fall into the two general categories "mountains" and "waters." One of Hsieh's favorite techniques is to juxtapose a "far-off" mountain scene with a "nearby" river scene, thus creating the picture of a traveler looking out to the distance from his river boat:

(1) White clouds embrace the shaded rocks; 白雲抱幽石
Green bamboos charm the clear ripples. 綠篠媚淸漣
(CHSK, II, 637)

(2) In the curvings of the stream, the flow keeps straying out of sight; 澗委水屢迷
By the distant forest, the cliffs cluster together. 林迥巖逾密
(CHSK, II, 639)

In example (1) the mountain scene is followed by a river scene, though the sense of distance is only implied. But example (2) clearly indicates that the cliffs are "distant." The force of such juxtaposition comes not only from a relative sense of distance that parallelism affords, but also from its tendency to call our attention to the panoramic scale of nature. One feels that the poet is never confined by his immediate surroundings; his ultimate joy comes from organizing the various aspects of nature—far and near, large and small—into a composite landscape. The T'ang poet Po Chü-i 白居易 (772–846) most aptly summed up Hsieh Ling-yün's accomplishments in this respect:

His large [images] always encompass the sky and the sea; 大必籠天海

His small [images] never leave out those of the grass and the trees.[40] 細不遺草樹

By definition, the object-oriented parallelism emphasizes natural objects themselves and their picturesque attributes. But good descriptions are never "plastic," and this is why Hsieh Ling-yün's couplets remain enduring models for emulation. One of the most important qualities of Hsieh's parallel couplets is something we might call "animation"—a quality that may be attributed mainly to his well-chosen *chü-yen*. Consider the following couplet just cited above:

Whit clouds embrace [*pao*] the shaded rocks; 白雲抱幽石
Green bamboos charm [*mei*] the clear ripples. 綠篠媚淸漣

The sense of liveliness embodied in the verbs *pao* (embrace) and *mei* (charm) lends to the descriptive couplet an animated effect. "Embrace" and "charm" are verbs referring to intense human feelings. In real life, one does not normally embrace another person unless there is affection involved. And the verb *mei* ("charm") specifically implies the seductive appearance or gestures of a woman. When these verbs are attached to such inanimate objects as clouds, rocks, bamboos, and ripples, the description of the landscape immediately becomes more vital and arresting. The art of transferring "life" from the perceiver to the things being perceived is one of the characteristics of Hsieh Ling-yün's description. This poetic accomplishment seems to draw on the basic idea of personality appraisal so overwhelmingly accepted by the Wei-Chin intellectuals.[41] When a poet achieves *hsing-ssu* successfully, he not only gives the fine details but also captures the essential spirit—the *shen* 神 or life—of things. This technique of description may be compared to that which one uses to comprehend a person's whole character in personality appraisal. Thus, to Hsieh, descriptive similitude must

[40] See Po Chü-i's 白居易 poem entitled "Tu Hsieh Ling-yün shih" 讀謝靈運詩, in *Po Chü-i chi* 白居易集, ed. Ku Hsüeh-chieh 顧學頡 (Peking: Chung-hua shu-chü, 1979), vol. 1, p. 131.

[41] See Tu Wei-ming's article "Profound Learning, Personal Knowledge, and Poetic Vision" in this volume; and Yü Ying-shih, "Individualism and the Neo-Taoist Movement in Wei-Chin China" (unpublished manuscript, 1982).

include that of the spirit of "life" as well. The following couplet of his has been admired for centuries precisely because of its quality of vitality created by the verbs *sheng* (grow) and *pien* (change):[42]

> By the pond spring grass is growing [*sheng*]; 池塘生春草
> In the garden willows cause singing birds to change [*pien*]. 園柳變鳴禽
> (CHSK, II, 638)

Some of Hsieh's descriptive techniques were not so innovative, but he did attempt to bring conventional devices into full play, to experiment with new variations, and to produce a marked effect which might otherwise be hidden from the view. A case in point is his use of reduplicative compounds in the descriptive couplets:

(1) *Mei-mei* the orchid-covered banks are surrounded by rapid flow; 莓莓蘭渚急
Miao-miao the moss mountain is high. 藐藐苔嶺高
(CHSK, II, 640)

(2) *Huo-huo* the roaring currents rush on at dusk; 活活夕流駛
Chiao-chiao the apes cry shrilly through the night. 噭噭夜猿啼
(CHSK, II, 643)

The device of using reduplicative compounds to describe the essential qualities of natural objects can be of course traced back to the *Book of Songs*. Such compounds of earlier times were usually used to highlight general appearances rather than to bring out the particular details of things, as Liu Hsieh points out in his *Wen-hsin tiao-lung*:

> *Cho-cho*, "brilliant," is used to depict the brilliance of peach blossoms; *i-i*, "feeling of attachment," to describe the sweeping willow trees; *kao-kao*, "brightly burning," to describe the coming out of the sun; *piao-piao*, "fast and heavy," to suggest

[42] For a discussion of "verb and the dynamic image" in relation to Hsieh Ling-yün's use of verbs, see Yu-kung Kao and Tzu-lin Mei, "Syntax, Diction, and Imagery in T'ang Poetry," *Harvard Journal of Asiatic Studies* 31 (1971), 95.

> an image of rain and snow; *chieh-chieh*, "chirping," to imitate the sound of orioles; *yao-yao*, "buzzing," to imitate the sound of insects. . . .[43]

Hsieh's innovation lies in his combining this old conventional device with his symmetrical arrangement of "mountains" and "waters." The reduplicative compounds in Hsieh's poetry are no longer limited to the descriptions of plants, flowers, insects, etc. They have now entered the larger world of the *shan-shui* landscape, and help to heighten the qualities of the parallel elements. For instance, in example (1) above, the river scene is juxtaposed with the mountain scene, and *mei-mei* and *miao-miao* serve to emphasize the qualitative differences between the external "appearances" of the two scenes. In example (2), it is through the "auditory" effect of *huo-huo* and *chiao-chiao* that the paired relation between a river scene and a mountain scene becomes more pronounced.

Hsieh's crafted art of parallelism was a breakthrough in the five-character line *shih* tradition. Never before was a *shih* poet so skillful in producing parallel couplets with such a wide range of variety.[44] His poetic talent was in keeping with the taste of the time, for parallelism was held in great esteem during the Six Dynasties. In Chinese literary history Hsieh Ling-yün represented the culmination of a poetic trend, for the ideal of *ch'iao-ssu* in description was finally realized in his vivid depiction of the well-balanced world of "mountains and waters." Later landscape poets, notably Pao Chao and Hsieh T'iao, modeled their *shan-shui* poetry largely on Hsieh Ling-yün's work, although Hsieh T'iao's poems are usually free from Taoist allusions.[45] Speaking generally, it was the painstaking artistry of parallel couplets that formed the very core of Hsieh Ling-yün's descriptive realism which later poets came to learn most from him.

[43] See Vincent Yu-chung Shih, trans., *The Literary Mind*, p. 349. For a discussion of the poetic effect of reduplicative sounds in descriptive poetry, see Chou Chen-fu, *Shih-tz'u li-hua*, pp. 62–63.

[44] For example, Hsieh Ling-yün was the first Chinese poet in the five-character line poetry to have experimented with placing *chü-yen* in all five different positions.

[45] The influence of Hsieh Ling-yün's landscape poetry on that of Pao Chao and Hsieh T'iao has been admirably studied by Lin Wen-yüeh. See her *Shan-shui yü ku-tien*, pp. 23–61; pp. 93–123.

Lin Wen-yüeh

The Decline and Revival of *Feng-ku* (Wind and Bone): On the Changing Poetic Styles from the Chien-an Era through the High T'ang Period*

In one of his poems Li Po 李白 (701–762) once referred to "P'eng-lai literature and Chien-an *ku* (bone)" (蓬萊文章建安骨).[1] In another context, he commented that the dominance of highly ornamented style in literature after the Chien-an period (196–220) was not to be valued (自從建安來,綺麗不足珍).[2] There can be no doubt of Li Po's admiration for the literature of the Chien-an period. Even before Li Po, Ch'en Tzu-ang 陳子昂 (661–702) had remarked:

> The Way of literature has been declining for five hundred years. The *feng-ku* 風骨 (wind and bone) of the Han (206 B.C. to A.D. 220) and Wei (220–265) was lost in the Chin (265–420) and Liu Sung (420–479) dynasties. However, there are still some poems that can attest to the survival of the *feng-ku* manner of Han-Wei [i.e., *Chien-an*] literature. . . . I chanced upon "Ode on a Lonely Paulownia" 詠孤桐篇 by Ming

* I wish to express my gratitude to Stephen Owen, Arthur Tobias, and Shuen-fu Lin for their help in refining this English version of my study on *feng-ku*.

[1] Li Po 李白, "Hsüan-chou Hsieh T'iao lou chien-pieh chiao-shu Shu-yün" 宣州謝朓樓餞別校書叔雲, *Fen-lei pu-chu Li T'ai-po shih* 分類補注李太白詩 (SPTK ed.), fourth series, *chüan* 18, p. 262.

[2] See no. 1 of "Ku-feng wu-shih-chiu shou" 古風五十九首, *ibid.*, *chüan* 2, p. 47.

> Kung 明公 [his full name is Tung-fang Ch'iu 東方虬, a contemporary of Ch'en]. . . . Unexpectedly, it was imbued with the Cheng-shih 正始 (240–248) style. Even the Chien-an poets might well have smiled in approval.[3]

Chien-an is the last reign period of the last emperor of the Eastern Han. In literary historical terms, the Chien-an period spans the last years of the Han dynasty to the Wei dynasty. Therefore, "the *feng-ku* of the Han and Wei," referred to by Ch'en Tzu-ang, is exactly what Li Po meant by "Chien-an *ku*."

Long before the time of Li Po and Ch'en Tzu-ang, literary men of the Six Dynasties had already singled out the Chien-an period as a model for creative writing. Chung Hung 鍾嶸 (?-ca. 518) in the preface to his *Shih-p'in* 詩品 remarked:

> During the Yung-chia 永嘉 period (307–313), people prized Taoism and tended to philosophize in conversation. Since poets paid more attention to philosophical ideas than to their poetic language, their poetry was bland and tasteless. The trend persisted into the Chiang-piao 江表 period (Eastern Chin 東晉, 318–420). Poems by Sun Ch'o 孫綽 (314–371), Hsü Hsün 許詢 (fl. ca. 358), Huan Wen 桓溫 (312–373) and Yü Liang 庾亮 (289–340) are as prosaic as [Ho Yen's 何晏 (?–249)] "Tao-te lun" 道德論 (Discourse on the Way and its power): the *feng-li* 風力 (wind and strength) of Chien-an has come to an end.[4]

"The *feng-li* of Chien-an" in this context is by implication similar to Li Po's "Chien-an *ku*" and Ch'en Tzu-ang's "*feng-ku* of the Han and Wei." Liu Hsieh 劉勰 (ca. 465–ca. 532) in *Wen-hsin tiao-lung* 文心雕龍 (The Literary Mind and the Carving of Dragons) did not explicitly refer to the *feng-ku* or *feng-li* of Chien-an, yet he described the literature of the Chien-an period favorably as being "heroic in

[3] Ch'en Tzu-ang 陳子昂, "Yü Tung-fang tso-shih Ch'iu hsiu-chu p'ien ping-shu" 與東方左史虬修竹篇并書, *Ch'en Po-yü ch'üan-chi* 陳伯玉全集 (SPTK ed.), fourth series, *chüan* 1, p. 12.

[4] Ku Chih 古直, *Chung Chi-shih shih-p'in chien* 鍾記室詩品箋 (Taipei: Kuang-wen shu-chü, 1968), p. 5.

giving free play to their vitality, open and artless in the application of their talents" and "full of feeling and life."[5] In another chapter, "Feng-ku," Liu Hsieh also cited the representative poets of the Chien-an period as positive illustrations of his poetics. P'ei Tzu-yeh's 裴子野 (469–530) "Tiao-ch'ung lun" 雕蟲論, too, observed that "Ts'ao and Liu abound in *feng-li*."[6] Thus in advocating a literary taste modeled on the Chien-an period, the two great T'ang poets were following a long tradition. Gradually, the *feng-ku* of Chien-an became an established criterion of poetry; for example, the term appears prominently in the *Ts'ang lang shih-hua*[7] 滄浪詩話 by Yen Yü 嚴羽 (fl. thirteenth century) of the Sung dynasty (960–1279) and the *Shih sou*[8] 詩藪 by Hu Ying-lin 胡應麟 (1551–1602) of the Ming dynasty (1368–1644).

But why should the T'ang literati have singled out the *feng-ku* of Chien-an as a means to invigorate the literature of their own time? This is a question I would like to answer in the following pages, from the standpoint of poetics.

I. *Feng-ku*

The term *feng-ku* was originally used to describe a person's demeanor and appearance. Shen Yüeh 沈約 (441–513) records in "The Chronicle of Emperor Wu" in the *Sung shu* 宋書武帝紀: "He distinguished himself by his *feng-ku*. Though poor, he was filled

[5] My quotations from Liu Hsieh 劉勰, *Wen-hsin tiao-lung* 文心雕龍 are all from Vincent Yu-chung Shih, trans., *The Literary Mind and the Carving of Dragons* (Taipei: Chung-hua shu-chü, 1970). The first remark is from the chapter "An Exegesis of Poetry," p. 46; the second remark is from the chapter "The Literary Development and Time," p. 339.

[6] P'ei Tzu-yeh's 裴子野 comment can be found in "Ch'üan Liang wen" 全梁文 in Yen K'o-chün 嚴可均, *Ch'üan shang-ku san-tai Ch'in-Han San-kuo Liu-ch'ao wen* 全上古三代秦漢三國六朝文 (hereafter *CSSCSLW*) (rpt. Taipei: Shih-chieh shu-chü, n.d.), *chüan* 53, p. 16.

[7] The term *feng-ku* is used in the "Shih-p'ing" 詩評 chapter in Yen Yü 嚴羽, *Ts'ang-lang shih-hua* 滄浪詩話. See *Li-tai shih-hua* 歷代詩話, ed. Ho Wen-huan 何文煥 (Taipei: I-wen ch'u-pan-she, 1956), p. 450.

[8] Hu Ying-lin 胡應麟, *Shih-sou* 詩藪 (rpt. Taipei: Kuang-wen shu-chü, n.d.), p. 441.

with ambition."[9] *Feng-ku* in this context refers to the overall impression that demeanor and physical appearance made on others. This broader application of *feng-ku* is simply one case of a wide range of terms shared by both traditional literary criticism and the appraisal of personality. Although this shared vocabulary has the advantage of suggestiveness and flexibility, it is also imprecise and loose. But what is *feng-ku*? What kind of work may be judged as characterized by *feng-ku*? This issue has long been the subject of much controversy.

The chapter on *feng-ku* in the *Wen-hsin tiao-lung* is considered to be the first full treatment of the term in Chinese literary criticism. Liu Hsieh opens this chapter with a direct statement about the concept of "wind and bone."

> The *Book of Poetry* contains six elements, and of these *feng*, or wind, stands at the head of the list. It is the source of transformation, and the correlate of emotion and vitality. He who would express mournful emotions must begin with the wind, and to organize his linguistic elements he must above all emphasize the bone. Literary expressions are conditioned by the bone in much the same way as the standing posture of a body is conditioned by its skeleton; feeling gives form to the wind very much as a physical form envelops the vitality which animates it. When expressions are organized on the right principles, literary bone is there; and when the emotion and vitality embodied are swift and free, there we find the purity of the literary wind.[10]

Liu Hsieh finds his most obvious source for the term *feng* in the *Book of Songs* (i.e., the *Book of Poetry*, or *Shih ching* 詩經), and he draws on the term's canonical association with a process of "transformation" asserted in the preface to the Mao version of this classic ("Mao-shih hsü" 毛詩序). However, he does not draw in another interpretation of the Han Confucians, who understood *feng* as a way for the ruler to transform his subjects and for the subjects to criticize the ruler. Instead he quickly goes on to explain *feng* as "the

[9] Shen Yüeh 沈約, *Sung Shu* 宋書 (SPPY ed.), *chüan* 1, p. 1a.
[10] Vincent Yu-chung Shih, *The Literary Mind*, p. 227.

correlate" or expression of "emotion and vitality." Unable to give *ku* the same canonical authority as *feng*, Liu Hsieh explains *ku* in parallel antithesis to *feng*. This passage seems to indicate that while *feng* refers to the emotion and will ("vitality") revealed by the content, *ku* refers to literary expression. For this reason Huang K'an's 黃侃 *Notes on the Wen-hsin tiao-lung* 文心雕龍札記 makes the distinction that "*feng* is meaning and *ku* is expression."[11] But the issue remains largely unsettled.

Liu Hsieh further elaborates his definition by explaining *feng* and *ku* from both positive and negative points of view:

> If a literary piece has nothing but rich and brilliant colors, without wind and bone to keep it air-borne, then one shaking is enogh to destroy its splendor, lacking as it does the vigor which can justify fame.... He whose bone structure is well exercised will always be versed in rhetoric; and he who is deep of wind will always be articulate in expressing his feelings. To be firm and exact in diction, and in resonance sure without being heavy: this is what is meant by vigor of wind and bone. Now to be thin in ideas and fat in words, or confused and disorganized, without unity, are sure signs of lack of this kind of bone. And when ideas are incomplete and incomprehensive, lifeless and without vitality, it is an evidence of the absence of the wind.[12]

It is apparent that we can hardly draw a clear line between either *feng* and *ku* or between content and form. In actuality, all works are composed of literary expression. As Liu Hsieh makes clear in his chapter on "Emotion and Literary Expression" 情采篇, "emotion is the warp of literary pattern, linguistic form the woof of ideas."[13] Emotion and expression are no more in opposition than the warp and woof of a fabric; rather, they are organically related. Liao Wei-ch'ing 廖蔚卿 observes in "Feng-ku lun" 風骨論 (Discourse on Wind and Bone) in her *Liu-ch'ao wen-lun* 六朝文論 (Six Dynasties Literary Criticism) that: "the co-called *feng* refers to the work's

[11] Huang K'an 黃侃, "Wen-hsin tiao-lung cha-chi" 文心雕龍札記, in *Wen-hsin tiao-lung chu* 文心雕龍注 (Taipei: K'ai-ming shu-chü, 1967), *chüan* 6, p. 15a.

[12] Vincent Yu-chung Shih, *The Literary Mind.*

[13] *Ibid.*, pp. 246–247.

content, a profound and vigorous expression of sentiments and thoughts; it has to do with the writer's idea and thinking. The so-called *ku* refers to the work's form, a vigorous expression in diction and composition; it has to do with the technique of rhetoric. A masterpiece is never merely rich in rhetorical ornamentation and poor in *feng-ku*."[14] Liao Wei-ch'ing not only contrasts *feng* with *ku* but emphasizes the connection between *feng-ku* and vigor. To judge from Liu Hsieh's repeated expositions of *feng* and *ku* in relation to their presence in or absence from a literary piece, it is evident that the phrase is not an empty generality but stresses a kind of vigorous expression. Thus *feng-ku* resembles the quality of *feng-li*, as in Chung Hung's remark that "the *feng-li* of Chien-an has come to an end." In reference to the same quality, P'ei Tzu-yeh gives special praise to Ts'ao and Liu for the way in which their work "abounds in *feng-li*."

It is impossible to talk about Chien-an *feng-ku* without reference to Liu Hsieh's ideas about *feng-ku*. However, any consideration of the term *feng-ku* in isolation is unlikely to yield a concrete understanding of the category. What, exactly, are the characteristics and features of Chien-an *feng-ku* which in critical hands has been a term of praise? In order to answer this question, it is necessary to examine certain literary pieces in juxtaposition with the theory.

II. The *Feng-ku* of Chien-an

Chien-an literature covers the period from the end of Han rule to the Wei dynasty. Yen Yü in the section on "Poetic Style" in his *Ts'ang-lang shih-hua* lists Chien-an and Huang-ch'u 黃初 (220–226) separately. However, there are notes under each entry. Under the section entitled "the style of Chien-an," we read: "the title of the last reign of the Han dynasty, represented by the Ts'ao family and the seven literary men of Yeh 鄴";[15] but under "the style of Huang-ch'u," Yen Yü comments: "the reign title of the Wei

[14] Liao Wei-ch'ing 廖蔚卿, *Liu-ch'ao wen-lun* 六朝文論 (Taipei: Lien-ching shu-chü, 1978), p. 72.

[15] Ho Wen-huan, *Li-tai shih-hua*, p. 444.

dynasty: connected with Chien-an, sharing the same literary style." From this it is clear that Yen Yü considers the so-called "poetic circle of Chien-an" as extending from the first year of Chien-an to the seventh year of Huang-ch'u (196–226). The Chinese consider every thirty years a generation. This implies that the format of literature in every thirty years will manifest a distinctive style of its own. Most of the extant Chien-an works were composed either by members of the Ts'ao family or by the seven literary men of Yeh, although the poetic circle of Chien-an was not formed exclusively by these people.

The Ts'ao family not only encouraged creative writing, it also played the leading role among the literati. Together with the "seven literary men" attached to them, the Ts'aos formed a kind of literary salon in Yeh, the capital of Wei. Ts'ao Ts'ao 曹操 (155–220) was their helmsman. With his bravery and intellect, Chien-an literature launched itself fearlessly. The grand gathering of literati in Yeh, the vitality of the works of the group, and their literary features were recorded in the preface to the *Shih-p'in* and in the chapter entitled "Shih-hsü" 時序 or "Literary Development and Time" in the *Wen-hsin tiao-lung*.

Ts'ao Ts'ao, an iconoclast in his own time, was politically anti-Confucian: his words and deeds were everything but "tender and gentle" (the qualities appropriate to a Confucian statesman). He judged people by their ability alone, regardless of morality; nor did he even feel shamed at proclaiming his desire for achievement and fame. The influence of his political values on literature was reflected in a style called *ch'ing-chün t'ung-t'o* 清峻通脫 or "simple, forthright, and free."[16] The spirit of writing advocated by Ts'ao Ts'ao in effect provided a free but solid stage for contemporary literati. In addition to Ts'ao's personal influence, his sons' admiration for literary men encouraged writers to gather around the Ts'aos. Fortunately, these writers were not the self-effacing literary courtiers of later ages. Although they relied on the Ts'aos for their liveli-

[16] According to T'ai Ching-nung 臺靜農, *ch'ing-chün* refers to "simple and forthright" (簡練明快) and *t'ung-t'o* to "free expressions" (自由抒寫). See his "Wei-Chin ssu-hsiang te shu-lun" 魏晉思想的述論 in *Chung-kuo wen-hsüeh shih lun-wen hsüan-chi* 中國文學史論文選集, 2 vols. (Taipei: Hsüeh-sheng shu-chü, 1978), vol. 2, p. 450.

hood, in their writing they were free to speak their own minds. In his "Tien-lun lun-wen" 典論論文, Ts'ao P'i (187–226) praised the seven literary men of Yeh in the following words: "In learning, they have covered everything important; in writing, they are free of borrowings. Like horses running side by side, they emulate one another."[17] Such mutual emulation was a particularly powerful force in Chien-an literature, and it won for the poets of the period the highest place in the estimation of later generations. In other words, at that time rank existed only in the socio-political world; in writing all were equal. In the field of literature, there was no need to fear giving offense to the Ts'aos; either by criticism or flattery a writer could speak his own mind without restraint. The quality that Liu Hsieh praised as "heroic in giving free play to their vitality, open and artless in the application of their talents" was rooted in the larger background of free competition.

Although the corpus that has come down to us is certainly incomplete, when we turn to the poetry produced against this background, the excitement of the times and misery of life can be discerned as the main issues that concerned the Chien-an poets. Ts'ao P'i in the preface to his *Tien-lun* described the chaos at the end of Han rule thus: "People died with their corpses exposed to the open air much like weeds covering the ground."[18] Ts'ao Ts'ao's "Hsieh-lu" 薤露 or "Dew on the Shallots" is typical of the poems describing the time and circumstances in which the poets lived.[19] "Hsieh-lu" was originally the name of a Han lament which Ts'ao Ts'ao adopted to describe the events of the day. In this *yüeh-fu* 樂府 poem, he states that the ambitious politicians of the late Han brought their country and people to ruin. Half narrating and half commenting, Ts'ao Ts'ao pours out his grief, ending the poem on a note of moral outrage. He castigates Ho Chin 何進 for his hesitation and Tung Cho 董卓 for his regicide. Another poem with a *yüeh-fu* title is "Hao-li hsing" 蒿里行 or "Song on the Village of the

[17] Ch'en Shou 陳壽, *San-Kuo chih* 三國志 with a commentary by P'ei Sung-chih 裴松之 (Peking: Chung-hua shu-chü, 1960), *chüan* 21, p. 602.

[18] *Ibid.*, *chüan* 2, p. 18.

[19] See "Ch'üan San-Kuo shih" 全三國詩 in *Ch'üan Han San-Kuo Chin Nan-Pei-Ch'ao shih* 全漢三國晉南北朝詩 (hereafter *CHSCNS*), ed. Ting Fu-pao, 3 vols. (rpt. Taipei: Shih-chieh shu-chü, 1962), vol. 1, p. 120.

Dead," which was also a Han lament adopted to describe contemporary events. In it, Ts'ao Ts'ao gives voice to his indignation at Yüan Shao 袁紹 and his brother, men who pursued fame and profit at the expense of the state and the people. Their actions were injurious to both soldiers and common people alike. Consider these lines in the latter part of the poem:

Lice larvae are born in armor worn by soldiers; 鎧甲生蟣蝨
Thousands of families end in death, 萬性以死亡
White bones are exposed to the open air; 白骨露於野
The land lacks even the crowing of roosters. 千里無鷄鳴
Only one survives among a hundred; 生民百遺一
To think of it breaks one's heart.[20] 念之斷人腸

These lines are clearly a variation of the theme of Ts'ao P'i's preface to the *Tien-lun*. Chung Hsing 鍾惺 therefore characterizes this poem as "a documentary on the late Han."[21]

Chung Hsing's remark applies not only to the work of Ts'ao Ts'ao, but also to many other Chien-an poets. The first of K'ung Jung's 孔融 (153–208) "Liu-yen shih san-shou" 六言詩三首 or "Three Hexasyllabic Poems" reads:

In the mid-Han, morality was on the decline. 漢家中葉道微
Tung Cho took the chance to rebel; 董卓作亂乘衰
He disregarded the emperor and oppressed the people. 僭上虐下專威
Being terrorized, officials dared not offend him; 萬官惶怖莫違
Common people were miserable and suffered.[22] 百姓慘慘心悲

Brief as it is, the poem shares with Ts'ao Ts'ao's "Dew on the Shallots" the same profound melancholy and righteous indignation. Ts'ao P'i's "Ling-shih" 令詩 or "Command" begins:

[20] *Ibid.*

[21] Quoted in Huang Chieh 黃節, *Han-Wei yüeh-fu feng chien* 漢魏樂府風箋 (rpt. Hong Kong: Shang-wu yin-shu-kuan, 1961), p. 78.

[22] Ting Fu-pao, "Ch'üan Han shih" 全漢詩, in *CHSCNS*, vol. 1, p. 45.

Turmoil has lasted more than ten years;	喪亂悠悠過紀
For miles and miles there are scattered bones.[23]	白骨縱橫萬里

This poem and his preface to the *Tien-lun* are mutually reinforcing. Ts'ao Chih 曹植 (192–232) in the first of his two poems entitled "Sung Ying-shih" 送應氏 or "Seeing Off Mr. Ying" has the following lines on the post-war spectacle:

How desolate the land is:	中野何蕭條
Not a single soul comes into sight.	千里無人煙
Recalling the place I used to live,	念我平常居
My breath chokes, I cannot utter a word.[24]	氣結不能言

Wang Ts'an 王粲 (177–217) in the first of three poems entitled "Ch'i-ai shih" 七哀詩 or "Seven Sorrows" also describes similar scenes of suffering:

I walk out with nothing in sight	出門無所見
But white bones covering the field.	白骨蔽平原
On the road a hungry woman	路有飢婦人
Takes her baby and abandons it among the grass.[25]	抱子棄草間

These poems bear testimony to the age: every word is a teardrop. Even Ch'en Lin's 陳琳 (d. 217) "Yin-ma Ch'ang-Ch'eng-k'u hsing" 飲馬長城窟行 (Song: I Watered My Horse at the Long Wall Caves) reflects the turbulent age, though apparently it describes how the construction of the Great Wall under the reign of Ch'in-shih-huang 秦始皇 (r. 221–210 B.C.) caused people misery.[26]

The literati of Chien-an confronted an age in turmoil. They either heard about or had been in the wars; each was a witness to the times in which they lived. Poets like Ts'ao Ts'ao, Ts'ao P'i, Wang Ts'an, and Ying Yang 應瑒 (d. 217) who wrote on war neither

[23] *Ibid.*, "Ch'üan San-Kuo shih,", vol. 1, p. 135.
[24] *Ibid.*, p. 162.
[25] *Ibid.*, p. 181.
[26] *Ibid.*, p. 182.

withdrew nor escaped. On the contrary, they were a part of the age and wrote down their personal experiences in a heroically tragic style. The pen expressed what the mind felt: it did not need to hunt for words or set phrases; rather, it followed the writer's direct pursuit of the feelings deep in his heart. The Chien-an poets therefore impress the reader with their tremendous vigor.

To judge from the socio-political background and the notable features of this period, the Chien-an literati deserve our admiration. Facing an eventful age, though they certainly felt sad, they had a deep social consciousness, and their compassion for the world is preserved in their poetry. Though only twenty-odd poems of Ts'ao Ts'ao have survived, many of them articulate his political ideals. "Tu kuan-shan" 度關山 or "Passing through the Mountain Passes," for instance, opens with high aspirations:

In the universe
Man is noblest.
My duty is to assist the emperor
And shepherd the people.[27]

天地間人爲貴
立君牧民爲之軌則

Here Ts'ao Ts'ao states the public obligations that are a consequence of his political power. "Tui-chiu" 對酒 or "Facing the Wine" is another example.[28] In his view, a prosperous state depends upon an orderly system with an able emperor to dispense rewards and punishments impartially. High and low work together to create social well-being. In one hundred and twenty-odd words, "Tui-chiu" evokes a Confucian utopia with some touches of Legalism and Taoism. In the first of three songs under the title of "Shan-tsai hsing" 善哉行 or "Song: How Splendid," Ts'ao Ts'ao marshalls twelve historical personages to illustrate the importance of having loyal and able men in high positions.[29] By using exemplary models, he again indicates his political ambition to right wrongs. The most noteworthy and best known among this type of poetry is the second of the two "Tuan-ko hsing" 短歌行 or "Short Songs."[30] The poem must have been written after the Battle of

[27] *Ibid.*, p. 117.
[28] *Ibid.*, p. 122.
[29] *Ibid.*, p. 118.
[30] *Ibid.*

Ch'ih-pi 赤壁之戰. This lost battle frustrated his undertaking of unifying China. In this context he laments aging and his unfulfilled dreams, unable to escape the feeling that life was too short. Yet the speaker is, above all, a hero, and, instead of giving way to melancholy, he urges his friends to join him for a drink, to forget sorrows and worries. The thought of having people from near and far joined under his rule inspires him. He explicitly compares himself with the Duke of Chou 周公 (fl. twelfth century B.C.), declaring his high aims. In the same way, the following lines from "Pu-ch'u tung-hsi-men hsing" 步出東西門行 or "Song on Walking Out of the Eastern and Western Gates" reveal an unyielding determination:

Old horse kept to the stable	老驥伏櫪
Still aspires to run a thousand miles;	志在千里
The passionate hero in his last years	烈士暮年
Has a mind still in the prime of its vigor.[31]	壯心不已

The courage to face reality and a positive attitude toward life mark the Chien-an literati. Ts'ao P'i usurped the throne of the Han, established the Wei, and changed the reign title to Huang-ch'u in 220. Although he reigned for only seven years, he cared deeply for his people. Having personally gone through the turmoil from the late Han to the Three Kingdoms period, Ts'ao P'i was deeply conscious of the need to rebuild the nation. By lessening punishments, cutting down taxation, advocating the simple life, and emphasizing agriculture, he carried out his aim after coming to the throne. Being a ruler himself, Ts'ao P'i spoke out repeatedly on the true way of government. "Huang-huang ching Lo hsing" 煌煌京洛行 or "Song on the Glorious Capital Lo-yang" employs historical allusions in a way much like Ts'ao Ts'ao's "Shan-tsai hsing."[32] But in contrast to his father, Ts'ao P'i was not only in power, he also mounted the throne in his lifetime. Thus it was natural for him to write as a titled emperor.

In the poetic circle of Chien-an, Ts'ao Ts'ao and Ts'ao P'i were real political leaders. Their poetry shows deep concern for uniting

[31] *Ibid.*, p. 119.

[32] *Ibid.*, p. 126.

people near and far under a single kingdom and for the employment of able men. Ts'ao Chih and the other poets, though in a subordinate position, were nonetheless concerned with politics and administration. Ts'ao Chih's view on poetry and political values, as seen in his early writing "A Letter to Yang Te-tsu"[33] 與楊德祖書, remained unchanged throughout his life. This letter is representative of Chien-an belles-lettres in its general concern with political achievements.

Though born in disjointed times, a man of ambition could not be an escapist. K'ung Jung aimed at neither Lü Wang's aloofness nor at Po I and Shu Ch'i's escapism. Rather, modeling himself on Kuan Chung 管仲 (d. 645 B.C.), he pursued a career in politics. The active attitude toward life was common to all the Chien-an poets. We have observed the straightforward proclamation of one's ambition in the above-mentioned poems by Ts'ao Chih. Ch'en Lin asserted his position in the second of his "Yu-lan erh-shou" 遊覽二首 or "Two Poems on Sightseeing" in much the same way:

How quickly the days and months rush away;	騁哉日月逝
Life like the setting sun is approaching its end.	生命將西傾
Were I not to attain achievements in my lifetime,	建功不及時
How could I be remembered in history?[34]	鍾鼎何所銘

Ts'ao P'i also remarked in "Yen-ko ho-ch'ang hsing" 艷歌何嘗行:

Born into this world	男兒居世
Man should try his best.	各當努力
Fleetingly the sun sets;	蹙迫日暮
Life is too short to stay.[35]	殊不久留

A pressing sense of life's brevity inspired the Chien-an poets to build careers in their own time. But another consequence was the impulse to "seize the day." This aspect of their life-style has left us a considerable number of poems on banquets and social intercourse. Yeh was a sort of literary salon where a galaxy of literati took joy in such activities as cockfighting, falconry, sightseeing, and compos-

[33] Yen K'o-chün, *CSSCSLW*, vol. 3, *chüan* 16, pp. 5–6.

[34] Ting Fu-pao, "Ch'üan San-kuo shih," in *CHSCNS*, vol. 1, pp. 182–183.

[35] *Ibid.*, p. 130.

ing poems. The poets labored to excel in every field of endeavor. They extended poetic subject matter, and at the same time made remarkable progress in versification. In the chapter on "An Exegesis of Poetry" 明詩篇 in the *Wen-hsin tiao-lung* Liu Hsieh says:

> Their common themes are love for the wind and the moon, excursions to gardens and parks, royal grace and favors, drunken revelry and feasts. Heroic in giving free play to their vitality, open and artless in the application of their feelings or in their descriptions of what they saw, and in harnessing language for their descriptions, aiming simply at lucidity—in all these ways they manifest the same spirit.[36]

This passage points out that, in addition to the grief of parting and the aspirations of the mind, social activities were themes for versification. However, even in poems on the joys of life, they were "heroic in giving free play to their vitality, open and artless in the application of their talents." The way they wrote and the way they lived were consistent, which distinguishes even the salon poetry of this period from that of the later generations. We will consider three poems from this perspective. Wang Ts'an's "Kung-yen shih" 公讌詩 or "My Lord's Feast" reads:

Nowadays I often hear people say:	常聞時人語
Don't go home unless you're already drunk.	不醉且無歸
If we don't make merry today,	今日不極歡
For whom do we wait, holding our feelings back?[37]	含情欲待誰

Ts'ao Chih's second poem in the "Seeing Off Mr. Ying" set reads:

Leisure is not often to be found;	淸時難屢得
Joyful gatherings are rare and few.	嘉會不可常
Heaven and earth are eternal;	天地無終始
Life is as brief as the morning dew.	人命若朝露
I'd like to present the lovable aspects,	願得展嬿婉
For my friend is leaving for the far-north. . . .[38]	我友之朔方

[36] Vincent Yu-chung Shih, *The Literary Mind*, p. 46.

[37] Ting Fu-pao, "Ch'üan San-Kuo shih," in *CHSCNS*, vol. 1, p. 179.

[38] *Ibid.*, p. 162.

Consider also the following lines in Ying Yang's "Cockfight" 鬬雞:

Heavy is my heart,	戚戚懷不樂
No way to relieve burdens.	無以釋勞勤
To join friends at the arena	兄弟遊戲場
I order the carriages ready for the guests.[39]	命駕迎衆賓

The feelings here are deeply rooted in the heart. Standing on the riverside, Confucius once sighed at the passing of time. To survive in troubled times is to suffer more than one's fair share. Hsieh Ling-yün 謝靈運 (385–433) observed in the preface to his "Ni Wei-t'ai-tzu Yeh-chung chi-shih pa-shou" 擬魏太子鄴中集詩八首 or "Eight Poems in Imitation of the Poems of the Wei Crown Prince's Gathering in Yeh": "There are four joyful aspects of life: a good day, beautiful scenery, a bosom friend, delightful amusement. They seldom visit a man simultaneously."[40] He keenly perceived the difficulty of attaining perfection. Such being the case, the Chien-an poets were willing to enjoy themselves to their heart's content, though they were born in a miserable world. Their courage to face life, imperfect as it was, is tragically heroic. Therefore Ts'ao Ts'ao exclaimed:

Sing while we drink.	對酒當歌
Life is too short.[41]	人生幾何

In all its celebration of feasts and natural charms, Chien-an poetry never degenerated into pettiness and triviality. Exposed to stimulating surroundings, the poets broadened their horizon, but never pursued a passive and mannered style, as later poets did.

To sum up, disjointed times inspired the Chien-an literati. Far from being aloof onlookers, they were passionately concerned with their time and circumstances. They were all eager to labor in a noble cause and felt deep sympathy for the misery of the common people. Their writings were drawn from heartfelt feelings and therefore read more impressively than a historical text. Mere senti-

[39] *Ibid.*, p. 197.

[40] *Ibid.*, "Ch'üan Sung shih" 全宋詩, in *CHSCNS*, vol. 2, p. 648.

[41] *Ibid.*, "Ch'üan San-kuo shih," in *CHSCNS*, vol. 1, p. 117.

mentality could never be so moving as this. The Chien-an poets were closely bound to their surroundings. Liu Hsieh has rightly pointed out in "Literary Development and Time" in the *Wen-hsin tiao-lung*: "An examination of their writings reveals that most of them are full of feeling. This is because they lived in a world marked by disorder and separation, and at a time when morals declined and the people were complaining; they felt all this deeply in their hearts, and this feeling was expressed in a style which is moving. For this reason their works are full of feeling and life."[42] Chi Yün 紀昀 (1724–1805), commenting on Liu Hsieh's idea of *feng-ku*, expostulates that "vigor 氣 is *feng-ku*."[43] Vigor marks not only the writings of this period but the individual poets. The Chien-an literati made clear in their work that they neither hesitated to declare their ambition nor abandoned pleasure. Neither escapist nor mincing, Chien-an poetry impresses us with its masculine beauty and powerful diction. To end this section, it is sensible to equate Chung Hung's "*feng-li* of Chien-an" with Liu Hsieh's view of "*feng-ku*," for they designate the same quality that characterizes poetry produced during this period in literary history.

III. The Decline of *Feng-ku*

Chien-an poetry is noted for *feng-ku*, all the more so in sharp contrast to the poetry in the succeeding age, when masculine beauty faded away, as Liu Hsieh and Chung Hung observed from their own perspective two centuries after Chien-an.

The time from the end of Chien-an down to the end of the Six Dynasties, a period covering more than three hundred years, departed even farther from *feng-ku*. For the present purpose, I will consider only the major literary trends instead of each individual writer or work. The major poetic categories of the period thematically were: *chao-yin* 招隱 (poetry summoning the recluse from or into reclusion), *hsüan-yen* 玄言 (poetry of Taoist discourse), *yu-*

[42] Vincent Yu-chung Shih, *The Literary Mind*, p. 339.

[43] See *Wen-hsin tiao-lung chu teng liu-chung* 文心雕龍注等六種 (Taipei: Shih-chieh shu-chü, 1980), p. 111.

hsien 遊仙 (poetry of wandering immortals), *t'ien-yüan* 田園 (rural poetry), *shan-shui* 山水 (landscape poetry), *yung-wu* 詠物 (poems on objects), and *kung-t'i* 宮體 (court-style poetry). Though they differ in subject matter and treatment, a notable similarity exists in their disregard for the present world and worldly affairs: poets showed concern for the faraway and the long ago, or they took interest in natural beauty and even personal trivialities. The more they were concerned about themselves, the farther they were removed from society.

We should note in passing that some of these categories already existed by the time of the Wei and the Chin, but they reached their peak after the period of T'ai-k'ang 太康 (280–289). For instance, an early practice of *chao-yin* poetry can be traced back to "Chao yin-shih" 招隱士 or "Invitation to a Gentleman in Hiding,"[44] written in the *Ch'u tz'u* 楚辭 tradition by Huai-nan Hsiao-shan 淮南小山 of the Han dynasty. In this poem, reclusion was described as undesirable and even painful, threatened by the attack of wild animals. The speaker hence dissuaded the hermits from staying in the remote mountains. By the time of T'ai-k'ang, the *chao-yin* and anti-*chao-yin* poets viewed hermitage in a perspective altogether different from Huai-nan Hsiao-shan's. To the T'ai-k'ang poets, mountains and waters struck a merry note; plants and animals offered pleasant company. Hermitage was no longer considered dangerous and painful but was seen as the inclination of a noble mind and refined taste.

The types of writing varied from poet to poet, yet "T'ai-k'ang" was a period most noted for *chao-yin* poetry. Among the extant *chao-yin* poems there are three pieces by Lu Chi 陸機 (261–303), two by Chang Hua 張華 (232–300) and Tso Ssu 左思 (fl. 300), respectively, one by Chang Tsai 張載 (fl. third century), Lü Ch'iu-ch'ung 閭丘沖 (d. ca. 311), and Wang K'ang-chü 王康琚 (fl. fourth century) each, and one anti-*chao-yin* by Wang K'ang-chü. The fact that *chao-yin* and anti-*chao-yin* poetry was specified as a category in *Chao-ming wen-hsüan* 昭明文選, *chüan* 22, though only four pieces were collected therein, indicates its wide appeal at that time. In the hands of the T'ai-k'ang poets, reclusion turned out to be a desirable

[44] Hsiao T'ung 蕭統, *Chao-ming Wen-hsüan* 昭明文選 (rpt. Taipei: I-wen ch'u-pan-she, 1955), *chüan* 33, p. 315.

situation, approaching the natural life of Taoism. The passivity which underlies *chao-yin* poetry was caused by the ephemeral calm during the Western Chin (317–420). The peace was only on the surface; the conflicts among the royal families were to lead to disorder and unrest. Threatened by the tangled intrigues of society, faced with the subtlety of its politics, poets had on the one hand to flatter people in power, while on the other hand to long for the quietude and peace of reclusion. *Chao-yin* poetry, which had been meant to summon those who had retreated to out-of-the-way places back to the mundane world, now became a eulogy of eremitism. The view that public life is burdensome and peace lies in reclusion marks the typical *chao-yin* poetry in the Six Dynasties.

Yu-hsien poetry differs only slightly from *chao-yin* poetry in that the latter has a remote natural setting while the former envisages a fairyland and fantastic scenes that exist only in imagination. *Yu-hsien* poetry began as early as the time of Liu An 劉安 (d. 122 B.C.), who wrote "Pa-kung ts'ao" 八公操 in honor of the immortals. However, this piece was unique in its time. Not until the time of the Eastern Han did mature *yu-hsien* poetry begin to appear within secular *yüeh-fu* poetry. The Ts'aos wrote some pieces on the wandering immortals, but touches of fantasy were only vaguely perceivable in the Chien-an era. Ts'ao Ts'ao's *yu-hsien* poetry, cast in the remote and unapproachable, shows casual traces of human frailty. His poetry on the whole shows titanic grandeur, as its writer intended it to. As for the second of his two poems entitled "Ch'iu Hu hsing" 秋胡行 or "Songs of Ch'iu Hu," the poem contradicts itself in maintaining that:

There is no ruler of a single land	萬國率土
But is the subject of the imperial rule.	莫非王臣
The kingdom is noted for benevolence and integrity,	仁義爲名
Cultured by rites and music.[45]	禮樂爲樂

Strangely, its tone is more of the anti-*yu-hsien* rather than of the *yu-hsien* modified. The only *yu-hsien* poem by Ts'ao P'i now extant is "Che yang-liu hsing" 折楊柳行 or "Song on Breaking a Willow

[45] Ting Fu-pao, "Ch'üan San-kuo shih," in *CHSCNS*, vol. 1, p. 123.

Branch," which is actually an anti-*yu-hsien* poem. As Ts'ao P'i put it:

Prince Ch'iao gave a futile hope; 王喬假虛辭
Red Pine left empty promises. 赤松垂空言
A wise man distinguishes true from false, 達人識眞僞
While the fool loves to spread what is untrue.[46] 愚夫好妄傳

Ts'ao Chih's *yu-hsien* poetry is comparatively stately and colorful. However, in the last of his set of seven poems entitled "Tseng Po-ma Wang Piao" 贈白馬王彪 or "Presented to Piao, the Prince of Po-ma," even he said that:

Vain is the search for immortality; 虛無求列仙
Master Red Pine has long deceived us.[47] 松子久吾欺

The tone was suspended between believing and suspicion in much the same way as the experience in one of the "Nineteen Old Poems:"

Those who take pills to attain immortality 服食求神仙
Are usually fooled by them.[48] 多爲藥所誤

Yu-hsien poetry became even more popular after the Chien-an era. Poets like Hsi K'ang 嵇康 (223–262), Juan Chi 阮籍 (210–263), Chang Hua, Ch'eng-kung Sui 成公綏 (231–273), Ho Shao 何邵, Lu Chi, Chang Hsieh 張協 (d. 307?), Kuo P'u 郭璞 (276–324), T'ao Ch'ien 陶潛 (365–427), Chan Fang-sheng 湛方生, and Su Yen 蘇彥 all tried their hand at this sub-genre of *shih*. It is recorded in the *Wen-hsin tiao-lung* that "during the reign of Cheng-shih of the Wei, the trend was to explain *tao*, and poetry of this period contains elements of the cult of immortality."[49] Though tried by many poets before, *yu-hsien* poetry reached its peak only in Kuo P'u's hands. "His *yu-hsien* writings were heroic in expression, but departed from orthodoxy"; Chung Hung continued to comment that they were "poems about one's misfortunes, far from pursuing

[46] *Ibid.*, p. 128.
[47] *Ibid.*, p. 168.
[48] *Ibid.*, "Ch'üan Han shih," in *CHSCNS*, vol. 1, p. 56.
[49] Vincent Yu-chung Shih, *The Literary Mind*, p. 46.

immortality."[50] However, poems of one's heart in the name of *yu-hsien* are like those on historical events, as in the case of Tso Ssu. Such is also the case with Juan Chi's ambivalent tone in "Yung-huai shih" 詠懷詩 or "Poems Expressing My Feelings." There is a guarded indirectness in their work, and the open-hearted and straightforward qualities that marked Chien-an poetry were missing from their poems. Most *yu-hsien* writings were motivated by (1) depression at the inevitability of human mortality and (2) a desire to find consolation in a fantastic world where a man neither grew old nor passed away.

The *chao-yin* poets prided themselves on a sort of self-imposed exile of seclusion, while the *yu-hsien* writers regarded the world as a dunghill, people as vulgarians, and life as transitory. In short, the *yu-hsien* poets longed for a fairyland which was more remote and more detached than the mountains and forests of *chao-yin* poetry. Such poets sought to make the acquaintance of Taoist adepts and immortals, and wanted no contact with the "vulgar herd." Since *yu-hsien* writing was motivated by escapism, the fairyland envisaged in these flights of fancy was inevitably peaceful and pleasant, charming, and carefree. The poets would rather be absorbed in a fictitious world than bestow a look at the "dunghill." Thus *yu-hsien* poetry was still farther removed from society at large and became little more than a momentary antidote to a painful poison.

Hsüan-yen poetry was a natural consequence of *ch'ing-t'an* 清談 or "pure conversation" in the Wei-Chin period. As Liu Hsieh observed, "metaphysical discussion was emphasized during the early Chin and reached its height in the Eastern Chin. Such discussions left their influence upon the literary trends of the time."[51] "Pure conversation" and Taoist discourse were already popular in the period of Cheng-shih. But at that time full-length treatments of *tao* were made in prose instead of verse. Though some poems by Hsi K'ang, Juan Chi, and other Cheng-shih literati had an element of concern for *tao* in them, especially the fifth of a set of seven poems entitled "Songs of Ch'iu Hu" by Hsi K'ang[52] and the third

[50] Ku Chih, *Chung Chi-shih*, p. 20.

[51] Vincent Yu-chung Shih, *The Literary Mind*, p. 342.

[52] Ting Fu-pao, "Ch'üan San-Kuo shih," in *CHSCNS*, vol. 1, p. 204.

and fourth of the four poems entitled "In Reply to Hsi K'ang" by Hsi Hsi 嵇喜 (mid-third century),[53] *hsüan-yen* poetry reached its full form only during the time of the Eastern Chin. Taoism was intensively and extensively treated in the prose works of Ho Yen 何晏 (ca. 190–249),[54] Juan Chi,[55] and Hsi K'ang.[56]

About sixty years after Cheng-shih, expositions of Taoism entered the realm of poetry and became the main subject matter for most poets. Shen Yüeh in "On the Biography of Hsieh Ling-yün" of the *Sung shu* records: "Within the one hundred years from Chien-wu 建武 to I-hsi 義熙 (317–418), verses were rendered in a variety of subtle ways. Nevertheless, there were none who did not set forth Taoist philosophy. Vigorous expressions were out of the picture."[57] This passage and the one from the *Shih p'in* quoted in the very beginning of this essay can illustrate one another. Liu Hsieh also said:

> During the period of the Chiang-tso [317–420] literary writings were burdened with metaphysical discussions. Writers ridiculed the desire for worldly attainments and indulged in talks on complete spontaneity, or total obliviousness to mental machination and schemes. Although Yüan and Sun and those who followed them had each his own particular way of carving and coloring his literary patterns, still, with respect to intense rhetorical interest, none was in the same class [with those who wrote prior to the Chiang-tso period].[58]

A quotation from *Hsü Chin yang-ch'iu* 續晉陽秋 in a note on the literary chapter of *Shih-shuo hsin-yü* 世說新語 reads "Hsü Hsün

[53] *Ibid.*, Ch'üan Chin shih," in *CHSCNS*, vol. 1, p. 287.

[54] See "Wu-ming lun" 無名論 in Yen K'o-chün, *CSSCSLW*, vol. 3, *chüan* 39, pp. 10–11.

[55] See "T'ung I lun" 通易論, "T'ung Lao lun" 通老論, "Ta Chuang lun" 達莊論, and "Ta-jen hsien-sheng chuan" 大人先生傳, in *ibid.*, vol. 3, *chüan* 45, pp. 3–7, 7–8, 8–11 and *chüan* 46, pp. 5–11.

[56] See "Yang-sheng lun" 養生論 and "Nan Chang Liao-shu tzu-jan hao-hsüeh lun" 難張遼叔自然好學論 in *ibid.*, vol. 3, *chüan* 48, pp. 1–3 and *chüan* 50, pp. 6–7.

[57] Shen Yüeh, *Sung Shu*, *chüan* 67, p. 19a.

[58] Vincent Yu-chung Shih, *The Literary Mind*, p. 47.

and Sun Ch'o were the master poets of their time. From then on, all the literary men followed their style."[59]

The four references mentioned above give evidence that *hsüan-yen* poetry had been in vogue for nearly a century when it reached its height in the early Eastern Chin. Representative writers were Hsü Hsün 許詢 (fl. ca. 358), Sun Ch'o 孫綽 (314–371), and their followers. Unfortunately very few *hsüan-yen* pieces survive. With what little remains, it is hard to piece together the whole picture of *hsüan-yen* poetry; however, we can still infer some of its characteristics from a typical poem. Sun Ch'o's "A Piece in Reply to Hsü Hsün" 答許詢一首 was written in the four-character line.[60] Every ten lines make a stanza. There are nine stanzas, three hundred and sixty words altogether. This long poem is devoted entirely to a conceptual treatment of *tao*. It is representative among extant *hsüan-yen* poems in being part of a verse exchange written in four-character lines. There are some other poems by Sun Ch'o presented to, for instance, Wen Ch'iao 溫嶠 (288–329), Yü Ping 庾冰 (296–344), and Hsieh An 謝安 (320–385). We find also "pure conversation" in verse in the poems exchanged between Hsieh An and Wang Hu-chih 王胡之 (d. ca. 364); "by the end of Yung-chia," as it is told, "the style of Cheng-shih revived."[61] Both Shen Yüeh and Liu Hsieh referred to the kind of *hsüan-yen* poetry loaded with metaphysical terminology.

Since the aim of writing was now merely to comment on Taoism, profound and detailed analyses of *tao* in simple language were sufficient. *Hsüan-yen* poetry therefore neither expressed personal ambition and emotion, nor was it colored by imagination. Although they both picture an ideal world, *yu-hsien* poetry offers us flights of fancy and magnificent dwellings, while *hsüan-yen* poetry appears much less inviting in comparison. Chung Hung rightly commented that the *hsüan-yen* poetry was more philosophy than literature, and offered little for the reader to savour. Such dryness

[59] Yang Yung 楊勇, ed., *Shih-shuo hsin-yü chiao-chien* 世說新語校箋 (rpt. Taipei: Ming-lun ch'u-pan-she, n.d.), p. 205.

[60] Ting Fu-pao, "Ch'üan Chin shih" 全晉詩, in *CHSCNS*, vol. 1, p. 432.

[61] Fang Hsüan-ling 房玄齡, "Wei Chieh chuan" 衛玠傳 in *Chin shu* 晉書 (Shanghai: Chung-hua shu-chü, 1923), *chüan* 36, p. 4a.

is perhaps its weakest point. By the same token, *hsüan-yen* poetry fell out of favor after its one-hundred-year prime of life, and many a piece was hereafter unknown.

Between the Chien-an and the Eastern Chin *chao-yin*, *yu-hsien*, and *hsüan-yen* poetry each underwent a period of waxing and waning; each in its turn offered unique challenges to its practitioners. However, all three had roots in Taoism, and there is no clear-cut boundary among them. To put it simply, *chao-yin* poetry follows the Taoist interest in seclusion; *yu-hsien* poetry draws on the mysticism of the Taoist occult; while *hsüan-yen* poetry expounds the hidden meanings of *tao*. None of the three could be entirely distinct since each drew inspiration from the same source. However, the shift from a deep concern for society to seclusion and from outspokenness to metaphysical indulgence was common to all three, so the leading critics in subsequent ages, such as Chung Hung and Shen Yüeh, lamented over the ever-deepening languor that permeated the poetic scene of the Six Dynasties.

Commenting on the literary trends of the Six Dynasties, Liu Hsieh observed that: "At the beginning of the Sung some development in the literary trend was evident. Chuang and Lao had receded into the background and the theme of mountains and streams then began to flourish."[62] This judgment became normative and was often repeated by later scholars. A literary style does not appear out of nowhere, and every trend sooner or later reaches a period of decline. After a century of dominance, by the close of the Eastern Chin *hsüan-yen* poetry had lost its freshness. Its proclivity for flat abstraction had been moderated by the group of supremely sophisticated writers who assembled at the Orchid Pavilion 蘭亭. The verses included in the "Orchid Pavilion" collection follow much the same pattern: all begin with descriptions of the scene and end with the discursive Taoist *hsüan-yen* style. Although "by the end of Yung-chia the style of Cheng-shih revived," there is a sharp difference between a poetry of private joys of life indulged in by the sophisticated aristocrats of the Eastern Chin and one which was motivated by escapism and a deep fear, as was the case with the "Seven Worthies of the Bamboo Grove." To members of

[62] Vincent Yu-chung Shih, *The Literary Mind*, p. 48.

distinguished families such as the Wang and the Hsieh, as Tso Ssu says in the second of two poems entitled "Invitation to a Gentleman in Hiding":

No need for strings and pipes—	非必絲與竹
Mountains and streams turn elegant notes.[63]	山水有清音

They delighted in forgetting care and spent their lives in joy. So it was natural for them to combine delightful scenery with an approach to Taoism.

The *t'ien-yüan* poetry advanced by T'ao Ch'ien, who drew on nature for his simple and unadorned verses, emerged almost at the same time as the lushly ornamented *shan-shui* poetry by Hsieh Ling-yün. However, T'ao's style did not share the major trends of Six Dynasties poetry; it was thus placed merely in the second rank in the *Shih-p'in*, and was totally overlooked by Liu Hsieh. In contrast, the *shan-shui* poetry that flourished at the hands of Hsieh Lin-yün was given an important position by the critics of the Six Dynasties. After the Yung-chia era *shan-shui* poetry took the place of the previously dominant *hsüan-yen* poetry. *T'ien-yüan* poetry diverged from the major poetic trends in this period, and manifestations of its influence were not to be seen until the time of High T'ang poets like Wang Wei 王維 (701–761), Ch'u Kuang-hsi 儲光羲 (707–759?), and others.

The difference in thought and writing style between *shan-shui* poets and *t'ien-yüan* poets was manifest in certain traits distinctive of each mode of writing. But as different as they are, both *shan-shui* and *t'ien-yüan* poetry have a common concern for nature, and the scent of Taoism equally fills the atmosphere of both. Liu Hsieh's remark that "Chuang and Lao had receded into the background and the theme of mountains and streams then began to flourish"[64] does not actually indicate a dichotomy or a definite turning point between the periods. Taoist discourse did not die out in *shan-shui* poetry; it only receded to a secondary role within the larger concern of natural scenery. A similar phenomenon can be seen in the "Orchid Pavilion" verses discussed earlier. Though there is no

[63] Ting Fu-pao, "Ch'üan Chin shih," in *CHSCNS*, vol. 1, p. 386.

[64] Vincent Yu-chung Shih, *The Literary Mind.*

mention whatever of *t'ien-yüan* poetry in Liu Hsieh's book, T'ao's poetry still had an obvious feeling for *tao*. "Chuang and Lao" (i.e., Taoism) did not disappear; instead they became part of mountains, streams, and farms, as was noted by Tsung Ping 宗炳 (375–443): "Mountains and streams beautify *tao* with their outlook."[65] In this way Taoism found a more artistic mode of expression. In other words, the insipid *hsüan-yen* poetry, with polish and animation added to it, took on a new aspect in which literary values and philosophical depth were conjoined.

Although nature poetry was a breakthrough in the dullness of metaphysical discursiveness that lasted almost a century, and although it breathed fresh life into poetry, the Taoist inclination toward aloofness from the mundane world remained unchanged. T'ao Ch'ien sometimes cast a backward glance, and left a few poems reminiscing on the vigor of youth. Consider, for instance, the following verses "Unititled Poems" 雜詩 and "Imitations" 擬古, respectively:

I recall when I was in my prime 憶我少壯時
I could be happy without cause for joy. 無樂自欣豫
My ambition ranged beyond the seas; 猛志逸四海
On widespread wings I thought to soar afar.[66] 騫翮思遠翥

I was strong and bold when young, 少時壯且厲
With sword in hand I journeyed alone. 撫劍獨行遊
Will anyone say the road was short— 誰言行遊近
West from Chang-i to Yu-chou in the east?[67] 張掖至幽州

"In Praise of Ching K'o" 詠荊軻 also reveals his youthful passion and vitality.[68] As in all of T'ao's writings, the theme of preserving one's purity by voluntary seclusion is central. Consider, for example, the following couplets, drawn from "On Reading *The Seas and Mountains Classic*" 讀山海經 and "Returning to the Farm

[65] See "Hua shan-shui hsü" 畫山水序 in Yen K'o-chün, "Ch'üan Sung wen" 全宋文, in *CSSCSLW*, *chüan* 20, p. 8.

[66] James R. Hightower, *The Poetry of T'ao Ch'ien* (Oxford: Clarendon Press, 1970), p. 191.

[67] *Ibid.*, p. 182.

[68] *Ibid.*, pp. 224–225.

To Dwell" 歸園田居:

In this world all I want	在世無所須
Is wine, and length of years.[69]	唯酒與長年
Wet clothes are not cause for complaint	衣沾不足惜
If things will only go as hoped.[70]	但使願無違

In Hsieh's Ling-yün's poetry, the praise of nature is closely linked to an enlightenment regarding *tao*. He remarked in "In the Southern Fields I Plant a Garden, with Running Water and a Hedge Set There" 田南樹園激流植援:

Hermits and woodcutters both live in the mountains,	樵隱俱在山
Though naturally for very different reasons.[71]	繇來事不同

He prided himself on being a recluse, as he says in "What I Saw When I Had Crossed the Lake on My Way from Nan-shan to Pei-shan" 於南山往北山經湖中瞻眺:

I do not regret that I live far away from people.	不惜去人遠
I am only sorry I have no one as a companion.[72]	但恨莫與同

These poems all reveal a sense of narcissism, isolating the poet's persona from the common run of people, while he seeks the company of mountains and streams as a manifestation of grace and dignity. Majestic but unapproachable, his *shan-shui* writings inevitably separated themselves from society and people. Hsieh's successors followed his descriptive realism and tried their best to achieve freshness and symmetry, but unfortunately they were getting farther away from humanity as they drew nearer to scenery.

The *shan-shui* tradition was inherited by Hsieh Huei-lien 謝惠連 (397–433), Pao Chao 鮑照 (414–466), and Hsieh T'iao 謝朓 (464–499) successively in a period of about one century, during

[69] *Ibid.*, p. 236.

[70] *Ibid.*, p. 52.

[71] Huang Chieh, *Hsieh K'ang-lo shih-chu* 謝康樂詩注 (rpt. Taipei: I-wen yin-shu-kuan, 1967), *chüan* 3, p. 106.

[72] *Ibid.*, p. 130.

which there were three changes of dynasty. Though the times were out of joint, few poets were passionately concerned about national affairs, regardless of whether their writing was in the adorned or unadorned style. They assumed the role of distinterested hermit or of detached onlooker. The active participation and the enterprising spirit which marked the Chien-an era had now died away entirely.

The latter part of the Six Dynasties saw the high point of *yung-wu* and *kung-t'i* poetry. Scattered traces of these two modes were already discernible in the early Six Dynasties. In "On Reading the Poems by Hsieh Ling-yün" 讀謝靈運詩 Po Chü-i 白居易 (772–846) credited Hsieh Ling-yün's poetry with being:

Broad enough to cover heaven and sea, 大必籠天海
Fine as not to miss a blade of grass.[73] 細不遺草樹

So fine and delicate is Hsieh's pen that it takes care of even the tiniest trees and grass. Hsieh Ling-yün's poetry is characterized by a grand air in presenting the whole universe before one's eyes, but the subject matter of later *yung-wu* poetry is comparatively limited and simplified. The objects chosen as topics were often a part of the natural world or extracted from nature, yet they were given the most detailed illustration. Topics like "The Inner Garden of the North Residence" 北宅秘園, by Hsieh Chuang 謝莊 (421–466), "On Looking at a Lonely Stone" 望孤石, by Pao Chao, and "A Fragrant Tree" 芳樹, by Wang Jung 王融 (467–493)[74] are all concerned with garden scenery or a specific aspect of it. The following poems deal, on the other hand, with the scenes and atmosphere of a particular season: "On Watching the Moon" 望月, by Liu Hsiao-ch'o 劉孝綽 (481–539), "Ode on the Snow" 詠白雪, by Pao Chao, and "The Late Spring" 晚春, by Hsiao T'ung 蕭統 (501–531).[75] Still more pieces are on tiny indoor articles and decorations; to name but a few: "Mirror Stand" 鏡臺, by Hsieh

[73] Po Chü-i 白居易, *Po Hsiang-shan chi* 白香山集 (SPPY ed.), fourth series, vol. 1, *chüan* 7, p. 3a.

[74] Ting Fu-pao, "Ch'üan Sung shih" 全宋詩, in *CHSCNS*, vol. 2, pp. 623, 705, 780.

[75] Liu Hsiao-ch'o's poem can be found in *ibid.*, "Ch'üan Liang shih" 全梁詩, in *CHSCNS*, vol. 3, p. 1206; Pao Chao's in "Ch'üan Sung shih," vol 2, p. 703; and Hsiao T'ung's in "Ch'üan Liang shih," vol. 2, p. 877.

T'iao, "Ode on a Curtain" 詠簾, by Yü Yen 虞炎, and "Ode on a Candle" 詠蠟燭, by Wang Yün 王筠.[76]

The materials selected tended to be the petty and delicate articles which, to take a socially oriented view, might reflect the life of a luxurious nobility and their passion for architecture and gardening. However, in terms of the development of poetry, Hsieh Ling-yün's realism in description exerted a great influence on his followers, who followed contemporary fashion by imitating his mature style and, in doing so, produced many poems that describe objects in the minutest detail.

We have noted that *shan-shui* and *yung-wu* poetry differ both in the range of subject matter and point of view. There exists another distinction between the two modes: in Hsieh Ling-yün's poems we sense the surviving traces of Taoism, but these are totally lost in *yung-wu* poetry. Thus, Liu Hsieh's comments mentioned earlier should be qualified as follows: it was only in Ch'i-Liang times, when *yung-wu* and *kung-t'i* poetry rose to popularity, that Chuang and Lao fully receded. *Yung-wu* poetry differs from *kung-t'i* poetry in that the latter is thematically concerned with the gentle sex and love affairs, while the former is concerned with lifeless objects. Yet the two modes not only emerged at the same time; they also shared virtually the same style. When mature *kung-t'i* poetry was still taking shape, most *yung-wu* poets also practiced this mode. For instance, the same Pao Chao who wrote such verses as "Ode on the Swallow Couple" 詠雙燕 would address "The Charming One" 可愛.[77] T'ang Hui-hsiu 湯惠休 (fl. fifth century) left not only "The Autumn Wind" 秋風 but also "Song on Concubine Ming of the Ch'u" 楚明妃曲 (the above are Liu Sung poets);[78] Hsieh T'iao wrote both "Ode on the Rose" 詠薔薇 and "On Listening to a Songstress Sing at Night" 夜聽妓;[79] Ch'iu Chü-yüan 丘臣源 wrote "Ode on a Fan with Seven Decorations" 詠七寶扇 and "On Listening to a Neighboring Songstress" 聽鄰妓 (the above are Ch'i

[76] Hsieh T'iao's poem can be found in *ibid.*, "Ch'üan Ch'i shih" 全齊詩, in *CHSCNS*, vol. 2, p. 827; Yü Yen's on p. 843; and Wang Yün's in "Ch'üan Liang shih," vol. 3, p. 1189.

[77] *Ibid.*, vol. 2, p. 706.

[78] *Ibid.*, p. 725.

[79] *Ibid.*, p. 826.

poets).[80] The same is also true in the Liang dynasty, when members of the royal Hsiao family were the members of literary affairs. In Hsiao Kang's 蕭綱 (503–551) many *yung-wu* and *kung-t'i* poems, there is little real difference between the two categories except for the received distinction between human beings and objects.

There is a detachment in the versifying of *yung-wu* and *kung-t'i* poets; at times their work seems to serve no greater purpose than to add ornament to a social occasion. Playfulness can be seen in the titles of the poems by the Liang and their fellow courtier-poets: "Each Writes of the Same Musical Instrument" 同詠樂器, "Each Writes of One Object Seen by the Group" 同詠坐上所見一物, "A Playful Poem to a Beauty" 戲贈麗人, "A Playful Erotic Composition" 戲作艷詩, "Offhand Poems Done Together" 率爾同詠. To all appearances, poems were merely an amusement that had its place in a palace banquet after wine and dancing. Although such poetry lacks profound thought and compassion, it does excel in description. Feigned emotions occasioned verse that inevitably lacked vigor, and in which there was nothing more substantial than detailed descriptions of objects and subtle rhyme schemes. Like the case of *hsüan-yen* poetry, where philosophizing overshadowed the individuality of the poets, here an overemphasis on descriptive realism makes *yung-wu* poems appear uniform.

Yung-wu and *kung-t'i* poetry marked a thematic turn from Taoist themes to worldly affairs, yet its poetic range was narrowed down either to the triviality of *yung-wu* poetry or to the ornateness of *kung-t'i* poetry. From another perspective, impassioned verse became the impassive or playful observation of lifeless objects. The Hsiao family of the Six Dynasties occupied a position parallel to that of the Ts'aos of the Chien-an era: the political leaders were also distinguished poets. However, they sponsored a literary scene that was strikingly different from the Chien-an. Living in disjointed times, the Chien-an literati were inspired to passionate and heroic verse, while the emperors and courtiers of the Liang dynasty indulged in a brief peace, immobilized by sensual pleasures at the expense of the nation's fate. The Liang poets addressed the moon and the wind, wrote about beautiful women, and their own lan-

[80] *Ibid.*, p. 839.

guid melancholy. Gorgeous but superficial, their verse is merely a documentary record of the highest levels of society, its leisured literary class, which was unconcerned with the common people and the national interest.

The Six Dynasties, a period of over three hundred years, from the end of the Chien-an era to the close of the Ch'en dynasty (557–588), is distinguished by rich allusiveness and masterly versification: accomplishment on the artistic plane is tremendous. But the major trends, whichever poetic mode and subject matter it favored, were directed exclusively to the calm of sylvan escape or an indulgence in trivial objects at hand. If the grandeur of the Chien-an literati can be compared to the torrents of the Yangtze River running eastward to the sea, the literary scenes hereafter may be said to be little brooks which were ever dwindling until they finally dried up. Exceptions may be found in Juan Chi's poems on his feelings, Tso Ssu's verse on history, and even in Kuo P'u's *yu-hsien* poetry, but their style was independent of the vogue of the time. Because of the political dangers that attended direct expression of social criticism, their attitudes toward the age could be presented only indirectly. And such indirection was no match for the outspokenness of the Chien-an verse.

The only heir to the Chien-an *feng-ku* is perhaps Liu K'un 劉琨 (270–317), whose surviving poems number only three or so. His exchange of verse with Lu Ch'en 盧諶 and a poem titled "Fu-feng ko" 扶風歌 vigorously express his pain at the turmoil of the age and a profound melancholy that came from confronting a miserable end.[81] However, these scattered exceptions could not reverse the general trend.

IV. The Revival of *Feng-ku*

The periodization of literature does not always coincide with that of political history. The distinctive quality of Han literature, for example, did not fully appear until the period of Wu-ti 武帝 (140–87 B.C.). This means that, in spite of the change of dynasty,

[81] *Ibid.*, "Ch'üan Chin shih," vol. 1, pp. 415–417.

the literary trends of the Han dynasty in its first hundred years actually continued those of the Warring States Period 戰國 (403–221 B.C.). Following the decline of the Ch'en 陳 dynasty in A.D. 589 and the unification of China under Sui Wen-ti 隋文帝 (r. 589–604), the Six Dynasties period came to an end in terms of political history. But throughout the Sui period the literary scene was purely a continuation of the *kung-t'i* poetry of the Six Dynasties, such that one can hardly distinguish it from the literary trends of the Southern Dynasties. Emperor Yang-ti 煬帝 (r. 604–617) himself was a master of *kung-t'i* poetry. Delicate and soft in style, his poems do not show the poet's inner feeling but elaborate the superficial appearances of objects; hence they are no different from those by Liang Chien-wen-ti 梁簡文帝 (i.e., Hsiao Kang). Works by the courtiers of Emperor Yang-ti all exhibit a similar style.

If the last wave of *kung-t'i* poetry occurred in the Sui dynasty, we may well say that it still "haunted" the early T'ang poetic scene. Most of the early T'ang poets and literati were Sui dynasty courtiers. Therefore, although the T'ang empire had been established, it still inherited the literary trends of the Southern Dynasties. According to Liu Su's 劉肅 *Ta-T'ang hsin-yü* 大唐新語, Emperor T'ai-tsung 太宗 told his courtiers, "We enjoy writing *yen* 艷 poetry." Yü Shih-nan 虞世南 (558–638) criticized this: "Though your majesty is good at *yen* poetry, the format and style are not elegant. If the rulers are fond of this kind of poetry, the subjects will definitely follow. I am afraid this will corrupt our people, once this kind of poetry becomes popular."[82] Although Yü Shih-nan could make such a straightforward criticism of his emperor, his own poetic works are mostly in a frivolous court style. In fact, at the beginning of the T'ang dynasty, the restoration of peace after a long period of political turmoil and the court fashion for elaborate literature constituted favorable ground for the growth of *kung-t'i* poetry. Under such circumstances, elaborate, overly ornamented poetry could not be supplanted. Even Shen Ch'üan-ch'i 沈佺期 (ca. 656–714) and Sung Chih-wen 宋之問 (ca. 656–712), who are

[82] Liu Su 劉肅, *Ta-T'ang hsin-yü* 大唐新語 (rpt. Taipei: I-wen yin-shu kuan, 1971), *chüan* 3, p. 3a.

generally considered to be the inventors of the T'ang *lü-shih* 律詩, show a continuation of the court style in their works.

Even at the earliest stages of the popularity of the *kung-t'i* poetry, Hsiao Kang had sensed its defects. According to the *Ta-T'ang hsin-yü*, "when Liang Chien-wen-ti was a prince, he was so fond of writing *yen* poetry that the whole country tended to follow the fashion, which was eventually called 'court style.' In his later years, he changed his style, but still he was unable to reform the fashion. To enlarge the limits of *kung-t'i* poetry, he ordered Hsü Ling 徐陵 (507–583) to edit the *Yü-t'ai chi* 玉臺集."[83] But the publication of the *Yü-t'ai hsin-yung* 玉臺新詠 did not manage to change the literary fashion; instead, *yen* poetry prevailed all over China until the early T'ang dynasty—altogether more than one hundred years. This phenomenon, like *hsüan-yen* and *shan-shui*, proves that the occurrence of a literary fashion never takes place by accident, and it must run its full course. No one can arbitrarily suppress it. So Li E 李諤 proposed in vain to Sui Wen-ti to change the literary fashion by law, but the court style went on for many years.

If we examine this phenomenon from a different perspective, we will realize that every literary style has its inherent contour of rise and fall. In the words of Ku Yen-wu 顧炎武 (1613–1682): "It is natural that literary trends change from time to time. When one period of literary trends has reached its full term, there is no room for further improvement."[84] This principle is evident in the thematic changes of Six Dynasties poetry. However, the motivation and timing of such changes are due not only to the completion of a certain literary style but also to the assistance of perceptive and talented men. Hsieh Ling-yün played such a role in the end of the fashion for metaphysical (*hsüan-yen*) poetry and the appearance of *shan-shui* poetry. In spite of its popularity in the Six Dynasties, *kung-t'i* poetry came to seem wearily familiar by the time of the early T'ang dynasty. In literary evolution, *kung-t'i* poetry was bound to be displaced; the only factor missing was the right person to bring about the revolution.

[83] *Ibid.*

[84] Ku Yen-wu 顧炎武, *Yüan-ch'ao-pen jih-chih-lu* 原抄本日知錄 (rpt. Taipei: Ming-lun ch'u-pan-she, 1970), *chüan* 22, p. 606.

When the early T'ang historians compiled the official history of the Six Dynasties, they all attacked the decadence of *kung-t'i* poetry, considering it a principal cause of the downfall of the preceding dynasties. For example, Wei Cheng 魏徵, Yao Ssu-lien 姚思廉, and Li Pai-yüeh 李百藥 criticized Six Dynasties literature, but historians' comment on literature is inevitably limited by the didactic motives of Confucian values. It was talk without action: they could not change the literary mode.

Ch'en Tzu-ang and Li Po are the major inventors of the T'ang style. They were not only advocates of literary revolution but also talented poets. Theory and practice came together in their works. Where before there had been merely ineffectual criticism, literary style was now changed. It is especially noteworthy that Ch'en and Li both took Chien-an *feng-ku* as their literary standard. In Ch'en Tzu-ang's "Hsiu-chu p'ien-hsü" 修竹篇序, he points out two factors: "Classical literture has been declining for five hundred years. The *feng-ku* of the Han and Wei was lost in the Chin and Liu Sung dynasties."[85] "In the Ch'i and Liang dynasties, poems sought for artifice and decadence, and poems of metaphors and overtones faded away."[86] These two quotations resemble the views of the historians mentioned above, but the historians criticize literature from a political standpoint, while Ch'en is genuinely concerned with literature itself and is not making remarks on political grounds. Also, Ch'en Tzu-ang concretely observes that the defects of contemporary literature lie in "artifice and decadence," and that "poems of metaphors and topical reference faded away." Why had the literary mode degenerated while literary form flourished in excess? In his chapter on *feng-ku*, Liu Hsieh remarks that: "To be thin in ideas and fat in words, or confused and disorganized, without unity, are sure signs of lack of this kind of bone. And when ideas are incomplete and incomprehensive, lifeless and without vitality, it is an evidence of the absence of the wind."[87] In the chapter on *pi hsing* 比興 (metaphor and allegory), he thus observes:

> *Pi* involves reasoning by analogy, and *hsing* response to a

[85] See n. 3.

[86] *Ibid.*

[87] Vincent Yu-chung Shih, *The Literary Mind*, p. 227.

> stimulus. When we reason by analogy, we group things by comparing their general characteristics; and when we respond to stimuli, we formulate our ideas according to the subtle influences we receive. The *hsing* is the result of our responding to a stimulus, and the *pi* a consequence of reasoning by analogy. Formally, the *pi* is a linguistic expression charged with accumulated indignation, and the *hsing* is an admonition expressed through an array of parables.[88]

The two remarks made by Liu Hsieh help to explain Ch'en Tzu-ang's theory of *feng-ku* and *hsing-chi* 興寄, while at the same time serving as an overview of the period immediately after the Chien-an, which went from robust realism to metaphysical generalization and materialistic description of desire. Why does Ch'en Tzu-ang say that the poem by Tung-fang Ch'iu "may well make the Chien-an poets smile in approval"? Because Chien-an poems have compassion, a reflection of contemporary reality and powerful expression—which were gradually lost after the Han-Wei times.

With his intention to renovate T'ang literary modes in the manner of Han and Wei poetry, Ch'en Tzu-ang not only pointed out the trend of the preceding five hundred years, in which poets gradually abandoned reality, giving up the road to *feng-ku* and losing themselves in the blind alley of artifice and decadence. He also transformed the remaining Six Dynasties habit by his own creative practice. His "Thirty-eight Responses to Experience" 感遇詩三十八首 were by and large poems criticizing reality, reflecting the human condition, rich in thought and emotion, and robust and strong in tone. For example, in his popular poem "A Song on Climbing the Gate Tower at Yu-chou" 登幽州臺歌, he writes:

I fail to see the ancients before my time,	前不見古人
Or after me the generations to come.	後不見來者
Thinking of the eternity of Heaven and Earth,	念天地之悠悠
All alone, sadly I shed tears.[89]	獨愴然而涕下

[88] *Ibid.*, p. 276.

[89] Wu-chi Liu and Irving Y. C. Lo, eds., *Sunflower Splendor: Three Thousand Years of Chinese Poetry* (New York: Anchor Press, 1975), p. 88.

Yang Shen 楊愼 (1488–1559), a Ming scholar, in his *Sheng-an shih-hua* 升菴詩話, comments: "His expressions are straightforward, reflecting Han and Wei trends."[90] This best shows Ch'en Tzu-ang's effort to fulfill theory with practice. In terms of the development of T'ang poetry, Chen Tzu-ang's renovation was invaluable, but his promotion of Han and Wei *feng-ku* was most important for subsequent poets. Because he set up a paradigm that put an end to fruitless carping about court-style decadence, thus relieving later poetic generations of the need to search for a new, clear style, his contribution was active and constructive.

Following Ch'en Tzu-ang, Li Po, the genius of T'ang poetry, raised the banner of "P'eng-lai literature and Chien-an *ku*." Li Po describes his own view of poetry in the first of the "Fifty-nine Old-Style Poems" 古風五十九首; but in fact these poems indicate nothing but his self-conceit.[91] His comment on the declining trend of classic poetry was a repetition of what had been said before. As for his statement that the prevalence of an overly ornamented style of literature after the time of Chien-an is of little value—his opinions resemble Ch'en Tzu-ang's. So, given Ch'en Tzu-ang's priority, Li Po's judgment is no literary breakthrough. But one thing deserves our attention: after five hundred years of decline in classical literature, within a matter of a few decades both Li Po and Ch'en Tzu-ang advocated Chien-an style poetry as the creative model of T'ang poets. Their influence on contemporary and later literary development was extremely significant. Therefore Meng Ch'i 孟棨 makes the significant remark in *Pen-shih shih* 本事詩: "Li Po was a genius; he and Ch'en Tzu-ang enjoyed the same kind of popularity. Their judgments matched."[92]

Li Po and Ch'en Tzu-ang are not always alike. In terms of content and style, Li Po is recognized as an incredible genius and incomparable artist; his subjects range from heaven to earth, his emotions run the full gamut, he has universal tastes, not limited to certain styles and schools. His literary renovations are best shown in

[90] Yang Shen 楊愼, *Sheng-an shih-hua* 升菴詩話 in *Hsü li-tai shih-hua* 續歷代詩話, ed. Ting Fu-pao (rpt. Taipei: I-wen yin-shu kuan, n.d.), *chüan* 6, p. 13a.

[91] Li Po, "Ku-feng wu-shih-chiu shou."

[92] Meng Ch'i 孟棨, *Pen-shih shih* 本事詩, in *T'ang-tai ts'ung-shu* 唐代叢書, ed. Ch'en Shih-hsi 陳世熙 (rpt. Taipei: Hsin-hsing shu-chü, 1968), p. 373.

his dedication to revival of the old forms. He gave up the bad habits of court-style poetry in admiration for natural and robust language. So Fan Wen 范溫 praised him, saying: "Tu Fu (712–770), Li Po, Han Yü (768–824)—all started as disciples of the Chien-an style and eventually became masters of their own styles."[93] Although both Ch'en Tzu-ang and Li Po admired the Chien-an style, their efforts at renovation did not mean a retreat to an old position. Rather, they took from the spirit of *feng-ku* a new paradigm and foundation of the T'ang literary scene, replacing the bad habits of *kung-t'i* poetry. Therefore, the Ch'ing scholar Yeh Hsieh 葉燮 (1627–1703) noted, in the *Yüan Shih* 原詩, that the decadent style did not change until a breakthrough was made by the K'ai-yüan 開元 (713–741) and T'ien-pao 天寶 (742–755) poets. According to Yeh Hsieh, every literary trend undergoes its cyclic rise and fall. The fact that the High T'ang poets chose not to rigidly imitate Chien-an poems contributes to their achieving a Han-Wei spirit in their "old-style" poems 古詩.[94] In his preface to the *Ts'en Chia-chou chi* 岑嘉州集, Tu Ch'üeh 杜確 says, "when things reach an extreme, they are bound to change.... All great poets from the K'ai-yüan to T'ien-pao periods write in a style similar to Chien-an."[95] In terms of the social and political background, after one hundred years of peace and prosperity, all cultural, official, political, and diplomatic systems reached their peak in the K'ai-yüan and T'ien-pao periods, and T'ang relations with foreign countries had become more and more complicated. Such an environment provided poets with sources of inspiration, provided scholars with competition and mutual reinforcement, and led to the greatest moment of Chinese poetry. Hence the achievements of T'ang poetry far surpassed those of the Chien-an period.

From what we have just discussed, we have seen how, in the five hundred years from Chien-an to T'ang, Chinese poetry changed from vigorous *feng-ku* style through decadence and depravity to

[93] Fan Wen 范溫, *Ch'ien-hsi shih-yen* 潛溪詩眼 in *Sung shih-hua chi-i* 宋詩話輯佚, ed. Kuo Shao-yü 郭紹虞 (Peking: Harvard-Yenching Institute, 1937), p. 390.

[94] Yeh Hsieh 葉燮, *Yüan shih* 原詩 in *Ch'ing shih-hua* 清詩話, ed. Ting Fu-pao (rpt. Taipei: Ming-lun ch'u-pan-she, n.d.), p. 569.

[95] Tu Ch'üeh 杜確, "Preface" to *Ts'en Chia-chou chi* 岑嘉州集 (SPTK ed.), fourth series, p. 1.

rebirth and rejuvenation. Ssu-ma Ch'ien 司馬遷 (145–90 B.C.) says, "It took five hundred years to have a Confucius after Chou Kung's 周公 (the Duke of Chou) death; it is now another five hundred years after Confucius' death."[96] Five hundred years is a long span of time in the history of human civilization; five hundred years constitute a great cycle of rise and fall. However, the end of such a cycle does not mean a return to its beginning. At least, to judge by the great cycle of poetic history mentioned above, High T'ang poetry, in its vigor, does not mean a retreat to the Chien-an style, but a new mode. Literature always develops along a crooked path, but its ultimate direction is always forward.

[96] Ssu-ma Ch'ien 司馬遷, "T'ai-shih-kung tzu-hsü" 太史公自序, *Shih-chi* 史記, 10 vols. (Peking: Chung-hua shu-chü, 1972), vol. 10, p. 3296.

Paul W. Kroll

Verses from on High: The Ascent of T'ai Shan

"Les montagnes sont, en Chine, des divinités." Thus Edouard Chavannes (1865–1918) began his magnificent monograph on T'ai Shan 泰山, reminding us that the most prominent features of the Chinese landscape are not merely natural, but numinous, objects.[1] One of the great virtues of Chavannes' classic study—and one apparent also in the more recent monographs on the important peaks Lo-fou Shan 羅浮山 and Mao Shan 茅山, by Michel Soymié and Edward H. Schafer, respectively[2]—is the detailed documentation and evocation of the manifestly sacred climate that traditionally invested China's "notable mountains" (*ming shan* 名山). Indeed it was not only the most eminent alps but lesser mounts as well that commonly called forth, in the men of ancient and medieval times, varying kinds and degrees of religious feeling. It is no accident, for instance, that virtually all of Meng Hao-jan's 孟浩然 (689–740)

[1] Edouard Chavannes, *Le T'ai chan; essai de monographie d'un culte chinois* (Paris: E. Leroux, 1910), p. 3. Chavannes' treatise remains one of the true monuments of Western sinology, standing at the head of a schólarly tradition—more influential in Europe than in America—that has sought to accord religion its due importance in studies of ancient and medieval China. Since, however, Chavannes neglected to discuss the *shih* poems of medieval writers (or those of any other age) written about Mount T'ai, a significant gap remains in his great work. It is hoped that the present essay may supply this deficiency in a manner not out of keeping with the spirit of Chavannes' study.

[2] Michel Soymié, "Le Lo-feou shan; étude de géographie religieuse," *Bulletin de l'École Française d'Extrême-Orient* 54 (1956), 1–132; Edward H. Schafer, *Mao Shan in T'ang Times* (Society for the Study of Chinese Religions, Monograph No. 1, 1980). These two informative and fascinating studies can hardly be neglected by any serious student of medieval culture.

poems set in alpine environs (excepting only those works celebrating the familiar hills of Hsiang-yang, his native place) are imbued with explicit Buddhist or Taoist imagery.[3] Likewise, the mountain verses of most medieval writers are rarely the simple portrayals of landscape—mere "nature poems" (to use a critically useless term)—that many scholars would have us believe.

In an article published in 1965, the late Paul Demiéville briefly surveyed the historical evolution of the treatment of mountains in Chinese literature.[4] Interested readers are encouraged to review his findings for themselves. In the context of the present study, however, it is worthwhile to recall that as late as the first quarter of the fourth century A.D., Ko Hung 葛洪 (283–344),[5] that industrious collector of the occult traditions of southern *fang-shih* 方士, did not see mountains as picturesque regions conducive to carefree excursions but as a "zone of sacred horror."[6] Witness the following:

> Of all those who compound drugs for the sake of [pursuing] the Way, as well as those who dwell in hiding to escape from disturbance, there are none who do not enter the mountains. Yet, those who are not aware of the procedures (法) for entering the mountains many times come to hazard and harm. Hence there is the proverb: "At the foot of Grand Flower (太華[山]), / Bones of white are strewn in a clutter." ... Mountains, whether large or small, are in all cases possessed of divine numina. If the mountain be large, then the divinity is a greater one; if the mountain be small, then the divinity is a lesser one. Entering a mountain without being in possession of the [proper] technique (術), one is certain to find calamity and harm.[7]

[3] Paul W. Kroll, *Meng Hao-jan* (Boston: Twayne, 1981), p. 95.

[4] Paul Demiéville, "La Montagne dans l'art littéraire chinois," *France-Asie* 183 (1965), 7–32; reprinted in Paul Demiéville, *Choix d'études sinologiques (1921–1970)* (Leiden: E. J. Brill, 1973), pp. 364–389.

[5] On Ko Hung's 葛洪 dates, which are disputed, I follow Ch'en Kuo-fu 陳國符, *Tao-tsang yüan-liu k'ao* 道藏源流考 (rev. ed. Taipei: Ku-t'ing shu-wu, 1975), p. 97, whose argument I find convincing.

[6] The phrase is Demiéville's, *op. cit.*, p. 15 (372).

[7] *Pao-p'u tzu nei-p'ien* 抱朴子內篇, 17.1a (SPPY ed.).

This passage begins Ko Hung's chapter, in the *Pao-p'u tzu*, on "Ascending [Mountains] and Wading Through [Streams]" (登涉), which includes descriptions of various spirits and dangers one may encounter in the hills and provides explanations of numerous effective methods—along with illustrations of several potent talismans—which may avail to preserve one's person unharmed while sojourning there. We shall have occasion later on to examine more closely this individualistically oriented strain of sierran awe and mystery and some of the poems in which it appears. For the moment, however, let us concentrate instead on the state-oriented aspect of the great mountains—particularly Mount T'ai.

In recognizing the "divine numina" of greater or lesser power that inhabited and energized the mountains, Ko Hung was only adhering to accepted tradition. The ethereal essences of the peaks—particularly those of the four (later, five) "marchmounts" (*yüeh* 嶽),[8] at the cardinal points of the classical Chinese ecumene—had been propitiated and sacrificed to since Chou times. In fact, according to the *Canon of Documents* (*Shu ching* 書經), these primary mountains had first been ritually visited in the dawn of history by the great Shun 舜, who worshipped on each of them in turn, while making a formal progress and tour of inspection through his domains.[9] As is well known, later sovereigns at times contemplated the revival of Shun's legendary circuit of alpine landmarks. Only Ch'in Shih Huang 秦始皇 and Han Wu Ti 漢武帝 seem to have seriously attempted the feat and, of course, neither of them completed the full itinerary.

The Marchmounts, among the most powerful of the deified natural forces of ancient China, had been regarded as important

[8] On "marchmount" as an English equivalent for *yüeh*, see E. H. Schafer, *Pacing the Void: T'ang Approaches to the Stars* (Berkeley: University of California Press, 1977), p. 6.

[9] See *Shu ching* 書經, "Shun tien" 舜典. It is significant that the first office and title mentioned in the *Shu* is that of the *szu-yüeh* 四嶽, denoting one of the highest—if not the highest—ministers of the sage-king Yao; it was to the anonymous incumbent of this position that Yao went for advice on whom to employ to tame the great flood, as it was to him that Yao first offered to resign the throne (before abdicating eventually in Shun's favor). See "Yao tien" 堯典 in the *Shu ching*.

protectors of the state. By medieval times, only T'ai Shan—which had from early on been recognized as *primus mons inter pares*—still retained this attribute in observable fashion, for it was on its summit and at its foot alone that the grand *feng* 封 and *shan* 禪 sacrifices were performed. Strictly speaking, these sacred rites were properly to be performed only by monarchs whose exceptional virtue had been validated by unequivocal signs from above and whose rule had resulted in the unquestionable attainment of an era of supreme concord and prosperity; the *feng* and *shan* were announcements to Heaven and Earth, respectively, that the sovereign had successfully fulfilled his regnal charge.[10] Although tradition had it that seventy-two rulers of ancient days had carried out the sacrifices,[11] in the eleven centuries from Han through T'ang only four emperors had the requisite confidence in their own merit to perform the rites. These were Han Wu Ti (in the years 110, 106, 102, 98, and 93 B.C.), Kuang Wu Ti 光武帝 of the Later Han (in A.D. 56), Kao Tsung 高宗 of T'ang (in 666), and Hsüan Tsung 玄宗 of T'ang (in 725).[12] T'ai Shan was, thus, closely tied to the state cult itself. This is a fact clearly manifest in most of the medieval poems written about the peak.

Let us look first at a poem composed in honor of the mountain by Lu Chi 陸機 (261–303):

A Chant of Mount T'ai	太山吟
Mount T'ai—how very tall!	太山一何高
Farther and farther, attaining Heaven's Court!	迢迢造天庭
Its pinnacled apogee wholly distant now,	峻極周已遠
With tiered clouds clustered gloom upon gloom.	曾雲鬱冥冥

[10] The classic introduction to the history of these rites is, of course, the twenty-eighth chapter of the *Shih chi* 史記.

[11] Ssu-ma Ch'ien 司馬遷, *Shih chi* (Peking: Chung-hua shu-chü, 1972), 28.1361. According to a separate tradition, it was only the Yellow Thearch (Huang Ti 黃帝), among the seventy-two ancient kings who performed the *feng-shan*, who actually carried out the *feng* atop Mount T'ai (*Shih chi*, 28.1393).

[12] During this millennium, other emperors, such as T'ai Tsung 太宗 of T'ang, seriously considered observing the *feng* and *shan* but realized—sometimes under duress—their unworthiness or, at least, the inadvisability of the action.

On Liang-fu, for its part, there is a hospice;
On Hao-li, for its part, there is a pavilion.
The shrouded route detains a myriad
revenants,
And the haunt of spirits collects a hundred
numina.
—But I prolong my chant by the side of
Mount T'ai,
With brave forbearance, projecting the
sounds of Ch'u.[13]

梁甫亦有館
蒿里亦有亭
幽塗延萬鬼
神房集百靈
長吟太山側
慷慨激楚聲

In emphasizing T'ai Shan's height in the first four lines of his poem, Lu Chi is not only describing the mountain's physical altitude; he is also presenting the peak in its spiritual aspect—as intermediary between the mundane beings of this earthly realm and the more rarefied and mysterious powers housed in the heavens. This is pointed up by his careful use in line two of the phrase "Heaven's Court" 天庭, which is a traditional, alternative designation of the important constellation known as "Grand Tenuity" 太微, representing the palace of Heaven's lord, with which Mount T'ai communicates.[14] It is also well to remember here that, during the *feng* sacrifice, the spirit of T'ai Shan in fact played the role of intermediary between the emperor and Heaven.[15] Indeed, Chang Hua 張華 (232–300), a writer contemporaneous with Lu Chi, identifies T'ai Shan as "the grandson of Heaven's Thearch" (天帝孫).[16] We

[13] "T'ai Shan yin;" see Ting Fu-pao 丁福保, *Ch'üan Chin shih* 全晉詩 (in *Ch'üan Han San-kuo Chin Nan-pei-ch'ao shih* 全漢三國晉南北朝詩 [Taipei: I-wen yin-shu-kuan, 1968]; all references to the "complete poems" of pre-T'ang dynasties will be to this collection), 3.4b, p. 436; also Kuo Mao-ch'ien 郭茂倩, *Sung-pen yüeh-fu shih chi* 宋本樂府詩集 (Taipei: Shih-chieh shu-chü, 1961); hereafter *YFSC*, 41.5a.

[14] See *Li chi* 禮記, "Yüeh ling" 月令; Fan Yeh 范曄, *Hou Han shu* 後漢書 (Peking: Chung-hua shu-chü, 1974), "chih," 10.3219; and especially Fang Hsüan-ling 房玄齡 et al., *Chin shu* 晉書 (Peking: Chung-hua shu-chü, 1974), 11.291–92. The latter reference describes in detail the astral arrangement of the constellation.

[15] Chavannes, *Le T'ai chan*, p. 435. A later development of this role takes place after about the eleventh century, when the spirit-lord of Mount T'ai comes to be regarded as the earthly regent of the Jade Resplendent One (Yü huang 玉皇). See Henri Maspero, "Mythologie de la Chine moderne," in Maspero, *Le Taoisme et les religions chinoises* (Paris: Gallimard, 1971), pp. 117–118.

[16] *Po-wu chih* 博物志, 1.3b (SPPY ed.).

see that there is more to Lu Chi's diction in this line than a polite variation on the cliché "the mountain reaches to the sky." Or to put it another, and perhaps more accurate, way, there is more to that cliché itself, when set in its proper cultural and religious context, than we may be accustomed to realize: the sacred mountain, rising from the ground into the sky, is, quite literally, a locus of contact between the powers of Heaven and those of Earth. Nuances such as this, which would have been alive and, I imagine, readily responded to by contemporary readers, are crucial to the full understanding of medieval poetry. Much of this essay will be devoted to the attempt to recapture some of these faded—or unperceived—tints of meaning in poems on T'ai Shan. In line three, "pinnacled apogee" (*chün chi* 峻極) is a direct verbal borrowing from *Shih* 259, whose opening couplet reads: "Exalted and tall is the Marchmount, / Its pinnacled apogee reaching to heaven." We shall see variations of these classic verses employed by other medieval poets writing about T'ai Shan.

The poem's second quatrain descends from the heights, to focus on two foothills of Mount T'ai—viz., Liang-fu 梁甫 and Hao-li 蒿里. The former had been the site of an imperial sacrifice to the Presider of Earth (*ti chu* 地主) by Han Wu Ti just prior to that monarch's first observance of the *feng* in 110 B.C.;[17] the latter was the site of a *shan* sacrifice by the same ruler six years later.[18] The "hospice" and "pavilion" of lines five and six are remnants of the martial emperor's temporary habitation at these knolls. But they are also, within the setting of the poem, suggestive of the dark gathering-place of the "revenants" (*kuei* 鬼) and "numina" (*ling* 靈) of the next two lines. For it was a popular belief, since at least Late Han times, that upon death one's soul returned to Hao-li ("Wormwood Village")[19] or to the other low hills near T'ai Shan's

[17] *Shih chi*, 28.1398.

[18] *Ibid.*, 28.1402. In this year, only the *shan* sacrifice was carried out, unaccompanied by the *feng*.

[19] There remains an old song from Han times, called "Hao-li," whose four lines (in 5-7-7-7 syllabic count) read roughly as follows:

Wormwood Village is the land of everyone's home,
Which brings together all souls, whether they be wise or stupid.
Ghostly sires—oh how they are hurried on and hastened!

base. The poem is therefore divided equally, giving us a dual view of Mount T'ai: the first quatrain shows the celestial connection of the towering mountain; the second quatrain exhibits its earthly and nether affiliations. The concluding couplet of the piece portrays the poet himself, undaunted by the awful spectacle of T'ai Shan, giving voice to his defiant song.[20]

Somewhat over a century after Lu Chi's death, Hsieh Ling-yün 謝靈運 (385–433) also wrote a "Chant of Mount T'ai." His version goes as follows:

Tai the Revered—flourishing is the Marchmount;
Sublimely spiring, to pierce the cloudy heavens.
Precipitous and acclivitous, both hazardous and high;
Its jostled rocks, in every case luxuriant and lush.

岱宗秀維岳
崔崒刺雲天
岝崿既嶮巇
觸石輒芊綿

Ascending for the *feng*—interment at the exalted altar;
Descending for the *shan*—a cache at Solemn State.
Stone Wicket is very obscure and hazy;
And in the Hall of Light a numinous tract is secreted.[21]

登封瘞崇壇
降禪藏肅然
石閭何晻藹
明堂祕靈篇

This poem, too, begins with an emphasis on T'ai Shan's great

The fates of men cannot for a moment hesitate or halt.

YFSC, 27.5b. "Hao-li" is the traditional companion piece of the song "Hsieh lu" (薤露, "Shallot Dew"). Both were mourners' songs.

[20] "Defiant" because "prolonged," just as the poet's very vitality is itself a defiance in this place ("by the side of Mount T'ai," i.e., at its foot) of expired lives. The "sounds of Ch'u" (楚聲) were traditionally distinguished by their resolute and zealous tones. Note that Lu Chi's own background (he hailed from the south) was such as to enable him to consider himself poetically, with a little stretching of geographical fact, a native of Ch'u. But perhaps there is also in this poem a political and topical undercurrent that escapes us today.

[21] *Ch'üan Sung shih* 全宋詩, 3.2b, p. 800; *YFSC*, 41.5a/b.

height.[22] And, again as in Lu Chi's poem, we hear an echo of *Shih* 259—in the consciously archaic diction that ends the opening verse ("flourishing is the Marchmount" 秀維嶽; cf. "Eminent and tall is the Marchmount" 崧高維嶽).[23] We are not surprised either to come upon references, in lines five and six, to the *feng* and *shan* sacrifices. In the second half of the poem, however, Hsieh Ling-yün's strict adherence to syntactic parallelism as a principle for organizing the couplets of the work seems to lead him into a static and rather unsatisfying closure. Yet, these last lines are productive of two ingenious onomastical juxtapositions that display the poet's knowledge of "official" T'ai Shan lore. First, we have the clever matching of "exalted altar" (*ch'ung t'an* 崇壇), where the emperor's report to Heaven would be buried, with "Solemn State" (Su-jan 肅然), the proper name—here semantically revivified—of the hill at the northeast foot of Mount T'ai, where Han Wu Ti delivered his report to Earth during his first performance of the *shan* rite in 110 B.C.[24] Next, we have the matching, in the final couplet, of "Stone Wicket" (Shih-lü 石閭) and the "Hall of Light" (Ming-t'ang 明堂). Stone Wicket, at the southern foot of T'ai Shan, was where the *shan* sacrifice of 102 B.C. was carried out.[25] The Hall of Light referred to here is the structure erected at the northeast base of the mountain in 107 B.C., at Han Wu Ti's behest. He had been convinced that, in having this symbolic edifice (the prototype of which, according to devoted *Ju*-ist scholars, had first been raised by the legendary culture-hero Shen Nung 神農) built on this spot, he was siting his Ming-t'ang precisely where that of the Yellow Thearch (Huang Ti 黃帝) had been many, many centuries ago.[26]

The name by which T'ai Shan is called in the opening words of Hsieh's poem—Tai Tsung 岱宗—deserves some attention also.

[22] In fact, it is not a particularly lofty mountain, measuring only 1,524 meters (about 5,000 feet) above sea-level.

[23] This use of 維 as a copula is a feature of archaic texts, used in medieval times only for antique effect.

[24] *Shih chi*, 28.1398.

[25] *Ibid.*, 28.1403.

[26] Henri Maspero, "Le Ming-t'ang et la crise religieuse chinoise avant les Han," *Mélanges chinois et bouddhiques* 9 (1951), 4–5. The building is described in *Shih chi*, 28.1401; this description is repeated verbatim in the sixth-century *Shui ching chu* 水經注 (Taipei: Shih-chieh shu-chü, 1962), 24.314.

The second element in the name poses no problems: it means "revered ancestor" and indicates T'ai Shan's senior position among all the mountains of China. The key term is the first element of the phrase, *tai*, which may stand alone in reference to the sacred mountain. I have left it untranslated in my rendering of the poem. But the significance of this name was commented on by various scholars during the first centuries of our era. Hsü Shen 許慎 (fl. 100) takes what seems to be the simplest view: *tai* 岱 merely means "the Greatest Mountain" (*t'ai shan* 太山).[27] If we follow Hsü's somewhat tautological definition, we might wish to English the word as "Paramount." Other writers, however, had different, more suggestive explanations of the name. Ying Shao 應劭 (fl. 178), for instance, glosses *tai* 岱 (archaic **d'âi*) as *t'ai* 胎 (**t'âi*), "womb" or "gestator."[28] This definition is not as odd or fanciful as it may at first glance appear: lexicographical tradition, at least, verified the idea that mountains were conspicuous loci of nascent life. Thus, Hsü Shen defines the general term *shan* (**săn*) 山, "mountain," as *hsüan* (**siwän*) 宣, "diffuser," explaining that it "diffuses vital breath, dispersing and engendering the myriad beings" (宣气, 散生萬物).[29] And Liu Hsi 劉熙 (late second/early third century) in his *Shih ming* 釋名 glosses **săn*, "mountain," paronomastically as **săn* 產, "generant."[30] Mount T'ai was naturally assumed to possess this life-giving quality in greater abundance than other heights, since it was the Marchmount of the East, the east being regarded as the cardinal direction of incience for all creatures. One therefore sees why the souls of the newly dead were believed to make their way to T'ai Shan: they are returning back to their original place of animation. Closely related to these ideas is the definition given the character *tai* 岱 by Ts'ui Ling-en 崔靈恩 (fl. 520), one of the greatest classical scholars and teachers of the first half of the sixth century. He derives the word from the phrase *tai-hsieh* 代謝 "to supersede successively," and explains that, since

[27] Ting Fu-pao, *Shuo-wen chieh-tzu ku-lin* 說文解字詁林 (Taipei: Shang-wu yin-shu-kuan, 1976), 9B.5819a.

[28] *Feng-su t'ung-i* 風俗通義, 10.1b, in Ch'eng Jung 程榮, *Han Wei ts'ung-shu* 漢魏叢書 (Kyoto: Chūbun shuppansha, 1971).

[29] *Shuo-wen chieh-tzu ku-lin*, 9B.5817a.

[30] *Shih ming* 釋名, 1.5b (SPTK ed.).

spring is the time when new life replaces old, T'ai Shan—as the eastern sacred peak (in the traditional system of *wu-hsing* correspondences, the east correlates symbolically with springtime)—is called Tai 岱 because it is where "the myriad beings, born in turn, supplant each other" (萬物更生相代).[31] But it is easy to see that Ts'ui's definition is little more than an elaboration of the basic theme established by earlier scholars.[32] Deriving *tai* 岱 from the sense of *tai* 代, then, we have a name for Mount T'ai which seems to mean something like "Mountain of [Animate] Interchange" or "Alp of Transition"—T'ai Shan as presider over the transmutations of life and death.

Mount T'ai's role as arbiter of fate may be noted, after the obligatory opening lines on its sky-grazing stature, in the following work by the late fourth-century poet Hsieh Tao-yün 謝道韞,[33] entitled "Ascending the Mountain:"

Upborne aloft, the Marchmount of the East is high!	峨峨東嶽高

[31] *San-li i-tsung* 三禮義宗, quoted in Chang Ying 張英 et al., *Yüan-chien lei-han* 淵鑑類函 (Taipei: Shih-chieh shu-chü, 1978), 27.20b. This work was preserved through T'ang times, as verified by notices of it in the bibliographic monographs of the *Sui shu* 隋書, ed. Wei Cheng 魏徵 et al. (Peking: Chung-hua shu-chü, 1973), 32.924; Liu Hsü 劉昫 et al., *Chiu T'ang shu* 舊唐書 (Peking: Chung-hua shu-chü, 1975), 46.1975; and Ou-yang Hsiu 歐陽修 et al., *Hsin T'ang shu* 新唐書 (Peking: Chung-hua shu-chü, 1975), 57.1433. These notices uniformly refer to a thirty-*chüan* edition, although in Ts'ui's official biography (*Liang shu* 梁書, ed. Yao Ssu-lien 姚思廉 [Peking: Chung-hua shu-chü, 1973], 48.677) the original text is stated to have been in forty-seven *chüan*.

[32] In particular, the words of Pan Ku 班固 (32–92) in the *Po-hu t'ung* 白虎通: "Whereby is it that [the king] is obliged to [perform the *feng-shan*] at T'ai Shan? [Because] it is the inceptor of the myriad beings, the place of successive interchange" (所以必於泰山何. 萬物之始, 交代之處也). *Po-hu t'ung-i* 白虎通義, 6.228 (*Kuo-hsüeh chi-pen ts'ung-shu*).

[33] This lady, from the illustrious and influential Hsieh clan, was perhaps the best educated and most literarily adept woman of her day. For her biography, see *Chin shu*, 96.2516–17. Her father was Hsieh I 謝奕 (d. 358), close companion of the dictator Huan Wen 桓溫; her brother was the famous general Hsieh Hsüan 謝玄, and her paternal uncle the great statesman Hsieh An 謝安. She was married to Wang Ning-chih 王凝之, son of the renowned calligrapher Wang Hsi-chih 王羲之. The poem quoted here is one of only three by her that remain to us. An "appraisal" (*tsan* 讚) by her of the *Lun-yü* may be found in Ou-yang Hsün 歐陽詢 et al., *I-wen lei-chü* 藝文類聚 (Peking: Chung-hua shu-chü, 1974), 55.985.

Its flourishing apogee surges up to azure heaven.	秀極冲青天
Among its cliffs are spaced the eaves of the void;	巖中間虛宇
Still and null—both shrouded and mysterious.	寂寞幽以玄
Not the work of artisan, nor again that of builder,	非工復非匠
Its cloudy beams have been thrown up spontaneously!	雲構發自然
An image made from vital pneuma—what being art thou,	氣象爾何物
That duly causes myself to be many times transported?	遂令我屢遷
—I swear I shall take up abode under these eaves,	逝將宅斯宇
Allowing me to finish fully my heaven-ordained years.[34]	可以盡天年

We may recognize by now certain key words that regularly punctuate the introductory verses of T'ai Shan poems—"high" (*kao* 高), "apogee" (*chi* 極), and "heaven" (*t'ien* 天), all three finding their origin in *Shih* 259. Hsieh Tao-yün accepts this convention in the first couplet of her poem, while fashioning her own variation.[35] In the lines that follow, the poet contrives a poem that—in my view—is more successful and tightly knit than either Lu Chi's or Hsieh Ling-yün's effort. Especially interesting in the present context is the descriptive epithet addressed to the mountain itself in line seven—"An image made from vital pneuma." The two-word Chinese phrase that this rendering attempts to capture is *ch'i hsiang* 氣象. It is of course quite possible to read the phrase simply as "a vaporous shape" or "a vaporous simulacrum"—portraying the

[34] "Teng shan" 登山, in *Ch'üan Chin shih*, 7.15b, p. 670.

[35] It may be that Hsieh Ling-yün's choice of the word "flourishing" (*hsiu* 秀) in the opening line of his poem quoted earlier was inspired by Hsieh Tao-yün's "flourishing apogee" (*hsiu chi* 秀極), a variation of course on the classical "pinnacled apogee" (*chün chi* 峻極) from *Shih* 259.

contours of the mountain wrapped in mist.[36] But I believe there is more involved here: the image behind the poet's diction in this case is surely Hsü Shen's familiar (to a medieval writer) definition of mountains as "diffusers of vital breath" (*hsüan ch'i* 宣气) which give life to all creatures. To Hsieh Tao-yün, T'ai Shan is a symbolic figure that has been formed "spontaneously"—"Not the work of artisan, nor again that of builder"—from life-giving pneuma. Nicely done also in this piece is the careful patterning of the architectural imagery ("eaves," "artisan," "builder," "beams," and "eaves" again) that finally leads to the poet's vow to make the mountain her "abode."[37]

Our sampling of pre-T'ang verses on Mount T'ai, and some of the cultural, religious, and lexical background to them, has perhaps given us now an adequate perspective from which to view the handling of the same topic by Tu Fu 杜甫 (712–770), one of the greatest of T'ang wordsmiths. The poem in question, which is one of the earliest extant examples of Tu Fu's work (most commentators date its composition to the year 736, when the poet was twenty-four), is called "Gazing Afar at the Marchmount:"

Tai the Revered—now, what to compare it with?	岱宗夫如何
Over Ch'i and Lu, its azure never ending.	齊魯青未了
In it the Shaping Mutator concentrated the flourishing of divinity;	造化鍾神秀
Shaded and sun-lit it cleaves the dusk from the dawn.	陰陽割昏曉
A heaving breast—giving rise to cumulus clouds;	盪胸生層雲

[36] Cf., for instance, the line 日出氣象分, "The sun shows forth and vaporous shapes resolve," in Meng Hao-jan's poem "Starting Early from the Tarn at Fisher's Reach" 早發漁浦潭, *Meng Hao-jan chi* 孟浩然集, 1.8a (SPTK ed.); see the translation in Kroll, *Meng Hao-jan*, p. 70.

[37] Note that the phrase *shih chiang* 逝將 in the penultimate line (逝將它斯宇) is a classical locution from the refrain of *Shih* 113 (逝將去女), meaning "swear to [do X] in future"—not, as one might be tempted to read, a reference to the soul's return to T'ai Shan at death ("Passed on, I shall ..."). The latter interpretation would, moreover, make no sense in conjunction with the final line of the poem.

Bursting eye-sockets—giving entrance to homing birds.
Someday I will surmount its incomparable crest—
And in a single scanning the host of hills will dwindle![38]

決眥入歸鳥
會當凌絕頂
一覽衆山小

To understand this poem's verbal craft properly, we must see it in the context of the T'ai Shan verses that preceded it.[39] We may begin by noting how Tu Fu opens his poem, as did Hsieh Ling-yün, with the declaration of Mount T'ai's alternate name—Tai Tsung. But he immediately breaks off, expressing his uncertainty over what course of metaphorical description to pursue—thus rejecting, temporarily at least, the standard formula used by poets preceding him, of explicitly extolling the mountain's height. However, he then proceeds in the second line with an image which indeed serves to suggest—but obliquely—the verticality of T'ai Shan. I say "obliquely," because not one word of this line in fact mentions the concept of height directly: it merely says that the *color* of the mountain[40] goes on and on, visible from both the states of Ch'i and Lu (since Mount T'ai was on the boundary between these two regions). Bypassing the now common images drawn from *Shih* 259, Tu Fu's vision here is reminiscent of a couplet from a different song of the *Shih ching*—viz., "Mount T'ai is steep and brant, / Looked up to by the state of Lu" 泰山巖巖, 魯邦所詹), from *Shih* 300. And we are reminded, too, of the statement from *Shih chi* that "Sunward (i.e., south) of T'ai Shan is Lu, shadeward

[38] "Wang yüeh" 望嶽, in *Chiu-chia chi-chu Tu shih* 九家集註杜詩 (rpt. in *A Concordance to the Poems of Tu Fu* [Cambridge: Harvard-Yenching Institute Sinological Index Series, Supplement no. 14, vol. 2]), 1.5–6.

[39] We will not, then, be induced to consider it a "Confucian" reworking of a vague Buddho-Taoist tradition of ascent poems (as does Stephen Owen, *The Great Age of Chinese Poetry* [New Haven: Yale University Press, 1980], p. 188). As I hope the comments below will show, the poem is not an isolated or novel counter to a loosely defined tradition of "mountain verses"—it rather takes its place squarely within the discrete tradition of T'ai Shan poems.

[40] Note that, while "azure mountains" are a commonplace of T'ang poetry, the color is particularly appropriate here, since *ch'ing*, "azure," is the symbolic hue of the east and T'ai Shan is the Eastern Marchmount.

(i.e., north) of it is Ch'i."[41] Line three of the poem affirms the sacred nature of Mount T'ai, preeminent among alpine divinities; it owes its prominence to, and is the handiwork of, the mysterious selecting and synthesizing principle of Nature, known as the "Shaping Mutator" (*tsao hua* 造化).[42] We should also note specially here the epithet "flourishing" (*hsiu* 秀), encountered already in the T'ai Shan verses of Hsieh Tao-yün and Hsieh Ling-yün. Tu Fu, however, uses the word not—as did his Mount T'ai predecessors—to describe the upward flowering elevation of the peak but rather to describe the complete and perfect holiness of the mountain. But this phrase, *shen hsiu* 神秀 ("flourishing of divinity"), was not original with Tu Fu, either; in this, the young poet was appropriating a usage earlier applied to Mount T'ien-t'ai 天台山 in Sun Ch'o's 孫綽 (ca. 310–397) celebrated rhapsody on that important peak.[43] The fourth line of the poem points to the seemingly massive physical structure of T'ai Shan, characterizing it almost as an *axis mundi*, or at least an *axis luminis*, whose northern and southern flanks ("shaded" and "sun-lit," respectively) divide night from day.

The lexical crux of the poem rests in the fifth and sixth lines (盪胸生層雲, 決眥入歸鳥), where the poet's diction attains its richest and most compact density. (The reader may have noticed that my rendering of the lines is—intentionally—ambiguous.) The corporal imagery in these two lines has long been regarded by commentators as referring to the poet himself: he is so high up that the

[41] *Shih chi*, 129.3265.

[42] Also referred to commonly as the "Fashioner of Creatures" (*tsao wu che* 造物者). On the concept of this creative force, see Edward H. Schafer, "The Idea of Created Nature in T'ang Literature," *Philosophy East and West* 15, no. 2 (1965), 153–160.

[43] 天台山者, 蓋山嶽之神秀也. See Sun Ch'o 孫綽, "Yu T'ien-t'ai Shan fu" 遊天台山賦, in *Wen hsüan* 文選, ed. Hsiao T'ung 蕭統 (Hong Kong, 1936), 11.223. The phrase was also applied to the western peak of Mount Sung, the Central Marchmount, by Yang Chiung 楊炯 (650–694), two generations before Tu Fu: 少室山者, 山岳之神秀也; see his "Shao-shih Shan i miao pei" 少室山姨廟碑, in *Ch'üan T'ang wen* 全唐文, ed. Tung Kao 董誥 et al. (Taipei: Hui-wen shu-chü, 1961), 192.17b. (On Yang Chiung's dates, about which there is argument, I follow Yang Ch'eng-tsu 楊承祖, "Yang Chiung nien-p'u" 楊炯年譜, *Journal of Oriental Studies* 13, no. 1 [1975], 57–72.)

alpine clouds seem born from his chest, and his eyes seem to burst as he strains his vision to follow the flight of birds returning to their roosts on the mountain. Since this interpretation has been hallowed by centuries of critical acceptance, one hesitates to subscribe to a contrary view. Yet I admit I do not think the traditional interpretation accounts adequately, much less entirely, for Tu Fu's particular—and, we must suppose, careful—arrangement of words in this couplet.

It is, of course, possible to read the lines with the poet as the understood subject, and it may well be that Tu Fu had this reading in mind. But at the same time it must be conceded that this reading poses some difficulties, both artistically and logically. Artistically, it is at least unnecessary, if not infelicitous, to shift the focus of the poem, which has till this point been wholly on T'ai Shan, so conspicuously toward the speaker himself. Logically, this reading is rather problematic also in that, if we take it to be at the level of the poet's breast that the mountain's cumulus clouds come forth, we must assume the poet to be somewhere up the slope of the mountain itself. But if so, the title of the work ("*Gazing Afar* at the Marchmount") is invalidated and, perhaps more troublesomely, the apparently long-range view of the homing birds in line six is called into question (for, why should the poet need to strain his eyes to follow the flight of birds that are coming *closer* to him?).[44] There is, though, an alternate reading of this couplet, which seems to alleviate these difficulties. And that is to read the lines with T'ai Shan itself as the subject—in the same manner as it had been the continuous subject of the poem's first four lines. If we do so, line

[44] These problems are not, by the way, avoided by reading *tang* 盪 as "washing; cleansing; scouring" (Middle Chinese **t'ang-*) instead of "heaving; agitated" (**dang-*). That reading could indeed place the poet at some distance from Mount T'ai (since the *locus classicus* for the phrase 盪胸, with *tang* meaning "washing," implies a confrontational posture (see Chang Heng's 張衡 [78–139] "Nan tu fu," in Hsiao T'ung, *Wen hsüan*, 4.73: 淯水盪其胸). However, then we must assume the poet to be on a mountain peak barely less tall than T'ai Shan itself, which would be clearly inappropriate in the context of a poem celebrating the "incomparable" Marchmount. I think David Hawkes is quite right in reading *tang* here as "heaving" (Hawkes, *A Little Primer of Tu Fu* [Oxford: Oxford University Press, 1967], p. 4), although I cannot agree with him that it refers only to a "climber's" breast or that lines five and six are merely a case of "poetical inversion."

five resolves itself nicely: "Its heaving breast gives rise to cumulus clouds." We may recall here that a standard property of mountains in the traditional Chinese view is that they "engender" or "give rise to" clouds. But while most readers will have no trouble accepting this rather mild form of anthropomorphism, many may balk at the similar—but somehow more extreme—personification then required in line six: "Its bursting eye-sockets give entrance to homing birds." Here one must allow the mountain's imagined caverns or grottoes to be "eye-sockets" into which, when seen from a distant perspective, birds seem to enter. Presumably it is because of the eccentricity of the latter image that traditional critics have chosen to disregard this reading. And yet it is, in fact, no more unusual than the "daring"[45] inversion of normal syntax and the logical incongruities necessitated by the approved interpretation. I confess to being attracted to the "anthropomorphic" reading, and this for two reasons: it requires no undue wrenching of either the syntax of the original text or of the focused subject of the poem. The change of subject to the poet comes much more naturally in the seventh line, with the explicitly stated ("Someday I will . . .") shift from present observation to deliberate imagination. Still, I am not convinced that Tu Fu himself made—or wished to make—a clear choice between the two possible meanings of his couplet; we may be dealing here with a conscious ambiguity which gives a layered depth to the words themselves.[46]

However we construe the poem's fifth and sixth lines, it is plain enough that with these lines the poet's distant contemplation of Mount T'ai has reached the limit of its capabilities. In the concluding couplet he can only imagine the ascent of its summit, which he promises himself to make "someday." (Note how this votive ending resembles that of Hsieh Tao-yün's poem.) And the view he shall then enjoy will affirm T'ai Shan's preeminence, in terms

[45] Hawkes, *loc. cit.*

[46] As far as I know, the only other scholar to consider seriously the syntactic and semantic ambiguity of these lines is Francois Cheng, *L'écriture poétique chinoise* (Paris: Seuil, 1977), p. 180, who observes "En réalité, le poète cherche justement à suggérer que le grimpeur 'fait corps' avec la montagne et vit la vision de la montagne de l'intérieur."

reminiscent of Confucius' experience ("On climbing T'ai Shan, [Confucius] considered the subcelestial realm to dwindle" 登泰山而小天下)[47] upon reaching the great mountain's summit long ago.

Tu Fu's view of Mount T'ai in the preceding poem was apparently the result of a private excursion. We know, however, of at least two poets of the T'ang who came to the mountain on formal occasions, in the entourage of their respective rulers, for the *feng* and *shan* sacrifices. Lu Chao-lin 盧照鄰 (ca. 635–684)[48] accompanied Li Chih 李治 (posthumously Kao Tsung 高宗, reg. 649–683) there in 666 and has left us a set of four heptasyllabic quatrains, called "Songs for the Great Refection upon the Ascent for the *feng*,"[49] which were composed for the celebratory banquet that followed Kao Tsung's performance of the *feng* on T'ai Shan. But the mountain itself barely appears in these songs; the poet's interest is rather on the pious evocation of the sovereign's royal virtue. In 725, when Tu Fu was a lad of thirteen, Kao Tsung's imperial grandson Li Lung-chi 李隆基 (pht. Hsüan Tsung 玄宗, reg. 712–756), also carried out the *feng-shan*. Coordinating all aspects of the imperial progress to, encampment at, and sacrifice on Mount T'ai on this occasion was the famous writer and statesman Chang Yüeh 張說 (667–731).[50] It was Chang also who conceived the words for the fourteen solemn songs performed to bring down, welcome, entertain, and finally send off the divinity of the moun-

[47] *Mencius*, 7A.24.

[48] His dates are far from definite; see Takagi Masakazu 高木正一, "Ryo Shōrin no denki to bungaku" 盧照鄰の傳記と文学, *Ritsumeikan bungaku* 立命館文学 196 (October 1961), 777–809, esp. 777–785, for a conscientious attempt to establish the facts. Recently, Fu Hsüan-tsung 傅璇琮 has sought to establish 630–680 as the span of Lu's life; see Fu's "Lu Chao-lin, Yang Chiung chien-p'u" 盧照鄰楊炯簡譜, in *Lu Chao-lin chi, Yang Chiung chi* 盧照鄰楊炯集, ed. Hsü Ming-hsia 徐明霞 (Peking: Chung-hua shu-chü, 1980). In any event, the traditionally accepted dates of 641–680, based on Lu's *Chiu T'ang shu* biography (190A.5000), can hardly be upheld.

[49] "Teng feng ta-p'u ko, szu shou" 登封大酺歌四首, in *Ch'üan T'ang shih* 全唐詩 (hereafter *CTS*) (Peking: Chung-hua shu-chü, 1960), 42.532.

[50] Although Chang's dates are given in all reference works as 667–730, he actually died on 9 February 731; see Paul W. Kroll, "On the Date of Chang Yüeh's Death," *Chinese Literature: Essays, Articles, Reviews* 2, no. 2 (1980), 264–65.

tain during the rites on T'ai Shan.[51] Chang Yüeh further composed, at his lord's command, a long "altar hymn" (壇頌) for the *feng* sacrifice, which was carved on a memorial stele at the Marchmount.[52] However, these works, like Lu Chao-lin's four songs, are turned more toward conveying a sense of the grandeur and majesty of the emperor than that of Mount T'ai. We might remark, though, that it was on this occasion that T'ai Shan received from Hsüan Tsung the exalted title "Prince Equal to Heaven" (*t'ien-ch'i wang* 天齊王)—an alternate appellation for the mountain which was to endure in official use long past the T'ang dynasty.[53]

So far we have surveyed that strain of T'ai Shan verses which derives its inspiration from this alp's traditional standing as the foremost of China's mountains, arbiter of life and death, and supreme intermediary between Heaven and Emperor. We shall now examine a divergent order of poems about this peak, poems that feature Mount T'ai as the setting for specifically Taoist episodes of transcendence and transformation. We begin with a poem by

[51] For these lyrics, see "T'ang feng T'ai Shan yüeh-chang" 唐封泰山樂章, *CTS*, 85.918–920. The eight similar songs performed for Hsüan Tsung's *shan* sacrifice at Mount She-shou 社首山 had lyrics composed (the first seven of them) by Ho Chih-chang 賀知章 (659–744) and (the last one) by Yüan Ch'ien-yao 源乾曜 (d. 731); see "Shan She-shou yüeh-chang" 禪社首樂章, *CTS*, 12.111–12.

[52] *Chiu T'ang shu*, 23.904; *Hsin T'ang shu*, 125.4408. The text of this hymn may be found in *Ch'üan T'ang wen*, 221.14a–18b, and also—with numerous interesting and often helpful variants—in the late sixteenth-century *Tai shih* 岱史 (HY 1460), 8.8b–14a, preserved in the *Tao tsang* 道藏. (All *Tao tsang* texts cited in this paper will be identified by their "HY number," i.e., their number in Weng Tu-chien, *Combined Indices to the Authors and Titles of Books in Two Collections of Taoist Literature* [Cambridge: Harvard-Yenching Institute Sinological Index Series, no. 25], pp. 1–37). The *Tai shih*, in eighteen *chüan*, is the most comprehensive and valuable of all monographs on T'ai Shan; Chavannes unfortunately did not know of this work.

It might also be noted here that Chang Yüeh was a practiced hand at putting words to official court music: he had earlier composed the lyrics for the songs to be sung in Hsüan Tsung's ancestral temple (see *CTS*, 85.920–923). For more on some of Chang's other lyrics for official occasions, see Paul W. Kroll, "The Dancing Horses of T'ang," *T'oung Pao* 67, nos. 3–5 (1981), 240–268.

[53] Of all medieval monarchs, Li Lung-chi was perhaps the most solicitous toward the sierran spirits of his realm, granting new and loftier titles and enfeoffments to the major peaks than they had previously possessed. Prior to Mount T'ai's change of title

in 725, the emperor in 713 had designated the Western Marchmount, Hua Shan, "Prince of the Heaven of Metal" (*chin-t'ien wang* 金天王). In 746 Mount Sung 嵩 was created "Prince of the Central Heaven" (*chung-t'ien wang* 中天王), Mount Heng 桓 "Prince of the Sedate Heaven" (*an-t'ien wang* 安天王), and Mount Heng 衡 "Prince Administrator of Heaven" (*szu-t'ien wang* 司天王). The five Marchmounts having all been raised to princely status, Hsüan Tsung in later years turned his attention to several other peaks—in 748 Mount Chao-ying 照應山 was made "Lord of Mystic Virtue" (*hsüan-te kung* 玄德公), and in 751 the following promotions were effected: Mount T'ai-po 太白山 was made "Lord of Divine Responsiveness" (*shen-ying kung* 神應公), Mount I 沂山 was made "Lord of Eastern Stability" (*tung-an kung* 東安公), Mount Kuai-chi 會稽山 was made "Lord of Eternal Ascendance" (*yung-hsing kung* 永興公), Mount Huo 霍山 (the original Southern Marchmount of ancient times) was made "Lord Responsive to the Peerless One" (*ying-sheng kung* 應聖公), and Mount I-wu-lü 醫巫閭山 was made "Lord of Extensive Peace" (*kuang-ning kung* 廣寧公). See *T'ang hui-yao* 唐會要, 47.834–35 (TSCC ed.) (and, in the case of Sung Shan, *Chiu T'ang shu*, 24.934), where the enfeoffments granted to mountains by all other T'ang rulers combined do not approach in number those bestowed by Li Lung-chi.

Li Lung-chi's interest in properly denominating and dignifying these peaks was due partly to the fact that he was convinced the great mountains concealed within their rocky frames the terrestrial headquarters (the "grotto archives," *tung fu* 洞府) of those sublime and perfected beings, the Realized Persons of the Heaven of Highest Clarity (*shang-ch'ing [t'ien] chen-jen* 上清[天]眞人)—the Taoist divinities who were the lords behind the stars above and the true superintendents of the holy mountains. He had first been persuaded of this fact by the influential "patriarch" of the Shang-ch'ing school, Szu-ma Ch'eng-chen 司馬承禎 (647–735), who is reported to have advised Li Lung-chi after the latter's 725 visit to T'ai Shan that "At present the divine bethels of the Five Marchmounts are in all cases for [the propitiation of] the divinities of mountain and grove; but these are not the true and real divinities [of those peaks]. Every one of the Five Marchmounts has a Grotto Archive, within each of which are Realized Persons of Highest Clarity who have come down to discharge their responsibilities." In response to a subsequent suggestion of Szu-ma Ch'eng-chen, the sovereign decreed the establishment on these peaks of shrines called "Bethels of the Realized Lords" (*chen-chün tz'u* 眞君祠), in honor of these prepotent divinities. See *Chen hsi* 眞系 (by Li Po 李渤, preface dated 805), as preserved in the eleventh-century *Yün-chi ch'i-ch'ien* 雲笈七籤 (HY 1026), 5.15b. The *Chen hsi* biography of Szu-ma Ch'eng-chen is the basic source for his "official" biography in the *Chiu T'ang shu*, 192.5127–29, where this incident is also recorded. For more on this important Taoist prelate, see Ch'en Kuo-fu, *Tao-tsang yüan-liu k'ao*, pp. 52–59; Paul W. Kroll, "Szu-ma Ch'eng-chen in T'ang Verse," *Society for the Study of Chinese Religions Bulletin* 6 (1978), 16–30; Kroll, "Notes on Three Taoist Figures of the T'ang Dynasty," *Society for the Study of Chinese Religions Bulletin* 9 (1981), 19–22; and, most recently and thoroughly, J. Russell Kirkland, "Taoists of the High T'ang: An Inquiry into the Perceived Significance of Eminent Taoists in Medieval Chinese Society" (Ph.D. diss., Indiana University, 1985), pp. 55–168.

Ts'ao Chih 曹植 (192–232), which effectively mixes these two aspects of T'ai Shan. The first five stanzas of the poem are very much in line with the type of approach to which we have become accustomed, but the final two stanzas lead us into a different realm.

Urge on the carriage, lash the worn-out steeds,
Eastward to arrive at the enceinte of Feng-kao.
Divine, oh, is Mount T'ai in that place!
Among the Five Marchmounts its name is special.

驅車揮駑馬
東到奉高城
神哉彼泰山
五嶽專其名

Arched and high—threading the clouds and rainbows;
Upborne and abrupt—emerging into Grand Clarity.
Coursing round about it are twice six watch-mounds,
And placed atop them are kiosks ten and two.

隆高貫雲蜺
嵯峨出太淸
周流二六候
間置十二亭

Above and below are springs of gushing ale,
With stones of jade displaying their floriate blooms.
To the southeast one gazes on the countryside of Wu;
Looking west, one observes the germ of the sun.

上下涌醴泉
玉石揚華英
東南望吳野
西眺觀日精

It is where cloud-soul and spirit are tethered and attached—
In the passage away [of time], one feels this ongoing march.
They who are kings, in returning their allegiance to Heaven,
Devote to it (i.e., T'ai Shan) the completion of their principal deeds.

魂神所繫屬
逝者感斯征
王者以歸天
效厥元功成

In successive ages there are none who have not paid it honor,

歷代無不遵

For the rites and litations have their gradings
  of quality.
If one probes the divining slips, some are
  long-lived, others short;
It is only virtue that "succeeds and furthers
  through perserverance."

禮祀有品程
探策或長短
唯德亨利貞

Those that offered the *feng* were seven tens
  of thearchs,
But Hsüan the August was the primary,
  unmatched numen.
He partook of the aurorae, rinsed his mouth
  with cold-night damps,
And fur and feathers then mantled the form
  of his person.

封者七十帝
軒皇元獨靈
餐霞漱沆瀣
毛羽被身形

Rising up and away, he trod the outskirts
  of emptiness;
Aloof and afar, he ascended to sequestered
  tenebrity.
Equal in span of years to the Father in the
  East,
He wastes the ages now in perpetual pro-
  longation of life![54]

發舉蹈虛廓
徑庭升窈冥
同壽東父年
曠代永長生

Some of this may be obscure enough to warrant commentary. Feng-kao 奉高 is the name of the Han dynasty county (here, for rhyming purposes, called a *ch'eng* 城, "enceinte," instead of a *hsien* 縣) centered on Mount T'ai. "Grand Clarity" (*t'ai ch'ing* 太清) is the formal designation of the sky we see—the nearest to us of the vertically arranged Taoist heavens.[55] The twelve "watch-mounds" (*hou* 候) and "kiosks" (*t'ing* 亭) that stud the mountain are mile-

[54] "Ch'ü chü p'ien" 驅車篇, in *Ts'ao Tzu-chien shih chu* 曹子建詩注, ed. Huang Chieh 黃節 (Taipei: I-wen yin-shu-kuan, 1971), 2.33b–34a, pp. 170–171. In the eleventh line I emend 東北 to 東南, to make sense out of the geography; and in line 16 I accept the variant 禮祀 (in place of 禮記) given in *YFSC*, 64.5b.

[55] According to Ko Hung, the zone of Grand Clarity commenced at a distance of forty *li* above the earth. *Pao-p'u tzu nei-p'ien*, 15.7a/b. In the developed Taoist cosmology of medieval times, it would be surmounted by the heavens of Highest Clarity 上清 and Jade Clarity 玉清.

stones, set one *li* apart, which mark the route upward.[56] Of the marvelous "springs of ale" mentioned by Ts'ao Chih, one at least, issuing from the eastern talus of the mountain, is reported still to have been pouring forth its liquor four hundred years afterward; a drink from it would cleanse one's mind of worldly impurities.[57] "Germ of the sun" (*jih ching* 日精) is a kenning for the roseate clouds of dawn or evening; since the poet is looking west when he sees them, we may assume him to be viewing a sunset.[58] T'ai Shan "is where cloud-soul and spirit are tethered and attached" because, as we have seen, one's spiritual essence returns there—whence it issued—upon the death of one's body. This thought gives rise logically, in the line immediately following, to the poet's heightened sense of awareness of life's quick passage, expressed here in phrases compounded from the *Shih ching* and the *Lun yü*.[59] The "divining slips" referred to are those that, according to tradition, were to be found atop Mount T'ai and that listed the predestined term of everyone's years; Han Wu Ti was said to have once stolen a peek at his own.[60] "Succeeding and furthering through perseverance" is, of course, a quotation from the opening line of the *I ching*;[61] the import here seems to be that only a virtuous ruler could hope to enter into proper relations with Mount T'ai.

Up to this point and through the next two lines, where Huang Ti, the Yellow Thearch (here called by an honorific form of his given name)[62] makes his appearance, as the first of the seventy-plus sovereigns of antiquity to perform the *feng*, Ts'ao Chih's poem exhibits no unusual twists that would set it apart from the works we

[56] The setting up of such markers had been a Ch'in practice, continued under the Han. Huang Chieh (2.34a, p. 171) cites the relevant information as contained in Li Hsien's 李賢 (651–684) annotations to the *Hou Han shu*, 1B.60.

[57] *Tai shih*, 3.3b, quoting the late seventh-century Buddhist compendium, *Fa-yüan chu-lin* 法苑珠林. By Ming times, however, when the *Tai shih* was compiled, this spring had dried up (*Tai shih*, 4.9b).

[58] The equation of *hsia* 霞 and *jih ching* 日精 is noted in several medieval texts, all of Taoist provenance—to name only one, *Chen kao* 眞誥 (HY 1010), 2.6a.

[59] Cf. *Lun-yü*, 9.16, and *Shih* 196, stanza 4.

[60] *Feng-su t'ung-i*, 2.2a.

[61] Viz., the second, third, and fourth words of the text on the hexagram *ch'ien* 乾.

[62] Huang Ti's given name was Hsüan-yüan 軒轅 (*Shih chi*, 1.1), often respectfully altered by medieval writers to Hsüan the August 軒皇.

have already studied. But this Huang Ti is not a pale and bloodless imperial prototype, a mere name from the mists of mythology. He is, or rather he becomes, following his ascent of T'ai Shan, a Taoist superman. Sustained on auroral clouds and chill brumes—ethereal fare—he undergoes a bodily transformation which equips him with wings for the ultimate ascent—into the remote void of the heavens. For Huang Ti, then, the summit of Mount T'ai is but his last point of physical contact with the world of men. From there, lifting away effortlessly from this lower realm, he has become a true Transcendent (*hsien* 仙), matching in longevity the "Father in the East" (*tung fu* 東父). This latter and, for the moment, enigmatic figure will engage our attention at greater length in the third section of this essay. For now it will suffice to identify him as the male counterpart of the powerful Taoist goddess Hsi Wang Mu 西王母, "The Royal Mother in the West," and to appreciate the directional appropriateness of his connection with the Eastern Marchmount.

The Yellow Thearch's ascension into the heavens had been the concluding element in at least one tradition pertaining to this legendary ruler. But in the normal account of this event, recorded in the *Shih chi* chapter on the *feng-shan* rites and thereafter amplified in various other versions,[63] Huang Ti's translation to the celestial regions is always effected by means of a divine dragon, who graciously carries him aloft; he does not make this final climb unaided, as he does in Ts'ao Chih's poem. Nor, for that matter, is the place of his transcendence identified as Mount T'ai; it is noted, instead, as the foot of Mount Ching 荊山 (in Honan).

Ts'ao Chih seems to have been the first writer to portray Huang Ti in verse as a Taoist *hsien*. But perhaps more important for us is the suggestion of T'ai Shan as a site of spiritual—as well as

[63] *Shih chi*, 28.1394, where Han Wu Ti hears the story from the thaumaturge Kung-sun Ch'ing 公孫卿. This incident is not part of the more sober "annals" of Huang Ti recorded by Szu-ma Ch'ien in the first chapter of the *Shih chi*. However, it and many other uncommon episodes are recounted in numerous Taoist biographies of Huang Ti, from medieval times. See, for example, *Lieh-hsien chuan* 列仙傳 (HY 294), 1.2b–3a, but especially the more extensive T'ang dynasty work *Kuang Huang Ti pen-hsing chi* 廣黃帝本行記 (HY 290) and the lengthy "Hsüan-yüan pen-chi" 軒轅本紀 preserved in *Yün-chi ch'i-ch'ien*, 100.2b–32a.

physical—transformation. In another poem by Ts'ao Chih, Mount T'ai is again the setting for a transmutation to immortality; but this time the fortunate being is the poet himself:

In the morn I wandered to Mount T'ai; 晨遊太山
Clouds and fog were comely and coy. 雲霧窈窕
Of a sudden I came upon two lads— 忽逢二童
The beauty of their features fresh and fine. 顏色鮮好

They were mounted on that deer of white, 乘彼白鹿
Their hands were masked by polypore plants. 手翳芝草
I deemed that they were Realized Persons, 我知眞人
And I knelt down long and inquired of the Way. 長跪問道

We ascended westward to a hall of jade— 西登玉堂
Loft-buildings of gold, streets of mallotus trees! 金樓榎道
To me they transmitted drugs of transcendence 授我仙藥
That had been fashioned by their divine radiances. 神皇所造

They instructed me in their ingestion and eating, 教我服食
And in the cycling of sperm to supplete the brain. 還精補腦
With a life-span now equal to metal or stone, 壽同金石
For generations everlasting, it is impossible to age![64] 永世難老

Here we have a true encounter with divinity on T'ai Shan[65]—not, however, with the spirit of the mountain itself (that never happens in T'ai Shan poems) but with a pair of "Realized Persons" (*chen jen* 眞人, the highest grade of Taoist superbeings, more perfected even than *hsien*; their boyish appearances are, paradoxically, indications of their extreme age) who find Mount T'ai a suitably numinous

[64] "Fei lung p'ien" 飛龍篇, *Ts'ao Tzu-chien shih chu*, 2.32a, p. 167. The poem is in tetrasyllabic lines.

[65] Cf. M. Soymié, "Le Lo-feou shan," p. 2: "Les montagnes sont pour les Chinois des zones délimitées, des aires religieuses chargées elles-mêmes de puissance magique et où l'on va chercher le contact avec le divin."

locale for their activities. The polypore plants they hold are magic mushrooms that are one of the ingredients in the transcendent drugs that these two "divine radiances" will concoct. The white deer they ride is a conveyance often favored by Taoist gods when they must travel upon the earth (we will see it reappear later in a poem by Li Po). In the second half of this piece the two supernatural "lads" abruptly whisk the poet away to paradise, where they proceed to teach him pharmacological and physiological techniques conducing to immortality.[66]

At this point we might recall our earlier experience of T'ai Shan as an alp of transition, a passage-place between life and death. From that perspective it is not difficult to see why Ts'ao Chih should present Mount T'ai as an appropriate site for Taoist transformation: the transition to *hsien*hood is, indeed, an existential alteration, requiring as real a metamorphosis in one's being as that undergone when one comes into or leaves this world.

Ts'ao Chih was not the first poet to see T'ai Shan as an abode of Taoist divinities or as a place of encounters with transcendence—or transcendents. In the anonymous *yüeh-fu* poem called "Canzonet on Striding Out the Hsia Gate" (步出夏門行), we find, for example, a seeker of "the Way of the divine transcendents" who pays a visit to the "Royal Father and Mother" (that is, Hsi Wang Mu and the Father in the East) in their joint dwelling, located in a "niche of Mount T'ai"; he then meets—still on T'ai Shan—the famous immortal Red Pine (Ch'ih Sung 赤松) who "Grasps the reigns, to act as my driver, / And leads me to ramble above the heavens."[67] Similarly, Ts'ao Chih's father, Ts'ao Ts'ao 曹操 (155–220), begins the first of his three "Cantos on the Pneuma Emerging" (氣出唱) with the poet riding a chariot of wind and

[66] On the practice of "cycling sperm to supplete the brain" (*huan-ching pu-nao* 還精補腦)—a method of preventing the ejaculation of semen, and consequent diminution of *yang*-essence, during copulation—see H. Maspero, "Les procédés de 'nourrir le principe vital' dans la religion taoiste ancienne," in his *Le Taoisme et les religions chinoises*, p. 557.

[67] "Pu-ch'u Hsia men hsing," *YFSC*, 37.3a. This work is probably datable to the last decades of the Han dynasty. A useful general survey of Taoist thought in Han and Wei *yueh-fu* is Sawaguchi Takeo 澤口剛雄, "Kan Gi gakufu ni okeru Rō-Sō dōka no shisō" 漢魏樂府における老莊道家思想, *Tōhō shūkyō* 東方宗教 44 (October 1974), 14–32.

cloud, pulled by six dragons, "eastward to arrive at Mount T'ai," where "Transcendent persons and jade maidens come downward [to me] in meandering wander." He is then given a draught of "jade broth," fortifying him for his subsequent journey to P'eng-lai and beyond, eventually leading to the portals of Heaven.[68] Although we are restricting ourselves here to *shih* poetry, we may yet remark a like instance in Huan T'an's 桓譚 (43 B.C.to A.D. 28) "Rhapsody on Mountain Transcendents" (山仙賦), where we again see Red Pine, this time in company with his fellow immortal Wang-tzu Ch'iao 王子喬, sporting at "the terrace of Mount T'ai."[69] A similar recognition of T'ai Shan's pertinency as a home of ethereal beings can be seen in a rhyming inscription on a Han TLV mirror, which reads in part:

> Ascend Mount T'ai, to glimpse the Transcendent Persons
> Who feed on blooms of jade, quaff from springs of ale,
> Harness kraken dragons and ride the floating clouds;
> The white tiger leads them, oh, ascending straight to heaven.[70]

The literary culmination of this motif in *shih* poetry is to be found in Li Po's 李白 (701–762?) marvelous suite of six poems entitled "Wandering on Mount T'ai." In the concluding section of this essay, we shall apply ourselves to a close reading of these works. But, before we do so, it will be helpful to contemplate briefly the specifically Taoist contours of T'ai Shan as they appeared in medieval times.

One of the most practically potent periapts of early Taoism was

[68] "Ch'i-ch'u ch'ang" 氣出唱, no. 1, *Wei Wu Ti, Wen Ti, Ming Ti shih chu* 魏武帝文帝明帝詩注, p. 3; in *Wei Chin wu-chia shih chu* 魏晉五家詩注 (Taipei: Hsin-hsing shu-chü, 1962). The title refers to the poet's witnessing, in the first poem, the wonderful sight of an astral "pneuma" emanating from the "heart" star—our Antares (see Diether von den Steinen, "Poems of Ts'ao Ts'ao," *Monumenta Serica* 4 [1939–40], 169).

[69] *I-wen lei-chü*, 78.1338. For an English translation of this *fu*, see Timotheus Pokora, *Hsin-lun (New Treatise) and Other Writings by Huan T'an* (Ann Arbor: Center for Chinese Studies, The University of Michigan, 1975), pp. 231–232.

[70] The inscription is from the mirror classed as C 4311, in Michael Loewe, *Ways to Paradise: The Chinese Quest for Immortality* (London: George Allen and Unwin, 1979), p. 201.

"The Real Form of the Eastern Marchmount," showing its mystic caves and subterranean waters. (From *Tung-hsüan ling-pao wu-yüeh ku-pen chen-hsing t'u*, in *Tao tsang*, HY 441)

that known as "The Plans of the Real Forms of the Five Marchmounts" (*wu-yüeh chen-hsing t'u* 五嶽眞行圖).[71] This talisman, mentioned often in the *Pao-p'u tzu* of Ko Hung, kept its owner and his family from physical harm (especially—but not only—when entering the mountains), through the good offices of spiritual emissaries sent by the presiding deities of the great peaks. These spirits also reported periodically to the lords of the mountains on the proper or improper conduct of the possessor of the talisman—this an outgrowth of an ancient belief that the five holy alps were overseers of morality and guarantors of convenants.[72] Following the Shang-ch'ing and Ling-pao 靈寶 reformations of Taoism in

[71] The different uses and traditions pertaining to the "cult" of this talisman have been exhaustively studied by K. M. Schipper, "'Gogaku shinkeizu' no shinkō" 五嶽真形図の信仰, *Dōkyō kenkyū* 道教研究 2 (1967), 114–162.

[72] *Ibid.*, pp. 122–123.

the fourth and fifth centuries, this talisman underwent a shift, or evolution, in character.[73] As Schipper has stated, the "plans" (or "charts") of the five peaks began then to assume most importantly the function of aids to mystic orientation, allowing the adept to visit the sacred mountains in meditation.[74] To one who would thus reach T'ai Shan in meditation, its "true form" is revealed in the representation shown on page 193, according to one medieval text.

The source from which this illustration is taken identifies the lord of the Eastern Marchmount as the leader of 5,900 congregated spirits, chief counselor of the hundred revenants, and controller of life and death. It goes on to describe his apparel as follows: "He is arrayed in a long azure gown, wearing a 'Seven Correspondences' cap of cyan-blue and watchet; he wears a pendant seal of great luminosity and penetrating solarity, and rides an azure dragon."[75]

[73] On the Shang-ch'ing synthesis, which profoundly affected the course of medieval Chinese cultural, political, and literary history, see especially Isabelle Robinet, "La révélation du Shangqing dans l'histoire du taoisme," 2 vols. (Ph.D. diss., The University of Paris, 1981)—an extremely thorough and wholly admirable study which is a treasury of material on all aspects of Shang-ch'ing Taoism. It has recently (1984) been published as vol. CXXXVII in the series of Publications de l'École Française d'Extrême-Orient. See also Michel Strickmann, "The Mao Shan Revelations; Taoism and the Aristocracy," *T'oung Pao* 63 (1977), 1–64, and his *Le Taoisme du Mao Chan; chronique d'une révélation* (Paris: l'Institut des Hautes Etudes Chinoises, 1981). On the less well studied Ling-pao synthesis, see Stephen R. Bokenkamp, "Sources of the Ling-pao Scriptures," in *Tantric and Taoist Studies, in Honour of R. A. Stein*, vol. 2, ed. M. Strickmann (Brussels: Mélanges chinois et bouddhiques 21, 1983), pp. 434–486.

[74] Schipper, "'Gogaku shinkeizu,'" pp. 142–144. The point is also convincingly made here that Joseph Needham (*Science and Civilisation in China, Vol. 3: Mathematics and the Sciences of the Heavens and the Earth* [Cambridge: Cambridge University Press, 1959], p. 546) is mistaken in supposing these "charts" to be early exercises in contour mapping. In an earlier publication Schipper noted the symbolic identification in medieval China of the Five Marchmounts on earth with the five viscera of the human body and the five planets in the heavens—all manifestations of the great thearchs of the five cardinal points (Schipper, *L'empereur Wou des Han dans la légende taoiste* [Paris: l'École Française d'Extrême-Orient, 1965], p. 29). Isabelle Robinet, *Méditation taoiste* (Paris: Dervy-Livres, 1979), pp. 274–276, reminds us of this and also of the historically close connection between the Marchmounts and the "isles of the immortals."

[75] *Tung-hsüan ling-pao wu-yüeh ku-pen chen-hsing t'u* 洞玄靈寶五嶽古本眞形圖 (HY 441), 2a/b. The same description is repeated in *Wu-yüeh chen-hsing hsü lun* 五嶽

Some additional details of dress and equipage are added in another medieval text which also informs us that the deity's surname is Ch'ang 常 ("Constant") and his ineffable name Ching-meng 精萌 ("Essential Germinator")—one notes the references here to a by now familiar attribute of T'ai Shan. This latter text, by name the *Most High Scripture of the Dappled Talisman of the Nine Incarnadines and the Interior Realization of the Five Thearchs*, is an extremely interesting work from the Shang-ch'ing tradition, in which the sovereigns of the five sacred peaks are seen as keepers of the rosters of immortality. Two meditations—or visualizations—on the lord of T'ai Shan are described therein. Both are to be practiced on the first day of spring (the power of the east having then attained ascendancy), when the Lord Azure Thearch of the Eastern Quarter 東方青帝君—the god of Mount T'ai in his greater guise as Lord of the East—mounts his nine-dragon cloud-chassis of auroras of the cyan sky and, attended by twelve azure-waisted jade maidens, proceeds to T'ai Shan, where he collates and certifies the celestial registers containing the names of Realized Persons and Transcendent Magistrates.

In the first meditation, the adept who would have himself certified as a transcendent being is advised, after purifying and calming himself and burning incense in his meditation room, to ingest the Dappled Talisman of the Nine Pneuma for Entering Wood with Chia and I 甲乙入木九氣班符.[76] He must then clack his teeth together nine times (to bring to attention his corporal divinities) and visualize the Lord Azure Thearch descending on his celestial conveyance into the room, filling the chamber with a densely stifling azure pneuma. In the words of the text, the adept must then

Actualize as visible the center of the Lord Thearch's azure

眞形序論 (HY 1271), 23a; and in the "Wu-yüeh chen-hsing t'u hsü" 五嶽眞形圖序 contained in *Yün-chi ch'i-ch'ien*, 79.2a/b. Such descriptions of the outfits of spirit-beings are a regular feature of Taoist "visualization" texts, necessary so that the adept can distinguish precisely which high lord of the heavens he is encountering in a particular meditation.

[76] *Chia* and *i* are the two "celestial stems" that correspond to the East, whose "activity" or "phase" is that of wood.

> pneuma transmuted into a red light—like the germ of the year-star—doubly rutilant and splendidly luminous, which, descending from the summit of your head passes into your own body, the luminosity of its light penetrating and glinting amidst the space of one's liver sector.[77] Then, conduct the pneuma and gulp it down nine times, being conscious of a fumulous warmth within your body. Soon afterward, the red light will dissipate from within. Emerging from your nine apertures, it will return back *en bloc* above the summit of your head, where it will be transmuted to form an azure cloud. Be conscious of your own body residing within this azure cloud, and rise up along with the cloud. In a good while, you will be conscious of your certification [as a *hsien*], passing freely through space as though treading the emptiness.[78]

The adept will then raise his head and pronounce a rhymed incantation, after which he clacks his teeth twelve times and swallows his salival liquor twenty-four times. The meditation is then finished. Regular performance of this exercise over the space of eighteen years will, the adept is assured, render him capable of proceeding in flight to the heaven of Highest Clarity.

The second ritual to be carried through on this day, according to our scripture, involves the burying of a vermilion-transcribed copy of the aforementioned talisman, plus another incantation to the visualized great lord, and thirty-six circulations through one's body of the azure pneuma that fills one's room upon his appearance. This procedure is then to be followed by another, on the day of the vernal equinox, the date when the Azure Thearch presents his registers to the All-highest Lord Thearch 高上帝君. The meditation to be performed on this day will result in the god of T'ai Shan inscribing one's name on those registers before they are presented to the All-highest. It will also entail one's obtaining nine "divine lads" as familiars, as well as the acquisition of divine mushrooms that will appear for one spontaneously and the knowledge

[77] The liver is the bodily organ associated with the East, just as the "year-star," i.e., Jupiter, is the symbolic planet of that direction.

[78] *T'ai-shang chiu-ch'ih pan-fu wu-ti nei-chen ching* 太上九赤班符五帝內眞經 (HY 1318), 6b–7a.

of all affairs within the myriad *li* of the Eastern Quarter. After eighteen years of practice of these methods, a dragon-chassis will come to enable one to mount the emptiness and ascend to the heaven of Jade Clarity.[79] Similar meditation exercises are associated with the lords of the other four Marchmounts.

In the *Chen kao*, one of the seminal texts of the Shang-ch'ing canon, it is recorded that the grotto-heaven below Mao Shan 茅山—the most important peak for Shang-ch'ing Taoism—is the mid-point of a quincunx of connected subterranean heavens. We might expect the other four to be under the four "classical" marchmounts, but such is not the case: of the traditional quartet only Mount T'ai is honored with a link to Mao Shan.[80] This too is surely an indication of the sacred prominence of T'ai Shan, undeniable even in Taoist circles.

The mountain, however, was not a notable center of Taoist activities in medieval times. In fact, among humans there seem to have been only two "gentlemen of the Way" remembered for any particular association with T'ai Shan. One of these was Hsü Chün 許峻, who lived during the early second century A.D. Widely renowned as a master of divinatory practices, he was said to have acquired his skill in this art on Mount T'ai, having been taught it by Chang Chü-chün 張巨君, a transcendent whom he encountered during a pilgrimage there.[81] More closely tied to the mountain was Chang Chung 張忠, a well-known expert in Taoist respiratory

[79] *Ibid.*, 8a–9a. For a summary and analysis of this entire scripture, see Robinet, "La révélation du Shangqing," vol. 2, pp. 175–178.

[80] *Chen kao*, 11.7a. T'ai Shan was the northern point of this underground communications system, which also included Mounts Lin-wu 林屋 to the east of Mao Shan, O-mei 峨嵋 to the west, and Lo-fou 羅浮 to the south. But, according to Tu Kuang-t'ing 杜光庭 (850–933), the informed Taoist geo-mythographer of five and a half centuries later, Mount T'ai's grotto-heaven (called *P'eng-hsüan tung-t'ien* 蓬玄洞天 and measuring a thousand *li* in circumference) did not rank among the ten "major" *tung-t'ien*, only among the thirty-six lesser cavern paradises. See Tu's *Tung-t'ien fu-ti yüeh tu ming-shan chi* 洞天福地嶽瀆名山記 (HY 599), 6b.

[81] *Hou Han shu*, 82B.2731; translated in Ngo Van Xuyet, *Divination, magie et politique dans la Chine ancienne* (Paris: Presses Universitaires de France, 1976), p. 111. A much fuller version of the incident may be found in Chang Chü-chün's own "biography" in *Yün-chi ch'i-ch'ien*, 110.12b–13b. Hsü Chun was one of the early ancestors of the Hsüs who played such a crucial role in the Shang-ch'ing movement of the fourth century; see Strickmann, *Le Taoisme du Mao chan*, p. 88.

techniques who made T'ai Shan his home during the first half of the fourth century.[82] It was partly because of him that the bonze Chu Seng-lang 竺僧朗 (ca. 315–400) went to Mount T'ai in 351, establishing an important Buddhist monastery there that was to be influential for centuries in that region.[83] I have not found the names of any Taoist "observatories" (*kuan* 觀) established on T'ai Shan in medieval times, although doubtless there were some: a late source records, for instance, that during the reign of "Empress" Wu of the T'ang (690–705) the marchmount's own shrines were converted to serve the interests of the Taoist clergy.[84]

As befitted a mountain of such venerable sanctity, T'ai Shan was supposed to abound in jade on its upper slopes, gold on its lower—or so said the *Shan-hai ching* 山海經, which included the mountain in its mythographical survey of marvelous alps and seas.[85] And in a now lost Taoist text, quoted in Chang Shou-chieh's 張守節 standard commentary (published in 737) to the *Shih chi*,[86] we are told that Mount T'ai "teems with polypore plants, stones of jade, sweet springs of long ichor, and dwellings of Transcendent Persons."[87] At the same time, however, the innards of the mountain contain six prisons for the examination and ostracism of malefic revenants and spirits.[88] T'ai Shan could be both heaven and hell. But for poets it was the forces of light that prevailed there.

[82] *Chin shu*, 94.2451–52.

[83] On Chu Seng-lang's Buddhist establishment at T'ai Shan during the Six Dynasties period, see Miyakawa Hisayuki 宮川尚志, *Rikuchōshi kenkyū: shūkyō-hen* 六朝史研究:宗教篇 (Kyoto: Heirakuji Shoten, 1977), pp. 255–278, esp. pp. 258–261 for Chu in relationship to Chang Chung.

[84] *Tai shih*, 9.15b.

[85] *Shan-hai ching chiao-chu* 山海經校注, ed. Yüan K'o 袁珂 (Shanghai: Ku-chi ch'u-pan-she, 1979), 4.104, also noting a singular beast "whose appearance resembles a snork (i.e., a pigling) but [covered] with pearls, called by name *t'ung-t'ung* 狪狪," which lives only on Mount T'ai. The creature seems never to have been spotted on the mountain in medieval times.

[86] On Chang's *cheng-i* 正義 commentary, see E. Chavannes, *Les Mémoires historiques de Se-ma Ts'ien* (Paris: Librairie d'Amérique et d'Orient, 1895), vol. 1, pp. ccxvi–ccxvii, who notes specially that Chang's work is remarkable for the geographical information it furnishes.

[87] *Shih chi*, 6.242. The text Chang cites is the anonymous "Records of the Fortunate Lands" (*Fu-ti chi* 福地記), apparently a forerunner of Tu Kuang-t'ing's similar work from the tenth century (see n. 80).

[88] *Ibid.*

It remained to Li Po to compose the grandest and most vivid vision of the theme already exploited by Ts'ao Chih and touched on in various earlier poems, that of the transcendent encounter on Mount T'ai. The set of six poems he devoted to the subject was written in the early summer of the year 742.[89] The poems are replete with Taoist references and terminology, much of which has been overlooked or inadequately explained by commentators, even including the admirable Wang Ch'i 王琦 (1696–1774) whose annotated edition of Li Po's works is far superior to any other. Part of our task, in examining these poems, will be to restore to them their full religious context, which must be understood if we are properly to interpret Li Po's experience of Mount T'ai.

The first of the series reads as follows:

In the fourth month I ascend Mount T'ai;
Its stones are leveled—the autocrat's road opens out.
The six dragons traverse a myriad straths;
Ravines and races wind in due course round about.

四月上太山
石平御道開
六龍過萬壑
澗谷隨縈迴

Horses' footprints wreathe the cyan peaks
That are at present overflowing with azure lichens.
Flying streams shed their spray over steep stacks;
Waters rush, and the voice of the pine-trees is poignant.

馬跡遶碧峯
於今滿青苔
飛流灑絕巘
水急松聲哀

The view to the north—singular bluffs and walls;

北眺崿嶂奇

[89] Chan Ying 詹鍈, *Li Po shih-wen hsi-nien* 李白詩文繫年 (Peking: Tso-chia ch'u-pan-she, 1958), p. 25; Huang Hsi-kuei 黃錫珪, *Li T'ai-po nien-p'u* 李太白年譜 (Peking: Tso-chia ch'u-pan-she, 1958), p. 12. It was just after this that Li Po journeyed to K'uai-chi, where he became acquainted with the Taoist priest and poet Wu Yün 吳筠 (d. 778), who was summoned to court soon afterward and promptly persuaded Hsüan Tsung to send for Po as well. 742 was the first year of the T'ien-pao 天寶 ("Heavenly Treasure") reign-period, which had been inaugurated to honor the discovery of a celestial token vouchsafed the sovereign by the deified Lao Tzu and which witnessed the beginnings of Li Lung-chi's avid attachment to Taoist hierology. See Kroll, *Meng Hao-jan*, pp. 132–133.

Canted banks toward the east topple away.
The grotto gates—closed door-leaves of
  stone;
From the floor of the earth—rising clouds
  and thunder.

傾崖向東摧
洞門閉石扇
地底興雲雷

Climbing to the heights, I gaze afar at P'eng
  and Ying;
The image imagined—the Terrace of Gold
  and Silver.
At Heaven's Gate, one long whistle I give,
And from a myriad *li* the clear wind comes.

登高望蓬瀛
想象金銀臺
天門一長嘯
萬里清風來

Jade maidens, four or five persons,
Gliding and whirling descend from the Nine
  Peripheries.
Suppressing smiles, they lead me forward by
  immaculate hands,
And let fall to *me* a cup of fluid aurora!

玉女四五人
飄颻下九垓
含笑引素手
遺我流霞杯

I bow my head down, salute them twice,
Ashamed for myself not to be of a
  transcendent's caliber.
—But broad-ranging enough now to make
  the cosmos dwindle,
I'll leave this world behind, oh how far
  away![90]

稽首再拜之
自媿非仙才
曠然小宇宙
棄世何悠哉

The poet begins this first ascent of T'ai Shan (there will be others in the succeeding poems) by following the "autocrat's road" up the mountain—that is, the route taken by Hsüan Tsung for his *feng* sacrifice seventeen years earlier and by other emperors before him. It was traditionally the prerogative only of the Son of Heaven to ride in a carriage pulled by six horses;[91] that Li Po is conveyed upward

[90] "Yu T'ai Shan" 遊太山, no. 1, *Li T'ai-po ch'üan-chi* 李太白全集 (hereafter *LTPCC*), ed. Wang Ch'i 王琦 (Taipei: Hsin-hsing shu-chü, 1975), 20.447. B. Belpaire, "Le Taoisme et Li T'ai Po," *Mélanges chinois et bouddhiques* 1 (1931–1932) 2–4, comments briefly on, and translates a few lines from, the poems, but his remarks are vitiated by his lack of first-hand knowledge of Taoist sources.

[91] Shen Yüeh 沈約, *Sung shu* 宋書 (Peking: Chung-hua shu-chü, 1974), 18.495.

here by "six dragons" alerts us that his will be a journey even more magnificent than that of the sovereign.[92] We recall, too, that this sextuple team of dragons had earlier wafted Ts'ao Ts'ao to Mount T'ai; thus there was literary precedent for their harnessing. But we note in this first poem of Li Po's hexad that the gates of T'ai Shan's grotto-heaven are initially closed. It is only halfway through the poem, when he stands on the mountain's brow, above the clouds and above the thunder, and moreover only after gazing far off at the paradise isles of P'eng-lai and Ying-chou in the Eastern Sea, that images from the celestial regions begin to envelop him.

The "Terrace of Gold and Silver" fixed in mind by Li Po[93] is the same estrade remarked by Kuo P'u 郭璞 (276–324) when that inspired poet beheld P'eng-lai in the sixth of his famous series of *yu-hsien* 遊仙 ("Roaming to Sylphdom") verses.[94] Once this visionary contact with the higher realms is established by Li Po, the pace of events quickens. He stands now at the aptly named arête Heaven's Gate.[95] In response to his "long whistle"—an old and respected method of calling up desired atmospheric and spiritual phenomena[96]—a "clear wind" arrives from afar. But this uncanny

[92] As I have pointed out elsewhere, horse and dragon are congeners—differing symbolically only in that the former treads the earth, the latter the sky. See Kroll, "The Dancing Horses of T'ang," pp. 252–253.

[93] William G. Boltz, "Philological Footnotes to the Han New Year Rites," *Journal of the American Oriental Society* 99, no. 3 (1979), 431, has some pertinent comments on the basic meaning of the word *hsiang* 想 in classical texts. Often misrendered (by analogy, one supposes, with modern Mandarin usage) as "to think; thought," it properly indicates "to draw up a mental image, vision."

[94] "Yu hsien shih" 遊仙詩, no. 6, in *Ch'üan Chin shih*, 5.7b, p. 562.

[95] Chavannes, *Le T'ai chan*, p. 45, also p. 46, fig. 12.

[96] For the history of this technique, see Aoki Masaru 青木正兒, "'Shō' no rekishi to jigi no hensen" 嘯の歴史と字義の變遷, *Aoki Masaru zenshū* 青木正兒全集 (Tokyo: Shunjusha, 1971), vol. 8, pp. 161–168; and Sawada Mizuho 澤田瑞穂, "Shō no genryū" 嘯の源流, *Tōhō shūkyō* 44 (October 1974), 1–13. An interesting early T'ang text, the *Hsiao chih*, or "Directives on Whistling," describes in some detail the different types of "whistling" and the proper times of year at which to perform them; this text has been studied by E. D. Edwards, "'Principles of Whistling'— 嘯旨 *Hsiao chih*—Anonymous," *Bulletin of the School of Oriental and African Studies* 20 (1957), 217–229. "Long whistling" is mentioned in many medieval poems, but translators generally convert it into a dull "humming." For example, it is unfortunate that, given the scores of books and articles written about Wang Wei (701–761), it has not been noticed that, in his celebrated quatrain "A Lodging in the

breeze (it is a rarer, more remote, wind than that which sounded through the pines on the climb up) is merely the herald of a group of "jade maidens" come from heaven's farthest bounds—or are they members of the troupe of jade maidens we have already seen as attendant upon the lord of T'ai Shan himself? These ethereal damsels, with their suppressed smiles, seem to share a private joke—perhaps they are amused at the sight of the poet who has invoked their presence (he is not, as he himself realizes, "of a transcendent's caliber"). Nevertheless, they have a celestial gift for him. The "fluid aurora" (*liu hsia* 流霞) he receives from their hands is a supernal liquor, a draught of solar essence. A fundamental scripture of medieval Taoism, the *Purple Text of the Numinous Writ* (*Ling-shu tzu-wen* 靈書紫文), describes the procedures required to obtain this pentachrome pneuma which, when imbibed, suffuses one's body with solar energy.[97] Li Po, however, is here awarded it freely, an act of pure kindness on the part of the jade girls. it is significant that the word used for the transferral of the gift is *wei* 遺 ("let fall"), a more casual verb than the formal *shou* 授 ("confer") usually employed in religious contexts to indicate the transmission of doctrine, scripture, or token. The poet's bowed head and double salute may seem mere politesse, but in fact are the ritually correct actions to make after taking in the "fluid aurora," as indicated in the *Ling-shu tzu-wen*.[98] Similarly, the poet's acknowledgment of his

---

Bamboo" ("Chu-li kuan" 竹里館, in *CTS*, 128.1301), the "luminous moon" that appears in the final line of the poem has in fact shown itself in consequence of the poet's "long whistling" in line two. This is not just quaint "nature imagery."

[97] The original *Ling-shu tzu-wen* is scattered in four different works in the present *Tao tsang*; see Robinet, "La révélation du Shangqing," vol. 2, pp. 101–110, for analysis and discussion. The technique for absorbing the "fluid aurora" is found in *Huang-t'ien shang-ch'ing chin-ch'üeh ti-chün ling-shu tzu-wen shang-ching* 皇天上清金闕帝君靈書紫文上經 (HY 639), 4a–5a. The ingestion of aurorae is an exercise predating the Shang-ch'ing synthesis. We have seen it referred to above in Ts'ao Chih's first poem; and *Pao-p'u tzu nei-p'ien*, 20.4b, notes the "cup of fluid aurora" given by a transcendent to one Hsiang Man-tu 項曼都, which relieved the latter of all hunger and thirst. The poetic prototype is a line from the "Yüan yu" 遠遊: "Rinsing my mouth with [the essence of] True Solarity, I take in the aurora of dawn" 漱正陽而含朝霞. *Ch'u tz'u chi-chu* 楚辭集註 (Taipei: Kuang-wen shu-chü, 1956), p. 136.

[98] HY 639, 5a.

spiritual unworthiness is not routine self-depreciation (there would be no need to waste words over that); it is expressed in the exact words applied to Han Wu Ti when he, though considered undeserving, was granted celestial secrets by Hsi Wang Mu some eight centuries earlier.[99] Finally, we see in the last couplet another variation on the same passage from the *Mencius*—about Confucius' view from atop T'ai Shan making the subcelestial realm seem to dwindle—that Tu Fu had used to close his poem. But, while Tu Fu imagined that "the host of hills" would dwindle in his sight, for Li Po—energized now with solar essence—it is the whole cosmos that dwindles, and he feels himself ready to take leave of this paltry world.[100]

The second poem of the suite, only half as long as the first, presents a second ascent:

At clear daybreak I rode upon a white deer, And ascended straight to the mount of Heaven's Gate. At the mountain's edge I happened on a plumed person, With squared pupils, with handsome face and features.	淸曉騎白鹿 直上天門山 山際逢羽人 方瞳好容顏
Holding onto the bindweed, I would have attended to his colloquy; He nevertheless concealed himself with a barrier of clouds from the blue. But he let fall to me a writ formed of avian tracks, Which dropped down aflutter in the midst of the rocky heights.	捫蘿欲就語 却掩靑雲關 遺我鳥跡書 飄然落巖間

[99] Schipper, *L'empereur Wou des Han*, p. 111.

[100] Arthur Waley, *The Poetry and Career of Li Po* (London: George Allen and Unwin, 1950), p. 17, in a very brief and error-prone paraphrase of the content of the first three poems of the series, misinterprets this last line as saying the poet was "not yet ready to turn his back altogether upon the world." His mistake apparently derives from reading *yu* 悠 (棄世何悠哉) as "sad" instead of "far away." But the latter reading is confirmed not only by common sense, but also by the comparable diction at the end of the poem "Hsün shan seng pu-yü tso," *LTPCC*, 23.517: 了然絕世事, 此地方悠哉, where *yu* can only mean "far away."

Its script, it turned out, was of highest antiquity;
In construing it, I was absolutely unpracticed.
Sensible of this, I thrice breathed a sigh;
But the master I would follow has till now yet to return.[101]

其字乃上古
讀之了不閑
感此三嘆息
從師方未還

The poet's conveyance this time is a white deer, popular carrier, as we have noted, of earth-bound transcendents.[102] Progress is being made in his spiritual climb: this time he "ascends straight" to Heaven's Gate, arriving there quickly, in the second line of the poem. And he immediately meets a "plumed person," an angelic sylph whose "squared pupils" confirm his great age despite his youthful features.[103] This transcendent being wraps himself in clouds, wishing to avoid the poet's direct gaze. But he too, like the jade maidens of the preceding poem, turns over to Li Po an encouraging gift (again the verb is *wei*, "let fall"). It is a writing, and hence intrinsically more valuable than the auroral potion received in the first poem,[104] but it is indecipherable to him, being in "bird-track" script of ancient times (the earliest manuscripts were traditionally said to have been inspired by the observation of bird tracks). The poet is left sighing and frustrated: the path to transcendence is not as easy as it seemed to be at the end of the first poem. He needs the tutelage of a "master." He must persevere.

Poem three:

In the level light I climbed to the Belvedere of the Sun,

平明登日觀

[101] "Yu T'ai Shan," no. 2, *LTPCC*, 20.448.

[102] Curiously, one T'ang text says that Hsüan Tsung had ridden a white mule up the mountain for his *feng* rites. Cheng Ch'i 鄭棨 (d. 899), *K'ai-T'ien ch'uan-hsin chi* 開天傳信記, 2a (*T'ang-tai ts'ung-shu* 唐代叢書, 1806 ed.).

[103] *Yün-chi ch'i-ch'ien*, 19.19b, in a list of attributes attaching to each hundred years of a transcendent's existence, records that at 500 years of age the pupils of the eye become square.

104 See Robinet, *Méditation taoiste*, pp. 29–44, on the supreme importance of revealed writings in Taoism; also the comments of John Lagerwey, *Wu-shang pi-yao; somme taoiste du VIe siècle* (Paris: l'École Française d'Extrême-Orient, 1981), p. 38.

Raised my hand and opened up the barrier of clouds.
My germinal spirit lifted up four directions in flight,
As though emerging from between heaven and earth!

舉手開雲關
精神四飛揚
如出天地間

The Yellow River comes here from out of the west,
Winsome but withdrawn it passes into the distant hills.
Leaning against a high bank, I scanned the Eight Culmina;
Vision exhausted its limits, idling in lasting emptiness.

黃河從西來
窈窕入遠山
憑崖覽八極
目盡長空閑

By an odd chance then I beheld the Azure Lad,
His virid hair done up in twin cloud-coils.
He laughed at me for turning late to the study of transcendence;
My unsteadiness and unsureness have brought the fading of ruddy features.

偶然值青童
綠髮雙雲鬟
笑我晚學仙
蹉跎凋朱顏

Halting I stood and hesitant—suddenly he was gone from sight;
So careless and uninhibited—it is hard to pursue and detain him.[105]

躊躇忽不見
浩蕩難追攀

The very first line takes the poet to T'ai Shan's peak this time. The "Belvedere of the Sun" (*jih kuan* 日觀) is the southeast crest, from which the view of the rising sun was most spectacular.[106] We note that Li Po can now "open up the barrier of clouds" that in the preceding poem concealed the plumed person from him, and that

[105] "Yu T'ai Shan," no. 3, *LTPCC*, 20.448.

[106] Chavannes, *Le T'ai chan*, p. 60; also Li Fang 李昉, et al., *T'ai-p'ing yü-lan* 太平御覽 (Taipei: Hsin-hsing shu-chü, 1968), 39.5a, quoting Ying Shao's *Han kuan i* 漢官儀. A rhapsody on the Sun's Belvedere ("Jih-kuan fu" 日觀賦), composed by Ting Ch'un-tse 丁春澤 (*chin-shih* 775), is preserved in *Ch'üan T'ang wen*, 457.13b–14b.

his spirit—though not yet his body—is flightworthy now, its lift-off point "between heaven and earth" at the top of Mount T'ai. Gazing about, he sees the line of the Yellow River some two hundred *li* in the distance[107] and casts his sight even farther, to the extremes of the eight directions.

And now for the third time he is rewarded with an encounter with a celestial figure: no anonymous jade maidens or plumed persons this time, but the great Azure Lad himself.[108] We have met this deity before, as the "Father in the East" in one of Ts'ao Chih's poems on Mount T'ai. It is time now to take a closer look at him. As mentioned earlier, he is the male counterpart of Hsi Wang Mu, but that is the least of his attributes. He is known by a variety of alternate designations, among them "Lord Azure Lad, Supreme Minister" (*Shang-hsiang ch'ing-t'ung chün* 上相青童君), "Little Lord, Azure Lad" (*Ch'ing-t'ung hsiao-chün* 青童小君), "Little Lord, Azure Realized One" (*Ch'ing-chen hsiao-t'ung* 青眞小童), and "Royal Sire in the East" (*Tung wang kung* 東王公). In T'ao Hung-ching's 陶弘景 (456–536) systematized Taoist hierarchy, he delights in the resounding title "Lord Little Lad of Azure Florescence, King of the Eastern Sea, Master of the Lofty Dawn, Great Supervisor of Destinies, Supreme Minister of the Golden Pylons, Jade Conservator King of the Greatest Realization of Ninefold Tenuity" (*Chiu-wei t'ai-chen yü-pao wang chin-ch'üeh shang-hsiang ta szu-ming kao-ch'en shih tung-hai wang ch'ing-hua hsiao-t'ung chün* 九微太眞玉保王金闕上相大司命高晨師東海王青華小童君), and is highly placed among the most exalted divinities of the Heaven of Highest Clarity.[109] He resides in the Azure Palace of the Square [Moondew-] Speculum of Eastern Florescence (*Tung-hua fang-chu ch'ing-kung* 東

[107] Visible "like a belt" from the summit, according to Ying Shao. *T'ai-p'ing yü-lan*, 39.6b.

[108] As we shall see, he is rather more than the simple "fairy boy dressed in green" referred to by Waley, *loc. cit.* Like those of Belpaire (n. 90), Waley's remarks on these poems—indeed, on much of Li Po's poetic corpus—are defective largely because of his unfamiliarity with Taoist texts. It is a failing, alas, that mars nearly all modern studies on Li Po, whether Oriental or Western.

[109] *Tung-hsüan ling-pao chen-ling wei-yeh t'u* 洞玄靈寶眞靈位業圖 (HY 167), 3b.

華方諸青宮), located in the Eastern Sea.[110] He is, cosmologically, the lord of the principle of growth and fruition; doctrinally, he is one of the Shang-ch'ing deities most often involved in the transmission to lesser divinities and to human adepts of celestial texts and teachings.[111] Like Mount T'ai, then, he is associated with the east and is an intermediary between Heaven and Earth. His "virid hair" is a sign of his perpetual juvenescence, as are the "twin cloud-coils" in which his hair is bound (hair-coils being normal dress for a prepubescent boy). Unlike the jade maidens who had "suppressed" their smiles, he laughs openly at the opsimathic and already aging poet. But one senses that this is an encouraging mockery, a gentle goading, on the part of the Azure Lad, meant to prod the poet into greater seriousness in his Taoist studies. This is indeed the "master" Li Po "would follow," but again, at the conclusion of the poem, Li Po is left behind.

The meeting with the Azure Lad has, however, fortified the poet's will to pursue the path of transcendence. Some of the happy results are evident in poem four of the series:

Purified and purged for three thousand days, I strip plainsilk to copy the scriptures of the Way. Intoning and reciting I hold what I have won, As a host of spirits guards the physical form that is mine.	清齋三千日 裂素寫道經 吟誦有所得 衆神衛我形
Proceeding with the clouds, I trust to the lasting wind, Wafted on as though I'd spawned plumes and wings!	雲行信長風 颯若羽翼生

[110] His paradise domain is described in *Tung-chen shang-ch'ing ch'ing-yao tzu-shu chin-ken chung-ching* 洞眞上淸靑要紫書金根衆經 (HY 1304), 2.10b–13a; also *Tung-chen t'ai-shang pa-su chen-ching san-wu hsing-hua miao-chüeh* 洞眞太上八素眞經三五行化妙訣 (HY 1311), 9b–10b; and *Chen kao*, 9.20b–21b.

[111] A more detailed investigation of this divinity and his paradise realm may be found in Paul W. Kroll, "In the Halls of the Azure Lad," *Journal of the American Oriental Society* 105, no. 1 (1985) 75–94.

Clinging now to the high bank, I ascend the Sun's Belvedere;
Bending by the railing, I peer over the Eastern Gulf.

攀崖上日觀
伏檻窺東溟

A sheen on the sea animates the distant mountains;
The Cockerel of Heaven has already given his first call.
A silvery terrace emerges out of inverted luminescence,
Where white-capped waves roll over the long leviathan.

海色動遠山
天鷄已先鳴
銀臺出倒景
白浪翻長鯨

—Where is one to acquire the drug of immortality?
Fly away on high toward P'eng and Ying![112]

安得不死藥
高飛向蓬瀛

The poet has now at last committed himself to basic practices—purging and purifying his body and mind in long retreat, and diligently transcribing sacred texts. But what scripture is he "intoning and reciting" in the third line, that enables him "to hold what [he] has won," with "a host of spirits guard[ing his] physical form?" Although Li Po does not tell us, we can make a reliable guess. It is almost certainly the *Ta-tung chen-ching* 大洞眞經 or "Realized Scripture of the Great Grotto." This most fundamental text of the Shang-ch'ing revelation consists of verses and incantations in honor of thirty-nine celestial deities and the corollary (in point of fact, identical) corporal spirits that watch over the mortal gaps in one's body. Recitation of the text, accompanied with proper "visualization" techniques, serves to fixate these corporal spirits and close the fissures out of which one's vital forces slowly seep.[113] This is what Li Po is doing in the third and fourth lines. The *Ta-tung chen-ching* is a text that must be approached with great

[112] "Yu T'ai Shan," no. 4, *LTPCC*, 20.448–49.

[113] On the *Ta-tung chen-ching* (also called the *Shang-ch'ing ching* 上淸經), see Robinet, *Méditation taoiste*, pp. 151–160, and "La révélation du Shangqing," vol. 2, pp. 29–44.

reverence: when Wei Hua-ts'un 魏華存, a holy mistress of the fourth century A.D. who would eventually transcend her mortal state to be apotheosized as the divine "Lady of the Southern Marchmount" (*Nan-yüeh fu-jen* 南嶽夫人) and ranked in the Shang-ch'ing pantheon, was still studying on this earth, she was advised by the Azure Lad to recite this scripture but not before "purifying and purging" herself for five hundred days.[114] Considering the far less advanced state of our poet, it is not surprising that he should need "three thousand days" to refine himself sufficiently, before intoning the text.

With his physical form now secure (momentarily, at least) against decay, Li Po finds himself capable at last of bodily flight and soars off on the wind—a plumed person himself. His airborne journey takes him, of course, to the top of Mount T'ai. (Contrast this aerial ascent with the three earlier ones—carried by dragon or horse, by deer, and on foot.) By the Belvedere of the Sun he looks out upon the Eastern Sea, as he had done in the first poem. The "distant mountains" are the enchanted seamounts of P'eng-lai and Ying-chou, shimmering now in the first light of dawn upon the waters. "Inverted luminescence" (*tao ching* 倒景) is a phrase used with two different referents in Li Po's poetic vocabulary. First, it describes the play of reflected sunlight on water, used this way in two of his poems.[115] Second, in two other poems, both with strong Taoist overtones,[116] it signifies the farthest realms of heaven, out beyond the stars, where the light of the heavenly luminaries is seen

[114] Li Fang 李昉, et al., *T'ai-p'ing kuang-chi* 太平廣記 (Peking: Wen-yu-t'ang shu-fang, 1934), 58.122b, quoting the *Chi hsien lu* 集仙錄 (that is, Tu Kuang-t'ing's *Yung-ch'eng chi-hsien lu* 墉城集仙錄, the extant version of which does not contain a biography of Wei Hua-ts'un) and the *Pen-chuan* 本傳 (presumably the lost *Nan-yüeh fu-jen nei-chuan* 南嶽夫人內傳). See E. H. Schafer, "The Restoration of the Shrine of Wei Hua-ts'un at Lin-ch'uan in the Eighth Century," *Journal of Oriental Studies* 15, no. 2 (July 1977) 124–137, for a discussion of the lady's career, the sources of her biographies, and a translation of one account of her life and transcendence (which does not include the *Ta-tung chen-ching* incident) by the T'ang writer Yen Chen-ch'ing 顏眞卿.

[115] "T'ung yu-jen chou hsing," *LTPCC*, 20.451; "Ch'un-jih p'ei Yang Chiang-ning chi chu-kuan yen Pei-hu kan ku tso," *LTPCC*, 20.455.

[116] "Ku feng," no. 20, *LTPCC*, 2.56; "Ch'ou Ts'ui Wu lang-chung," *LTPCC*, 19.427.

reversed.[117] In the present context Li Po seems to have combined these two meanings neatly: while the terrace of P'eng-lai appears to emerge out of the aqueous glimmer of the Eastern Sea, it is also true that P'eng-lai is a celestial paradise beyond the world we know. (Indeed, some late illustrations show the island floating in the air above the ocean or, again, placed upon an elongated pedestal whose base is below the waves but whose capital is in the heavens.) The "long leviathan" is the great sea-monster that was said to guard jealously the oceanic approaches to P'eng-lai.[118] The extraordinary nature of the view taken in by the poet in lines 10–12 is emphasized phonetically in the original text by the fact that the last word of the odd-numbered line 11 ("luminescence" 景, Middle Chinese **kyăng*), which should not be a rhyme-word, here does match the proper rhyme-words of lines 10 ("call" 鳴, **mywăng*) and line 12 ("leviathan" 鯨, **gyăng*). This unusual phonetic correlation, although not strictly acceptable in the canons of *shih* poetry, serves to lay a special stress on these three lines. Surely this is a conscious action on Li Po's part to make the lines sound as unusual as is the scene they describe. The poem closes with Li Po's voice hopeful and assured. He is ready to journey on to paradise.

Poem five begins with the poet still on T'ai Shan's summit:

The Belvedere of the Sun inclines north and east; Its pair of high banks—twinned stone hemmed about. The sea's waters drop away before one's eyes; The sky's light spreads far in the cyan-blue of the void.	日觀東北傾 兩崖夾雙石 海水落眼前 天光遙空碧
A thousand peaks, vying, throng and cluster round; A myriad straths are cut off from traverse and transit.	千峯爭攢聚 萬壑絕凌歷

[117] This is the normal sense of the term in Taoist literature.

[118] Li Po mentions it in three other poems: "Ku feng," no. 3, *LTPCC*, 2.45; "Ku yu so-szu," *LTPCC*, 4.119; "Tseng seng Chao-mei," *LTPCC*, 12.306.

Thread-thin in the distance, that transcendent on his crane—	緬彼鶴上仙
Upon departing he left no tracks among the clouds.	去無雲中跡
Long pines enter here into the Empyreal Han,	長松入霄漢
The "distant view" is now no more than a foot away.	遠望不盈尺
The mountain's flowers are different from those in the human realm—	山花異人間
In the fifth month they are white amidst the snows.	五月雪中白
—I am bound in the end to come upon An-ch'i,	終當遇安期
Refining at this very place the liquor of jade.[119]	於此鍊玉液

This poem is something of a pendant to the preceding piece, furnishing a description of the proximate scene, to balance the remote vista of poem four. Only a few remarks are necessary. We should note the emphasis in these lines on the solitary, removed, and superb qualities of Mount T'ai. It is sundered from all other mountains and valleys, its peak but a foot away from the "Empyreal Han" (i.e., the sky river, our Milky Way). The fifth-month snows on its lofty slopes are an indication of its extreme height (the summer sun cannot warm its crest)[120] and also, even more importantly, an image of T'ai Shan's true crystalline nature, akin to the cold, white, celestial palaces of which it has become a visible, reachable simulacrum.[121] It is here that the poet feels confident that he shall encounter An-ch'i 安期, the mysterious alchemist of classical times. A seller of drugs in Lang-yeh 瑯琊 during the Ch'in

[119] "Yu T'ai Shan," no. 5, *LTPCC*, 20.449.

[120] Interestingly, the *Tai shih*, 3.6a, comments that in the fifth and sixth months of the year one must still wear cold-weather, quilted clothing on the mountain, as the climate is like that of deepest autumn.

[121] The symbolism of snow on holy mountains has been explicated, with special reference to Mao Shan, in Schafer's *Mao Shan in T'ang Times*, pp. 33–35.

dynasty, An-ch'i was reported to have had an audience—which stretched on for three days and nights—with Ch'in Shih Huang when that monarch was on his way to sacrifice at T'ai Shan (!). After this meeting with the prince of men, he took leave of the world, announcing that thereafter he was to be looked for on P'eng-lai.[122] His ingestion of a personally compounded potion of "liquor of gold" is mentioned by Ko Hung;[123] this elixir enabled him to live a thousand years on earth. An-ch'i is one of the figures most closely associated with the tradition and transmission of this famous "liquor of gold" (*chin i* 金液),[124] so it is a bit puzzling to have Li Po identifying him with the "liquor of jade" (*yü i* 玉液). But the two phrases are virtually interchangeable in T'ang poetic diction, the primary image in either case being the quality of incorruptibility imparted by the mineral-based elixir. Here again the poem closes on a highly expectant note, as did the last. But now the poet has discerned the true nature of Mount T'ai—it is itself a transcendent paradise; it is "at this very place" that An-ch'i and others of his kind are to be found.

We turn finally to poem six:

At sunup I drank from the Royal Mother's pool, In the gloaming took refuge by the pylons of Heaven's Gate. In solitude I held close the Green Tracery zither, At nighttime strode out in moonlight on the azure mountain.	朝飲王母池 暝投天門闕 獨抱綠綺琴 夜行青山月
The mountain was luminous—moonlit dew was white; The night was still—the pine-tree wind had died away.	山明月露白 夜靜松風歇

[122] *Lieh-hsien chuan*, 1.14b–15a; also *Pao-p'u tzu nei-p'ien*, 13.3a/b. In T'ao Hung-ching's official hierarchy, An-ch'i holds a place in the sphere of Grand Culmen (*t'ai-chi* 太極), just below Highest Clarity. *Tung-hsüan ling-pao chen-ling wei-yeh t'u*, 8b.

[123] *Pao-p'u tzu nei-p'ien*, 3.5b; the recipe for this elixir is recorded by Ko Hung at 4.9b–10b.

[124] Robinet, "La révélation du Shangqing," vol. 1, pp. 10–11.

Transcendent persons were roaming the cyan
peaks;
From place to place songs of reed-organs
issued forth!

仙人遊碧峯
處處笙歌發

In subdued stillness I took pleasure in the
clear candescence,
As Jade Realized Ones linked up on the
halcyon heights.
The image imagined—a dance of phoenixes
and simurghs;
Tossing and swirling—in raiment of dragon
and tiger.

寂靜娛清輝
玉眞連翠微
想象鸞鳳舞
飄颻龍虎衣

Touching the sky, I plucked down the
Gourd[-star];
Distracted and delirious, reflecting not on
my return.
Lifting my hand, I swished it in the clear
shallows,
And inadvertently caught hold of the
Weaving Maid's loom!

捫天摘匏瓜
恍惚不憶歸
舉手弄清淺
誤攀織女機

—Next morning I sat in forfeit of it all;
Only to be seen—pentachrome clouds
floating away.[125]

明晨坐相失
但見五雲飛

In this culmination of Li Po's T'ai Shan experience the time of a full day (from one morning to the next) is contained, just as the entire spatial expanse of the mountain (from the Royal Mother's Pool at its base to Heaven's Gate at its peak) is traversed. To begin with, let us note the symbolic appropriateness of the place-names mentioned in the opening couplet. It is fitting that the poet begin this final ascent from the "Royal Mother's Pool":[126] as we saw at the conclusion of poem five, he seems sure now of his elect status and is consequently able to picture himself as starting out from—instead of merely ending at—a paradisal spot. Twilight finds him, in the

[125] "Yu T'ai Shan," no. 6, *LTPCC*, 20.449.

[126] Chavannes, *Le T'ai chan*, pp. 87–88.

second line, settling in on the threshold of Heaven. This is the first time the poet has been on T'ai Shan at night: the place is transformed as—he imagines—he is too.

Evening begins with Li Po going out for a stroll on the peak, where he intends to amuse himself with some solitary music on the zither he brings along. The zither itself is no ordinary one; it is the famous instrument, called "Green Tracery" (*lü-ch'i* 綠綺), that had belonged to Ssu-ma Hsiang-ju 司馬相如 (179–117 B.C.), the magnificent rhapsodist of Han times.[127] The scene is quiet—luminous and white. Even the wind in the pines, which we recall had sounded with a "poignant" voice in the first poem of the series, has subsided. But suddenly the poet is aware of other night-roamers on the mountain and of sounds *behind* the silence—the pipings of transcendent music! This shift of consciousness is deftly enhanced by Li Po with a shift of rhyme at this point (there are no rhyme-changes within any of the other poems); and it is a major modulation, across the binary division of deflected and level tones (in this case, from M.C. **-ăk* to **-ĕi*), not merely a change of homotonic rhyme-groups.[128]

The festive gathering of "Jade Realized Ones" witnessed by the poet appears to him—as did his vision of P'eng-lai's terrace in poem one, which was the catalyst of his initial meeting with the "jade maidens"—as a fixed mental image or conjuration. This nocturnal celebration resembles in part the merriment described in the *Chen kao* as enjoyed by the fortunate residents of the Azure Lad's domain: when those transcendent beings, whose bodies have the brightness of gold and jade, play their reed-pipes in concert, all kinds of animals come to dance before them and phoenixes harmonize their voices with the sounds of the heavenly orchestra.[129] But our poet is not to be a mere observer; he must join in the celestial revel. And he is now capable of doing just that. He can

[127] Fu Hsüan 傅玄 (217–278), "Ch'in fu" 琴賦, *Ch'üan Chin wen* 全晉文, 45.5b, in *Ch'üan Shang-ku San-tai Ch'in Han San-kuo Liu-ch'ao wen* 全上古三代秦漢三國六朝文 (1886 ed.).

[128] As will be evident, I accept the rhyme variants in lines two and four given in the Miao Yüeh-ch'i 繆曰芑 edition of the text; see *Li T'ai-po wen-chi* 李太白文集, 17.9a.

[129] *Chen kao*, 9.21b.

"touch the sky" and pulls down the asterism of the "Gourd" (our Delphinus) for a wine-stoup. Delirious with joy, he thinks no more of the vulgar world below, at home now in the celestial regions. He swishes his fingers playfully in the Heavenly River's "clear shallows." But, quite by accident, he overturns the sidereal loom of the Weaving Maid. (It is instructive here to note the precision of Li Po's stellar geography: the "Gourd" [Delphinus] hangs to one side of the Heavenly River [the Milky Way], directly opposite the location of the "Weaving Maid" [our Vega] on the other side. If one were to flick his hand across the course of the sky river from the site of the Gourd-star he would indeed risk catching a fingernail on the Weaver's loom.) With this unwitting blunder, the poet's wonderful vision, the fantastic revel, dissolves into nothingness. When dawn arrives he is forlorn, the only reminder of the night's Elysian gaiety the rainbow-hued clouds that now drift away from the mountain. Although this final work of Li Po's sequence on T'ai Shan has seen the poet successfully enter the realm of the transcendents, his careless behavior there has cast him out again. As he himself anticipated in the first poem, he is in the end "not of a transcendent's caliber."[130]

Despite the fond desires of the New Critics, no poem exists completely in a vacuum. While we may rightly fault (as it has lately become fashionable to do) the bulk of traditional Chinese criticism for its predominantly biographical approach that diverts critical attention from the text itself, this ought not to lead us into making the equally parochial mistake of assuming we can understand a medieval poem properly without resort to all manner of extra-poetic materials. It is the most grievous critical myopia to suppose that, in studying medieval Chinese verse, we need only read poetic texts or belletristic writings. We must rather seek to know as much as possible about the *entire* cultural context of medieval times, that real and multi-faceted world in which our poets had their being.

The study of literary history alone is not enough for this en-

[130] For two further studies of Li Po's use of Taoist motifs in his poetry, see Kroll, "Li Po's *Rhapsody on the Great P'eng-bird*," *Journal of Chinese Religions* 12 (1984), 1–17, and "Li Po's Transcendent Diction," *Journal of the American Oriental Society* 106, no. 1 (1986), 99–117.

deavor; we also must become familiar with the social, material, and, especially, religious history of the times. I say especially religious history (including scriptures and liturgies, hymns and hagiographies, filiations, etc.), because it is the area that has been most ignored by students of Chinese literature—even though, as we are beginning to realize, it was of the most profound importance to medieval poets. The present essay represents a mere excursion into the overlapping terrains of medieval Chinese poetry and religion. Whole continents remain to be opened up or, in some cases, extensively recharted. Only when we possess both territories will we begin to see the magic and dignity of individual poems in their true fullness.

Ching-hsien Wang

The Nature of Narrative in T'ang Poetry

I. Origins

Narrative poetry constitutes a significant category of T'ang literature. Here social concerns, intellectual judgment, and artistic sensitivity find effective expression in a comprehensive form to define momentous events in plot. The general nature of narrative is complex; and it is particularly so in T'ang poetry, which is most famous for its unyielding lyricism. To investigate the nature of narrative in T'ang poetry, therefore, we will inevitably attend to the nature of that lyricism and, with due caution, we may have to question the meanings commonly attributed to both. I do not intend to rewrite the definition of T'ang lyricism, but I will attempt to examine the origins, essence, and scope of narrative poetry by looking at the conventional differences drawn between various literary genres, lyric poetry included. I aim to reconsider the validity of established definitions and to propose a preliminary principle of generic distinction from which a creative reading of poetry may proceed.

The primordial origin of T'ang narrative poetry can be traced back to the comprehensive and forthright style of the *Shih ching* 詩經: the technique *fu* 賦 (narrative display), in contrast with *pi* 比 (direct metaphor) and *hsing* 興 (indirect metaphor). While the term *fu* had existed in *Shih ching* scholarship ever since the "Great Preface" 大序 took its shape, probably during the Later Han 後漢 period, it did not function as a note on poetic technique, as *hsing* did, until Chu Hsi 朱熹 (1130–1200) used it to describe the rhetorical style of *Shih ching* 2 葛覃.[1] This poem falls into three stanzas. In

[1] For the early definitions of *fu* as it is written out in the "Great Preface" to *Shih ching* and further in the "Grand Master" 大師 and "Lesser Master" 小師 in *Chou Li*

the first, the poet, assuming the voice of a woman, sings of a certain creeping plant and of orioles, with plentiful images pertinent to their beauty. In the second stanza the quality of the plant itself is developed by specifying its use—its suitability for making cloth for dresses, of which she will never tire. The last stanza picks up the image of the dresses, which she is washing and arranging in preparation to leave for her parents' home to make her first ceremonial visit after the wedding. According to Chu Hsi, each stanza is composed in the style of *fu*.[2] When we look at the three stanzas closely, however, we find that they are somewhat different, both in terms of technique and intent. The first stanza, with its lavish presentation of two objects free from any action taken by the persona, is *fu* in the sense of a "display." The second stanza turns the display of natural objects to a statement of purpose and allows the persona to interfere by passing judgment on the material value of one of the objects. Finally, in the third stanza, the straightforward telling of an event relates the action the persona takes—it is *fu* in the sense of "narration."

In this poem we can appreciate the principal mode of narrative poetry in the Chinese tradition: a mixture of narration and display, and also of the participation of a persona, assessing the object in the *display* in order to anticipate its full operation in the *narration*. There are some variations. When the poet assumes the role of the persona, as in *Shih ching* 58 氓, the development of the story conforms to more restrictive definitions: narrative poetry involves a complete plot with appropriate characters, including the poet-persona or narrator. Consequently, it also reveals the problem of "point of view," as does any narrative.[3] Yet even in this more conventional narrative aspect, *Shih ching* 58 is unique: the poet leaves the plot in the third stanza to indulge in a highly emotional utterance of self-pity and, in the sixth, she turns from her role as narrator to become

---

周禮, see Shih-hsiang Chen, "The *Shih ching*: Its Generic Significance in Chinese Literary History and Poetics," *Bulletin of the Institute of History and Philosophy* (hereafter *BHIP*) 39, pt. 1 (1969) 381, n. 33.

[2] Chu Hsi 朱熹, *Shih chi-chuan* 詩集傳 (rpt. Taipei: I-wen yin-shu-kuan, 1970), 1.5b–6b, pp. 10–12.

[3] Cf. Robert Scholes and Robert Kellogg, *The Nature of Narrative* (Oxford: Oxford University Press, 1966), p. 240.

a suppliant, addressing her husband directly and thus closing the poem in a murmuring tone. These different stances make the poem both narrative and lyrical, and perhaps even dramatic. Similar to the narrator of *Shih ching* 58, but still more astonishing, is the poet of *Shih ching* 237 緜, an omniscient narrator of a great epic adventure undergone by ancestors in time past. After singing of the tale at length, consistently in the third person, the poet, before he finishes singing, suddenly steps forward to identify himself to the audience. On the other hand, when the poet assumes the role of observer and offers a "display" of what he sees, as in *Shih ching* 281 潛, he does not limit himself simply to cataloguing; the poet comments on the ritualistic and symbolic values of the fish according to a definite point of view. The same practice is found in a powerful poem of display, *Shih ching* 297 駉. The poem is essentially a catalogue of horses, and yet the catalogue is gracefully intensified in a steady intent to offer praise. The display is characteristic of early narrative poetry in the art of *fu*, and the crescendo of praise, moreover, is so markedly picturesque that it is comparable to Pindaric lyricism with its "vigorous, weighty, and dignified" verses.[4]

The origins of narrative poetry are also found in the expansive, allegorical mode of the *Ch'u tz'u* 楚辭 songs. From these sources, in particular, T'ang poetry derives its psychic, mythical dimension, traversing the realistic world to discover fantastic realms. The sequential structure of the *Chiu ko* 九歌, for instance, provides a comprehensive frame for the depiction of an even greater variety of personae, presented in a strong dramatic movement. In its elaborate depiction of gods and spirits, it not only extends the scope of poetic display, but also deepens the psychological meaning of the rite by putting stress on the mutual approach of man and the supernatural, on a yearning for contact, and on the eventual failure of the quest which, in turn, always serves as the climax of the narrative. Moreover, in the *Li sao* 離騷 the complex progress of Ch'ü Yüan 屈原 (ca. 340–278) adds to the complement of Chinese poetic narrative a new dimension of allegorical structure, joined with a

[4] Dionysius of Halicarnassus, *De Compoitione Verborum*, c. 22. The English translation is from a quote in *The Odes of Pindar Including the Principal Fragments*, ed. Sir John Sandys (Cambridge: Harvard University Press, The Loeb Classical Library, 1961), p. xvii.

strict, complete plot. Despite the unnecessary question in the meta-poetic exercises about Ch'ü Yüan's identity, the poem is complete in its own right, including a principal introduction of the hero, a flashback to his confrontations with other forces, a number of consultation scenes disclosing the philosophical basis of his anxiety, and several journeys through the ethereal and mundane levels of the universe.[5] Although its phases are not always balanced in length and depth, there is an unmistakable narrative progress depicted in the plot. In the *Li sao* we see the capacity of early Chinese narrative poetry to engage and provoke us by its rejection of linear symmetry without ever losing an organic harmony in structure. Moreover, when the poem calls for it, lyricism emerges to complement the narration. Another feature, equally salient in *Shih ching* poetry, is the ellipsis of information, making the active collaboration of the audience necessary to bring its imaginative world to full maturity.

A third origin of narrative poetry are the diverse categories of poetic literature since the Han period, including the *fu* 賦, *yüeh-fu* 樂府, and a new type of literary verse known to the T'ang poets as *ku-shih* 古詩. Strictly speaking, they are significant in the formation of T'ang narrative not because they created any new standard in imaginative literature, but because they made innovations on traditional forms established in *Shih ching* and *Ch'u tz'u*. In other words, they represent for T'ang poetry a point of historical reference rather than any aesthetic principle. As a poetic genre, *fu* draws upon the narrative display of *Shih ching* and the dynamic progress of *Ch'u tzu*, to take on a grand, erudite quality that expands into rhapsodic composition. This may take the form of discourse, depiction, lament, or eulogy to attend to the purpose of admonition inherent in the name. But it easily turns extravagant and trivial when the classical norms of narrative display and imaginary progress are misunderstood and abused. In retrospect, it seems that *yüeh-fu* and *ku-shih* together provided the most immediate

[5] The myth of Ch'ü Yüan has dwindled, in modern days, into the doubt as to whether he is himself the hero of his poetry. The doubt is repeatedly expressed in James J. Y. Liu's review of *China and the West: Comparative Literature Studies*, ed. William Tay et al. (Hong Kong: The Chinese University Press, 1980). Liu's statements were published in *Comparative Literature Studies* 18, no. 2 (1981) 201–207.

legacy to T'ang poets in their pursuit of narrative poetry. A revival of classical poetry, *yüeh-fu* involved either direct recording or literary imitation of the folk spirit, as it reflected the common impulse to express emotion and thought through poetic story-telling. The *ku-shih*, on the other hand, advanced steadily through both the poet's ambition to exhaust the classical models and his grasp of an immediate or "modern" sense of literary evolution so as to identify himself against a broader intellectual background. In both *yüeh-fu* and *ku-shih* we find the clear formative elements, as well as a variety of perennial themes, inherited from the narrative poetry of the *Shih ching* and *Ch'u tz'u*.

A logical conclusion, therefore, is that poetry before the T'ang, despite the diverse forms that evolved from one or more origins, tended markedly to narrative. Of the three classical devices of poetic composition exhibited in the *Shih ching*, as narrative display *fu* is more decisive than *hsing* and *pi*, and, along with the imaginary progress elevated by *Ch'u tz'u*, it contributed most greatly to the direction of narrative poetry in terms of tone, voice, and structure. Sometimes it takes as its primary goal the display of a plenitude of images, supported by an energetic force to complete the plot. Whenever appropriate, *fu* displays a definite tendency toward lyrical digressions, thus perpetuating the model of classical poetry as a standard of what was good and effective. Sometimes it revises the classical models, as it were, to formulate a story in verse, though it never surpasses many old traits born with the art. Nevertheless, the narrative quality of Chinese poetry was actually weakened, and almost destroyed, by the establishment of the phonetic, prosodic principles in the early sixth century. This development led to the rise of what is known as *chin-t'i shih* 近體詩 (modern-style poetry), including *lü-shih* 律詩 and a minor class of *chüeh-chü* 絕句, to which I will return later.

II. Essence

The mixed style of narrative display, which grew out of the *fu* technique of *Shih ching* poetry, became an enduring mode for the poet who sought to encounter social realities with an artistic capacity to both describe and assess. By using elements of the *fu* technique, usually in the form of conventional phraseology in which the substance of the event was presented, the poet had the freedom to draw in personal emotion, scholarly erudition, and philosophical concerns. He became, to a certain degree, both poet and historian. A few examples from the early T'ang will be sufficient to exemplify the advance of narrative poetry from the rhapsodic *fu* literature written since the Han dynasty (which we may call the "secondary *fu*") to the rebirth of a vital poetry inspired and supported by the classical mode of narrative display embedded in *Shih ching* (which we may call the "primary *fu*") and *Ch'u tz'u*.

"Composition on the Imperial Capital" 帝京篇, by one of the most audacious poets in Chinese history, Lo Pin-wang 駱賓王, attests to the strength of narrative display in the expression of historical judgment, social concerns, and poetic sensitivity.[6] The poem can be regarded as an early T'ang version of the traditional rhapsodic poems about capitals, abundant in the *Wen hsüan* 文選, developing, as it does, the subject in the order characteristic of those early writings.[7] It starts with a grandiloquent generalization of what an imperial capital is like, in terms of geographical layout, and then proceeds to elaborate on the pageantries of palaces and mansions, the extravagant life-style of nobles and commoners, with observations on the mutability of power and wealth. The sequence is concluded by a final lament full of conceits wrought from historical allusions. This technique elicited the observation that Lo Pin-wang, as did some of his contemporaries, adopts the art of the secondary *fu* to write *shih* (以賦爲詩).[8] However, the poem rises

[6] Lo's poetical works are collected in *Lo Pin-wang wen-chi* 駱賓王文集, 10 *chüan* (SPTK ed.). An annotated version of the poem in question is found in Fan K'uang 范况, *Chung-kuo shih-hsüeh t'ung-lun* 中國詩學通論 (rpt. Hong Kong: Shang-wu yin-shu-kuan, 1959), pp. 19–23. I follow Fan's text. For a partial translation and discussion of the poem, see Stephen Owen, *Poetry of the Early T'ang* (New Haven: Yale University Press, 1977), pp. 111–115.

[7] For some examples in English, see Xiao Tong, *Wen Xuan or Selections of Refined Literature, Volume One: Rhapsodies on Metropolices and Capitals*, trans. David R. Knechtges (Princeton: Princeton University Press, 1982).

[8] Wen I-to 聞一多, "*Kung-t'i shih te tzu-shu*" 宮體詩的自贖, in *Wen I-to ch'üan-chi* 聞一多全集, 4 vols. (Shanghai: K'ai-ming shu-chü, 1948), vol. 3-A, p. 17.

beyond the great complexity of the secondary *fu* to reach a stylistic clarity. Lo's parallelism is not restricted to the array of ornate phrases and weighty objects; it extends to the contrast of major and minor actions and, further, to that of numerical symbols.[9] An abstract, fluid quality is evident in this aspect of his poetry (*shih*) that differs from the static grandeur of the secondary *fu* about capitals. Although the parallelism of numbers seems to be a stylistic trait of *ku-t'i* poetry alone, it anticipates a significant technique also found in *chin-t'i* poetry, most saliently in the work of Tu Mu 杜牧 (803–852). The importance of the classical narrative display in the general revitalization of Chinese poetry is evident here.

Lo Pin-wang infuses life into the "Composition" primarily by adopting a definite, subjective tone in the passages where he comments on phenomena described externally. The tone is stern, supported by the vigorous verses, which are primarily heptasyllabic, in a continually complicating structure. When Li P'an-lung 李攀龍 (1514–1570) praises the heptasyllabic verse of the early T'ang for its vital style, he obviously refers to the poetry of Lo Pin-wang and Lu Chao-lin 盧照鄰.[10] Here, immediately after Lo Pin-wang writes about the prodigal life-style once practiced in the imperial capital, he steps forward, in the manner of a *Shih ching* poet, to announce:

Since antiquity glory and wealth have been compared to drifting clouds,	古來榮利若浮雲
Bane and boon are truly undistin- guishable in life.[11]	人生倚伏信難分

Moreover, in a later passage, he departs from the narrative to elaborate on this theme with examples from philosophical texts, histories, anecdotes, and folk songs. As he is closing the composition he suddenly bursts into an exclamation: "It is all over! Let us return!" 已矣哉，歸去來! The objectivist principle of the secondary *fu* on capitals, where at the most the author would let the rival personae

[9] Lo's maneuver of numbers is pointed out in *T'ang shih chi-shih*, ed. Chi Yu-kung 計有功 (SPTK ed.), 7.10b–11a.

[10] Li P'an-lung 李攀龍, in the "Preface" to his *T'ang shih hsüan* 唐詩選. See *Tō shih sen* 唐詩選, ed. Mekeda Makato 目加田誠 (Tokyo: Meiji shōin, 1973), p. 159.

[11] Fan, *Chung-kuo shih-hsüeh*, p. 21.

contend in an enthusiastic rhetorical dialogue, is replaced by a personal utterance derived from the emotional phrases of T'ao Ch'ien's 陶潛 (365–427) poem.[12] Lo Pin-wang's adoption of the two phrases attests to a subjectivist attitude toward the scenes and events which he has classified in the narrative display, redirects our attention to his own mind, and sets a manifest principle for the correct interpretation of his allusion to Chia I 賈誼 (201–169 B.C.). He emerges at the end of the poem to identify himself unashamedly with the most brilliant young man of Lo-yang 洛陽 nine centuries earlier, who was unjustly misunderstood in the imperial capital.

Lu Chao-lin wrote "A Reminiscence of Old Ch'ang-an" 長安古意 during the early T'ang period, when the return of the capital to Ch'ang-an suggested a proud analogy between the present dynasty and the glorious Han, whose capital had also been Ch'ang-an. Having once been *the Capital*, since the beginning of the Later Han dynasty Ch'ang-an had been rendered inferior to other cities. After six centuries of vicissitudes, it has become *the Capital* again. The identity of the T'ang with the Han is a convention in T'ang poetry, and the collective imagination of poets carefully documents the political and cultural dimensions which Ch'ang-an embodied during the Han. Lo Pin-wang's "Composition on the Imperial City" has its basis in the imaginary unity of the Han and T'ang capitals, and Lu Chao-lin's poem shows even more clearly the heavy burden assumed by the early T'ang poet.

"Reminiscence" is basically a narrative display of the capital in the past, as Lu Chao-lin imagines it should have been. Ch'ang-an is drawn in those elements found in earlier praise of the capitals: its avenues, chariots, mansions, and social activities. It likewise refers to the ultimate expression of the imperial dream: the golden columns and the dewpan, symbolic of the vanity of wealth and power in the face of time. Stylistically, however, the poem is rather free from the dense diction typical of the secondary *fu* since the

[12] T'ao Ch'ien writes at the end of his preface to "Kuei-ch'ü lai hsi tz'u" 歸去來兮辭: "Observing the events according to the direction of my mind, I have entitled the poem 'Kuei-ch'ü lai hsi.'" The text and some revealing comments are included in *T'ao Yüan-ming chüan* 陶淵明卷, 2 vols. (Peking: Chung-hua shu-chü, 1961), vol. 2, pp. 326–338. For a brilliant interpretation of the two phrases adopted by Lo Pin-wang, see especially p. 335.

Han dynasty (especially the Later Han), and it is even more lucid and transparent than Lo Pin-wang's "Composition." This is due apparently to Lu Chao-lin's profound appreciation of the mercurial style of *ku-shih* and *yüeh-fu*, especially such poems as Ts'ao Chih's 曹植 (192–232) "Composition on the Famed Capital" 名都篇. This reflects both the contrast with the parallelism of the secondary *fu* and also Lu's continued use of the mixed tone typical of the *Shih ching* narrative. The poet is not hesitant, for example, to offer lyrical amplification of a love theme woven from the images of fish (*pi-mu* 比目) and birds (*yüan-yang* 鴛鴦). These are so powerful in themselves in the development of the theme that the narrative seems, as is sometimes true of *Shih ching* poetry, to halt for a moment. However, as the familiar theme diffuses, the poem properly returns to the narrative display. Then, in a later passage, Lu Chao-lin writes, "A thousand outriders of the Royal Herald have arrived from the Han dynasty" 漢代金吾千騎來, thereby changing the prospect of the entire poem, as though time past had transformed into time present. The ghosts of the Han, invoked by poetic imagination (or in this case fantasy), enter the world of the T'ang to be met by the living host in Ch'ang-an. With the breakdown of a strict narrative about the Han, a songlike lyricism is generated to celebrate the identity of time past and present, when the masculine power of the past merges with the feminine beauty of the present to give birth to a new meaning of life and history. The scene points directly to the connotation of *ku-i* in the title of the poem, which is translated here as "reminiscence." There is a strong reminiscence of Han power in the procession of a thousand horsemen, who eventually relax their discipline in the competitive pursuit of voluptuous joy and resulting indignation.

All these are vanity. Lu Chao-lin summarizes the concept of mutability in the following lines:

The charm of things is seasonal; it will not stay—	節物風光不相待
Mulberry fields and green seas interchange in an instant.	桑田碧海須臾改
The golden stairs and jade halls of the past	昔時金階白玉堂

Have now been replaced by the blue pines only.[13] 即今惟見青松在

Thereupon he ends the poem with an affirmation of eremitism. Citing Yang Hsiung 揚雄 (53 B.C. to A.D. 18) as an exemplar of intellectual life, he gives an anagogical interpretation of the permanence of the solitary in contrast to all extravagant monuments and lavish pursuits. The impermanence of the historical Ch'ang-an should strike a warning to the present inhabitants of the city.

In a discussion of narrative display as an essential mode for blending the narrative and the lyrical, one cannot neglect Chang Jo-hsü's 張若虛 (ca. 683–740) "Spring River in the Flower Moon Night" 春江花月夜. Little is known about the poet, for whom we have only two extant poems. "Spring River" is so unique in structure and imagery that scholars never fail to mention it, if only briefly and sometimes cryptically, in their historical surveys of T'ang poetry.[14] I propose to take it as an example to illustrate the meaning of narrative display growing out of the folk *yüeh-fu* tradition, as opposed to Lo Pin-wang's "Composition," which is emancipated from the secondary *fu*, and Lu Chao-lin's "Reminiscence," which evolved from the literary *ku-shih*.

A *yüeh-fu* poem is, by nature, capable of the direct expression of emotion, the complete portrayal of a scene, and the narration of events. Like a good number of *Shih ching* songs, it develops meaning through direct or indirect metaphors; but it seems that more

[13] Lu Chao-lin 盧照鄰, *Lu Sheng-chih chi* 盧昇之集 (*Chi-fu ts'ung-shu* 畿輔叢書), 2.7a. All references to Lu's poem are made to this edition. The *Yu-yu-tzu chi* 幽憂子集 (SPTK ed.) presents an undesirable variant in the last line of the citation. For other interpretations of the poem, cf. Hans Frankel, *The Flowering Plum and the Palace Lady: Interpretations of Chinese Poetry* (New Haven: Yale University Press, 1976), pp. 130–143; and Stephen Owen, *Poetry of the Early T'ang*, pp. 105–111.

[14] The poem is collected in *Yüeh-fu shih chi* 樂府詩集, ed. Kuo Mao-ch'ien 郭茂倩 (SPPY ed.), 47.1b–2a. It is reprinted with Chang's second poem in *Ch'üan T'ang shih* 全唐詩, *chüan* 117. I follow the text in *Yüeh-fu shih chi*. See, for example, Wen I-to's enthusiastic comments in *Wen I-to ch'üan-chi*, vol. 3-A, pp. 20–22. Two extensive monographs on the poem have appeared recently: Cheng Chi-hsien, *Analyse formelle de l'oeuvre poétique d'un auteur des Tang: Zhang Ruo-xu* (Paris: Mouton, 1970); and Ch'ai Fei-fan 柴非凡, "Lun Chang Jo-hsü Ch'un-chiang hua-yüeh yeh" 論張若虛春江花月夜, *Wen-hsüeh p'ing-lun* (Taipei: Shu-p'ing shu-mu ch'u-pan-she, 1975), vol. 2, pp. 23–80.

often than not a *yüeh-fu* poem tends to present succinctly and inclusively a mood, a landscape, or a story without recourse to excessive, digressive figures of speech. The evolution of the tune-title, "Ch'un-chiang hua-yüeh yeh," as shown in the poems connected with it, exhibits some of the stylistic features of antecedents dating back to the Six Dynasties period. The simple displays of emotion, scenes, and events, primarily individual entities before the T'ang, are blended in the production of an artistic *tour de force*. In addition to Chang Jo-hsü's work, the *Yüeh-fu shih-chi* collects six poems under that common title, beginning with two quatrains by Emperor Yang of the Sui dynasty 隋煬帝 (r. 604–17).[15] The first is a rather static portrayal of an evening scene over the Yangtze: the spring flowers bloom, the ripples flow away with the moon, and the tides wash the stars back to the observer. The portrayal of the scene is complete, but, with the exception of an implicit passage of time, it presents no action as such. The second quatrain is composed in equally florid diction, with the first couplet depicting a night filled with scented, fragrant dew near a spring lake, wherein the moonlight fluctuates. In the second couplet the poet is inspired to think that such a romantic atmosphere is conducive to an idyllic, amorous meeting with certain goddesses. The introduction of a love theme markedly widens the scope of the poem, but the theme stays muted, to be developed only through an act of imagination. It does not grow into an event through which a plot, in its unfolding, might form the basis of a narrative.

The poem by Chu-ko Ying 諸葛穎, a poet-musician in Emperor Yang's court, is almost identical with the first quatrain mentioned above. Even the two pieces by Chang Tzu-jung 張子容, a contemporary of Chang Jo-hsü, are based on the mood and diction of the Sui emperor's poem, each following its precedent faithfully (except for expanding the length from the four-line structure into a kind of awkward hexastitch). In this historical and literary context,

[15] (A) 暮江平不動, 春花滿正開. 流波將月去, 潮水帶星來. (B) 夜露含花氣, 春潭瀁月暉. 漢水逢遊女, 湘川値兩妃. For an excellent search into the original type of the tune "Ch'un-chiang hua-yüeh yeh" prior to the Sui dynasty, see Ch'ai Fei-fan, "Lun Chang Jo-hsü," pp. 25–36. Of the six poems, the last one by Wen T'ing-yün 溫庭筠 (ca. 820–870) is evidently collected here by mistake; it should belong to the tune-title "Yü-shu hou-t'ing hua" 玉樹後庭花.

therefore, we see how Chang Jo-hsü's work is unusual and why it has always appealed to Chinese readers.[16]

"Spring River in a Flower Moon Night" is comprised of thirty-six heptasyllabic lines. Structurally it can be divided into two equal sections, each tightly linked by common tone and imagery. The first section (lines 1–18) is further divided into two parts, switching gradually with the introduction of a mood in the landscape, in preparation for the theme to appear in the second section (lines 19–36). The first ten lines establish a familiar scene, derived from the Sui verses, which the poet describes exhaustively with all the best figurative images in a cyclic arrangement. The spring tides are as brimful and high as the ocean, from which the moon rises to flood the scene, including the spring river, which in turn flows around the flowering gardens under the moonlight. Bright as sleet and quiet as frost, the moon makes the white sand on the islet fade away, mixing the sky and the river into an absolute clarity in which, again, there is the full, lonely moon. Here ends the first part of the first section, with the moon significantly qualified as a *lonely* disc high in the transparent sky. The pathetic fallacy marks a turn in the poem from an objective portrayal of the scene to the expression of emotion. Indeed, in line 11 the poet begins to suggest the lamentable fact that, enveloped in such a beautiful scene, there is always someone struck by grief in the expectation of a returning boat. Line 18, the end of the first section, ushers in the note of *grief* to pave the way for the large-scale narrative in the second section. Up to this point, however, Chang Jo-hsü has only amplified the traditional modes set up by the Sui poets; the first part is equivalent to Emperor Yang's first quatrain and the second to his second quatrain.

It is in the second section that Chang Jo-hsü generates an emotionally charged event which widens and deepens the common theme of "Ch'un-chiang hua-yüeh yeh," elevating it, in a sense, from a conventional exercise of poetic diction to a poignant narrative display about a woman's sorrowful anticipation of the re-

[16] A modern appraisal by Wang Chung 汪中 speaks for the traditional reader's fascination with it. See *Yüeh-fu shih chi* 樂府詩紀 (Taipei: Hsüeh-sheng shu-chü, 1968), pp. 166–167.

turning boat. The second section of the poem both continues the florid imagery and dreamlike tone established at the outset and shifts the poem from picturesque to narrative, as it portrays in detail a lonely woman with thoughts about the past, a resentment of the present, and a faint wish for the future. There is a "plot" involved in the lines, though it may be more implicit than explicit. The poem is no longer concerned simply with the landscape, nor is it operating through empathy. It concentrates on the presentation of a familiar story about a longing woman enclosed in a courtyard or tower, a theme treated repeatedly in *yüeh-fu* poetry before and after Chang Jo-hsü.[17] The poem is, consequently, infused with a strong psychological meaning in an increasingly broadening dimension. By the presentation of a longing woman and a presumably returning boat, the five elements in the tune-title are no longer composite images, but substantive elements in the narrative. As spring quickens thoughts of love, so do the flowers; the river is the thoroughfare from which the boat may appear. The night is still and lonely, but the moon shining all over the world brings two souls together by its all-encompassing power.

The essence of narrative poetry is, therefore, discernible in the various types of narrative display. It grows out of different genres of pre-T'ang poetry, including the secondary *fu*, the literary *ku-shih*, and *yüeh-fu* (or the folk *ku-shih*), the latter two commonly classified as *ku-t'i shih* 古體詩 (ancient-style poetry). One of their most salient common stylistic features is found in the blending of narrative and lyrical elements in a single composition.

In comparison with modern-style poetry, the ancient-style appears to be more inclined to narrativity. This is true not only of T'ang poetry, but of Chinese poetry in general, ever since the distinction was made. A long poem written in the ancient style is clearly provided with the mechanisms necessary to develop a plot and with the other elements required of the narrative. If the ancient style is employed to determine structure and tone, even when the poem is relatively short and compact, it often contains a quasi-narrative quality. The three poems examined above are each

[17] E.g., "Yin ma ch'ang-ch'eng k'u hsing" 飲馬長城窟行(青青河邊草); Li Po 李白, "Ch'ang-kan hsing" 長干行.

extensive narratives in their own way. The quasi-narrative is found in both pentasyllabic and heptasyllabic ancient-style poems, even when they are relatively short. First, there is "Mountain Rock" 山石 by Han Yü 韓愈 (768–824). As an ancient-style poem, it is comprised of twenty heptasyllabic lines telling of a rare experience in mobile style. The poet specifies the time of day he arrived at the monastery, yesterday in the evening. In his abundant description of the small world, we are to infer from the vegetation that the monastery is in south China. He tells of observing some obscure Buddhist drawings (probably a value judgment as well, considering the poet's resentment of Buddhism). The night is extremely quiet, and the moon shining through the window into his chamber is bright. He leaves the monastery at dawn, venturing into the exotic atmosphere created by mist, colorful hills and streams, huge pines and oaks, and is inspired by the wilderness to express the daring lyricism of the concluding passage:

Life is certainly enjoyable in this way:	人生如此自可樂
Why is it necessary to be pent, controlled by others?	何必局促爲人鞿
Alas, for the two or three of us!	嗟哉吾黨二三子
But shall we not be returning home in old age?[18]	安得至老不更歸

Following this extended narrative, the lyrical expression is distinct. It is filled with more poetic, historical, and philosophical allusions than the other part of the poem.

A similar quasi-narrative can be detected in "Coming Across Feng Chu in Ch'ang-an" 長安遇馮著 by Wei Ying-wu 韋應物 (ca. 737–791). Feng Chu has arrived from the east, his clothes wet with the rain of Pa-ling. The poet asks him why he should bother to come into town, and he replies: "To clear the hills I need to buy some axes." Looking around, they see that flowers are blooming among the dense foliage and young swallows are flying agilely in the air:

[18] Han Yü 韓愈, *Han Ch'ang-li chi* 韓昌黎集 (rpt. Hong Kong: Shang-wu yin-shu-kuan, 1964), 3.1–2.

We bade farewell to each other last year. It is spring again:	昨別今已春
See how much gray hair has grown on our temples![19]	鬢絲生幾縷

The narrative is incomplete, but notwithstanding there is an inferable story behind the poem. As the poet proceeds with a highly intimate exchange of thoughts with his friend, the story unfolds itself gradually: Feng Chu left for a hermit life in the hills a year ago, when the poet saw him for the last time, and the place he has supposedly lived is east of the city. In a poem as short as this one, there is a progression of time and space, all condensed in precise images charged with unmistakable emotion, telling a tale about the conflict of life-styles and fear of aging.

The essence of narrative is, finally, to be appreciated in a type of *chüeh-chü*, which, for all its artistic intent and technique, is understood here as "ultimate verse."[20] While some scholars may regard it as a verse form split from *lü-shih* (regulated verse), and consequently label it modern-style poetry, Fan K'uang dismisses the assumption categorically.[21] Originated in the Six Dynasties quatrain, "ultimate verse" proliferates in several types as it was adopted and refined by the T'ang poets. An "ultimate verse" is far-reaching and demanding, but it is often indirect and implicit, and usually more suggestive than descriptive. Of the four lines (either penta- or heptasyllabic) that define its length, there may be an antithetical couplet in strict parallelism or, occasionally, even two. However, an "ultimate verse" can also be completely free from parallelism, and

[19] Wei Ying-wu 韋應物, *Wei Su-chou chi* 韋蘇州集 (rpt. Taipei: Shang-wu yin-shu-kuan, 1965), *chüan* 5, pp. 237–238. The dates of Wei Ying-wu are disputable. I follow Fu Hsüan-ts'ung 傅璇琮, *T'ang-tai shih-jen ts'ung-k'ao* 唐代詩人叢考 (Peking: Chung-hua shu-chü, 1980), p. 276.

[20] For some relevant discussions on the artistic intent and technique of *chüeh-chü*, and for different interpretations of the term, see, e.g., Liu Hsi-tsai 劉熙載, *I kai* 藝概 (rpt. Taipei: I-wen yin-shu-kuan, 1969), 2.14a–14b.

[21] Fan K'uang, *Chung-kuo shih-hsüeh t'ung-lun*, p. 80. Cf. also, Wang Yün-hsi 王運熙, "Han Wei Liu-ch'ao yüeh-fu tui Li Po te ying-hsiang" 漢魏六朝樂府對李白的影響, in *Li Po shih lun ts'ung* 李白詩論叢 (Hong Kong: Wen-yüan shu-wu, 1962), pp. 94–95.

it can run on in four syntactically independent, solid lines. In this particular type of "ultimate verse," which proceeds freely without reliance on sophisticated parallelism and which is structurally derived from *ku-shih* and *yüeh-fu*, we can discern a strong narrative quality in the perfect planning of the poem. This type of "ultimate verse" belongs properly to the category of ancient-style poetry. Given its narrative vitality and scope, I propose to call it the "dynamic quatrain."

Li Po 李白 (701–762) writes "Setting out from Po-ti City at Dawn" 早發白帝城 in "ultimate verse" without recourse to antithetical parallelism.[22] It is dynamic and action-filled, as suggested in the powerful, successive lines, without halting to elaborate on poetic diction. The poet left Po-ti at dawn and, as he was going aboard, turned his head around for a last view of the city on high, which he found veiled in colored clouds. The journey downstream was rapid: in a day he has gotten back to Chiang-ling, a thousand *li* away, and he realizes that while the cries of the monkeys along the river banks remain hauntingly in his mind, the boat has already passed through myriad gorges. The tempo of the poem is furiously fast, but the poetry it achieves is calm and graceful. This demanding form encourages the poet to be suggestive and, through an indirect method, to attain the highest density and speed possible in a poem. The essence of narrative is revealed in the completion of an experience, a plot, expressed in the fast succession of energetic and original phrases. The nature of the "dynamic quatrain" is equally manifest in some of the six poems entitled "Songs Below the Frontier" 塞下曲 by Lu Lun 盧綸 (ca. 748–799), as they are collected in the *Yüeh-fu shih chi*.[23] The most dynamic of them is the

[22] 朝辭白帝彩雲間，千里江陵一日還；兩岸猿聲啼不住，輕舟已過萬重山. See *Fen-lei pu-chu Li T'ai-po shih* 分類補注李太白詩, ed. Hsiao Shih-yün 蕭士贇 (rpt. Taipei: Shih-chieh shu-chü, 1962), 22.8b.

[23] *Yüeh-fu shi-chi*, 93.2a. The title and arrangement of the poems appear to follow the *Yü-lan shih* 御覽詩, ed. Ling-hu Ch'u 令孤楚 (765–836), reprinted in *T'ang-jen hsüan T'ang shih* 唐人選唐詩 (Peking: Chung-hua shu-chü, 1962), pp. 216–217. These poems are sometimes entitled differently in other collections and anthologies. For other discussions on the poem quoted below, see Yu-kung Kao and Tsu-lin Mei, "Meaning, Metaphor, and Allusion in T'ang Poetry," *Harvard Journal of Asiatic Studies* 38, no. 2 (1978), 305–306; and Stephen Owen, *The Great Age of Chinese Poetry: The High T'ang* (New Haven: Yale University Press, 1981), pp. 278–279.

one that follows:

The woods are dark, grasses startled by the wind:	林暗草驚風
The general drew his bow by the night.	將軍夜引弓
At daybreak we went to retrieve the white arrow,	平明尋白羽
And found it sunk deep in a mighty rock.	沒在石稜中

The brevity of an "ultimate verse" does not limit the full development of a narrative, but turns it to extreme precision and solidity, with the typical ellipsis of superfluous details and an awesome suspension leading toward the eventual climax. In contrast with some of the other poems in the sequence, the poem above is more dynamic and akin to narrative poetry because it is free from parallelism. It uses a style close to *yüeh-fu*, as does Li Po's work cited earlier, that defies the principles of modern-style poetry represented eloquently by "regulated verse." In other words, an "ultimate verse" is not always ready for narrative; it can be static, picturesque, and lyrical too. It is only in the type of "dynamic quatrain" defined here that we find it embodying another essence of narrative in T'ang poetry.

III. Scope

While a narrative poem is centered on an event, in the case of T'ang poetry the event is not always presented through the objective delineation of any plot. Chinese poets are reluctant to undertake the sequential unfolding of a tale in detail. Rather, they bring forth the most momentous aspect of the event, linger over it, exhaust all its artistic and philosophical possibilities, and leave it when a principle of equilibrium is fulfilled, either thematically or stylistically. The ellipsis of information is not considered to be a defect in narrative or lyrical poetry: when artfully intended with taste and erudition, it forms the basis of an ideal agreement that poetry challenges before it delights.

In my search for the scope of narrative poetry, I seek to identify the furthest areas the poem can reach, or must reach, in order to discover and define a narrativity in the imaginative, intellectual world of the T'ang. At times a poem is narrative because it attends to an eventful world in the psyche; at times it can be narrative when linked with other works to become a group in a large structure. Historical and geographical references, of course, provide narrative perspectives for the poet to recount events. In other words, the areas toward which a poet reaches to identify his narrative can be abstract or concrete, in time or in space. It certainly happens, too, that a poet combines some or all of the different scopes in a single composition.

The psychic scope of T'ang narrative poetry is exemplified by Li Po's "Valediction: A Journey through Mount T'ien-mu in Dream" 夢遊天姥吟留別.[24] The T'ang convention of a valediction speaks to the sorrow of parting, embellished with a depiction of the present scene to which the poet expresses his emotional tie; it laments the remoteness of the place to which he goes as well as the uncertainty of a date for future reunion.[25] The poem by Li Po makes a major break with convention. This "Valediction" is comprised of three basic parts: an introduction briefly describes what lies ahead in the imagined direction of T'ien-mu; a main body relates the dream experience; and an end tells of his abrupt awakening, followed by his emphatic yearning to return to the dream world. The poem follows scarcely any device or motif relevant to the valediction, departing from the realistic to intensify the psychic aspect of poetic literature.

The introduction has immediate associations with the real Mount T'ien-mu, whose height is greatly exaggerated, and with the Ying-chou 瀛洲, a mythical, fairy island long part of the repertoire of Chinese imagination. Li Po admits that the latter is hard to seek; but the former, drifting in the clouds and mist in southeast China, may be reachable. The transformation of the real object to the mythical completes the preparation for a spiritual ascent to be narrated in the main body of the poem. The pivot of the poem is stressed in the two lines beginning the dream vision:

[24] *Fen-lei pu-chu Li T'ai-po shih*, 15.2a–3b.

[25] Fan K'uang, *Chung-kuo shih-hsüeh t'ung-lun*, pp. 150–151.

I wish to follow it in a dream to Wu
and Yüeh,
Flying by night over the moon of Lake
Mirror.

我欲因之夢吳越
一夜飛渡鏡湖月

However, the historical reminiscences in the area are haunting, especially those related to Hsieh Ling-yün 謝靈運 (385–433) and his exploits of the wilderness. Li Po, unable to overlook these historical realities, turns them ingeniously into a medium to bridge the real and the mythical. He traces the path taken by Hsieh in time past to approach the height in the space beyond common knowledge. Once there, Li Po, as though carried up to an ultimate peak of spiritual existence, lets go all his powerful imagination to portray the awesome landscape in a revitalized meter derived from the poetry of *Ch'u tz'u*, the archetype of Chinese poetry about spiritual soaring in the psychic domain. The style is perfectly compatible to the theme; the form and content merge into a unity. Although it is obvious, up to this point, that the poem savors of Sun Ch'o's 孫綽 (fl. 310) secondary *fu* on wandering into Mount T'ien-t'ai (upon which Li Po presumably looks as an antecedent in the creation of visionary writing), the T'ang poet goes beyond him. He depicts the landscape upon reaching the highest peak, as opposed to Sun's stylistic halt in order to devote himself to a complex discourse on Buddhist and Taoist philosophy.[26] Both Sun Ch'o's and Li Po's depictions of the landscape on high are grand and profound presentations of the individual poets' mental awareness of nature and life. However, whereas Sun Ch'o relaxes into expository prose on the concept of immortality and dilutes his work at its crucial point with excessive versification on morality, epistemology, and ontology, Li Po advances steadily through the passage in lucid language to an encounter with a host of the immortals themselves. A significant class of Chinese poetry is saved by the exploratory narrative style of Li Po set in the psychic scope.[27]

[26] "*Fu* on Wandering into Mount T'ien-t'ai" 遊天台山賦, in *Wen hsüan, chüan* 11.

[27] For an example of unfavorable criticism on the fashion represented by Sun Ch'o, see Chung Hung's 鍾嶸 preface to *Shih p'in* 詩品, in *Li-tai shih-hua* 歷代詩話, ed. Ho Wen-huan 何文煥 (rpt. Taipei: I-wen yin-shu-kuan, 1971), p. 7.

The adventure is signalled to end with another switch:

Suddenly my soul was agitated, my spirit shaken: 忽魂悸以魄動
I was startled to awake, dejected, with a long sigh. 怳驚起而長嗟

The awakening occurs abruptly in the middle of a list of visions, following the structure of *Li sao*, and breaks up the climactic appearance of the immortals as it brings the dream to an end. The mysterious world is gone, leaving the poet in bed. With reference to *Li sao* again, however, it is obvious that what Li Po refers to as a dream is not to be taken literally. Rather, the dream is a poetic dimension qualified by the poet's imagination to enable a flight into the visionary world; it is a stylistic device, as it is for Dante in *Divina Commedia*, to carry out an allegorical narrative in the psychic scope. The narrative ends where the dream ends. Consequently, Li Po concludes the poem with a return to the lyricism expected of a valediction. The acquired knowledge is that, having had such a contact with the spiritual elements, there is nothing in life more joyful than the pursuit of freedom in nature. The emphasis on spiritual abandon and personal integrity is an echo of the philosophy revealed in the earlier poems by such masters as Kuo P'u 郭璞 (277–324) and T'ao Ch'ien; and it is undoubtedly imitated by Han Yü in his quasi-narrative poem, "Mountain Rock," with the Taoist intention and psychic phenomena deleted.

A grand scope of narrative is achieved, too, in the structural unity of a sequence of poems. The best example in this respect is Tu Fu's "Autumn Meditations" 秋興.[28] This is a cycle of eight poems in heptasyllabic "regulated verse," the type of poetry least capable of generating and sustaining narrative. In its sophisticated lyricism, "regulated verse" is a sterling example of a form of modern-style poetry which, though endowed with a nearly perfect prosodic mechanism for the poet to exercise his literary craftsmanship in rhetoric and style, is also the force most destructive to the develop-

[28] *Tu shih ching ch'üan* 杜詩鏡詮, ed. Yang Lun 楊倫 (rpt. Taipei: Hsüeh-sheng shu-chü, 1971), 13.23b–26b.

ment of poetic narrative.[29] It is not my intention to devalue "regulated verse" here, since even the great effort made by Hu Shih 胡適 (1891–1962) to dismiss it as a serious poetic form has proved to be in vain.[30] Suffice it to say that the parallelism required of the two antithetical couplets (lines 3–4 and lines 5–6) effectively prevents the poem from narrative progression and turns it, instead, into an ideal stationary form for the presentation of the conceptual and picturesque phases of poetry. Accordingly, each piece in the "Autumn Meditations" cycle is a static, lyrical poem. Nevertheless, the eight poems may be linked together into a sequence (imaginably what Tu Fu would intend them to be) to achieve a structural scope demonstrating a part of the nature of narrative in T'ang poetry.

"Autumn Meditations" is composed of a number of contrasts, of time past and present, of place north and south, and of emotion *ethos* and *pathos*. Through these contrasts Tu Fu attains a comprehensive framework to set forth his interpretation of China in changing times, observed from a distance away in the south. Of the contrasts, the most poignant is, of course, his own fate illuminated in light of the national catastrophe. Thus the first poem is generally devoted to the description of time present, in such powerful images as dew, wounded maples, chilly air, and chrysanthemums, all marking the onset of autumn. The second locates the place in the south, where the poet "often relying on the dipper, gazes toward the capital." The third advances to lament his pathetic fate in terms of personal career, in sharp comparison with the success enjoyed by his friends, who "by the Five Mausoleums ride tall horses in their sleek cloaks." All the references up to this point are made to

[29] For recent examples of the positive appraisal of the "regulated verse" in T'ang poetry, see Ch'en Shih-hsiang 陳世驤, "Shih-chien yü lü-tu tsai Chung-kuo shih chih shih-i tso-yung" 時間與律度在中國詩之示意作用, *BIHP* 29, no. 2 (1958), 793–808; and, especially relevant to the present topic, Tsu-lin Mei and Yu-kung Kao, "Tu Fu's 'Autumn Meditations:' An Exercise in Linguistic Criticism," *Harvard Journal of Asiatic Studies* 28 (1968) 44–80.

[30] Hu Shih 胡適, *Pai-hua wen-hsüeh shih* 白話文學史 (rpt. Taipei: Hu Shih Chi-nien-kuan, 1969). See especially his criticism of Tu Fu's work in this category, pp. 299–302.

immediate, current factors: in autumn, a poet, alienated from the capital, sighs over his hardships. The rest of the cycle, five poems in all, takes up the construction of a large backdrop, against which these factors are further explicated and intensified to become a truly autobiographical narrative, intended to reflect the fate that had befallen China during the preceding decade. The complex interaction of these contrasts circumscribes an event and leads to the final portrait of the poet himself:

With this sparkling brush I once enlivened a scene:	綵筆昔曾干氣象
Chanting, gazing, I now grieve with a white head drooping.	白頭吟望苦低垂

The larger structure of "Autumn Meditations" is established in such a manner as to make the poems a significant narrative about the poet himself, set in a history of national turmoil. On the other hand, Tu Fu remains close to the smaller, relational structure of the poems in a sequence. The first poem, while stressing the symbolic meaning of autumn to set the melancholy tone of the narrative, draws to an end with the nostalgic sound of the pounding blocks in the Po-ti City, late in a dusky afternoon. The next poem picks up the effect of the passage of time: the setting sun slants behind the lone city of K'uei-fu, the Dipper gradually becomes visible, and the Milky Way, too, appears. Moreover, amidst the poet's anguished thoughts of the past and the present, the moon has stealthily glided through the sky to "shine upon the reed blossoms before the islets." The rich imagery in the procession strongly suggests that the poet, suffering from insomnia, has been watching the stars and the moon, listening to the mournful bugles, and brooding on a sense of his own failure. The narrative continues into the third poem, as the day dawns quietly with sunshine over clustered houses on the hills—the steady progression of time determines an unbroken plot in which the poet is the hero. It is in this third poem that Tu Fu, having located himself precisely in a narrative context, unreservedly sets forth his thoughts, which are only hinted at previously and which will rise to become the major theme of the rest of the poems. The fall of Ch'ang-an and its aftermath are reexperienced in a mixture of objective narrative, where the identity of the T'ang empire is again approached through the mirror of the Han, with the most sophisticated, purest lyricism, possible only in the mature form of "regulated verse" in sequential structure.

The sequential structure is the singular strength that broadens the generic meaning of the "Autumn Meditations," carrying it from lyricism, which characterizes each of the eight poems individually, to a provocative telling of a poet's deep awareness of personal duress under the fierce attacks of national catastrophe. The diverse contrasts in the larger structure and the linear progression of the sense of time in the smaller structure are equally important in the formation of a narrative scope. Here the poet assumes the role of historian, or, from another point of view, a historian speaks with all the sensibility of a poet. Either way, Tu Fu has manifested the genuine quality of a Chinese intellectual, combining the two highest ambitions in the tradition of Confucian humanism. In addition, it appears that Tu Fu has created a new dimension in terms of poetic craftsmanship in the refinement of "regulated verse." A "regulated verse" is complete with eight carefully ordered lines, with two antithetical couplets in the middle. Writing a sequence of "regulated verse" in eight parts for an expression of the self and public may suggest to us, in retrospect, that "Autumn Meditations" be taken as an expanded "regulated verse," each poem to be construed as a line in the decorous form aimed at formulating an advanced "regulated verse" in the structural scope of T'ang poetry.

The masterful "Song of Everlasting Sorrow" 長恨歌 by Po Chü-i 白居易 (772–846) presents itself with some of the problems intrinsic in the historical scope of T'ang narrative poetry.[31] It is with this poem that the balance of history and poetry becomes a problem in literary criticism and, to a certain degree, our approach to narrative poetry demands a consideration of the more abstract issues of *Dichtung* and *Wahrheit*.

The poem is comprised of 120 lines in heptasyllabic structure. The plot is adequately summarized by Lin Wen-yüeh 林文月 as follows: Part One (lines 1–32) depicts the extremely merry life

[31] Po chü-i 白居易, *Po-shih ch'ang-ch'ing chi* 白氏長慶集, 3 vols. (rpt. with supplementary collation, Taipei: I-wen yin-shu-kuan, 1971), vol. 1, *chüan* 12, 1.276–283.

which the rapturous Emperor Hsüan-tsung 玄宗 led with Yang Kuei-fei 楊貴妃, his devoted glamorous consort. Part Two (lines 33–50) relates how the felicitous love was lost as a consequence of the rise of the An Lu-shan 安祿山 Rebellion, the haste in which the emperor fled the capital, and the grief he experienced when he was forced to let Kuei-fei be killed at Ma-wei-p'o 馬嵬坡. Part Three (lines 51–74) describes the melancholy thoughts harbored by Hsüan-tsung over the dead. Part Four (lines 75–120) introduces a Taoist from Lin-ch'iung 臨邛 who, at the order of Hsüan-tsung, made a visit to the dead in a fairyland and returned with certain tokens of love, as well as with knowledge of the secret pledges made between the emperor and his consort, and ends with the notion of unending sorrow.[32] As Lin's synopsis shows, there is a clearly defined "plot" underlying the poem. Part One is the beginning of the narrative, in which the lovers are portrayed in an imperial aura with no fear of any sorrow. Parts Two and Three form the main body of the narrative: a disastrous blow demands the hero to recognize death and the vanity of power, wealth, and, above all, love. Part Four is an emphatically prolonged conclusion, which attains a new meaning for the poem through the supernatural interpretation of life. The plot, as is customary in Chinese narrative poetry, is not organized according to linear symmetry; rather, it is completed in response to thematic requirement. Thematically, the poem is not about the empire, but of love. It is not intended to admonish reckless government, but to lament the loss of love. As Lin Wen-yüeh points out with specific evidence, the category to which Po Chü-i assigns the poem is "kan-shang" 感傷 rather than "feng-yü" 諷諭.[33] This explains why the poet is devoted more to the amplification of the love theme than to the serial narration of a momentous historical event.

The "Song" bespeaks the general meaning of what we call the historical scope of T'ang narrative poetry. Against a national crisis so elaborately documented in history, literature, and folklore, Po Chü-i has elected to write a poem focused on an ahistoric touch of

[32] Lin Wen-yüeh 林文月, *Shan-shui yü ku-tien* 山水與古典 (Taipei: Ch'un-wen-hsüeh ch'u-pan-she, 1976), pp. 246–247.

[33] *Ibid.*, p. 249.

emotion, making the theme more universal. As Ch'en Yin-k'o 陳寅恪 remarks when he tries to explain the value of the spiritual contact of the lovers after the heroine was killed, the historical event becomes more "perpetual and beautiful than ever."[34] However, the question remains whether the poet is truly willing to ignore the opportunity to offer a historical admonition when telling such a revealing tale. The historical scope of T'ang poetic narrative is such that the poet, while drawing the tale from a historical, realistic event familiar to the audience, would not have hesitated to use it to produce an interpretation he believed to be the most urgent and relevant. This is as true for Po Chü-i in the composition of the "Song" as it is for Euripides in his drama.

Imperial adventures and princely romances provided the poet with eventful plots for the composition of narrative poetry, as did any "true story" of the commoners, albeit on a smaller political scale, but often with equal ethical and emotional weight. Sometimes the former may not lead the poet to a narrative poem of a length comparable to "Song of Everlasting Sorrow," but rather to the spontaneous verses known in Chinese poetry as *yung-shih* 詠史. Similarly, a "true story" which the poet has heard directly or indirectly may constitute the major plot of a generally narrative poem, such as Po's "Song of the P'i-p'a" 琵琶行. It may also become the interpretive principle of a narrative display such as "Spring River in a Flower Moon Night," or simply the framework of an imitation ballad. In general, it seems that the literati poet is more inclined to undertake the interpretation of an event in accordance with his taste and philosophy than to retell the story in a strictly detailed plot. The latter was a common practice among the folk singers, as shown in the domestic tragedy of "Southeast Fly the Peacocks" 孔雀東南飛, which belongs to the era prior to the T'ang dynasty. Accordingly, what is shown in Po Chü-i's "Song of Everlasting Sorrow" is the poet's conscientious choice of what he deemed the most significant themes to be drawn from the rebellion that had occurred half a century before he wrote it in 806. Enough time had passed for Po to take a private view of the event and to

[34] Ch'en Yin-k'o 陳寅恪, *Yüan Po shih chien-cheng kao* 元白詩箋證稿 (Hong Kong: Shang-wu yin-shu-kuan, 1950), p.12.

offer an original comment on the single theme he had chosen. In treating the events, the poet assumed a responsibility entirely different from that which Tu Fu did in "Journey to the North" 北征, written in 757, only two years after the outbreak of the rebellion. While both poems concern the same incident, the historical scope within which Po Chü-i's imagination and erudition operate is only a framework to study love, as opposed to the pressing circumstances under which Tu Fu writes about the immediate aftermath of the rebellion in the highest style of a poetic travelogue. A narrative poem such as "Song of Everlasting Sorrow" attains its meaning in the historical scope, but it is not a historical poem. Despite the narrative plot, it belongs properly in the category *yung-shih*, the genuine favorite of all Chinese intellectuals, which allows them to be selective in the assortment of materials and to be individualistic in the amplification of themes.

To pursue the topic a little further, we should add that, to a poet composing narrative poetry in the historical scope, the imperial, princely adventures recorded in annalistic literature are not necessarily more compelling than the commoner's poignant stories. "Song of Everlasting Sorrow" is a better poem than "Song of P'i-p'a," not because its subject matter is an imperial romance, but because it is selective in the formulation of the plot, concentrated in its treatment of an eternal theme (so much so that it makes the plot assymetrical), and because its overall design is original. In contrast, "Song of P'i-p'a" is only a narrative elaboration on an old story, filled with specific, situational details for the progression of the plot, and containing much unabsorbed sentimentality in the poet's direct reflection on his own sense of alienation. The faithful presentation of facts and details has turned out, ironically, to be a defect in what we call the narrative poem composed in the historical scope. To Chinese aesthetic values, overt moralizing and unabashed sentimentality, along with the serial concatenation of facts, reduce the impact of a narrative poem. This is true in reference to narrative poetry in the folk tradition. It is also true of the literati traditions, as evident in the conventional thinness of a composition entitled "A Song in Narration of the Story of Ou-yang Hsing-chou, with Preface" 詠歐陽行周事幷序, by Meng Chien 孟簡, a contemporary of Po Chü-i.[35] Meng Chien's desire to add a didactic dimension to his narration of a recent tragedy by identifying it with "Southeast Fly the Peacocks" and by supporting it with a preface to authenticate its historicity, has created a tedious document unworthy of its hero, another contemporary who happens to be the first poet in Chinese history to come from today's Fukien area.[36]

T'ang narrative poetry also has its geographical scope. The poet locates himself in a certain area, encountering present reality there as he proceeds to describe, to imagine, and often to comment on historical events or legends associated with the place. The result of such a work may be limited to a static narrative display of the poet's observations or it may expand to embody a dynamic narrative poem, its plot defined by his actual movement through the area and by historical or legendary references.

"A Poem in One Hundred Rhymes Written on a Journey through the Western Fields" 行次西郊作一百韻, by Li Shang-yin 李商隱 (812–858), is a narrative poem presented subjectively by the poet moving through an area, in the course of which both historical judgments and social criticism of current political prob-

[35] *Ch'üan T'ang shih* (rpt. Taipei: Chung-wen ch'u-pan-she, 1969), 9.2849–2850.

[36] *Hsin T'ang shu* 新唐書 (Peking: Chung-hua shu-chü, 1975), 203.5786–5787. Hsing-chou is the *tzu* of Ou-yang Chan 歐陽詹, from Chin-chiang 晉江, who is known to be the first man in history from that area to obtain the *chin-shih* 進士 degree and become distinguished as a poet. He was active at the end of the eighth century and the beginning of the ninth century, during the Chen-yüan 貞元 era. According to Meng Chien's preface to the poem, Ou-yang Chan was once invited by the General of T'ai-yüan 太原 to a banquet, in which he came to be fascinated by a chanteuse, "a beauty from the North," and remained with her in T'ai-yuan for months to fulfill their love. When he had to leave for the capital, he rejected the girl's request to travel with him, in fear of gossip, but promised to come back to fetch her immediately after he reached the capital. Somehow afterwards, Ou-yang was delayed from returning to the love-sick chanteuse, who eventually died in grief, leaving a lock of her hair to wait for him. At the sight of his beloved's hair, Ou-yang lamented so violently for over ten days that he also died of heartbreak. Meng Chien points out that Ou-yang Chan is mentioned by Han Yü in the "Biography of Ho Fan;" see "T'ai-hsüeh-sheng Ho Fan chuan" 太學生何蕃傳, in *Han Ch'ang-li chi*, pp. 14, 35–36. The poetical works of Ou-yang Chan can be found in *Ch'üan T'ang shih*, 7.2056–2064.

lems are formed.[37] It starts with a prosaic quatrain in the form of an introduction:

In the year of the Snake, the month of the Boar,	蛇年建丑月
I returned from the land of Liang to Ch'in:	我自梁還秦
I traveled south down to the Ta-san Pass,	南下大散關
And north across the waters over the bank of Wei.	北濟渭之濱

These four lines reveal problems in terms of geographical location and narrative style. The month of the Boar in the year of the Snake falls at the beginning of 838, when Li Shang-yin returned from the funeral of Ling-hu Ch'u, which had been held in Liang (Hsing-yüan 興元, approximately 250 kilometers southwest of Ch'ang-an).[38] The title indicates that the poem will concern itself with his experiences during the journey from Liang back to Ch'in, that is, Ch'ang-an. Judged according to its realistic context, therefore, the expression *nan-hsia* in the third line is ambiguous if not incorrect. In the journey from Liang to Ch'in, one does not go "down south" through Ta-san Pass, but "up north." We may outline the following corrected itinerary: he set forth from Hsing-yüan due north through the pass until he reached the River Wei, crossed it, and turned east, traveling along the north bank until he approached the vicinity and city proper of Ch'ang-an. The road he covered measures approximately 380 kilometers, all belonging to the so-called "Western Fields" of the capital. Consequently, the expressions *nan-hsia* and *pei-chi* suggest the limits Li Shang-yin intends to cover, the geographical scope for the narration of the poem. The scenes described follow along the Wei from north of Ta-san Pass to Ch'ang-an, the river valley devastated by almost a century of periodic military upheavals since the T'ien-pao 天寶 era.

Having so located himself in time and space, Li Shang-yin sets aside the prosaic element to commit himself directly to the poetic narration of the journey, constantly giving attention to past inci-

[37] Feng Hao 馮浩 ed., *Yü-hsi sheng shih chien-chu* 玉谿生詩箋注 (SSPY ed.), 1.37a–42a.

[38] Chang Ts'ai-t'ien 張采田, *Yü-hsi sheng nien-p'u hui-chien* 玉谿生年譜會箋 (Peking: Chung-hua shu-chü, 1963), pp. 43–45.

dents in order to intensify present horrors. In his account, "Western Fields" enjoyed peace and prosperity until the mid-K'ai-yüan 開元 era, when the court began to replace scholar-governors throughout China by military officials summoned from the frontiers, including some barbarian generals. Due to its location between the frontiers and the capital, the district most affected by the misgovernment of these recent officials is the "Western Fields." The journey structure of the poem has prompted Feng Hao 馮浩 to remark that it is comparable to Tu Fu's "Journey to the North."[39] Indeed, like Tu Fu, Li Shang-yin responds exhaustively to scenes as he sees them in his movement through the region; his experience is transformed into a startling poetic travelogue, heavily loaded with personal comments. However, unlike the "Journey to the North," Li Shang-yin's poem is not limited to a display of present scenes and the assumption of a reversal of fortunes expected from imperial wisdom. The poem has no single plot; it is woven with a variety of historical episodes, both long past and recent, and a series of emotional, pathetic descriptions of current reality. Against the wasted villages and devastated towns, Li Shang-yin, a young man of twenty-six, tells one tale after another in a simple, plain style characteristic of the old *yüeh-fu* and one quite free of the rich, ambiguous texture which would earmark his later poetry. The subjects of these tales are diverse, but they are also closely tied to the main theme, the suffering of the people, which is unmistakable in his recurrent historical awareness of the area as a geographical locus. Hsü Fu-kuan 徐復觀 believes that the poem is not simply an imitation of Tu Fu's "Journey to the North," but an expansive work harshly criticizing political realities, a work analogous to the powerful effect achieved combinedly by Tu Fu's three poems on officials (三吏) and three on partings (三別).[40]

"Western Fields" is unique in yet another respect. While moving through a sequence of different tales woven tightly by a common theme to a singular purpose, to criticize imperial misgovernment, it ends with one of the most desperate comments made in Chinese

[39] *Yü-hsi sheng shih chien-chu*, 1.42a.

[40] 新安吏, 潼關吏, 石壕吏; 新婚別, 垂老別, 無家別. See Hsü Fu-kuan 徐復觀, *Chung-kuo wen-hsüeh lun chi* 中國文學論集 (Taichung: Tung-hai ta-hsüeh, 1966), p. 235.

poetry. The air of despair is so strong, and yet so murky, that it is evident that the empire, as Li Shang-yin witnesses it, lacks any hope of survival. The meaning of "Late T'ang," as we use it in the study of literary history, can be fully appreciated in the whimper that marks the conclusion of this poem.

IV. "Lament of a Ch'in Woman"

Wei Chuang's 韋莊 (ca. 855–910) "Lament of a Ch'in Woman" 秦婦吟, an extensive work in heptasyllabic verse, sounds the final note in the complex development of T'ang narrative poetry.[41] Like many of its counterparts in the folk tradition, this poem was fated to disappear from the Chinese literary scene for almost a thousand years until the early twentieth century, when it was recovered in Tun-huang 敦煌.[42] The poem is important in Chinese literature, not only for the problem it presents in textual history, which is entangled with the political climate of an era and the problematic mentality of the intelligentsia common in all ages, but also for its monumental length in which it exemplifies the essence, scope, limits, and achievement of narrative poetry at the end of the T'ang dynasty.

"Lament of a Ch'in Woman" is a narrative poem in which the poet assumes the role of a scribe, recording a woman's tale of her experience during three years since Huang Ch'ao 黃巢 sacked Ch'ang-an in the spring of 882. The "Ch'in Woman" (poetic diction for a lady citizen of Ch'ang-an) was seized by the rebels when the capital fell, and was held in their camp for almost a year. When she managed to escape, the woman left Ch'ang-an and

[41] The text of the poem is best preserved in Ch'en Yin-k'o, *Ch'in-fu yin chiao-chien* 秦婦吟校箋 (K'un-ming: private edition, 1940), which is a revised, enlarged edition of his "Tu Ch'in-fu yin" 讀秦婦吟, *Tsing-hua hsüeh-pao* 清華學報 (*THHP*) 11 (1936), 951–968.

[42] For a summary of the details related to this important case in literary history, see Wang Ch'ung-min 王重民, *Tun-huang ku-chi hsü lu* 敦煌古籍叙錄 (Shanghai: Shang-wu yin-shu-kuan, 1958), pp. 303–308. The further investigation into the problem by Ch'en Yin-k'o is appraised in C. H. Wang, "Ch'en Yin-k'o's Approaches to Poetry: A Historian's Progress," *Chinese Literature: Essays, Articles, Reviews* 3, no. 1 (1981), 14–15.

wandered eastward to Lo-yang, where she encountered Wei Chuang and, at the poet's request, recounted the story in detail. The poem ends with her determination to travel farther east and eventually settle somewhere in the south, a region she believed to have remained peaceful despite the turmoil in the rest of the country.

The origins of the subject matter can be traced to the lamentation on ruins in such ancient poetry as *Shih ching* 65 黍離 or the *Ch'u tz'u* "Lament for Ying" 哀郢. It was repeatedly touched upon during the Chien-an and Six Dynasties periods by such poets as Wang Ts'an 王粲 (177–217), Ts'ao Chih (192–232), Pao Chao 鮑照 (414–466), and Yü Hsin 庾信 (513–581), each of whom mourned in his own way the destruction of old Ch'ang-an, Lo-yang, Kuang-ling 廣陵, and Chin-ling 金陵, respectively.[43] During the T'ang dynasty, the lament for the fallen capital continues to be found in the works of a large number of poets, including Lu Chao-lin's "The Hardship of Traveling" 行路難, Tu Fu's "Journey to the North," and Li Shang-yin's "A Poem in One Hundred Rhymes Written on a Journey through the Western Fields." There was, therefore, a rich tradition behind the composition of "Lament of the Ch'in Woman" when Wei Chuang undertook the project. In fact, by the end of the ninth century he had not only this rich tradition of classical models of literary expression and standard imagery, but also a set of established prosodic principles—the heptasyllabic verse structure had long since reached its perfection and was a versatile means to treat a wide range of topics. This, however, is not to say that Wei Chuang simply adds a new composition to the list of the laments upon ruins. Among other innovations, he creates a definite fictional character, the Ch'in woman. Allowing his subjective presence to withdraw from the suffering and destruction which would so naturally engage his response, he portrays the character with her own distinct personality and invests her with the capacity for emotional response. Like his predecessors, Wei Chuang displays the dire destruction of the city and country through a motif of traveling to or gazing at the scenes. Unlike them, he creates a fictional character out of his identification with

[43] 七哀詩, 送應氏, 蕪城賦, 哀江南賦.

the people in order to universalize the experience and enhance the credibility of the narration, thereby creating an equilibrium of subjective and objective voices in dramatic interaction. Moreover, even within the Ch'in woman's subjective voice yet another degree of objectivity is maintained as she introduces an old man, who, at her request, recounts the disaster that befell him in the wake of the bandits' passage through the villages—how the imperial troops followed and reduced the already stricken countryside into utter destitution. Wei Chuang has written a narrative poem in three dimensions, each voice contributing to the interpretation of the events. As he maintains complete objectivity in listening to the tale, he has the fictional Ch'in woman assume a subjective voice to narrate the events that occurred in Ch'ang-an and its vicinity. Later, as though reenacting the poet's calm attention, she also retreats to a distance when a character in her own tale cries bitterly in a straightforward subjective voice and tells *her* about the ravages suffered in the vast area between Ch'ang-an and Lo-yang. Wei Chuang has combined practically all the scenes and events described in the earlier poems on ruins, in both urban and rural areas, and has uncovered all the destroying forces mentioned by his predecessors in their works, forces which are focused in two paramount evils: rebellious bandits and corrupt imperial troops.

The structural scope of the poem appears in Wei Chuang's threefold picture: the horrors witnessed by an old man from the farming village, by a lady citizen of the capital, and by the poet serving as a scribe. These dimensions are woven into a unity, and their diversity in no way disrupts the plot. Through this design Wei Chuang is able to keep the poem from falling into stylistic monotony and, moreover, is able to widen the scope of social concerns in the critical judgment of the causes of disaster. Whereas the Ch'in woman laments the barbaric rebel attacks on urban civilization represented by Ch'ang-an, the old man, in his turn, reproaches the imperial troops for the final ruin of the rural areas. The areas, furthermore, are defined specifically, a backdrop of historical geography on which Wei Chuang allows the narrative action to unfold. Like Li Shang-yin's "Western Fields," the poem uses the journey motif: the heroine traveled the approximately 350 kilometers from Ch'ang-an to Lo-yang. Place names are given with historical accuracy, a credible record of those scenes where imperial troops, rather than the rebels, exercised brutality. This realistic, geographical scope is maintained steadily, providing the locus for the chronological order of events through which the heroine proceeds in a truly historical scope. In his continual attention to locating the events precisely, both in history and on the map, Wei Chuang has successfully maintained the genuine tradition of literati narrative poetry.[44] In retrospect, we see how the "Western Fields" of Ch'ang-an are described by Li Shang-yin as a completely devastated region; here, within fifty years, the "Eastern Fields" are also depicted in similar imagery with the same bitter effect. By the end of the ninth century, the great capital had become a ruin in the midst of a desolate land.

"Lament of a Ch'in Woman" is not merely a solid narrative account telling of the fall of the T'ang dynasty; it is also magnificent poetry. The dynamism of its lucid, flowing style generates and sustains the progress of the poem. The sure mastery with which its incidents are successively arrayed proves, probably for the first time in Chinese literature, that the heptasyllabic verse is capable of extended narration without slipping into either extravagantly ornamented poetic diction or flatness. The poem is free of the dense diction or constrained obscurity that characterize many literati works written in the late T'ang period. At the same time, it avoids the monotonous rhyme patterns found in most of the folk and religious pieces uncovered in Tun-huang, many of them roughly contemporary to Wei Chuang's work. Wei Chuang demonstrates that heptasyllabic verse is still powerful enough to combine the strength of the literati and the folk styles of narrative poetry, in an exuberant yet succinct and straightforward presentation of the plot. Two thousand years of slow but steady development of the form sustains Wei Chuang's alternation of plot-advancing elements with the display of picturesque and emotional moments; such alternation enriches the texture of the narrative while minimizing the

[44] For an expert examination in this regard, see Ch'en Yin-k'o, *Ch'in-fu yin*, pp. 10b–15a.

danger of dullness. No line or passage fails to contribute to the general effect of the poem as a testimony of the catastrophe of an empire and, above all, as an affirmation of the woman as the true heroine of a grand tale. Indeed, her sisters have always been heroines in the folk tradition of narrative poetry: in *Shih ching*, Han *yüeh-fu* poetry, "Southeast Fly the Peacocks," "Song of Mu-lan," and in such literati compositions as the two songs "Of Grief and Indignation" 悲憤詩, Fu Hsüan's 傅玄 (217–278) "Song of Ch'in Nü-hsiu" 秦女休行, and Yen Yen-chih's 顏延之 (384–456) "Song of Ch'iu Hu" 秋胡行.

The heroic adventure of the Ch'in woman is the primary theme in the plot of the poem. The national catastrophe serves as a backdrop, the old man's plaint as a supplement, and the poet's attention, a silent comment. In the process of the plot's unfolding the characterization of the heroine is fulfilled. The naive tone that marks her first reaction to the assault of the rebels dissolves with the description of the violent treatment she and other women received in its aftermath—she immediately assumes a stern voice to describe the starvation that followed the fall of the capital. The poignant lyricism in the transition indicates the growth of a feminine will to protest. When she assumes the authority to interpret the humiliation of the god, who fled the temple to hide himself from the human cataclysm, she becomes a Cassandra, released from all ethical codes to move in a fantastic realm. But the desperate, mystic tone subsides after she listens to the old man's story and realizes that the woe she has witnessed is a universal one. At that moment she matures, so much so that the concluding passage, in which she expresses her determination to proceed south, is narrated most calmly, careful to distinguish hearsay and true information, to weigh the pros and cons of seeking a foreign shelter and, in the gracious language that marks her gentle breeding, to encourage the listeners of her lament to consider joining the exodus. Wei Chuang has successfully portrayed a woman with distinctive temperament, love, and hatred who, having experienced violence, hunger, and inclemency, is as tragically resolute as her sisters in earlier narrative poetry. She is ready to abandon her homeland, the old Ch'ang-an, now in ruins, a city which we know in retrospect has never returned to its former grandeur and perhaps never will.

V. Conclusion

T'ang narrative poetry assimilated its heritage from earlier literature and from other cultural entities, such as music and graphic arts, using them to form a literary genre of the highest order. It appears to have evolved first from the folk and literati attempts to sing of extraordinary events celebrated in the Han *yüeh-fu*, *ku-shih*, and the secondary *fu*. On further investigation, however, we realize that T'ang narrative poetry possesses almost all the distinct stylistic and thematic features found in the poetry of the *Shih ching* and *Ch'u tz'u*. Insofar as Chinese poetic development is concerned, the periodization of literary history seems to have been done entirely for the sake of convenience, rather than to mark major shifts of literary taste and fashion of the sort obvious in the momentous change from the Medieval period to the Renaissance in European literature. There is an unquestionable continuity in classical Chinese poetry. Poets since the Han dynasty may have innovated upon earlier poetry for the attainment of a useful technique, but they did not change the principal method and function as upheld by their predecessors. A recognition of this continuity is essential to our appreciation of the nature of T'ang narrative poetry, and perhaps of lyrical poetry as well.

Narrative poetry, nonetheless, holds to that stylistic and thematic continuity more closely than does lyrical poetry. When Li Po criticizes the whimsical ornateness which marks many poetic works since the Chien-an 建安 era (196–220), he is obviously expressing a strong distaste for the latter-day indulgence in extravagant diction and decadent concerns characteristic of lyric poetry produced during the Six Dynasties period.[45] However, it was during the same period that narrative poetry steadily matured, owing first to the vital transmission of folk songs, some of which remain even today among the finest works of Chinese poetry, and, second, to the efforts of literati poets to form a synthesis between folk property and their traditional erudition and moral judgment. In place of the ornateness which diminishes the spiritual value and artistic integrity of much Six Dynasties lyric poetry, there is a certain dynamic tone

[45] See the first 古風 by Li Po in *Fen-lei pu-chu Li T'ai-po shih*, 2.1a.

which powerfully prepares narrative poetry throughout that long period in divided China to offer models, both extrinsic and intrinsic, for the T'ang poets. The continuity of this tradition is manifest in the essence and scope of T'ang narrative poetry. In terms of essence, we see how narrative display was practiced with tasteful sophistication by some ambitious early talents, how ancient-style poetry in general was always available for the poets to develop a kind of quasi-narrative in their compositions, and how the "ultimate verse" in particular never failed to sustain the serene homogeneity of ancient-style poetry, achieving at times narrative in the "dynamic quatrain." In terms of scope, we find the poet's energetic inquiry into myth, politics, history, and the enduring vastness of the Chinese land, though periodically attacked by the collective folly of a nation. Despite the difference of scope in which their imaginative, intellectual power inspects specific events, it is noteworthy that T'ang poets by and large share a unique style, a style that is mixed with the complementary alternation of lyric elements and narrative details. This style lends intensity and charm to most of the best narrative poems written during the T'ang dynasty, and it is accepted by the poets of subsequent ages as fundamental to the art.

The nature of narrative in T'ang poetry is such that, while it organizes an event or a number of events into the plot, it shows an inherent quality reminiscent of Chinese lyricism. We have not turned away from this quality in our investigation of narrative poetry, but have regarded it as a positive, characteristic feature worthy of our appreciation. By the same token, one wonders if this feature might not be central to our consideration of Chinese poetry in general and especially relevant to attempting a new definition for lyric poetry in particular.

III. Forms and Genres

Hans H. Frankel

The Development of Han and Wei *Yüeh-fu* as a High Literary Genre

Two phases may be discerned in the development of *yüeh-fu* 樂府 as a high literary genre in Han and Wei times.[1] During the first phase—from the beginning of Han rule in 202 B.C. to the last decade of the second century A.D.—a few educated men sporadically composed secular *yüeh-fu* for self-expression and entertainment. During the second phase—from the 190s to the end of the Wei dynasty in 266—*yüeh-fu* gradually separated itself from standard *shih* 詩 poetry and became a major literary genre in the hands of Ts'ao Ts'ao 曹操, his sons Ts'ao P'i 曹丕 and Ts'ao Chih 曹植, Ts'ao P'i's son Ts'ao Jui 曹叡, and some of their contemporaries.

Yüeh-fu is a vague, elusive term, encompassing both ritual hymns and secular, personal poetry. Although the division between these two kinds of *yüeh-fu* is not always clear, I will confine my discussion to secular, personal *yüeh-fu*. I will consider as a literary *yüeh-fu* any poem by a known author which possesses most if not all of the following characteristics: its author intended it to be sung; it bears a *yüeh-fu* title which distinguishes it from an ordinary *shih* poem; it is a member of a chain of *yüeh-fu* poems with a common title and affinities in form, theme, and wording; and it is included in *Yüeh-fu shih chi*[2] and/or other collections of *yüeh-fu* poetry. I will discuss fourteen literary *yüeh-fu* of this period in approximate chronological order, focusing primarily on the twenty-five *yüeh-fu* themes

[1] In writing and revising this article, I have received helpful suggestions and criticism from the other participants in the June 1982 conference at York, Maine, and also from Susan Cherniack and from my wife Chang Ch'ung-ho.

[2] *Yüeh-fu shih chi* 樂府詩集, compiled by Kuo Mao-ch'ien 郭茂倩 (died ca. 1126) toward the end of the eleventh century (Peking: Chung-hua shu-chü, 1979).

which I found by going through the extant *yüeh-fu* by Han and Wei poets, but paying attention also to forms, poetic devices, and styles, and to the place of individual poems in the *yüeh-fu* tradition.[3]

We will begin with a song by Li Yen-nien 李延年 (fl. late second to early first century B.C.), a professional musician at the court of Emperor Wu (reigned 141–87 B.C.):

Song
In the North there is a beautiful woman,
2 Unique, unequaled in the world.
With one glance she conquers a city of men,
4 With another glance a country of men.
Don't you know? A city and country conquering
6 Beauty cannot be found again.[4]

歌
北方有佳人
絕世而獨立
一顧傾人城
再顧傾人國
寧不知傾城與傾國
佳人難再得

Li Yen-nien recited this song to call the Emperor's attention to his younger sister, Lady Li 李夫人, who excelled not only in looks

[3] We need not consider improvised songs such as Hsiang Yü's 項羽 "Kai-hsia ko" 垓下歌 of 202 B.C. and Liu Pang's 劉邦 "Ta-feng ko" 大風歌 of 195 B.C. because they do not have enough of the characteristics of literary *yüeh-fu* as defined above. For "Kai-hsia ko" see Ssu-ma Ch'ien 司馬遷 (145?–90? B.C.), *Shih chi* 史記 (Peking: Chung-hua shu-chü, 1972), 7.333; *Yüeh-fu shih chi*, 58.849–850; translations by Yves Hervouet and Max Kaltenmark in *Anthologie de la poésie chinoise classique*, ed. Paul Demiéville (Paris: Gallimard, 1962), p. 61; and by Ronald Miao in *Sunflower Splendor: Three Thousand Years of Chinese Poetry*, ed. Wu-chi Liu and Irving Yucheng Lo (New York: Anchor Press, 1975), p. 29. For "Ta-feng ko" see *Shih chi*, 8.389; *Yüeh-fu shih chi*, 58.850. Translations by Hervouet and Kaltenmark in Demiéville, *Anthologie*, p. 62; and by Miao in Liu and Lo, *Sunflower Splendor*, p. 29.

[4] *Han shu* 漢書 by Pan Ku 班固 (32–92) (Peking: Chung-hua shu-chü, 1975), 97A.3951; *Yüeh-fu shih chi*, 84.1181; *Chien-chu yü-t'ai hsin yung* 箋注玉臺新詠, compiled by Hsü Ling 徐陵 (507–583), with commentary by Wu Chao-i 吳兆宜 (his preface dated 1675) (Taipei: Kuang-wen shu-chü, 1967), 1.12b–13a; Chang Shou-p'ing 張壽平, *Han-tai yüeh-fu yü yüeh-fu ko-tz'u* 漢代樂府與樂府歌辭 (Taipei: Kuang-wen shu-chü, 1970), pp. 94–95; Hervouet and Kaltenmark in Demiéville, *Anthologie*, p. 68; Anne Birrell, trans., *New Songs from a Jade Terrace: An Anthology of Early Chinese Love Poetry* (London: George Allen & Unwin, 1982), p. 41.

but also as a dancer. She became Emperor Wu's favorite. The phrase *ch'ing ch'eng* (line 5) comes from *Shih ching* 詩經, No. 264:

> A clever man builds a city wall/walled city, 哲夫成城
> A clever woman overthrows a city wall/walled city. 哲婦傾城

Li Yen-nien's poem has interesting metric and rhetorical features. Like many later *yüeh-fu* (and many standard *shih* 詩), its meter is the five-syllable line, with a caesura between the second and the third syllable, and an unchanging rhyme at the end of the even-numbered lines. (In addition, line 5 also rhymes.) *Ning pu chih* in line 5 in an early instance of a supernumerary phrase at the head of a line. (Later literary *yüeh-fu* often have extrametrical head phrases such as *chün pu chien* 君不見, "haven't you seen?") Note also the enjambement in the last two lines (if my reading of this couplet is correct). This is more common in *yüeh-fu* and other musical genres such as *tz'u* 詞 and *ch'ü* 曲 than in standard *shih*.

In lines 3 and 4 we have a rhetorical feature characteristic of oral poetry. The feature may be defined as a sequence of structurally and verbally similar statements, with progressive variations in each statement. The members of the sequence may be individual lines, couplets, or longer units. The feature occurs, for example, in the two anonymous Han *yüeh-fu* "Chiang-nan" 江南 and "Mo-shang sang" 陌上桑[5] and in modern folk songs, such as "Ho-nan chui-tzu shu" 河南墜子書.[6] It is common not only in China but also in the oral poetry of other countries.[7]

Li Yen-nien's "Song" exemplifies an important *yüeh-fu* theme:

[5] *Yüeh-fu shih chi*, 26.384 and 28.410–411.

[6] See Jaroslav Průšek, "Die *chui-tsï-shu*, erzählende Volksgesänge aus Ho-nan," in *Asiatica: Festschrift Friedrich Weller* (Leipzig, 1954), pp. 468–472.

[7] See Hans H. Frankel, "*Yüèh-fǔ* Poetry," in *Studies in Chinese Literary Genres*, ed. Cyril Birch (Berkeley and Los Angeles: University of California Press, 1974), pp. 87–88; and Hans Frankel, "Some Characteristics of Oral Narrative Poetry in China," in *Études d'Histoire et de Littérature choinoises offertes au Professeur Jaroslav Průšek*, ed. Yves Hervouet (Paris: Bibliothèque de l'Institut des Hautes Études choinoises, 1976), pp. 100–101. Examples from other cultures are an Irish "New Song on the Taxes" and an oral poem translated from the Yoruba language of West Africa, titled "Quarrel," in *A World Treasury of Oral Poetry*, ed. Ruth Finnegan (Bloomington: Indiana University Press, 1978), pp. 194–195 and 167.

the peerless beauty. The poem has inspired many generations of literati who relished the *double-entendre* of the woman who, like Helen of Troy, caused men and cities and states to fall.

We come now to a song composed in A.D. 49 by General Ma Yüan 馬援 (14 B.C. to A.D. 49) during a difficult campaign against a non-Chinese tribe at the Wu Stream (which runs from southern Hunan to northern Kwangtung).[8] The area was infested with a disease which killed many of the Chinese troops, including General Ma himself. The song and its origin are related in *Ku-chin chu* as follows:

> "The Wu Stream Is Deep" was made by Ma Yüan during a southern campaign. His subordinate Yüan Chi-sheng 爰寄生 was good at playing the horizontal flute; Ma Yüan made a song to harmonize with his [flute composition].[9] Its name is "The Wu Stream Is Deep" 武溪深. The words are:

Flooding, flooding, the Wu Stream—
  how deep!
Birds cannot fly across,
Beasts dare not come down to its
  banks.
Woe, the Wu Stream is rife with
  virulent plague.[10]

滔滔武溪一何深
鳥飛不度
獸不敢臨
嗟哉武溪兮多毒淫

In the song and its background there are several themes that will recur in later literary *yüeh-fu*: a forbidding, exotic landscape with lurking hostile barbarians; the forces and creatures of nature; a general relating his own difficult campaign, far from home; and the

[8] There is an account of the campaign in his biography, *Hou-Han shu* 後漢書 by Fan Yeh 范曄 (398–446) "Lieh-chuan" 列傳 (Peking: Chung-hua shu-chü, 1973), vol. 24, *chüan* 14, pp. 842–843.

[9] Variant in the *Yüeh-fu shih chi* version of the *Ku-chin chu* account: "Ma Yüan made a song and ordered Chi-sheng to play the flute harmonizing with it."

[10] *Ku-chin chu* 古今注 by Ts'ui Pao 崔豹 (late third century); photolithographic reproduction of Sung wood-block edition in *Ssu-pu ts'ung-k'an* 四部叢刊, third series, B.2a; *Yüeh-fu shih chi*, 74.1048; Yü Kuan-ying 余冠英, *Yüeh-fu shih hsüan* 樂府詩選 (rev. ed., Hong Kong: Shih-chieh shu-chü, n.d. [his preface to first ed. dated 1950, his postface to rev. ed. dated 1954], p. 149; Chang Shou-p'ing, *Han-tai yüeh-fu*, pp. 99–100.

threat of death. Three literary *yüeh-fu* imitating the title and atmosphere of this song are extant, all dating from the first half of the sixth century; their titles are "Wu hsi shen hsing" 武溪深行, "Pan tu hsi" 半渡溪, and "Pan lu hsi" 半路溪.[11]

The following poem was composed by the hermit Liang Hung 梁鴻 while passing the Eastern Han capital, Lo-yang, during the reign of Emperor Chang (75–88):

Alas Five Times
I climb that northern Mang Hill
2 Alas
And view the imperial capital.
4 Alas
The palaces loom high,
6 Alas
The people's toil
8 Alas
Is far from finished.
10 Alas[12]

五噫歌
陟彼北邙兮
噫
顧覽帝京兮
噫
宮室崔嵬兮
噫
民之劬勞兮
噫
遼遼未央兮
噫

Notable features are the refrain in the even-numbered lines and the enjambement in lines 7–10. We observe two new *yüeh-fu* themes: climbing to a high place and looking down; and the unending toil of the common people, contrasted here with the grandeur of the palaces that result from their labors. The refrain deftly anticipates the point of view in the conclusion.

One more poem from the first phase of literary *yüeh-fu* development remains to be considered.

The Palace Guard Officer
Once there was a servant in the house of
  Huo,
2 His name was Feng Tzu-tu.
Presuming on the general's power
4 He teased a foreign wineshop girl.
The pretty foreign girl was fifteen.

羽林郎
昔有霍家奴
姓馮名子都
依倚將軍勢
調笑酒家胡
胡姬年十五

[11] *Yüeh-fu shih chi*, 74.1048–1049.

[12] *Hou-Han shu*, "Lieh-chuan" vol. 83, *chüan* 73, pp. 2,766–2,767; *Yüeh-fu shih chi*, 85.1193; Yü Kuan-ying, *Yüeh-fu shih hsüan*, p. 149; J. D. Frodsham and Ch'eng Hsi, trans., *An Anthology of Chinese Verse* (Oxford: Clarendon Press, 1967), p. 23.

6 In spring she was tending the bar alone.
The halves of her long skirt were tied together with ribbons;
8 Her broad-sleeved coat had a floral design of happy union.
On her head she wore jade from Lan-t'ien,
10 Behind her ears, Byzantine pearls.
Her hair in two buns, so attractive,
12 Surely without equal in her time,
One bun worth five million,
14 Two buns more than ten million.
Surprise! An imperial guard officer,
16 A show-off, passes my bar.
His silver saddle, how it glitters!
18 His carriage, decked with kingfisher feathers, loiters in idleness.
He comes to me and asks for clear wine;
20 By the silk cord I lift the jade pot.
He comes to me and asks for a choice dish;
22 On a gold platter I serve him thin-sliced carp.
He gives me a green bronze mirror
24 And ties it to my red silk skirt.
I don't care if the red silk gets torn,
26 Not to mention my worthless body.
A man always desires a second wife,
28 A woman esteems her first husband.
In human life there is new and old;
30 Noble and base can't trespass on each other.
No, thank you, Officer of the Guard!
32 Such private amours are trifling and will get you nowhere.[13]

春日獨當壚
長裾連理帶
廣袖合歡襦
頭上藍田玉
耳後大秦珠
兩鬟何窈窕
一世良所無
一鬟五百萬
兩鬟千萬餘
不意金吾子
娉婷過我廬
銀鞍何昱爚
翠蓋空峙嶹
就我求清酒
絲繩提玉壺
就我求珍肴
金盤膾鯉魚
貽我青銅鏡
結我紅羅裾
不惜紅羅裂
何論輕賤軀
男兒愛後婦
女子重前夫
人生有新故
貴賤不相踰
多謝金吾子
私愛徒區區

[13] *Chien-chu yü-t'ai hsing yung*, 1.13b–14b; *Yüeh-fu shih chi*, 63.909–910; eight articles in *Yüeh-fu shih yen-chiu lun-wen chi* 樂府詩研究論文集, compiled by Tso-chia ch'u-pan she pien-chi pu 作家出版社編輯部 (Peking: Tso-chia ch'u-pan-she,

About the author, Hsin Yen-nien 辛延年, very little is known. No other works of his survive. According to *Yüeh-fu shih chi*, he lived during the Eastern Han. A work titled *Chi-shih chu* 記事珠 states that he was a professional singer from Chung-shan 中山, and that his parents and sisters were also professional singers.[14] Feng Yin 馮殷, courtesy name Tzu-tu (line 2), was in fact a subordinate of General-in-Chief Huo Kuang 霍光 (died 68 B.C.), and was known as a philanderer.[15] Thus Hsin Yen-nien uses here a method familiar to us from the works of countless literati of later times: he chooses a historical setting and historical names in creating a story that might have happened in his own day.

The poem takes up two themes encountered earlier: the peerless beauty and the exotic foreigner. But this foreigner (unlike the hostile barbarians in Ma Yüan's "The Wu Stream Is Deep") is portrayed sympathetically. Likeable, strong women often play dominant roles in *yüeh-fu* poetry. Hsin's alien is the topical woman triumphant, the virtuous beauty who thwarts the would-be seducer. Another woman triumphant is Ch'in Lo-fu 秦羅敷, the heroine of the anonymous Han *yüeh-fu* "Mo-shang sang" 陌上桑.[16] The two poems have much in common. A noteworthy shared feature is the initial demonstration of the heroine's attractions through her clothes, hairdo, and adornments.[17]

1957), pp. 84–137; *Liang Han wen-hsüeh shih ts'an-k'ao tzu-liao* 兩漢文學史參考資料, prepared by History of Chinese Literature faculty of Peking University (Shanghai: Kao-teng chiao-yü ch'u-pan-she, 1960), pp. 536–539; Yü Kuan-ying, *Yüeh-fu shih hsüan*, pp. 150–151; Marie Chan, "From the Folk to the Literary Yüeh-fu," *Tamkang Review* 5, no. 1 (April 1974) 45–49; anonymous translation (perhaps by André d'Hormon) in Demiéville, *Anthologie*, pp. 89–90; Hans Frankel, "Six Dynasties *yüèh-fǔ* and Their Singers," *Journal of the Chinese Language Teachers Association* 13 (1978) 192–193; Birrell, *New Songs from a Jade Terrace*, p. 42. Yü P'ing-po 俞平伯, in *Yüeh-fu shih yen-chiu lun-wen chi*, pp. 85–86, 100–102, gives a different interpretation of lines 25–26, which I find unconvincing.

[14] See Ching Yüan 靜淵 in *Yüeh-fu shih yen-chiu lun-wen chi*, p. 95. There are several works titled *Chi-shih chu*. I have not been able to find the one cited by Ching Yüan.

[15] See *Liang Han wen-hsüeh shih ts'an-k'ao tzu-liao*, p. 537, n. 2, and p. 487; *Han shu*, 8.251.

[16] *Yüeh-fu shih chi*, 28.410–411; Frankel, "Oral Narrative Poetry," pp. 98–105.

[17] See Marie Chan, "From Folk to Literary Yüeh-fu," pp. 31, 45.

Two other characteristic *yüeh-fu* features are noteworthy in Hsin's poem. In lines 13–14 and 19–22 we have progressive sequences of structurally and verbally similar statements (as in Li Yen-nien's "Song"). The sequence of lines 13–14 involves numbers, as is often the case in *yüeh-fu*.[18] The second *yüeh-fu* feature in Hsin's poem is the shift of viewpoint and manner of narration. In the first part (lines 1–14) the story is told by an outsider and set in the past ("Once there was . . ."). The second part (from line 15 to the end) is sung by the heroine herself, addressing first the audience, then her adversary. Such shifts are common in *yüeh-fu* and in ballads of other countries.[19]

Hsin's poem is followed in *Yüeh-fu shih chi*, 63.910–911, by four literary imitations, three titled "Yü-lin hsing" 羽林行 and one "Hu-chi nien shih-wu" 故姬年十五.

The second phase of literary *yüeh-fu* starts with Ts'ao Ts'ao 曹操 (155–220). Keenly interested in music, he chose to cast all his narrative and lyric poems in the form of *yüeh-fu* rather than ordinary *shih* 詩, using a wide variety of patterns and themes. According to a history written less than a half-century after his death, "whenever he composed poems, he had them set to wind and string accompaniment, so that they all became musical pieces."[20] We begin with an undated (perhaps early) *yüeh-fu* by Ts'ao Ts'ao which describes a utopia, an ideal state of government and society.

I Drink	對酒
I drink and sing of Great Peace and Equality:[21]	對酒歌太平

[18] See for example the first seven lines of "K'ung-ch'üeh tung-nan fei" 孔雀東南飛, *Chien-chu yü-t'ai hsin yung*, 1.24a.

[19] Frankel, "Oral Narrative Poetry," pp. 101–102; Frankel, "Six Dynasties," pp. 192–195.

[20] *Wei shu* 魏書 by Wang Ch'en 王沈 (died 266), cited in P'ei Sung-chih's 裴松之 (372–451) commentary to *San-kuo chih* 三國志 by Ch'en Shou 陳壽 (233–297) (Peking: Chung-hua shu-chü, 1975), 1.54, n. 2.

[21] For this meaning of *t'ai-p'ing*, see Max Kaltenmark, "The Ideology of the T'ai-p'ing ching," in *Facets of Taoism: Essays in Chinese Religion*, ed. Holmes Welch and Anna Seidel (New Haven: Yale University Press, 1979), p. 21.

2 Then tax collectors do not call at the door,[22]
Rulers are virtuous and sage,
4 Ministers—the rulers' arms and legs—are all loyal and good.
Everyone is courteous and willing to yield,
6 The people have no cause for quarrel and litigation.
After three-year periods of tilling there are reserve provisions for nine years;
8 Granaries are full.
Greyheads do not carry loads on their backs or heads.
10 Rains bring fertile wetness, thus
All grains are harvested.
12 Swift horses are withdrawn from war
And carry dung to the fields.
14 Men are enfeoffed as dukes, marquises, earls, viscounts, barons,
They all love their people,
16 Demote and promote according to merit,
Care for them like fathers and elder brothers.

時吏不呼門
王者賢且明
宰相股肱皆忠良
咸禮讓
民無所爭訟
三年耕有九年儲
倉穀滿盈
班白不負戴
雨澤如此
百穀用成
卻走馬
以糞其上田
爵公侯伯子男
咸愛其民
以黜陟幽明
子養有若父與兄

[22] Huang Chieh 黃節 (1873–1935) argues that the opening lines should be divided as follows: 對酒歌. 太平時. 吏不呼門. (Huang Chieh, *Wei Wu-ti Wei Wen-ti shih chu* 魏武帝魏文帝詩註 [Hong Kong: Commercial Press, 1961], p. 12, n.). Modern punctuated editions follow Huang Chieh. But this line division destroys the rhyme 平 / 明 and leaves the opening lines without any rhyme. The correct line division is confirmed by Wu Ching 吳兢 (670–749) in his *Yüeh-fu chieh-t'i* 樂府解題, where he quotes Ts'ao Ts'ao's poem by its first line: 對酒歌太平. (Cited in *Yüeh-fu shih chi*, 27.403; the citation is wrongly punctuated in the 1979 edition of *Yüeh-fu shih chi*.)

18 Violators of etiquette and law
Get the light or heavy punishment
they deserve.
20 No one pockets anything found
on the road;
Prisons are empty;
22 The winter solstice criminal courts
have no business.
People of eighty and ninety
24 All live out their natural lives.
Grace and virtue reach far, even
to plants and creeping
creatures.[23]

犯禮法
輕重隨其刑
路無拾遺之私
囹圄空虛
冬節不斷
人耄耋
皆得以壽終
恩德廣及草木昆蟲

The meter is complex. Lines vary in length from three to eight syllables. The title "Tui chiu" was used again by seven *yüeh-fu* poets, from Fan Yün 范雲 (451–503) to Li Po 李白 (701?–763). But they all employ simpler meters, with lines of five and seven syllables.[24]

Ts'ao Ts'ao presents his utopia both positively and negatively: the depiction of ideal conditions is balanced with the stated absence of undesirable phenomena. This literary *yüeh-fu* is replete with phrases that were the common property of educated men, contained in classical, historical, and philosophical works such as *Shu ching* 書經, *Meng Tzu* 孟子, *Li chi* 禮記, *Ta Tai li chi* 大戴禮記, *Shih chi* 史記, *Han shu* 漢書, and *Lao Tzu* 老子.[25]

[23] *Sung shu* 宋書 by Shen Yüeh 沈約 (441–513) (Peking: Chung-hua shu-chü, 1974), 21.606; *Yüeh-fu shih chi*, 27.403; Huang Chieh, *Wei Wu-ti*, pp. 11–12; *Wei Chin nan-pei-ch'ao wen-hsüeh shih ts'an-k'ao tzu-liao* 魏晉南北朝文學史參考資料, prepared by History of Chinese Literature faculty of Peking University (Peking: Chung-hua shu-chü, 1962), pp. 11–13; *Ts'ao Ts'ao chi* 曹操集 (Hong Kong: Chung-hua shu-chü, 1973), p. 4; *Ts'ao Ts'ao chi i-chu* 曹操集譯注, prepared by Anhui Po-hsien "Ts'ao Ts'ao chi" i-chu hsiao-tsu 安徽亳縣《曹操集》譯注小組 (Peking: Chung-hua shu-chü, 1979), pp. 15–17; Yü Kuan-ying 余冠英, *San Ts'ao shih hsüan* 三曹詩選 (rev. ed., Peking: Jen-min wen-hsüeh ch'u-pan-she, 1979), pp. 5–7; Chao Fu-t'an 趙福壇, *Ts'ao Wei fu-tzu shih-hsüan* 曹魏父子詩選 (Hong Kong: Joint Publishing Co., 1982), pp. 10–12; Diether von den Steinen, "Poems of Ts'ao Ts'ao Translated and Annotated," *Monumenta Serica* 4 (1939), 156–158.

[24] *Yüeh-fu shih chi*, 27.403–405.

[25] These are all duly noted by Huang Chieh, *Wei Wu-ti*, pp. 11–12.

The Prelude of the following composition has been interpreted by Ch'ing dynasty and more recent commentators as referring to Ts'ao Ts'ao's departure in the autumn of 207 on a campaign against the Wu-huan 烏桓 barbarians in northeastern China, and the Prelude has been said to reflect Ts'ao Ts'ao's hesitation between conflicting proposals offered by his subordinates: most of them urged him to march into Ching-chou 荊州 (modern Hupei and Hunan) rather than attacking the Wu-huan. But, as noted by Diény, these interpretations of the Prelude are untenable; the poem must have been written during or after the successful campaign against the Wu-huan, not at the start of the campaign. Mount Chieh-shih (Rock Pile Mountain) must be in the northeastern corner of modern Hopei, on the Gulf of Liaotung, but its exact location is uncertain.[26]

Stepping Out of the Hsia Gate 步出夏門行

Prelude 豔

Clouds travel, raindrops step
2 Across the hills of Nine Rivers.
Below I see different views:
4 Undecided in my mind,
I do not know which I should follow.
6 We move along to our Rock Pile
Mountain,
My heart is sad at our Eastern Sea.

雲行雨步
超越九江之臯
臨觀異同
心意懷遊豫
不知當復何從
經過至我碣石
心惆悵我東海

First Stanza 一解

8 Turning east, I look down from Rock
Pile Mountain
And view the dark green sea.
10 Such agitation in the water!
Hilly islands loom steep,
12 Trees in thick clumps,
A hundred kinds of plants in lush
growth.

東臨碣石
以觀滄海
水何澹澹
山島竦峙
樹木叢生
百草豐茂

[26] Jean-Pierre Diény, "Rapport sur les conférences," in Ecole pratique des Hautes Études, IVe Section: Sciences historiques et philologiques, *Annuaire 1970–1971* (103e année, Paris: Sorbonne, 1971), pp. 771–772; *Ts'ao Ts'ao chi i-chu*, pp. 40–41.

14 The autumn wind soughs;
Huge billows leap up.
16 Sun and moon in their movements
Seem to rise from them;
18 The Milky Way's splendor
Seems to rise from within.
20 Let happiness be perfect,
I sing of what is on my mind.

秋風蕭瑟
洪波湧起
日月之行
若出其中
星漢粲爛
若出其裏
幸甚至哉
歌以詠志

Second Stanza

22 In the first month of winter
The north wind lingers.
24 The weather is harsh and clear;
Frost is all around.
26 Cranes call at dawn;
Geese fly south.
28 Birds of prey hide in their roosts;
Bears stay in their caves.
30 Leveling and weeding tools are put
away;
The harvest is piled on the ground.
32 Inns make ready
To serve traveling merchants.
34 Let happiness be perfect,
I sing of what is on my mind.

二解

孟冬十月
北風徘徊
天氣肅清
繁霜霏霏
鵾鷄晨鳴
鴻雁南飛
鷙鳥潛藏
熊羆窟棲
錢鎛停置
農收積場
逆旅整設
以通賈商
幸甚至哉
歌以詠志

Third Stanza

36 Regions are not alike;
The land north of the Yellow River is
severe and cold.
38 Ice floes drift;
Boats move with difficulty.
40 Drills do not penetrate the soil;
Wormwood and turnips grow deep.
42 Water stops flowing;
Ice is firm enough to walk on.
44 Gentlemen are painfully poor;
Brave adverturers are prone to break
laws.

三解

鄉土不同
河朔隆寒
流澌浮漂
舟船行難
錐不入地
蘴藾深奧
水竭不流
冰堅可蹈
士隱者貧
勇俠輕非

46 My heart keeps lamenting and grieving, 心常歎怨
Sad, sad, so much sorrow. 慼慼多悲
48 Let happiness be perfect, 幸甚至哉
I sing of what is on my mind. 歌以詠志

Fourth Stanza 四解
50 The sacred tortoise, though long-lived, 神龜雖壽
Still comes to an end. 猶有竟時
52 The soaring serpent rides the mist 騰蛇乘霧
But finally turns to dust and ashes. 終爲土灰
54 The fleet horse, aging, lies in the stable 驥老伏櫪
But thinks of running a thousand miles. 志在千里
56 A hero in life's evening 烈士暮年
Constantly keeps his stout heart. 壯心不已
58 Whether his life-span be full or shortened 盈縮之期
Is not determined by Heaven alone. 不但在天
60 By nurturing the bliss of wholesome harmony 養怡之福
He can prolong his years. 可得永年
62 Let happiness be perfect, 幸甚至哉
I sing of what is on my mind.[27] 歌以詠志

Line 1, adapted from *I ching* 易經, equates the legitimate power represented by Ts'ao Ts'ao with rain from Heaven, according to Yü Kuan-ying.[28]

The poem achieves a marvelous integration of natural phenomena and personal concerns. On the eve of his departure, Ts'ao

[27] *Sung shu*, 21.619; *Chin shu* 晉書 by Fang Hsüan-ling 房玄齡 (578–648) and others (Peking: Chung-hua shu-chü, 1974), 23.714–715; *Yüeh-fu shih chi*, 37.545–546; Huang Chieh, *Wei Wu-ti*, pp. 26–29; *Wei Chin nan-pei-ch'ao*, pp. 10–11 (stanzas 1 and 4 only); *Ts'ao Ts'ao chi*, pp. 10–11; *Ts'ao Ts'ao chi i-chu*, pp. 40–45; Yü Kuan-ying, *San Ts'ao shih hsüan*, pp. 10–14; Chao Fu-t'an, *Ts'ao Wei fu-tzu*, pp. 23–29; von den Steinen, "Poems of Ts'ao Ts'ao," pp. 139–143; Robert Ruhlmann and Yves Hervouet in Demiéville, *Anthologie*, p. 113 (stanza 1 only); John A. Turner, S. J., *A Golden Treasury of Chinese Poetry* (Hong Kong: The Chinese University Press, 1976), pp. 62–63 (stanza 4 only).

[28] Yü Kuan-ying, *San Ts'ao shih hsüan*, pp. 10–11, n. 2.

Ts'ao identifies with the traveling clouds and the walking raindrops. This image combines the force and swiftness of wind with the beneficial properties of rain. The exciting sight of the sea reveals to the beholder a microcosm of the world familiar to him (lines 8–19). The "agitation in the water" (line 10) is analogous to his emotional state. As the army moves north and the season changes from autumn to winter, all living creatures withdraw to the safety of their homes and winter abodes; only merchants (and soldiers) are traveling, normal movements are blocked and frozen (lines 22–39). The contemplation of all those hardships leads the poet in the fourth stanza to a bold defiance of natural bounds: he is confident that a true hero can overcome the limitations to which ordinary men and even supernatural animals are subject.

Nature, with its creatures and phenomena, and particularly its changes of season and differences of climate, is one of the poem's themes. Others are: looking down from high places; exotic lands and their inhabitants; hardships of the common people; the brevity of life and the desire to prolong it. Two other *yüeh-fu* themes are also implied, though not openly stated: the general leading his army and the misery caused by war.

The refrain repeated at the end of every stanza is a typical *yüeh-fu* singer's formula. Beyond that, in the context of this poem, it is perhaps intended to suggest that the poet's mind is directed toward happiness, positive achievement, and triumph over natural limitations.

The title "Pu ch'u Hsia-men hsing" was not invented by Ts'ao Ts'ao, and was used again by Ts'ao Jui. Two anonymous Han *yüeh-fu* bear this title. One of them deals with Taoist immortals. Of the other, only two lines have been preserved; they speak of the brevity of human life.[29]

In the following poem, the principal human figure is an aging soldier.

Variation on the Songs of the East and West Gates 卻東西門行

The wild geese come from north of the passes,
From a land without men.

鴻雁出塞北
乃在無人鄉

[29] *Yüeh-fu shih-chi*, 37.545; *Wei Chin nan-pei-ch'ao*, p. 10, n. 1.

They raise their wings and fly more than
a myriad miles,
Traveling and stopping in natural files.
In winter they eat the rice of the south,
In spring they fly back north.
In the field there is the tumbleweed,
Borne by the wind, he drifts far and high,
Forever cut off from his native roots,
Not to meet them again in a myriad years.
What can he do, this soldier in the war,
To get away from the earth's four
corners?
His army horse is never unsaddled;
His armor never leaves his side.
Slowly, slowly old age comes upon him.
When can he go home?
The holy dragon hides deep in the abyss;
The fierce tiger paces the lofty ridge;
The fox, about to die, makes for his
burrow:
How can one forget his home?[30]

舉翅萬餘里
行止自成行
冬節食南稻
春日復北翔
田中有轉蓬
隨風遠飄颺
長與故根絕
萬歲不相當
奈何此征夫
安得去四方
戎馬不解鞍
鎧甲不離傍
冉冉老將至
何時反故鄉
神龍藏深淵
猛虎步高岡
狐死歸首丘
故鄉安可忘

The same Ts'ao Ts'ao who, in the previous poem, had presented himself as the commander-in-chief with the heavy burden of leading the campaign, gives us in this poem the common soldier who has no control whatever over the army's endless movements. An early instance of the tumbleweed image (which was to become one of Ts'ao Chih's favorite images) occurs, though in a different context, in the *Book of Lord Shang*: 今夫飛蓬遇飄風而行千里乘風之勢也. "Now when the tumbleweed meets a whirlwind it travels a thousand miles, riding the force of the wind."[31] Topical

[30] *Yüeh-fu shih chi*, 37.552; Huang Chieh, *Wei Wu-ti*, p. 30; *Wei Chin nan-pei-ch'ao*, pp. 9–10; *Ts'ao Ts'ao chi*, p. 10; *Ts'ao Ts'ao chi i-chu*, pp. 39–40; Yü Kuan-ying, *San Ts'ao shih hsüan*, pp. 14–15; Chao Fu-t'an, *Ts'ao Wei fu-tzu*, pp. 30–31; von den Steinen, "Poems of Ts'ao Ts'ao," pp. 144–145.

[31] *Shang Tzu* 商子, also called *Shang chün shu* 商君書 (third century B.C.?), attributed to Shang Yang 商鞅 (died 338 B.C.), photolithographic reproduction of wood-block edition from T'ien-i ko 天一閣 Library in *Ssu-pu ts'ung-k'an*, 5.9a (section 24, "Chin shih" 禁使). For this reference I am indebted to Professor Wang Shu-min 王叔岷.

phrases marking this poem as a literary *yüeh-fu* are line 15 (cf. *Li sao* 離騷, couplet 33: 老冉冉其將至兮 "Old age slowly, slowly is coming upon me")[32] and the adage about the dying fox heading for its burrow, which is in *Li chi* 禮記, *Huai-nan Tzu* 淮南子, *Chiu chang* 九章 ("Ai Ying" 哀郢),[33] and *Ch'i chien* 七諫 ("Tzu pei" 自悲).

The *yüeh-fu* themes of this poem are: the fate of animals and plants (matching and contrasting with the human condition); an inhospitable exotic region; the soldier's hard lot; old age and death; and homesickness. The title seems to indicate that this *yüeh-fu* (at least its music) is a variation on a combination of earlier *yüeh-fu* patterns, and Ts'ao Ts'ao's poem in turn inspired later *yüeh-fu* poets.[34]

We will consider one more poem by Ts'ao Ts'ao. It must have been written in or shortly after 215, when he passed by Mount San-kuan (in modern Shensi) during his campaign against the Taoist leader Chang Lu 張魯.

Song of Ch'iu Hu (first of two) 秋胡行(二首之一)

First Stanza
At dawn I go up Mount San-kuan;
2 How difficult is this road!
At dawn I go up Mount San-kuan;
4 How difficult is this road!
The oxen lie exhausted and will not rise;
6 The carriage sinks in the ravine.
I sit on a flat boulder,
8 Pluck the five-string zither,
Play the tune *ch'ing-chüeh*,

一解
晨上散關山
此道當何難
晨上散關山
此道當何難
牛頓不起
車墮谷間
坐盤石之上
強五弦之琴
作爲淸角韻

[32] Noted by Huang Chieh, *Wei Wu-ti*, p. 30, n. 4.

[33] *Wei Chin nan-pei-ch'ao*, p. 9, n. 6; von den Steinen, "Poems of Ts'ao Ts'ao," p. 145, n.; Huang Chieh, *Wei Wu-ti*, p. 30, n. 6.

[34] See the poems titled "Hsi-men hsing," "Tung-men hsing," "Ch'üeh tung-hsi-men hsing," "Hung-yen sheng sai-pei hsing" 鴻雁生塞北行, and "Shun tung-hsi-men hsing" 順東西門行, *Yüeh-fu shih chi*, 37.549–554.

Feel bewildered and vexed.
I sing to speak my mind.
At dawn I go up Mount San-kuan.

意中迷煩
歌以言志
晨上散關山

Second Stanza

Who is the triply venerable old man
Suddenly come to my side?
Who is the triply venerable old man
Suddenly come to my side?
He wears a cloak over a fur coat,
Looks like no ordinary man.
He asks: "What trouble has upset you?
What is it you seek in your anxiety
That has brought you to this place?"
I sing to speak my mind.
Who is the triply venerable old man?

二解

有何三老公
卒來在我傍
有何三老公
卒來在我傍
負掩被裘
似非恒人
謂卿云何困苦以自怨
徨徨所欲
來到此間
歌以言志
有何三老公

Third Stanza

I live on Mount K'un-lun
And am what they call a Perfected Man.
I live on Mount K'un-lun
And am what they call a Perfected Man.
The Way is profound, but some of it can be achieved.
Over famous mountains I pass and look;
I roam in all eight directions.
Rocks are my pillows, I wash in running water, drink from springs.

三解

我居崑崙山
所謂者眞人
我居崑崙山
所謂者眞人
道深有可得
名山歷觀
遨遊八極
枕石漱流飲泉

32 While I ponder deeply and
hesitate
He rises up to Heaven.
34 I sing to speak my mind.
I live on Mount K'un-lun.

Fourth Stanza
36 Gone, gone, he cannot be
pursued;
He always resents anyone who
would hang on to him.
38 Gone, gone, he cannot be
pursued;
He always resents anyone who
would hang on to him.
40 Night after night, how can I
sleep?
I grieve and feel personal
sorrow.
42 He who was "upright, not sly"
Found his man through a song.
44 The Histories record where he
passed; (?)
When he went west, this is
what they recorded. (?)
46 I sing to speak my mind.
Gone, gone, he cannot be
pursued.[35]

沈吟不決
遂上升天
歌以言志
我居崑崙山

四解
去去不可追
長恨相牽攀
去去不可追
長恨相牽攀
夜夜安得寐
惆悵以自悲
正而不譎
辭賦依因
經傳所過
西來所傳
歌以言志
去去不可追

By sitting on a flat boulder and playing the five-string zither (lines 7–8), Ts'ao Ts'ao assumes the position of a ruler on a punitive expedition, worrying about the lot of his subjects.[36] The tune

[35] *Sung shu*, 21.610–611; *Yüeh-fu shih chi*, 36.526–527; Huang Chieh, *Wei Wu-ti*, pp. 19–21; *Ts'ao Ts'ao chi*, p. 7; *Ts'ao Ts'ao chi i-chu*, pp. 26–29; Stefan (Étienne) Balazs, "Ts'ao Ts'ao: Zwei Lieder," *Monumenta Serica* 2 (1937), 415–419 (English version: "Two Songs by Ts'ao Tsao," in his *Chinese Civilization and Bureaucracy* [New Haven: Yale University Press, 1964], pp. 183–184); von den Steinen, "Poems of Ts'ao Ts'ao," pp. 153–156.

[36] *Ts'ao Ts'ao chi i-chu*, p. 27, nn. 5–6.

ch'ing-chüeh (line 9) should be played only when the ruler is virtuous, according to a story in *Han-fei Tzu* 韓非子.[37] *San-lao* (lines 13, 15, 23) in antiquity and Han times often signifies a venerable old man;[38] *san lao kung* could of course also mean "three old men,"[39] but that seems less fitting here. The second and third stanzas make clear that the old man is a Taoist immortal. Line 42 alludes to *Lun-yü* 論語, Section 14, "Hsien wen" 憲問：子曰. 晉文公譎而不正. 齊桓公正而不譎. "The Master said, 'Duke Wen of Chin was sly, not upright; Duke Huan of Ch'i was upright, not sly."[40] Line 43 refers to Ning Ch'i 寧戚, who made himself known to Duke Huan of Ch'i by singing a song while feeding his oxen, and consequently became one of Duke Huan's ministers.[41] Duke Huan, anxious to find able men and marching west to subdue an enemy (line 45), becomes a model for Ts'ao Ts'ao during his western expedition against Chang Lu.[42]

Notable are the regular repetitions of whole lines at the beginning and end of every stanza. The *yüeh-fu* themes of this poem are: the commander-in-chief leading his army; an ascent; the hardships of travel; a musical performance; a meeting with a Taoist immortal and the immortal's activities; and insomnia. Two other *yüeh-fu* themes—the lord worrying about his subjects and about perfecting his rule and models from history—are alluded to in this poem, and treated more explicitly in other *yüeh-fu* by Ts'ao Ts'ao and others.

The title "Ch'iu Hu hsing" derives from a story about a man named Ch'iu Hu which has nothing to do with Ts'ao Ts'ao's two poems. The same title was used again by many *yüeh-fu* poets after Ts'ao Ts'ao.[43] Noteworthy among them are seven poems by Hsi

[37] *Ts'ao Ts'ao chi i-chu*, pp. 27–28, n. 7.

[38] Balazs, "Ts'ao Ts'ao," p. 416; Derk Bodde, *Festivals in Classical China: New Year and Other Annual Observances during the Han Dynasty 206 B.C.–A.D. 220* (Princeton: Princeton University Press, 1975), pp. 372–380.

[39] *Ts'ao Ts'ao chi i-chu* takes it in this sense.

[40] Huang Chieh, *Wei Wu-ti*, p. 21, n. 16.

[41] Huang Chieh, *Wei Wu-ti*, p. 21, n. 17; von den Steinen, "Poems of Ts'ao Ts'ao," p. 156.

[42] *Ts'ao Ts'ao chi i-chu*, p. 28, nn. 18 and 20.

[43] See *Yüeh-fu shih chi*, 36.526–534.

K'ang 嵇康 (223–262). They are close to Ts'ao Ts'ao's in form, and set forth Taoist philosophy.[44]

Ts'ao Ts'ao's poems touch on nearly all the themes of Han and Wei *yüeh-fu* poetry, with one conspicuous exception: the themes connected with women. But these are well represented in the *yüeh-fu* of his sons Ts'ao P'i and Ts'ao Chih. Ts'ao P'i 曹丕 (born winter 187–188, died 226, reigned 220–226, known as Wei Wen-ti 魏文帝), unlike his father, wrote both *yüeh-fu* and regular *shih*. We will consider four of his twenty-three full-length *yüeh-fu*.

Good! (second of four)
There was one beautiful woman,
2 Fine bright eyes, graceful brows,
Attractive looks, coquettish smile,
4 Pleasing, heart-captivating.
She knew notes, was versed in tunes,
6 An excellent musician.
Her melancholy strings were subtle and wonderful;
8 Her clear breath carried fragrance.
In flowing strains of Cheng and rousing tunes of Ch'u
10 The notes *kung* and *shang* were never off,
Heart-moving, ear-stirring,
12 Her beauty hard to forget.
A separated bird roosts in the evening
14 On yonder island.
It stretches its neck and beats its wings,

善哉行(四首之二)
有美一人
婉如清揚
妍姿巧笑
和媚心腸
知音識曲
善爲樂方
哀弦微妙
清氣含芳
流鄭激楚
度宮中商
感心動耳
綺麗難忘
離鳥夕宿
在彼中洲
延頸鼓翼

[44] For a translation and thorough discussion of the seven poems, see Donald Holzman, "La poésie de Ji Kang," *Journal asiatique* 268 (1980), 333–342.

Sadly calling, looking for its mate.
With longing I look toward it,
It makes my heart grieve.
Alas, the people of the past,
How did they ever get over their sorrow?[45]

悲鳴相求
眷然顧之
使我心愁
嗟爾昔人
何以忘憂

The poem consists of two parts, audibly set apart by a different rhyme for each part. The meaning of each part becomes clear only in conjunction with the other part. When one reads the first part (lines 1–12), one may think that this is simply a poem in praise of a fascinating woman (in the tradition of Li Yen-nien's "Song") and a fine musician. Only in the second part does one realize that the heart she has captivated is the speaker's, and that he is unhappily separated from his love. This throws the entire first part into the past. The lone bird (its species and sex not specified in this case) is a common *yüeh-fu* image for a man or woman separated from a friend, companion, relative, lover, or spouse. Its specific significance here is made clear by the context.

The first two lines of our poem are adapted from *Shih ching*, Song No. 94. "Shan tsai hsing" was the title of an anonymous Han *yüeh-fu*, and was used by *yüeh-fu* poets from Ts'ao Ts'ao down to T'ang times.[46]

Different twists are given to bird imagery in the following poem by Ts'ao P'i.

I Look Down from the High Terrace 臨高臺

The terrace from which I look down is high,
High with a distant view. (?)
Below there is a body of water,
Clear and cold.

臨臺高
高以軒
下有水
淸且寒

[45] *Yüeh-fu shih chi*, 36.538; Huang Chieh, *Wei Wu-ti*, pp. 37–38; Yü Kuan-ying, *San Ts'ao shih hsüan*, p. 23; Chao Fu-t'an, *Ts'ao Wei fu-tzu*, pp. 60–61; Wilfried Schulte, *Ts'ao P'i (187–226): Leben und Dichtungen*, dissertation, Bonn 1971 (Bonn: Rheinische Friedrich-Wilhelms-Universität, 1973), pp. 87–88.

[46] *Yüeh-fu shih chi*, 36.535–540.

On it there are brown swans, about to leave, flapping their wings.
6 As a subject
I must be loyal to the end.
8 I wish His Imperial Majesty to live three thousand years
As is fitting, residing in this palace.
10 The swan wants to migrate south;
His mate cannot fly with him.
12 "I want to carry you myself in my beak,
But my bill is shut tight, I cannot open it."
14 He wants to carry her on his back,
But his feathers are broken and ruined.
16 After five miles he looks back once;
After six miles he hesitates.[47]

中有黃鵠往且翻
行爲臣
當盡忠
願令皇帝陛下三千歲
宜居此宮
鵠欲南遊
鴜不能隨
我欲躬銜汝
口噤不能開
欲負之
毛衣摧頹
五里一顧
六里徘徊

Ts'ao P'i's immediate model is the sixteenth of the eighteen anonymous Han "Nao ko" 鐃歌:

I Look Down from the High Terrace 臨高臺

I look down from the high terrace with distant view. (?)

臨高臺以軒
下有清水清且寒

[47] *I-wen lei-chu* 藝文類聚, compiled by Ou-yang Hsün 歐陽詢 (557–641) (Shanghai: Chung-hua shu-chü, 1965), 42.761; *Yüeh-fu shih chi*, 18.258–259; Huang Chieh, *Wei Wu-ti*, pp. 51–52; Schulte, *Ts'ao P'i*, pp. 95–96. Lines 6–9 show that the poem must be earlier than 220, when Ts'ao P'i became emperor. The meter is complex, and there are textual problems. In the first line (and in line 3 of the "Nao ko" below) I have adopted the emendations proposed by Wen I-to 聞一多 (1899–1946), "Yüeh-fu shih chien" 樂府詩箋, in *Wen I-to ch'uan-chi* 聞一多全集 (Shanghai: K'ai-ming shu-chü, 1948), vol. 4, p. 111.

2 Below there is a clear body of water, clear and cold.
In the river there are fragrant plants, angelica and orchid.
4 Brown swans fly up, away, soaring.
I bend the bow and shoot a swan
6 To make my lord live ten thousand years.[48]

江有香草茝以蘭
黃鵠高飛離哉翻
關弓射飛鵠
令我主壽萬年
收中吾

The three themes of Ts'ao P'i's poem—the view from the terrace, the bird couple, and loyalty to the emperor—are not well integrated. In the anonymous model, there is a connection between the shooting of the bird and the wish for the emperor's longevity, a connection which is even clearer in the story of General Wang Chi 王吉 shooting a crow to insure long life for Emperor Ming (reigned 58–75).[49] In Ts'ao P'i's poem no bird is shot, but the wish to prolong the emperor's life remains. The motif of the bird couple, tragically separated because the female is too sick to fly, occurs in several anonymous *yüeh-fu* poems. One of them, titled "Yen-ko ho-ch'ang hsing" 艷歌何嘗行, opens with a passage resembling Ts'ao P'i's rather closely, and is probably older than his.[50] In Ts'ao P'i's composition, there is no obvious connection between the bird couple and the rest of the poem. An analogy is perhaps intended between the conjugal loyalty of the migratory birds and the subject's loyal devotion to his emperor. After Ts'ao P'i, the same

[48] *Sung shu*, 22.643; *Yüeh-fu shih chi*, 16.231–232; Wen I-to, *Wen I-to*, p. 111. I have left line 7 untranslated; it is believed to be the remnant of a musical notation or filler.

[49] See Wen I-to, *Wen I-to*, p. 111, quoting Ch'en Hang 陳沆 (1785–1826), who cites the story from *Feng-su t'ung-i* 風俗通義 by Ying Shao 應劭 (ca. 140–ca. 206). But it is not to be found in the extant *Feng-su t'ung-i* text as concordanced in *Feng-su t'ung-i t'ung-chien* 風俗通義通檢 (Peking: Centre franco-chinois d'études sinologiques, 1943). Cf. also *Shih ching* 詩經, No. 216, where flying ducks are associated with the lord's longevity.

[50] *Sung shu*, 21.618–619; *Yüeh-fu shih chi*, 39.576–577. For this and related poems, see Jean-Pierre Diény, *Aux origines de la poésie classique en Chine: Étude sur la poésie lyrique à l'époque des Han* (Leiden: Brill, 1968), pp. 142–146, and Hans Frankel, "The Chinese Ballad 'Southeast Fly the Peacocks,'" *Harvard Journal of Asiatic Studies* 34 (1974), 267–271.

title "Lin kao-t'ai" and some of the same motifs were used again by ten *yüeh-fu* poets down to the T'ang.[51]

Our third example of Ts'ao P'i's *yüeh-fu* is distinguished by a refrain, and laments the fate of the poor.

Song of Shang-liu-t'ien
How much difference is there in life!
2 Shang-liu-t'ien
The rich eat rice and millet,
4 Shang-liu-t'ien
The poor get dregs and chaff.
6 Shang-liu-t'ien
How it hurts to be poor and humble!
8 Shang-liu-t'ien
Fate is suspended in blue Heaven.
10 Shang-liu-t'ien
Thus I lament today, who will complain in future?
12 Shang-liu-t'ien[52]

上留田行
居世一何不同
上留田
富人食稻與粱
上留田
貧子食糟與糠
上留田
貧賤亦何傷
上留田
祿命懸在蒼天
上留田
今爾歎息將欲誰怨
上留田

Shang-liu-t'ien was originally a place name, with a story and an anonymous poem about an orphan.[53] "Shang-liu-t'ien hsing" was used as a *yüeh-fu* title by poets from the Chin dynasty down to the T'ang, with reminiscences of the old themes and phrases, and sometimes of the refrain.[54]

Our final selection from Ts'ao P'i's *yüeh-fu* is a moving lament on his father's death. It must have been written shortly after Ts'ao Ts'ao's death in 220. (Ts'ao Ts'ao had written a *yüeh-fu* on the death of *his* father, titled "Shan-tsai hsing" 善哉行 [second of three].)[55]

[51] *Yüeh-fu shih chi*, 18.259–262.

[52] *I-wen lei-chü*, 41.745; *Yüeh-fu shih chi*, 38.563; Huang Chieh, *Wei Wu-ti*, p. 53; Yü Kuan-ying, *San Ts'ao shih hsüan*, pp. 24–25; Chao Fu-t'an, *Ts'ao Wei fu-tzu*, p. 64. Line 11 is punctuated correctly in the 1965 edition of *I-wen lei-chü* and in the 1979 edition of *Yüeh-fu shih chi*. It is split into two lines in other punctuated editions. Making it a single line gives the poem a neat pattern: the odd-numbered lines rhyme, the even-numbered lines constitute the refrain.

[53] See *Yüeh-fu shih chi*, 38.563 and the sources cited there.

[54] *Ibid.*, 38.563–565.

[55] *Ts'ao Ts'ao chi*, p. 9

Song in Short Meter	短歌行
First Stanza	一解
I look up and see the curtains;	仰瞻帷幕
I look down and view the table and mat.	俯察几筵
The objects are as before,	其物如故
The man is no more.	其人不存
Second Stanza	二解
His spirit has suddenly	神靈倏忽
Abandoned me, vanished, gone.	棄我遐遷
No one to look up to, no one to depend on,	靡瞻靡恃
Tears flow and flow.	泣涕連連
Third Stanza	三解
Yu yu cry the roving deer,	呦呦鹿鳴
Troubled, troubled, they call their fawns.	草草鳴麑
Flap flap go the birds' wings,	翩翩飛鳥
Covering their young in the nest.	挾子巢棲
Fourth Stanza	四解
Only I am all alone,	我獨孤煢
Harboring these hundred sorrows.	懷此百離
My grieving heart suffers,	憂心孔疚
No one knows how much.	莫我能知
Fifth Stanza	五解
People have a saying:	人亦有言
"Grief makes men old."	憂令人老
Alas, my white hair,	嗟我白髮
How early it grows!	生一何早
Sixth Stanza	六解
Long I sigh, always I lament,	長吟永歎
I miss my noble father.	懷我聖考
It's said the benevolent live long—	曰仁者壽
Why was *his* life not preserved?[56]	胡不是保

Note the enjambement in lines 5–6, and the many allusions

[56] *Sung shu*, 21.609; *Yüeh-fu shih chi*, 30.448; Huang Chieh, *Wei Wu-ti*, pp. 33–34; Yü Kuan-ying, *San Ts'ao shih hsüan*, pp. 17–18; Chao Fu-t'an, *Ts'ao Wei fu-tzu*, pp. 49–50; Schulte, *Ts'ao P'i*, pp. 83–84.

throughout the poem. Lines 1–4 derive from *Hsün Tzu*:俛見几筵. 其器存 . 其人亡. "Looking down you see the tables and mats; the [ancestors'] implements are still there but the men are dead."[57] Line 7 alludes to *Shih ching* 詩經, Nos. 197 and 202 (note the deft repetition of *chan* 瞻 in lines 1 and 7); line 9 to *Shih ching*, No. 161; line 14 to *Shih ching*, No. 70; line 15 to *Shih ching*, No. 167 or 169; line 16 again to *Shih ching*, No. 167; and line 23 to *Lun-yü* 論語, Section 6, "Yung yeh" 雍也. (These allusions are noted in the commentaries.)

The *yüeh-fu* themes of this poem are personal grief, death, aging, and analogies from animal life. The title "Tuan-ko hsing" means, I believe, "song in short meter." The early instances are all in lines of four syllables. It contrasts with "Ch'ang-ko hsing" 長歌行 "song in long meter" (five-syllable lines). *Yüeh-fu shih chi* has twenty-five poems with the title "Tuan-ko hsing," the oldest by Ts'ao Ts'ao.[58]

A new development of literary *yüeh-fu* was brought about by Ts'ao Chih 曹植 (192–232). Whereas Ts'ao Ts'ao had made *yüeh-fu* the exclusive vehicle for all his narrative and lyric poetry (and Ts'ao P'i for most of it), Ts'ao Chih made a distinction between *shih* 詩 and *yüeh-fu*. His extant poems are about equally divided between the two genres. Though some of his poems are borderline cases, the distinction is nevertheless clear: Ts'ao Chih uses *shih* for lyric self-expression and to communicate with brothers and friends; when he writes *yüeh-fu* he creates poetic worlds of fiction, taking up the tradition of anonymous Han narrative *yüeh-fu* and of Hsin Yen-nien's "Palace Guard Officer," and blazing a trail for later generations of *yüeh-fu* poets. In the following poem he creates, first, a merry dandy who shows off his incredible skills, and then an ideal feast.

Some Famous Cities	名都篇
Some famous cities boast seductive women;	名都多妖女

[57] *Hsün Tzu* 荀子, attributed to Hsün Ch'ing 荀卿 (ca. 298–ca. 238 B.C.), photolithographic reproduction of *Ku-i ts'ung-shu* 古逸叢書 wood block ed. in *Ssu-pu ts'ung-k'an*, 20.21a (section 3a, "Ai kung" 哀公), noted by Schulte, *Ts'ao P'i*, p. 146, n. 401.

[58] *Yüeh-fu shih chi*, 30.446–453.

2 The capital Lo-yang produces fine young men.
My precious sword is worth a thousand gold;
4 The clothes are handsome and bright.
I watch cockfights on the road to the eastern suburbs,
6 Then canter down the long catalpa-lined avenue.
Less than halfway on the galloping ride,
8 A couple of hares pass in front of me.
I grasp my bow and place a singing arrow,
10 Then a long chase up South Mountain.
I draw on my left and let fly on my right: (?)
12 A single arrow pierces both animals.
More skill is yet to be displayed:
14 I reach up with one hand and snatch a hawk in flight.
The onlookers are unanimous in their praise;
16 The experts concede my excellence.
Now we go back for a feast at the Palace of Peace and Pleasure,
18 With fine wines, worth ten thousand a peck,
Minced carp, a soup of shrimp with roe,
20 Roast turtle, and broiled bears' paws.
We shout to our friends, call to our companions
22 Along the whole length of the banquet mat.
Continuous games are played with balls and boards,
24 With nimble skills of myriad kinds.
The bright sun speeds southwest,
26 Its splendor cannot be arrested.

京洛出少年
寶劍直千金
被服麗且鮮
鬬鷄東郊道
走馬長楸間
馳騁未能半
雙兎過我前
攬弓捷鳴鏑
長驅上南山
左挽因右發
一縱兩禽連
餘巧未及展
仰手接飛鳶
觀者咸稱善
衆工歸我妍
我歸宴平樂
美酒斗十千
膾鯉臇胎鰕
炮鼈炙熊蹯
鳴儔嘯匹侶
列坐竟長筵
連翩擊鞠壤
巧捷惟萬端
白日西南馳
光景不可攀

Like clouds the company scatters back to
town,
28 To come again tomorrow morning.[59]

雲散還城邑
淸晨復來還

The title of the poem is taken from the opening words (as in other *yüeh-fu* by Ts'ao Ts'ao and Ts'ao Chih) and was not used again by other poets. The dashing young hero of this poem is surely a fictional creation, though he may have some traits in common with persons known to the poet, or with the poet as he saw himself. In this and other *yüeh-fu*, Ts'ao Chih creates ideal, fictional characters and situations, following in the tradition of Ts'ao Ts'ao's utopian "I Drink."

In the next poem Ts'ao Chih presents one of his favorite types, the faithful, good wife who has lost her husband's affection. In much of his work, Ts'ao Chih is obsessed with the notions of unrecognized loyalty and unjust neglect.[60]

The Floating Duckweed

浮萍篇

The floating duckweed lodges on clear
water,
2 Drifting east and west with the wind.
I bound up my hair, took leave of my

浮萍寄淸水
隨風東西流
結髮辭嚴親

[59] *Wen hsüan chu* 文選注, compiled by Hsiao T'ung 蕭統 (501–531, Crown Prince Chao-ming of Liang 梁昭明太子), with commentary by Li Shan 李善 (died 689) (Taipei: Shih-chieh shu-chü, 1962), 27.382–383; *Yüeh-fu shih chi*, 63.912; Ting Yen 丁晏 (1794–1875), *Ts'ao chi ch'üan-p'ing* 曹集銓評 (Peking: Wen-hsüeh ku-chi k'an-hsing-she, 1957), 5.61–62; Huang Chieh, *Ts'ao Tzu-chien shih chu* 曹子建詩注, in *Ts'ao Tzu-chien chi p'ing-chu erh chung* 曹子建集評注二種 (Taipei: Shih-chieh shu-chü, 1962), 2.71–73; *Wei Chin nan-pei-ch'ao*, pp. 85–87; Yü Kuan-ying, *San Ts'ao shih hsüan*, pp. 57–58; Chao Fu-t'an, *Ts'ao Wei fu-tzu*, pp. 156–158; Erwin von Zach, *Die chinesische Anthologie: Übersetzungen aus dem Wen hsüan*, ed. Ilse Martin-Fang (Cambridge: Harvard University Press, 1958), 27.32; Itō Masafumi 伊藤正文, *Sō Shoku* 曹植 (Tokyo: Iwanami, 1958), pp. 134–138; Frodsham and Ch'eng, *Chinese Verse*, pp. 42–44; George W. Kent, *Worlds of Dust and Jade: 47 Poems and Ballads of the Third Century Chinese Poet Ts'ao Chih* (New York: Philosophical Library, 1969), p. 65; Hugh Dunn, *Ts'ao Chih: The Life of a Princely Poet* (Taipei: China News, n.d.; his preface dated 1970), pp. 34–35; Eric Sackheim, *... the Silent Zero, in Search of Sound ...: An Anthology of Chinese Poems from the Beginning through the Sixth Century* (New York: Grossman, 1971), p. 100; Mok Wing-yin, "Three Poems by Ts'ao Chih," *Renditions*, no. 2 (Spring 1974), 52.

[60] For a study of this theme, see David Roy, "The Theme of the Neglected Wife in the Poetry of Ts'ao Chih," *Journal of Asian Studies* 19 (1959) 25–31.

stern parents,
4 And came to you to be your mate, my prince.
Diligent and respectful morning and evening,
6 I was blamed without cause.
I used to get affection and favor;
8 Our joy harmonized like music of *se* and *ch'in*.
Who would have expected the present ruin,
10 Putting us as far apart as Antares and Orion!
Dogwood has its own fragrance,
12 But it is not as good as cassia and orchid.
A new love, though attractive,
14 Is not as good for happiness as the old spouse.
For wandering clouds there is a time of return;
16 My lord's favor will perhaps come back.
Unhappy I look up to Heaven and sigh;
18 Whom shall I tell what is in my sad heart?
Sun and moon are not in constant locations;
20 Man's life changes suddenly, like an adventure.
A mournful wind comes through the curtains;
22 My tears drop like suspended dew.
I go through my trunk to make him new clothes,
24 Cut and sew lustrous and plain silks.[61]

來爲君子仇
恪勤在朝夕
無端獲罪尤
在昔蒙恩惠
和樂如瑟琴
何意今摧頹
曠若商與參
茱萸自有芳
不若桂與蘭
新人雖可愛
不若故人歡
行雲有反期
君恩儻中還
慊慊仰天歎
愁心將何愬
日月不恒處
人生忽若遇
悲風來入帷
淚下如垂露
散篋造新衣
裁縫紈與素

[61] *Chien-chu yü-t'ai hsin yung*, 2.6b–7a; *Yüeh-fu shih chi*, 35.524; Ting Yen, *Ts'ao chi ch'üan-p'ing*, 5.69–70; Huang Chieh, *Ts'ao Tzu-chien shih chu*, 2.94–95; Yü Kuan-ying, *San Ts'ao shih hsüan*, pp. 45–46; Chao Fu-t'an, *Ts'ao Wei fu-tzu*, pp. 182–183; Itō, *Sō Shoku*, pp. 165–168; Roy, "The Neglected Wife," pp. 29–30; Kent, *Worlds of Dust and Jade*, pp. 72–73; Birrell, *New Songs from a Jade Terrace*, pp. 69–70.

The poem bears one of the marks that distinguish literary *yüeh-fu* from popular anonymous *yüeh-fu*: It has literary antecedents, or, to put it more accurately, it contains phrases which had already been used in literary works that were the common property of the literati. As noted by Huang Chieh, the opening image—we may call it a *hsing* 興—derives from *Ch'u tz'u*, namely, from the end of the fifth poem ("Tsun chia" 尊嘉) of *Chiu huai* 九懷 by Wang Pao 王褒 (first century B.C.); and line 8 derives from *Shih ching*, No. 164.

Let me recapitulate now the twenty-five themes encountered in the Han and Wei literary *yüeh-fu*: (1) climbing up high and looking down; (2) nature and its relation to human affairs; (3) exotic places and their inhabitants; (4) barbarians; (5) hardships of travel; (6) homesickness; (7) the commander of a military campaign; (8) the soldier on campaign; (9) hardships caused by war; (10) sufferings of the common people; (11) immortals; (12) the brevity of life and the desire to prolong it; (13) old age and death; (14) personal grief; (15) insomnia; (16) feasts; (17) music; (18) ideal situations and persons; (19) the wish to be a perfect ruler; (20) the wish to be a perfect subject; (21) models from history; (22) beautiful women; (23) the woman triumphant; (24) a faithful woman rejected by her husband or lover; and (25) a loyal bird couple.

I have deliberately used the rather vague term "themes," rather than differentiating between topics, topoi, motifs, archetypes, and other categories. Some of the themes are closely related to each other, and some differ with respect to their social, historical, and literary backgrounds. For example, themes Nos. 1, 11, 16, 20, and 21 belong exclusively to the literati, while Nos. 8 and 10 are inherited from the anonymous Han *yüeh-fu* and voice the concerns of the common people. The feelings of insecurity that pervaded all classes of Chinese society from the end of Han through the Wei and Chin make themselves heard in Nos. 12, 15, and 18. The prominence of theme No. 17 is not surprising, since early *yüeh-fu* is by definition a musical genre.

Before the literati fully adopted this genre, the creation and performance of *yüeh-fu* must have been the nearly exclusive prerogative of professional singers and musicians. The earliest *yüeh-fu* poet discussed above, Li Yen-nien, was a professional musician, and

Hsin Yen-nien is said to have been one also. Tso Yen-nien 左延年 was a musician during Ts'ao P'i's reign.[62] He is also the author of "Ch'in Nü-hsiu hsing" 秦女休行, a powerful narrative *yüeh-fu* of family revenge and a brilliant elaboration of the woman triumphant theme.[63] P'o Ch'in 繁欽 (died 218), the author of "Ting-ch'ing shih" 定情詩,[64] which may be considered a literary *yüeh-fu*, wrote an interesting letter to Ts'ao P'i, dated February 1, 217, telling him about a gifted fourteen-*sui*-old driver who was a marvelous singer.[65] The detailed account testifies to both men's interest in music and musicians. Since Ts'ao Ts'ao, Ts'ao P'i, and Ts'ao Chih did more than any other poet to secure a place for *yüeh-fu* in high literature, it is plausible that they had direct contact with professional musicians. Such contact may have been provided by Ts'ao Ts'ao's consort née Pien 卞, the mother of Ts'ao P'i and Ts'ao Chih. Before entering Ts'ao Ts'ao's household at the age of twenty *sui* she was a professional singer (*ch'ang-chia* 倡家).[66]

Finally, as a barbarian interested in *yüeh-fu*, I would like to call attention to the barbarian connection of this genre. Despite the low opinion in which foreigners were generally held in regard to cultural achievements,[67] there are indications of foreign elements in *yüeh-fu* songs (and in the dances that went with some of them); and among the professionals who created and performed *yüeh-fu* there may have been aliens. Non-Chinese entertainers, musicians, singers, and dancers were popular at the Chinese court and with the upper classes throughout the Han dynasty (and also before and afterward).[68] The woman triumphant of Hsin Yen-nien's "Impe-

[62] *San-kuo chih*, 29.807; *Chin shu*, 22.679. The fact that these three musicians had the same name Yen-nien is just a coincidence, I believe; it was a common name at the time.

[63] *Yüeh-fu shih chi*, 61.886–887; Frankel, "Six Dynasties," pp. 193–195.

[64] *Chien-chu yü-t'ai hsin yung*, 1.22a–23b; *Yüeh-fu shih chi*, 76.1076–1077.

[65] *Wen hsüan chu*, 40.562–563; von Zach, *Die chinesische Anthologie*, 40.5.

[66] See her biography, *San-kuo chih*, 5.156–159. Her possible connection with the Ts'aos' interest in *yüeh-fu* is suggested by Honda Wataru 本田濟, "Sō Shoku to sono jidai" 曹植とその時代, *Tōhōgaku* 東方学, no. 3 (January 1952), 53–60.

[67] For many instances of this prevailing view, see *China und die Fremden: 3000 Jahre Auseinandersetzung in Krieg und Frieden*, ed. Wolfgang Bauer (Munich: C. H. Beck, 1980).

[68] See Diény, *Aux origines*, pp. 56–64.

rial Guard Officer" was a non-Chinese girl. Ts'ao Chih once performed a barbarian dance and show "in several thousand words" for the scholar Han-tan Ch'un 邯鄲淳, whom he wanted to impress.[69] There is even the intriguing possibility that Ts'ao P'i and Ts'ao Chih were partly of non-Chinese descent: their brother Ts'ao Chang 曹彰 (died 223), born to Ts'ao Ts'ao by the same mother, nee Pien, is said to have had a brown (or blond?) beard (*huang hsü* 黃鬚).[70]

[69] *Wei lüeh* 魏略 by Yü Huan 魚豢 (third century), quoted in P'ei Sung-chih's commentary to *San-kuo chih*, 21.603, n. 1.

[70] *Wei lüeh*, quoted in P'ei's commentary to *San-kuo chih*, 19.556, n. 2; and in Liu Chün's 劉峻 (462–521) commentary to *Shih-shuo hsin yü*; see *Shih-shuo hsin yü chiao-chien* 世說新語校箋, ed. Yang Yung 楊勇, "Yu hui" 尤悔 (Hong Kong: Ta-chung shu-chü, 1969), section 33, item 1. But it is also possible that *huang* in this case signifies nothing more than a lighter shade of black.

Zhou Zhenfu

The Legacy of the Han, Wei, and Six Dynasties *Yüeh-fu* Tradition and Its Further Development in T'ang Poetry

Translated from Chinese by Kang-i Sun Chang and Hans H. Frankel

In discussing the development of *yüeh-fu* 樂府 poetry, the Ming critic Hu Ying-lin 胡應麟 (1551–1602) asserts that the stylistically embellished *yüeh-fu* of the Wei are inferior to the plain, unembellished *yüeh-fu* of the Han. He goes on to say that because they are full of parallelism and antithesis, Chin *yüeh-fu* are inferior to those of Wei and that T'ang *yüeh-fu* are inferior even to those of Chin.[1] It is clear that Hu's criterion for relative excellence is the proportion of plain style and ornamentation—a one-sided criticism, in my opinion.

In the more balanced view of the Ch'ing poet and theorist Wang Shih-chen 王士禛 (1634–1711), Han *yüeh-fu* still follow in the tradition of *Shih ching* 詩經, but during the T'ang definite changes occur in *yüeh-fu* poetry, as can be seen in Li Po's 李白 (701–762) "Infinite Separation" ("Yüan pieh-li" 遠別離)[2] and "The

[1] Hu Ying-lin 胡應麟, "Nei-pien" 內編, in *Shih sou* 詩藪 (Peking: Chung-hua shu-chü, 1959), *chüan* 6, pp. 101–102.

[2] Li Po 李白, *Li T'ai-po ch'üan-chi* 李太白全集, 3 vols. (Peking: Chung-hua shu-chü, 1977), vol. 1, *chüan* 3, pp. 157–159.

Hardships of the Road to Shu" ("Shu-tao nan" 蜀道難),[3] or in Tu Fu's 杜甫 (712–770) "Separation of the Newlyweds" ("Hsin-hun pieh" 新婚別),[4] "No Home to Take Leave of" ("Wu chia pieh" 無家別),[5] "The Recruiting Officer at Shih-hao" ("Shih-hao li" 石壕吏),[6] "The Recruiting Officer at Hsin-an" ("Hsin-an li" 新安吏),[7] "Lament on the River Bank" ("Ai chiang-t'ou" 哀江頭),[8] and "Ballad of the Army Carts" ("Ping-chü hsing" 兵車行).[9] In Wang's opinion, *yüeh-fu* should not slavishly copy lines and phrases from earlier *yüeh-fu*, but should innovate.[10] Generally speaking, the language of Han *yüeh-fu* was plain, lines of five syllables and of varying length taking the place of the four-syllable line of *Shih ching*, and narrative replacing the lyricism of *Shih ching*. Then, toward the end of the Eastern Han, the *yüeh-fu* style changed, becoming increasingly ornate and lyrical. During the Chien-an era (196–220), the seven-syllable line became common, embellishments were more elaborate, and some poems were characterized by passionate outbursts of emotion. By the Chin dynasty, parallelism and antithesis became even more common in *yüeh-fu*, though the outstanding creations of the epoch were such simpler lyric songs as the "Tzu-yeh Songs" ("Tzu-yeh ko" 子夜歌). During the Ch'i and Liang dynasties, tonal patterns became important, and literary style was excessively ornamented. T'ang *yüeh-fu* at once continued the traditions of *Shih ching*, *Ch'u tz'u*, and the *yüeh-fu* of the Han, Wei, and Six Dynasties, but at the same time added many new developments of their own. I will now separately discuss the *yüeh-fu* of Early, High, Middle, and Late T'ang.

Early T'ang poets reacted against the excessive ornamentation of Ch'i and Liang *yüeh-fu*. These efforts manifested themselves in

[3] *Ibid.*, vol. 1, *chüan* 3, pp. 162–168.

[4] Ch'iu Chao-ao 仇兆鰲, *Tu shih hsiang-chu* 杜詩詳注, 5 vols. (Peking: Chung-hua shu-chü, 1979), vol. 2, *chüan* 7, pp. 530–534.

[5] *Ibid.*, pp. 537–539.

[6] *Ibid.*, pp. 528–530.

[7] *Ibid.*, pp. 523–526.

[8] *Ibid.*, vol. 1, *chüan* 4, pp. 329–330.

[9] *Ibid.*, *chüan* 2, pp. 113–118.

[10] Wang Shih-chen 王士禛, "Shih-yu shih ch'uan-lu" 師友詩傳錄, in *Ch'ing shih-hua* 淸詩話, ed. Kuo Shao-yü 郭紹虞 (Peking: Chung-hua shu-chü, 1963), pp. 127–128.

two ways:

(1) "The Four Talents of the Early T'ang" opposed delicate artifice and overwrought refinement; although they sought a firm, strong style,[11] they still showed concern for the Southern Dynasties' sense of literary craft. The couplet:

The green leaves put to shame the painted eyebrows; The flowers are redder than the cheeks.	葉翠本羞眉 花紅强如頰

from Wang Po's 王勃 (650?–676) "Return from Picking Lotus Blossoms" ("Ts'ai lien kuei" 採蓮歸) is an example of such craft. But in the same poem, the couplet:

The soldier at the frontier has not yet returned; South of the Yangtze, the picking of lotus blossoms is over for the day.[12]	塞外征夫猶未還 江南採蓮今已暮

associates the soldier on campaign at the frontier with the picking of lotus blossoms. The simplicity of these lines contrasts strongly with the decadently ornate style of Lu Ssu-tao's 盧思道 (535?–586?) couplet in his "Song on Picking Lotus Blossoms" ("Ts'ai lien ch'ü" 採蓮曲):

At the winding river bank seductive women play; Their movements are lissome, without restraint.[13]	曲浦戲妖姬 輕盈不自持

(2) The following lines from Chang Jo-hsü's 張若虛 (ca. 660–ca. 720) "Spring-River Blossom-Moon Night" ("Ch'un-chiang hua-yüeh yeh" 春江花月夜) are a good example of how the mannered style dominant during the Ch'i and Liang dynasties was purged by the pure and fresh poetry of Early T'ang:

[11] Yang Chiung 楊烱, "Wang Po chi hsü" 王勃集序, in *Yang Ying-ch'uan chi* 楊盈川集, *chüan* 3; see *Chung-kuo li-tai wen-lun hsüan* 中國歷代文論選 (Hong Kong: Chung-hua shu-chü, 1979), p. 335.

[12] Kuo Mao-ch'ien 郭茂倩, *Yüeh-fu shih chi* 樂府詩集, 4 vols. (Peking: Chung-hua shu-chü, 1979), vol. 3, *chüan* 50, p. 736.

[13] *Ibid.*, vol. 3, *chüan* 50, p. 732.

River and heaven are one color, without a speck of dust;	江天一色無纖塵
Clear and bright in the sky, the lone moon wheel.	皎皎空中孤月輪
Who first saw the moon at the river bank?	江畔何人初見月
In what year did the river moon first shine on man?	江月何年初照人
Human life goes on age after age, without end;	人生代代無窮已
The river moon just stays the same year after year.	江月年年望相似
I do not know for whom the river moon waits;	不知江月待何人
I only see the Long River sending the water on.[14]	但見長江送流水

As one can see, Wang Po and Chang Jo-hsü returned to the forceful style of Chien-an poetry and swept away the artificial style of Ch'i and Liang poetry.

During the High T'ang, *yüeh-fu* became more vigorous and were used for political satire. Examples are Li Po's "Infinite Separation" and Tu Fu's "Ballad of Beautiful Ladies" ("Li-jen hsing" 麗人行).[15] Since Li Po's "Infinite Separation" is included in Yin Fan's 殷璠 anthology *Ho-yüeh ying-ling chi* 河嶽英靈集, which was completed in 753, it is remarkable that the following lines seem to foresee the An Lu-shan Rebellion which broke out in 755:

August Heaven, I fear, ignores my sincere concern;	皇穹竊恐不照余之忠誠
Thunder is about to give out a loud, angry roar.	雷憑憑兮欲吼怒
Yao and Shun in their time also yielded the throne;	堯舜當之亦禪禹
When the ruler loses his subject's loyalty, the dragon becomes a fish;	君失臣兮龍爲魚

[14] *Ibid.*, vol. 2, *chüan* 47, p. 679.

[15] Ch'iu Chao-ao, *Tu shih hsiang-chu*, vol. 2, pp. 156–162.

When power falls to the subject, the rat turns into a tiger. 權歸臣兮鼠變虎
Some say Yao was imprisoned and Shun died in the wilderness. 或云堯幽囚舜野死
All parts of the Nine-Peak Range look the same; 九疑聯綿皆相似
Where is the lone grave of the double-pupiled Shun?[16] 重瞳孤墳竟何是

In this poem, one of the most outstanding of its time, Li Po predicts Emperor Hsüan-tsung's loss of power, confinement, and exile; and he laments that the emperor is unaware of the poet's sincere loyalty. Li Po's sorrow resembles Ch'ü Yüan's 屈原, and the poem recalls the style of *Li sao* 離騷, rather than continuing the tradition of Han and post-Han *yüeh-fu*.

In "Ballad of Beautiful Ladies" Tu Fu describes the ladies' finery:

Thin silk garments shine in late spring, 綉羅衣裳照暮春
Embroidered with gold peacock and silver unicorn designs. 蹙金孔雀銀麒麟

and the rare delicacies served to the party:

Purple camel's hump cooked in a greenish-blue pot; 紫駝之峰出翠釜
On crystal platters are laid out white fish.[17] 水精之盤行素鱗

Here Tu Fu is following in the tradition of earlier poems such as *Shih ching*, No. 57 ("Shih-jen" 碩人), which describes the beauty of Chuang Chiang 莊姜; the anonymous Han *yüeh-fu* "Mulberry by the Path" ("Mo-shang sang" 陌上桑), which details the charms of Lo-fu 羅敷; and "Officer of the Guard" ("Yü-lin lang"(羽林郎) by Hsin Yen-nien (Eastern Han), where choice dishes are served by an attractive and resourceful girl of foreign origin. But Tu Fu's poem is richer and more beautiful than those models, reflecting the sophisticated life-style of ladies of his own time. Characteristically he uses natural objects to convey a message of political satire:

[16] Li Po, *Li T'ai-po ch'üan-chi*, vol. 1, *chüan* 3, p. 157.
[17] Ch'iu Chao-ao, *Tu shih hsiang-chu*, vol. 2, pp. 156–162.

Willow blossoms fall like snowflakes, covering the white duckweed;	楊花雪落覆白蘋
The green messenger bird flies with a red kerchief in its beak.	青鳥飛去銜紅巾
His imperious hand scorches with unequaled heat;	炙手可熱勢絕倫
Don't come too close, lest you risk the Chancellor's wrath.	愼莫近前丞相嗔

The poem mixes realistic and imaginative elements. Tu Fu uses the blossoms of the willow (*yang* 楊) to allude to the illicit relations between Chancellor Yang Kuo-chung 楊國忠 and his female cousin Yang Kuei-fei 楊貴妃. In Chinese mythology, the green bird is the messenger of the Queen Mother of the West (Hsi Wang Mu 西王母), a divinity associated with the erotic infatuations of rulers. A red kerchief, often carried by fashionable ladies in Tu Fu's time, is used here to hint that Yang Kuei-fei sent secret love messages to her cousin, the chancellor.

The two most important *yüeh-fu* poets of the Middle T'ang are Po Chü-i 白居易 (772–846) and Yüan Chen 元稹 (779–831), known for creating the so-called "new *yüeh-fu*" (*hsin yüeh-fu* 新樂府). In his "Preface to the New *Yüeh-fu*," Po Chü-i says: "In these poems meaning is paramount, diction is secondary. The opening line of each poem states its subject, the final lines bring home its import. This is in fact the principle of the *Shih ching*." He thus asserts that meaning should always have priority over form. But it seems to me that, although artistic form should not predominate, it cannot be entirely ignored. The meaning should become clear in the course of the poem, but there should also be some indirectness and holding back. Some of Po's *yüeh-fu* are very successful precisely because he pays attention to artistic form and because he does not reveal everything in the closure; whenever he fails in these two respects, he is less successful. One of his most successful "new *yüeh-fu*" is "The Whitehead of Shang-yang" ("Shang-yang pai-fa jen" 上陽白髮人), from which I will quote a few lines:

They are sad and tired of listening to the hundred warblings of the orioles in the palace;	宮鶯百囀愁厭聞

They are old but should not be jealous 梁燕雙棲老休妒
of the paired swallows on the rafters.

The poet's use of birds as images for the frustrated palace ladies is an effective artistic device. The poem ends with the following couplet:

Have you not read the old *fu* 君不見昔時呂向美人賦
"The Beauty" by Lü Hsiang? 又不見今日上陽白髮歌
Have you not read the recent
song "The Whitehead of
Shang-yang"?[18]

Among his less successful "new *yüeh-fu*" may be mentioned "Catching Locusts" ("Pu huang" 捕蝗), which includes the following couplet:

I have heard that in old times good 我聞古之良吏有善政
officials administered well; 以政驅蝗蝗出境
Through their governance they
expelled locusts from their
territory.

The concluding couplet is no more successful:

One man's merit benefits myriads of 一人有慶兆民賴
people; 是歲雖蝗不爲害
That year, though there were locusts,
they did no harm.[19]

Despite such shortcomings, Po Chü-i's "new *yüeh-fu*" are on the whole successful, particularly when they focus on actual events. They build upon and expand the tradition of narrative Han *yüeh-fu*. While the Han poets restricted themselves to relating events, Po Chü-i often manages to bring out the significance that transcends the individual event.

During the Middle T'ang, the *yüeh-fu* of Li Ho 李賀 (790?–816?) added a new dimension to poetry through their daring diction, colorful imagery, and rich imagination. An example is "Loud

[18] Po Chü-i 白居易, *Po Chü-i chi* 白居易集, 4 vols. (Peking: Chung-hua shu-chu, 1979), vol. 1, *chüan* 3, p. 59.

[19] *Ibid.*, pp. 65–66.

Song" ("Hao ko" 浩歌), which begins as follows:

The South Wind blows and flattens mountains;	南風吹山作平地
The Emperor of Heaven sends the Water God to move oceans.	帝遣天吳移海水
The Queen Mother's peaches have blossomed a thousand times;	王母桃花千遍紅
How many times have P'eng Tsu and Wu Hsien died?[20]	彭祖巫咸幾回死

To bring out the speed of change, Li Ho's fertile imagination deploys mythological figures as the instruments of change; and thousands of years are condensed into a single panorama. Such fantastic literary treatment is not found in the *yüeh-fu* of the Han, Wei, and Six Dynasties. Li Ho draws on the mythological tradition of *Li sao* and *T'ien wen* 天問 to create a new kind of *yüeh-fu* poetry, which expresses his own ideas and feelings. To be sure, Taoist immortals had already appeared in earlier *yüeh-fu*, but in Li Ho's poetry they are unique.

Late T'ang *yüeh-fu*, with some modifications, return to the tradition of the sensual poetry of "Tzu-yeh ko" and the ornate palace poetry of the Liang dynasty. Li Shang-yin 李商隱 (813?–858), the most important Late T'ang *yüeh-fu* poet, uses more tightly structured language to create emotional situations more complex than earlier *yüeh-fu* poets. A good example is his "Lady Li" ("Li fu-jen" 李夫人), which opens as follows:

A single belt cannot bind two hearts;	一帶不結心
It takes two pins to fasten the hair.	兩股方安髻
Shame on you, Man of White Cottage!	慚愧白茅人
The moon has set, how can a star replace it?[21]	月沒教星替

According to Feng Hao's 馮浩 (1719–1801) commentary, Li Shang-yin wrote this poem after his wife's death; it alludes to a

[20] Li Ho 李賀, *Li Ch'ang-chi ko-shih* 李長吉歌詩 (Peking: Chung-hua shu-chü, 1976), p. 54.

[21] Feng Hao 馮浩, *Yü-hsi-sheng shih chien-chu* 玉谿生詩箋注 (Shanghai: Ku-chi ch'u-pan-she, 1979), p. 495.

story told about Emperor Wu of Han: after the death of the emperor's favorite, Lady Li, the Man of the White Cottage (Liu Chung-ying 柳仲郢) sent the emperor a singing girl, Chi-fu 吉服, but the emperor refused to accept her. The images of the belt and the hairpins had already been used in anonymous songs and palace-style poems of the Six Dynasties, but without the sophistication found in Li Shang-yin's poem.

In conclusion, we may note two fundamental differences between the *yüeh-fu* of T'ang and those of earlier periods. First, while most Han *yüeh-fu* and many *yüeh-fu* of the Wei, Chin, and Six Dynasties were composed by anonymous singers, T'ang *yüeh-fu* were written almost exclusively by men of letters, with the notable exception of the songs preserved at Tun-huang. Second, the lyrical mode was more deeply developed in T'ang *yüeh-fu*, as distinct from the narrative bent of many earlier *yüeh-fu*.

Shuen-fu Lin

The Nature of the Quatrain from the Late Han to the High T'ang

> The writing of *chüeh-chü* relies on the perfection of one's art. Furthermore, each poem must involve countless variations so that one knows it is naturally marvelous without knowing the reason why. Can this be easily done?
> *Ssu-k'ung T'u, "A Letter to Mr. Li on Poetry"* [1]

Chüeh-chü 絕句, or literally "broken-off lines," is one of the most important genres of poetry of the T'ang dynasty (618–907). The term designates the brief quatrains written in either five- or seven-character lines. In the *Chüan-T'ang-shih* 全唐詩 (Complete T'ang Poetry), *chüeh-chü* and *lü-shih* 律詩 or "regulated verse," the two major genres of *chin-t'i-shih* 近體詩 or "modern-style poetry," constitute the two largest categories of poems by genre.[2] Though much smaller than that of *lü-shih*, the number of *chüeh-chü* surpasses by a significant margin the total number of poems written in the various forms known collectively as *ku-t'i-shih* 古體詩 or "ancient-style poetry."[3] While the large quantity of *chüeh-chü* certainly indicates the relative popularity of the genre in the T'ang,

[1] Ssu-k'ung T'u 司空圖, "Yü Li-sheng lun-shih-shu" 與李生論詩書, quoted in *Sui-T'ang wen-hsüeh tzu-liao hui-pien* 隋唐文學資料彙編 (Taipei: Kuo-li pien-i-kuan, 1978), pp. 252–253. I wish to express my thanks to Arthur Tobias who carefully proofread an earlier draft of this paper and made useful suggestions for stylistic improvement.

[2] Shih Tzu-yü 施子愉, "T'ang-tai k'o-chü-chih-tu yü wu-yen-shih te kuan-hsi" 唐代科舉制度與五言詩的關係, in *Tung-fang tsa-chih*, 東方雜誌 40, no. 8 (1944), 37–40. The statistics are based on the works of those poets who are represented with one *chüan* or more of poetry in the *Ch'üan-T'ang-shih* 全唐詩.

[3] *Ibid.*

the importance of the T'ang quatrain lies chiefly in the ways in which T'ang poets have fully realized the aesthetic potential of this verse form. Since the late T'ang many scholars and poets have held a view on *chüeh-chü* similar to that of Ssu-k'ung T'u 司空圖 (837–908) quoted above. They have come to regard *chüeh-chü*, the briefest of the important Chinese verse forms, as most difficult to master.[4] They also have generally come to recognize that *chüeh-chü* was brought to an unsurpassable quality and perfection by the T'ang writers. I hope that it will become clear in the course of my discussion that *chüeh-chü*, perfected in the hands of the T'ang masters, is one of the lyrical forms that best characterize the Chinese poetic genius and spirit.

The evolution of a genre in any literary tradition is always a complex and dynamic process. It is intimately related to changing cultural and aesthetic contexts as well as to the creative contributions of individual talents through the centuries. A comprehensive treatment of the generic evolution of *chüeh-chü* is obviously beyond the scope of the present essay. What follows is chiefly an attempt to describe the nature of the quatrain from its beginning at the end of the Han dynasty (206 B.C. to A.D. 220) to its fruition in the High T'ang. I shall be focusing on those general properties that constitute the distinctive aesthetics of the quatrain as a genre. As E. D. Hirsch, Jr., has observed, "essential elements of all genres are historical and culture-bound. . . ."[5] It is important, therefore, to

[4] For example, Shen Kua 沈括 of the Northern Sung (960–1126) says, "Although the little *lü-shih* [*hsiao-lü-shih* 小律詩, another T'ang name for the *chüeh-chü*] is a trivial art, in learning the skill for writing it, unless one reaches all of its fine points, he will not become a master. This is why T'ang poets all worked on it as a life-long undertaking." See Shen Kua, *Meng-hsi pi-t'an chiao-cheng* 夢溪筆談校證, ed. Hu Tao-ching 胡道靜 (Shanghai: Shanghai ch'u-pan-kung-ssu, 1956), p. 488. Wang Fu-chih 王夫之 of the late Ming and the early Ch'ing, after having said that seven-character quatrain is twice as hard to write as the *lü-shih*, bluntly states, "Whether a person has talent and feeling or not, only this form can put him to the test. If one is unable to write five-character ancient-style poetry, he is unworthy to enter the realm of refinement and culture. If one is unable to write seven-character *chüeh-chü*, he simply should not write poetry at all!" See "Chiang-chia shih-hua" 薑齋詩話 in *Ch'ing shih-hua* 清詩話, ed. Kuo Shao-yü 郭紹虞 (Shanghai: Chung-hua shu-chü, 1963), p. 18.

[5] E. D. Hirsch, Jr., *Validity in Interpretation* (New Haven: Yale University Press, 1967), p. 107.

put the T'ang quatrain which represents the perfection of this verse form in its place, to trace its "intrinsic genre"[6] back to its antecedents, albeit in a somewhat cursory manner.

In T'ang times *chüeh-chü* was sometimes called "little regulated verse" (*hsiao-lü-shih* 小律詩).[7] As early as the mid-T'ang period, quatrains were sometimes even classified under the category *lü-shih* in the collections of poetry by individual poets.[8] These occasional practices of T'ang scholars have led some later Chinese critics to interpret *chüeh-chü* as having evolved from *lü-shih* by combining two couplets taken from the latter.[9] This view is incorrect, of course, as it goes against the historical developments of these two genres of the "modern-style poetry." *Chüeh-chü* was developed long before *lü-shih* and had a distinct generic history of its own. It is true that after *lü-shih* was firmly established as an important verse form during the seventh century, its aesthetics also greatly influenced the quatrain. The exigencies of tonal patterns required for *lü-shih* began to be imposed on the preexisting quatrain form. But T'ang poets also continued to write quatrains which did not observe the prosodic rules of the regulated verse. Thus there existed in the T'ang two distinct styles of *chüeh-chü*: the "regulated quatrain" and the "ancient-style quatrain" (*ku-t'i chüeh-chü*). Other structural rules of *lü-shih*, particularly verbal parallelism, were also used in *chüeh-chü*, but they were generally subsumed under the overall structural principles of the shorter verse form.[10] As we shall see later, these structural principles remain largely the same in the quatrains of both the "ancient" and the "regulated" styles. The inclusion of *chüeh-chü* in *lü-shih* by previous scholars is based essen-

[6] *Ibid.*, pp. 78–89.

[7] Shen Kua, *Meng-hsi pi-t'an*, p. 488.

[8] In Han Yü's 韓愈 *Ch'ang-li chi* 昌黎集, ed. Li Han 李漢, Po Chü-i's 白居易 *Po-shih ch'ang-ch'ing-chi* 白氏長慶集, and Yüan Chen's 元稹 *Yüan-shih ch'ang-ch'ing-chi* 元氏長慶集, *chüeh-chü* was classified under *lü-shih*. See Hung Wei-fa 洪爲法, *Chüeh-chü lun* 絕句論 (Shanghai: Shang-wu-yin-shu-kuan, 1934), pp. 32–33.

[9] See Hung Wei-fa's review of these views in *ibid.*, pp. 3–5.

[10] Wang Li 王力 thinks that regardless of whether *chüeh-chü* originated from the *lü-shih* or not, regulated *chüeh-chü* is to be considered as taking half of a *lü-shih* after the T'ang dynasty. My own view is that this is only true in terms of tonal structure. For Wang Li's argument see *Han-yü shih-lü-hsüeh* 漢語詩律學 (Shanghai: Chiao-yü ch'u-pan-she, 1958), p. 40.

tially on the prosodic structure rather than on the intrinsic aesthetics of the genre.

In a definitive study on the generic history of *chüeh-chu*, Lo Ken-tse 羅根澤 discusses three aspects of the origin of this verse form: first, the term originated in its relation to the practice of writing *lien-chü* 聯句 or "linked verse" during the Six Dynasties (222–589); second, its form and style came from the folk songs popular since the end of the Han dynasty; third, its prosody came from the developments in regulated tonal pattern and verbal parallelism during the T'ang period.[11] Lo Ken-tse isolates the second aspect as the determining factor in the evolution of *chüeh-chü* as a genre because "linked verse" merely explains the source of the term "broken-off lines" and prosodic rules are imposed upon the forms of the folk songs.[12] Unfortunately he has not provided any elaboration on this perceptive observation other than the comment that the four-line verse form comes from the folk songs. I intend to show below that *chüeh-chü*'s link to Six Dynasties folk songs goes far beyond the surface feature of the quatrain form. For the moment, let us take a closer look at the first aspect mentioned by Lo Ken-tse because it bears relevance to the meaning of the name of the genre.

During the Eastern Chin (317–420), the custom of several poets writing poetry together, known as *lien-chü*, emerged in China.[13] This custom evidently became very popular during the Southern Ch'i and Liang dynasties (479–501, 502–556). Only six pieces of *lien-chü* with seven-character lines have survived, but several tens of them with five-character lines still exist today. Each of the six seven-character pieces, which range from three to twenty-six lines, is a complete verse. In five of them each poet contributed only one line to a poem while in the remaining poem each poet contributed two lines. In the majority of the five-character *lü-shih*, however, each poet composed four lines at a time, and these four lines formed one integral poem with no apparent connection to the other units.

[11] Lo Ken-tse 羅根澤, "Chüeh-chü san-yüan" 絕句三源, in *Chung-kuo ku-tien wen-hsüeh lun-chi* 中國古典文學論集 (Peking: Wu-shih-nien-tai ch'u-pan-she, 1955), pp. 28–53.

[12] *Ibid.*, p. 51.

[13] *Ibid.*, pp. 37–43.

Although they were grouped together under the title *lien-chü*, they did not comprise a unified work. From the surviving examples, we can tell that poets could write on different subjects in their poems, and they sometimes wrote their "linked" poems in different locations and at different points in time. Thus the practice of writing *lien-chü* during the Six Dynasties was quite different from that in later Chinese literary history.

When a poet could not find anyone to write poetry that could be "linked" to a poem he had written, his own poem was then called a *tuan-chü* 斷句 or a *chüeh-chü*, both meaning "broken-off lines." We do not know for sure when these two terms were first used, but by the sixth century the term *chüeh-chü* was already widely used.[14] For instance, in the *Yü-t'ai hsin-yung* 玉臺新詠 (New Compositions from a Jade Terrace) compiled by Hsü Ling 徐陵 (507–583), four anonymous quatrains from the end of the Han or the early Wei (220–256) were called "ancient *chüeh chü*" (*ku-chüeh-chü* 古絕句), and the quatrains by the Southern Ch'i and Liang writers were referred to as "miscellaneous *chüeh-chü*" (*tsa-chüeh-chü* 雜絕句), *chüeh-chü*, or simply, *chüeh*.[15] The term *chüeh-chü* can be found in other sources as well.[16] In the *Yü-t'ai-hsin-yung*, all these quatrains, written in the five-character form, appear in the tenth chapter (*chüan* 卷), along with specimens of *lien-chü* and the imitations of five-character *yüeh-fu* 樂府 quatrains written by poets since the Eastern Chin times.[17] Here Hsü Ling left us a significant clue to the relationship between Six Dynasties folk songs and the development of *chüeh-chü* and *lien-chü*.

The five-character quatrain, which emerged in the folk tradition toward the end of the Han, became the dominant form of folk songs in the Southern and Northern dynasties period (220–589). Of the folk songs collected in Kuo Mao-ch'ien's 郭茂倩 *Yüeh-fu-shih-chi* 樂府詩集 (A Collection of *Yüeh-fu* Poetry), nearly eighty per-

[14] *Ibid.*, pp. 32–36.

[15] Hsü Ling 徐陵, *Yü-t'ai hsin-yung* 玉臺新詠 (Taipei: Kuang-wen shu-chü, 1967), *chüan* 10, pp. 1–28.

[16] For instance, the term was used in the *Nan-shih* 南史 and in the *Yü K'ai-fu chi* 庾開府集. See Lo Ken-tse, "Chüeh-chü san-yüan," pp. 36–37.

[17] Hsü Ling, *Yü-t'ai hsin-yung*.

cent are regular five-character quatrains.[18] Since poets greatly enjoyed these folk songs, they began to write imitations of them. They also began to write original poems, using the quatrain form but probably without any musical setting. Therefore, the term *chüeh-chü* had a rather restricted meaning during the late Six Dynasties, when it was first used as a literary concept. It was not used to refer to seven-character quatrains, though some such examples did exist. It was during the T'ang that the term came to be recognized as a broad generic name for quatrains in both five- and seven-character meter. Although the *chüeh-chü* poems of the late Six Dynasties probably lacked a musical setting, they reflected certain important characteristics of the folk songs, from which they had derived their verse form.

I should like to say something about the development of the seven-character form before I take up concrete examples to trace the evolving aesthetics of the *chüeh-chü* genre. Seven-character quatrains existed long before five-character ones in Chinese literature. Four-line songs in seven-character meter could already be found in the historical text *I Chou-shu* 逸周書 of the late Spring and Autumn period (722–481 B.C.).[19] These folk songs continued to appear during the Han and the early Southern and Northern dynasties.[20] But one of the features in which they differ from the seven-character quatrains of the T'ang is that they each contain a rhyme at the end of every line. This kind of rhyming pattern is a common feature of early seven-character *shih* poetry.[21] The pattern of using a rhyme only at the end of every even-numbered line is a prominent characteristic of early five-character *shih* poetry. In seven-character *shih* poetry, however, this rhyming pattern was not used until the Liu Sung period (420–479), first in one poem on a Buddhist theme written by Hsieh Ling-yün 謝靈運 (385–433), and

[18] Lo Ken-tse, "Chüeh-chü san-yüan," pp. 44–45.

[19] Shen Tsu-fen 沈祖棻, *T'ang-jen ch'i-chüeh-shih ch'ien-shih* 唐人七絕詩淺釋 (Shanghai: Ku-chi ch'u-pan-she, 1981), p. 3.

[20] *Ibid.*, pp. 4–5.

[21] Wang Yün-hsi 王運熙, "Ch'i-yen-shih hsing-shih te fa-chan ho wan-ch'eng" 七言詩形式的發展和完成, in his *Yüeh-fu shih lun-ts'ung* 樂府詩論叢 (Shanghai: Ku-tien-wen-hsüeh ch'u-pan-she, 1958), p. 159.

then more significantly in the sequence of eighteen poems under the title of "In Imitation of 'The Difficult Journey'" ("Ni-hsing-lu-nan" 擬行路難), by Pao Chao 鮑照 (414–466).[22] Pao Chao was perhaps the very first poet to have written an "ancient-style" seven-character *chüeh-chü*. In his quatrain "Listening to the Singing Girls at Night" ("Yeh-t'ing-chi" 夜聽妓), he used the rhyme scheme of *aaba*, which was later to become the dominant rhyme scheme in seven-character *chüeh-chü*.[23] The only other rhyme scheme is *abcb* which is the same as that used in most five-character quatrains. Wang Yün-hsi 王運熙 is probably correct in suggesting that Pao Chao developed the early seven-character *chüeh-chü* form from long poems in which every four lines used one rhyme and rhymes appeared only in even-numbered lines rather than from four-line folk songs.[24] Although the ancient-style seven-character quatrain appeared in the fifth century, its use was limited until the Liang period in the next century. The dominant poetic form during the Southern and Northern dynasties was five-character *shih* poetry. Consequently, seven-character *chüeh-chü* was not as popular as five-character quatrains. In fact, it was still not very popular during the early T'ang.

Beginning with the eighth century, seven-character quatrains were set to banquet music (*yen-yüeh* 燕樂) for entertainment.[25] This relation to popular entertainment led to the increasing popularity of seven-character quatrains during the remaining two centuries of the T'ang dynasty. Banquet music was different from the music to which Six Dynasties five-character quatrains were set. It came from Central Asia and later became associated with the rise of *tz'u* 詞 poetry. Even though seven-character *chüeh-chü* were not sung when they first emerged in the fifth and sixth centuries, they had grown out of the *yüeh-fu* tradition, especially the longer seven-character song forms such as Pao Chao's "In Imitation of 'The Difficult Journey.'" They would have been influenced as well by the four-line folk songs which used a rhyme scheme different from

[22] *Ibid.*, pp. 165 and 176.

[23] *Ibid.*, p. 170.

[24] *Ibid.*

[25] Glen Baxter, "Metrical Origins of the *Tz'u*," in *Studies in Chinese Literature*, ed. John Bishop (Cambridge: Harvard Yenching Institute Studies, 1965), pp. 186–224.

that used later in *chüeh-chü*. Thus seven-character quatrains also bear the characteristics of folk songs, as do *chüeh-chü* and *tuan-chü* in five-character poetry.

Having briefly discussed its early history, we may now examine closely the quatrain's evolving aesthetics. The following are among the earliest surviving five-character quatrains which possibly date from the end of the Han period:[26]

1 The withering fish passes the river, weeping;	枯魚過河泣
When will there ever be time for regret?	何時悔復及
He writes a letter to the breams and carps,	作書與魴鱮
Advising them to be careful when going out.[27]	相教愼出入
2 Wheat is planted on the plateau;	高田種小麥
In the end it produces no ears of grain.	終久不成穗
A young man is in a strange land—	男兒在他鄉
How can he not be haggard?[28]	焉得不憔悴
3 The dodder drifts in the strong wind,	菟絲從長風
But its root and stem are not severed.	根莖無斷絕
If even the insentient cling together—	無情尙不離
How could the sentient ever be separated?[29]	有情安可別

The third piece is one of the four quatrains labeled "ancient *chüeh-chü*" by Hsü Ling in the *Yü-t'ai hsin-yung* mentioned earier. Looking at all three poems, we can immediately find at least four common qualities. First of all, they tend to use rather simple and straightforward diction. This simplicity of diction is obviously the natural characteristic of the folk songs.

[26] For the possible date of Songs 1 and 2, see Wang Yün-hsi, "Han-tai te su-yüeh yü min-ko" 漢代的俗樂與民歌, in *Yüeh-fu-shih lun-ts'ung*, p. 82. For the date of Song 3, see Lo Ken-tse, "Chüeh-chü san-yüan," pp. 31–32.

[27] Ting Fu-pao 丁福保, "Ch'üan Han-shih" 全漢詩, in *Ch'üan Han San-kuo Chin Nan-Pei ch'ao shih* 全漢三國晉南北朝詩 (rpt. Taipei: Shih-chieh shu-chü, 1962), vol. 1, p. 84. Hereafter all references to this book will contain only the section (e.g., "Ch'üan Han-shih," volume, and page number).

[28] *Ibid.*, p.60.

[29] *Ibid.*

Secondly, we can find an interrogative sentence in every poem. The application of question form or the form of a question and an answer is a common device found in the *shih* poetry of the late Han and early Wei.[30] In each of the three examples above, the question is a rhetorical one, thus adding poignant sentiment to the poem. Clearly the question is asked not for informational purposes but for emotional effect. The question further serves as an important element in maintaining the coherence of each poem. This further function leads us to the third common quality of the quatrains.

Although each of the above quatrains is made up of four complete grammatical sentences, it actually consists of two separate couplets. Each couplet contains one integral set of ideas, descriptions, or experiences, complete within itself and separate from the couplet next to it. The couplet is the basic unit in the progression of a poem in most *shih* poetry, and the quatrain is no exception. It is therefore misleading to try to approach the quatrain as if it entails the progression from the opening (*ch'i* 起), to the continuation (*ch'eng* 承), to the turning point (*chuan* 轉), and then finally to the conclusion (*ho* 合).[31] Rather, the structural integrity of the quatrain depends upon the dynamic complementation of two juxtaposed couplets. The rhetorical question serves as the dynamic link between the two halves in each of the three quatrains. In the first example, the "withering fish" writes a letter to his friends because he hopes that they may learn from his fatal mistake. The implied comparison between the withering fish and someone who has carelessly fallen into trouble is indeed ingenious. In the second poem, the metaphorical relation between the wheat and the young man is not made clear until the last line. Both the wheat and the young man are displaced living things who are left to wither away in a strange land. While the displaced wheat cannot produce any grain, the displaced young man cannot retain his youth and health and perhaps thereby accomplish something in life. The integration of the two couplets, therefore, depends on this implied comparison. The last quatrain is even more interesting. In the third line there is a

[30] Lo Ken-tse, "Chüeh-chü san-yüan."

[31] Hung Wei-fa, *Chüeh-chü lun*, p. 28.

general observation derived from the nature imagery of the first couplet. Although the dodder is an insentient object, it does not allow its root and stem to be severed when being tossed by the strong wind. But the reader is not aware of the whole human dimension until he comes to the rhetorical question which follows logically the statement made in the third line. The force of this last line goes beyond the implied answer that the sentient must remain together. The fact that the question is asked clearly suggests that the speaker is separated from his or her beloved. In the end the dodder becomes both a symbol of and a contrast to the state the speaker is in. Like the dodder, the speaker is drifting in the strong wind, but, unlike the dodder, he or she is going through the suffering alone. A seemingly simple poem is thus given a dimension of depth and poignancy.

The last common quality of the three quatrains is the sense of dynamic continuity that one feels in reading them. Each line is a complete syntactic unit rather than a series of juxtaposed isolated images. There is no parallelism to break up the continuity by creating a centripetal pull between the lines within each couplet. In addition, the two halves of each quatrain are linked by the device discussed above. All these elements contribute to the continuity of the quatrains. Since the three examples dealt with are folk songs, this flowing quality is to be expected.

We shall see later that the above-mentioned properties are present in varying degrees in the quatrains produced during the subsequent historical periods. The interrogative sentence is not used in every quatrain, of course, but it is frequently used as an effective closural device in later quatrains. The pattern of juxtaposing one couplet describing a scene with another describing the poet's introspection is also widely used in later quatrains. Naturally, new aesthetic principles continued to be developed through time. But for my purpose in this essay, it is especially important to pay attention to those elements which have remained "intrinsic" to a genre since its beginning.

Let us now turn to look at a few folk songs from the Six Dynasties. In the following group of songs, the first two belong to the group called "Tzu-yeh Songs" ("Tzu-yeh ko" 子夜歌) and the last two to the group called "Plain Songs" ("Tu-ch'ü-ko" 讀曲歌):

1	Tonight I've parted from my love; When can we be together again? The bright lamp shines on the empty chessboard— For a long time there won't be any game.[32]	今夕已歡別 合會在何時 明燈照空局 悠然未有棋
2	My love has been taken away by someone. It's not just that he's turned his back on me— Leaving his door open without a latch, He has no intention of ever closing it.[33]	郎爲傍人取 負儂非一事 攡門不安橫 無復相關意
3	Since I parted from my love, I've been bedridden, unable to lift my head. A flying dragon alights on the medicine shop— Bones sticking out: all because of you.[34]	自從別郎後 臥宿頭不舉 飛龍落藥店 骨出只爲汝
4	It was unbearable to hear that you were leaving me; Much worse that I have to part from you now. The prostrate turtle speaks to the stone slab: You've just become a thousand-year tombstone.[35]	聞乖事難懷 況復臨別離 伏龜語石板 方作千年碑

The "Tzu-yeh Songs" are associated with a singing girl of that name of the Eastern Chin dynasty in the fourth century.[36] The "Plain Songs" date from the early fifth century.[37] Both of these groups belong to one of the two large categories of folk songs of the

[32] Ting Fu-pao, "Ch'üan Chin-shih" 全晉詩, vol. 1, p. 523.

[33] *Ibid.*

[34] Ting Fu-pao, "Ch'üan Sung-shih" 全宋詩, vol. 2, p. 740.

[35] *Ibid.*, p. 742.

[36] Burton Watson, *Chinese Lyricism* (New York: Columbia University Press, 1971), p. 60.

[37] Wang Yün-hsi, "Wu-sheng hsi-ch'ü tsa-k'ao" 吳聲西曲雜考, in *Liu-ch'ao yüeh-fu yü min-ko* 六朝樂府與民歌 (Shanghai: Ku-tien wen-hsüeh ch'u-pan-she, 1957), pp. 87–88.

Six Dynasties, namely the *Wu-sheng-ko* 吳聲歌 or "Songs in the Wu Dialect," which originated in the city of Chien-yeh 建業 (present-day Nanking).[38] The other category is the *Hsi-ch'ü-ko* 西曲歌 or "Songs from the Western Region," which originated in the middle Yangtze River valley and the Han River valley, centering around the city of Chiang-ling 江陵.[39] Today we have nearly five hundred surviving songs in these two categories.[40] This is a sharp contrast to the paucity of surviving songs—only sixty-six pieces total—of the Northern dynasties known as the *Liang ku chüeh heng-ch'ui ch'ü* 梁鼓角橫吹曲 (Liang Dynasty Songs Accompanied by Drums, Horns, and Horizontal Flutes).[41] While the northern songs cover a wide range of subjects, the southern songs are almost invariably about the theme of love. Nonetheless, as noted earlier, a large portion of these songs are composed in the five-character quatrain form. Although five-character quatrains had existed a couple of centuries earlier, this brief verse form was not greatly developed until the folk songs of the Six Dynasties.

In the four examples just cited, it should be easy to observe the same qualities of simplicity of diction and of dynamic continuity in progression as in the previous set of three songs. As a matter of fact, in the first couplet of each current example, the language used is even more straightforward and personal. But one new quality immediately reveals itself when we read through the songs. We are bound to be struck by the surface incongruity that seems to exist between the two halves of each song. Each third line stands out as a startling transition from something familiar and intimate to something strange, fantastic, or seemingly unrelated. The appearance of incoherence is actually the result of the presence of puns in the verse. In Chinese poetry, puns are occasionally used in the *Book of Songs* and in early *shih* poetry.[42] But it is in the *Wu-sheng-ko* and

[38] Wang Yün-hsi, "Wu-sheng hsi-ch'ü te ch'an-sheng ti-yü" 吳聲西曲的產生地域, in *ibid.*, pp. 23–32.

[39] *Ibid.*

[40] Wang Yün-hsi, "Nan-pei-ch'ao yüeh-fu chung te min-ko" 南北朝樂府中的民歌, in *Yüeh-fu-shih lun-ts'ung*, p. 110.

[41] *Ibid.*, p. 116.

[42] Wang Yün-hsi, "Lun Wu-sheng hsi-ch'ü yü hsieh-yin shuang-kuan yü" 論吳聲西曲與諧音雙關語, in *Liu-ch'ao yüeh-fu yü min-ko*, pp. 124–126.

Hsi-ch'ü-ko that punning becomes a significant poetic device for the first time. As soon as the reader understands the puns involved, he will have no difficulty perceiving the structural coherence in the songs.

In general, puns are used very seriously and for complex aesthetic effect. They usually appear in the second couplet of the quatrain. As a rule, the third line, usually cast in highly imagistic language, is metaphorical for a scene, situation, or event, and the last line brings out the pun, which not only explains the meaning of the metaphor but also integrates the second couplet with the first.[43] For example, in Song 1, two puns are found in the concluding line: *yu-jan* 悠然 (far away, for a long time) puns with 油燃 (the oil burns) and the last word *ch'i* 棋 (chess, chess game) puns on 期 (a date). Hence this line also means "The oil burns on but no date has yet been set" or "There won't be any date for a long time." On one level the second couplet is an answer to the question set forth in line 2: "When can we be together again?" After her lover has gone away, the speaker, perhaps Tzu-yeh herself, is left alone to face an empty chess board under the bright lamp light, wondering when she will ever see her lover again. Here the chessboard is an appropriate object to mention because playing chess was something a courtesan or singing girl like Tzu-yeh would do with a customer in addition to performing other forms of entertainment. The song ends with the sad awareness that she probably will never see her lover again. As we read the song more carefully, we can also see that its poetic strength does not rely simply on the poet's wit. The poetic situation forces us to perceive the metaphorical relation between the lamp and the speaker in the poem. The burning oil becomes a symbol of her burning passion for her lover, with whom there is no hope for reunion.

In Song 2 punning is again used simultaneously as a device to integrate the elements and to enrich the meaning of the whole work. The pun is the word *kuan* 關 in the last line, which can mean both "to shut a door" and "to be concerned about." Wang Yün-hsi suspects that the phrase *pu-an-heng* 不安橫, or "without putting on

[43] Hung Mai 洪邁 comments on this structural feature in his *Jung-chai san-pi* 容齋三筆. His comments are quoted in *ibid.*, p. 122.

a latch," in the third line probably puns on *pu-an-fen* 不安分, meaning "not to be content with what one is."[44] This song is clearly about the infidelity of one's lover. By use of an ingenious metaphor, the speaker in the song sees her lover as someone who keeps open his door which does not even have a latch. Obviously we have here a man who is never content with whatever situation he is in and cannot remain committed to any bond of affection. He waits for the opportunity to be "taken away" from his love by another woman. What's more, once he leaves his previous love, our poet, he is completely unconcerned about the suffering she might be going through. In this song, then, metaphor and puns are used to clothe in simple language the profound bitterness the poet feels toward her lover's unfaithfulness and lack of concern for her emotional well-being.

The modern reader is likely to find the images used in Songs 3 and 4 somewhat astonishing and fantastic upon first reading, though the Six Dynasties reader might not have felt so at all. In any case, the poet's imagination displayed in both songs is truly refreshing and exuberant. Song 3 begins with a straightforward statement that the speaker has fallen ill after she parted from her lover. The third line then introduces the wildly bizarre image of a flying dragon settling on the medicine shop. Although the image of the medicine shop is linked to the idea of her lying ill in bed, the reader cannot fully understand the meaning of this line until he grasps the double meaning implied in the last line. The word *ku* or "bones" is a pun referring to both the dragon's bones and the speaker's own cheekbones. *Lung-ku* or "dragon bone" is the name of petrified animal bones used in Chinese medicine, evidently capable of healing a variety of illnesses. One meaning that we can readily derive from this couplet is that the woman has become so emaciated from love-sickness that she will need some medicine to improve her condition. But a deeper level of meaning can perhaps be discerned also. Since love is the best cure for love-sickness, the speaker certainly hopes that her lover will return soon to save her from her predicament. Perhaps then the second couplet describes a fantasy in which her lover would suddenly appear and hand out some magical

[44] *Ibid.*, p. 132.

medicine to cure her illness. The song becomes a passionate but subtle expression of a woman's love for a man.

Song 4 is about the pang of separation from one's beloved. To judge from the opening line, the speaker is possibly abandoned by her lover, though we cannot detect in her any bitterness toward him. Just as in Song 3, the reader is likely to be baffled by the images of the prostrate turtle, the stone slab, and the tombstone that appear in the second half of the song. All of these are mortuary objects widely used by people during the Six Dynasties.[45] The very last word of the song, *pei*, or "tombstone," is homonymous with the word 悲, meaning "grief." Tombstones were usually made from stone slabs. This pun makes clear the comparison between separation and the burial of a dead person. The prostrate turtle is metaphorically the speaker in the song herself. Since she has no hope that her lover will ever come back to her, parting from him is like burying a deceased person. Because she loves him passionately, she will forever carry the burden of grief over the permanent separation. Wang Yün-hsi believes that the "Plain Songs" probably originated as elegies for the dead and then later were developed into popular love songs.[46] This speculation explains why the "Plain Songs" often employ mortuary objects as imagery and why their general tone is thus particularly mournful among the southern folk songs.

Many other puns can be found in the folk songs of the Six Dynasties.[47] As we have seen in the preceding four examples, puns lend great pathos, articulate vigor, and rich overtones to a poetry usually written in simple language. Indeed, puns constitute a significant element of the aesthetics of Six Dynasties folk songs, representing a landmark in the development of the quatrain. While in keeping with the conventions of dynamic progression and simplicity and naturalness of diction, the quatrain now begins to take on *sententiousness* as part of its aesthetics. In the hands of the Six Dynasties folk song writers, the quatrain has become the most concentrated and energetic poetic form in Chinese literature.

[45] Wang Yün-hsi, "Tu-ch'ü-ko k'ao" 讀曲歌考, in ibid., pp. 91–93.

[46] *Ibid.*

[47] Wang Yün-hsi offers a list of many puns in his article mentioned in n. 42.

Focusing on the most quintessential aspect of an experience in the limited space of twenty characters, the quatrain is now fully capable of evoking a rich world of imagination.

One cannot ignore the importance of *Wu-sheng-ko* and *Hsi-ch'ü-ko* in the evolution of *chüeh-chü*. The Yüan scholar Yang Shih-yüan 楊士元 says, "Five-character *chüeh-chü* was developed during the early T'ang out of the form of Six Dynasties 'Tzu-yeh Songs.'"[48] Historically, this comment is incorrect. Nevertheless, in terms of the development of an aesthetic of concentration and subtlety in the quatrain, Yang Shih-yüan's point is an apt one.

We will now examine some of the quatrains written by the literati of the late Six Dynasties. Since the fifth century, and especially since the Southern Ch'i and the Liang dynasties, an increasing number of poets wrote imitations of folk songs or original poems in the quatrain form. The literati also used punning as a literary technique, but they primarily relied on resources from their own tradition to write quatrains which nonetheless conformed to the conventional aesthetics of the genre.

The following poem is one of the earliest examples of *tuan-chü* or "broken-off lines:"

White clouds arrive filling the fortress;	白雲滿鄣來
Yellow dust arises darkening the sky.	黃塵暗天起
On all sides mountain passes are cut off—	關山四面絕
My old home, how many thousand *li* away?[49]	故鄉幾千里

This quatrain was written by Liu Ch'ang 劉昶 (fl. 5th c.), the ninth son of Sung Wen-ti 宋文帝 (r. 424–453) or Emperor Wen of the Liu Sung dynasty.[50] In the *Nan-shih* 南史 (History of the Southern Dynasties), it is recorded that when the Former Fei-ti 前廢帝 (r. 423–424) ascended the throne, he suspected Liu Ch'ang, then Prince Chin-hsi 晉熙王, of seditious intention.[51] When his forces were defeated by the emperor, Liu Ch'ang had to abandon his

[48] Quoted in Wang Yün-hsi, *Yüeh-fu shih lun-ts'ung*, p. 118.

[49] Ting Fu-pao, "Ch'üan Pei-Wei shih" 全北魏詩, vol. 3, p. 1470.

[50] Shen Te-ch'ien 沈德潛, *Ku-shih yüan* 古詩源 (Taipei: Hsin-lu shu-chü, 1963), *chüan* 2, p. 158.

[51] *Ibid.*

mother and wife and fled his own country with only one concubine accompanying him. On his way to the Northern Wei, he was overcome by passion and composed the above quatrain.

Despite its brevity, the poem has effectively expressed the powerful emotions of a man who was compelled by unhappy circumstances to flee his home. It begins with a syntactically parallel couplet seldom seen in four-line folk songs up until this time. By the fifth century the parallel couplet had become an important element in *shih* poetry. The landscape poet Hsieh Ling-yün, for instance, enjoyed writing poems which consisted of tightly woven parallel couplets. From the fifth century onward, parallelism is often used by poets in their quatrains. A rigidly parallel couplet, especially one in which tonal opposition between the two lines is observed, as in the "regulated verse," has a tendency to create a centripetal force within itself. A parallel couplet of this sort can obstruct the dynamic linear drive essential to the quatrain. Commenting on the parallel couplet in the quatrain, the early Ch'ing scholar Wang Fu-chih 王夫之 (1619–1692) says that it must be made "dynamic and unbridled" (*liu-tung-pu-chi* 流動不羈) rather than "balanced and substantial" (*p'ing-shih* 平實).[52] Wang Fu-chih clearly sees this dynamic quality as intrinsic to the quatrain genre. Returning to Liu Ch'ang's opening couplet, we find that the two lines parallel each other perfectly in meaning and syntax, though not in tonal contrast. This semantic parallelism does create a picture of a self-enclosed world. The word *chang* 鄣 refers to the fortresses built on China's frontiers for defense purposes,[53] suggesting that Liu Ch'ang may have been in a frontier fortress when he wrote the quatrain. In spite of the parallelism in the first couplet, the poem does have a flowing quality, for three reasons. First, the quatrain consists of four complete sentences, so it does not suffer from the fragmentation and discontinuity produced by weak syntax. Second, the images of white clouds "arriving" and "filling" the fortress and yellow dust "arising" and "darkening" the sky suggest that a dynamic process is just taking place. Lastly, the third line serves as an indissoluble link between the two couplets. That sense

[52] Wang Fu-chih, *Chiang-chai shih-hua*, p. 20.

[53] Shen Te-ch'ien, *ibid*.

of being blocked off on all sides is clearly derived from the scene of the fortress being enveloped by white clouds and yellow dust. In this situation, trapped in the fortress, the poet is suddenly hit by the painful thought of his old home far away. It is more effective for the poet to end in an interrogative rather than a declarative sentence. It harks back to that feeling of being "trapped" and "lost" in a frontier fortress described earlier—he does not know how far away from home he is. More important, the question also brings out the futility of the poet's desire to return home, a desire that must exist in the mind of someone in Liu Ch'ang's situation. Here, of course, both the poet himself and the reader know full well that distance is not the real barrier. If the last line had been cast in the declarative syntax, the poem would lose much of its subtlety.

While Liu Ch'ang's "broken-off lines" contains only one parallel couplet, the following quatrain titled "A Farewell" ("Hsiang-sung" 相送) by Ho Hsün 何遜 (?–518) is made up of two completely parallel ones:

The traveler's heart already has a hundred thoughts,	客心已百念
And his lonely journey piles up a thousand miles.	孤遊重千里
The river darkens, rain is about to fall;	江暗雨欲來
The waves whiten, the wind is just rising.[54]	浪白風初起

As we can see from the original Chinese text, the two lines of each couplet virtually parallel each other, word for word. The first two lines are two complete syntactic units, but each of the next two lines consists of two juxtaposed segments. Although there is a causal relationship between the two juxtaposed sets of images in lines 3 and 4, there is no syntactical element to relate them. Yet Ho Hsün has not destroyed that sense of dynamic continuity so prominent in the quatrain. The poem is not simply a series of four isolated lines. The continuity is still largely preserved. The use of the word *i* 已 or "already" in the first couplet is important because it makes the second line sequential in meaning, though structurally parallel, to

[54] Ting Fu-pao, "Ch'üan Liang-shih 全梁詩, vol. 3, p. 1163. The English translation here is an adaptation from Burton Watson's version in *Chinese Lyricism*, p. 89.

the first. This fact necessarily creates a linear flow within the first couplet. Each line of the second couplet does appear somewhat disjointed in rhythm. As a result, the parallelism between the corresponding images of the lines becomes significant as a device to maintain coherence within the couplet. Upon closer scrutiny, we can also find an underlying unity in the sequence of seemingly isolated images. The poet first becomes aware of the river getting darker, a phenomenon that anticipates the arrival of the rain. Then he notices the waves—an object on the river—turning white, suggesting that the wind is growing stronger and tossing the waves to rise. Hence there is a sequential order to the structurally disjointed image clusters. This structural disjunction of the gloomy images of the storm reinforces the anxiety experienced by the traveler stated in the first half of the poem. It is noteworthy that the ending in this poem is not concerned with the emotive state of a man, unlike the ending in most quatrains. Rather, it is a description of a scene suggestive of the hazardous situation the poet's friend is facing. Effective in its own right, this sort of "open closure" became more popular only after the late seventh century.[55]

We have seen that Ho Hsün's quatrain is still in keeping with the generic convention of dynamic continuity. This quatrain by Wu Chün 吳均 (469–520), however, has departed farther from this convention:

Miscellaneous Poem Written in the Mountain
Beside the mountain I see the mist approaching;
Through the bamboos I peep at the setting sun.
Birds fly toward the eaves of the house;
Clouds come out from inside the windows.[56]

山中雜詩
山際見來煙
竹中窺落日
鳥向簷上飛
雲從窗裏出

Apart from the words *chien* 見 (to see) and *k'uei* 窺 (to peep at), which of course refer to the lyric speaker himself, this poem is composed solely of nature images. Although the sets of nature

[55] See Stephen Owen's discussion on "open closure" in his *The Poetry of the Early T'ang* (New Haven: Yale University Press, 1977), pp. 127–133.

[56] Ting Fu-pao, "Ch'üan Liang shih," vol. 3, p. 1,138.

images are organized into four complete sentences, they remain separate. This quatrain is an objective description of the beauty and seclusion of a mountain retreat as seen by the poet himself whose presence is suggested by the two verbs *chien* and *k'uei*. It is a vignette made up of four selected aspects which are structured in two precisely parallel couplets. And there is almost no movement from the beginning to the end of the poem, other than the implied field of vision of the poet. Despite its lack of the tonal pattern of the "modern-style poetry," this quatrain can be compared to the middle two couplets in the "regulated verse." This sort of "static" quatrain is uncommon. We will have occasion to see that even in quatrains which consist of two perfectly parallel couplets each, poets usually make some attempt to create dynamic continuity within them. It should be noted here that Tu Fu 杜甫 (712–770) was the poet who started to write a high percentage of "rigid" and "static" quatrains. Thus he represented a drastic transformation within the development of the *chüeh-chü* genre.

Two more examples will suffice to illustrate the development of the five-character quatrain in the late Six Dynasties:

Grievance of the Jade Stairs 玉階怨
—Hsieh T'iao 謝朓 (464–499)

Evening in the palace, letting down the pearled screens; 夕殿下珠簾
Drifting fireflies fly then rest. 流螢飛復息
During this long night, sewing silk garments, 長夜縫羅衣
Thinking of you—when will it end?[57] 思君此何極

Parting Again from Grand Secretary Chou 重別周尚書
—Yü Hsin 庾信 (513–581)

On the ten-thousand-*li* road through the Yang Pass, 陽關萬里道
There is not a man to be seen going home. 不見一人歸
There are only the wild geese along the river 唯有河邊雁
Who have been flying south since autumn began.[58] 秋來南向飛

[57] Ting Fu-pao, "Ch'üan Ch'i shih" 全齊詩, vol. 2, p. 803.
[58] Ting Fu-pao, "Ch'üan Pei-chou shih" 全北周詩, vol. 3, p. 1607.

I have specially chosen these two examples because Hsieh T'iao's poem is written in a style very close to that of the T'ang masters and Yü Hsin's poem exhibits the standard tonal pattern of the T'ang "modern-style poetry." Several traditional Chinese critics have commented that Hsieh T'iao started a style of poetry that was to become more typical during the T'ang dynasty.[59] Hsieh T'iao's five-character quatrains, in particular, were recognized as having considerable influence on T'ang poets.[60] Of "Grievance of the Jade Stairs," Shen Te-ch'ien 沈德潛 (1673–1769) of the early Ch'ing says, "Surprisingly it turns out to be [like] a T'ang quatrain. It [would] rank among the very best when put in the works of T'ang authors."[61] The theme of this poem is the grievance of a court lady who has been taken away from her beloved and put in the imperial harem. The language is extremely simple and each sentence makes a complete syntactic whole. There is a graceful continuity from one line to the next that can be easily felt by the reader. The first couplet presents the setting the court lady is in. The poem begins with a description of the world inside: it is evening in the palace, so the lady lets down the pearled screens. Then the second line depicts an object in the world outside: the fireflies are flying with their lights going on and off. The fireflies are obviously seen by the lady as she is letting down the screens. But the screens do not shut off the world outside. Although she is physically inside the palace sewing silk garments in order to pass the long and miserable night, her mind is far away, thinking of the person she is in love with. Finally she is like the fireflies moving restlessly in the endless stretch of the dark night. The poem is a complaint against the fate of separation and loneliness of the palace ladies. However, this sense of grievance is not directly expressed anywhere in the quatrain. This approach of clothing a profound meaning in simple and almost transparent language became one of the dominant components of the T'ang

[59] Yen Yü 嚴羽, *Ts'ang-lang shih-hua chiao-shih* 滄浪詩話校釋, ed. Kuo Shao-Yü (Peking: Jen-min wen-hsüeh ch'u-pan-she, 1962), pp. 146–147. Yen Yü comments that Hsieh T'iao has written poems that completely resemble T'ang style. And Kuo Shao-yü cites other sources to show that other critics share the same opinion.

[60] *Ibid.* Hu Ying-lin 胡應麟 in particular holds this view.

[61] Shen Te-ch'ien, *Ku-shih yüan, chüan* 2, p. 84.

quatrain. Li Po 李白 (701–762) actually wrote a poem under the same title "Grievance of the Jade Stairs." It is a greater poem than the one by Hsieh T'iao, but it is admired by critics for the same reason: one really feels the woman's grievance even though there is no mention of it in the words of the poem.[62]

We can also discern the same aesthetics of subtlety and indirection, though to a lesser degree, in Yü Hsin's quatrain. "Parting Again from Grand Secretary Chou" is one of many poems he wrote about his frustrated desire to return to his home in southern China. The Yang Pass is outside China's border. In the first couplet, therefore, Yü Hsin presents a scene of the border where no man is to be seen returning home in the south. This scene directly contrasts that of the southward migrating wild geese depicted in the second couplet. By use of the contrast, Yü Hsin expresses his grievance of being compelled to remain in the cold north without any hope of ever returning south.

With the exception of Wu Chün's quatrain, all of the examples from the late Six Dynastics have followed the aesthetic conventions of the five-character folk songs. Of particular interest, the Six Dynasties literati poets have integrated new aesthetic principles such as parallelism without sacrificing the intrinsic dynamic quality of the quatrain; they have also maintained the subtlety and depth of feeling and meaning of the folk songs without resorting to the use of enigmatic puns. In this poem by Yü Hsin, we also see a tonal structure that is to become typical of one type of T'ang "modern-style poetry."

If we use a "+" to represent the *tse* 仄 or "deflected" tone and a "–" to represent the *p'ing* 平 or "level" tone, we can transcribe the tonal structure of Yü Hsin's quatrain as follows:

– – + + +
+ + + – –
– + – – +
– – – + –

As we can see from the above diagram, the tonal properties of the

[62] Shen Te-ch'ien, *T'ang-shih pieh-ts'ai chi* 唐詩別裁集 (Shanghai: Ku-chi ch'u-pan-she, 1979), vol. 2, p. 616.

corresponding second, fourth, and last syllables within each couplet are opposed to each other, and those of the corresponding second and fourth syllables in lines two and three are identical. Together with the rhyme scheme of *abcb*, this tonal pattern fulfills all the requirements for a "regulated" T'ang quatrain. By the second half of the sixth century, therefore, the distinct T'ang style of the five-character quatrain has already evolved.

Before we turn finally to the T'ang, we must take a brief look at some examples of the early seven-character quatrain. As noted earlier, the seven-character quatrain which resembled the ancient-style *chüeh-chü* could be found as early as the Liu Sung period in the fifth century, but the form was little used until the Liang dynasty. Thus the seven-character form attained maturity much later than the five-character form. Nonetheless, the seven-character quatrain does not differ significantly from the five-character quatrain in its underlying aesthetics. Let us consider the following two examples:

Looking at a Lonely Flying Wild Goose at Night —Hsiao Kang 蕭綱 (503–551)

夜望單飛雁

The stars are few tonight north of the Heavenly Frost River;
A wild goose cries hoarsely—where is he flying to?
Had he known that he would lose his flock midway,
He would have been better off to start out alone.[63]

天霜河北夜星稀
一雁聲嘶何處歸
早知半路應相失
不如從來本獨飛

A Parting Poem —Anonymous (Sui dynasty, 589–618)

送別詩

Green, green the willows droop sweeping the ground;
Everywhere the catkins fly stirring the sky.
When all the branches are plucked and

楊柳青青著地垂
楊花漫漫攪天飛
柳條折盡花飛盡
借問行人歸不歸

[63] Ting Fu-pao, "Ch'üan Liang-shih," vol. 2, p. 940.

all the blossoms have fallen,
I ask these travelers if they will ever
return home.[64]

It is true that the two extra characters in each line allows the poet of the seven-character quatrain to add more descriptive detail to his rendering of experience. Phrases such as *sheng-ssu* 聲嘶 (voice is hoarse), *ch'ing-ch'ing* 靑靑 (green and green), and *man-man* 漫漫 (boundless) often cannot be accommodated in the shorter five-character form. Consequently, the seven-character quatrain has more rhetorical flourish than does the five-character form. But, apart from this essential difference, does the seven-character quatrain have its unique aesthetics?

Even a cursory reading will tell us that each of the above examples is written in simple language, is divided into two complementary couplets, and exhibits a dynamic quality in the individual lines as well as in the progression of the whole piece. In both cases, the first couplet presents a scene, while the second one presents the poet's introspection. All of these properties are the same as those that constitute the aesthetics of the five-character quatrain. Now what about the most important element, the principle of subtlety? While Hsiao Kang's poem is not particularly subtle, it is not completely devoid of overtones either. The introspective tone of the second couplet certainly suggests that the poet has learned a lesson from observing the lonely wild goose flying at night. A metaphorical relation between the wild goose who has lost its flock and the poet can probably be established. The second poem is more interesting and deserves our serious attention. Upon first reading, the reader will surely be struck by the repetition of words in this short poem. Each of the words *yang* 楊, *liu* 柳, *ch'ing* 靑, *hua* 花, *man* 漫, *fei* 飛, *chin* 盡, and *kuei* 歸 are repeated twice. These repetitions, however, do not destroy the aesthetic interest the poem generates. The first couplet describes the setting where the poet sees someone off. The willow trees are gracefully sweeping the ground with their green branches as the catkins fill the sky. The crucial third line brings together the two objects—the willow branches and the catkins—that dominate the first couplet. It alludes to the old

[64] Shen Te-ch'ien, *Ku-shih yüan, chüan* 2, p. 197.

Chinese custom of breaking a willow branch to give to the person who is departing. The third line also implies that many people come to the location to part formally from each other and that the poet has stayed there for a long time; he sees that all the willow branches are plucked and all the blossoms (i.e., catkins) have blown away. The quatrain closes with the poet asking the travelers if they will ever come back. The poet's action is obviously prompted by his observation of the willow trees, whose branches are all plucked by people at parting and whose catkins have all fallen away. There is no doubt that it is the image of the catkins scattering in the air that makes him wonder if the travelers (his own friend included) will ever return. The logical conclusion one draws from the poetic context here is, of course, that the travelers will scatter away from home just like the willow catkins. Throughout the poem not a word is said about separation or the lack of stability in human life. But a sensitive reader will never fail to perceive the sense of all-embracing sadness that is subtly and powerfully expressed in the simplest and most common imagery set against a pointed question that ends the poem. It should be pointed out also that the tonal pattern of this poem is exactly that of a "regulated *chüeh-chü*." Shen Te-ch'ien again perceptively observes, "Surprisingly this quatrain could almost have come from the hand of a High T'ang poet."[65] This quatrain illustrates that, as is the case of the five-character quatrain, the seven-character quatrain has developed along the same distinctive line of the combined aesthetics of simplicity, dynamism, and sententiousness.

It should be clear from the preceding pages that the four-line verse form had already developed for several hundred years before the T'ang masters appeared on the scene. We have also seen that in the long history of the quatrain genre, new aesthetic possibilities continued to be discovered, but certain properties have remained intrinsic to it. These particular properties have remained intrinsic partly because the form demands them and partly because they have been so widely practiced by poets through the centuries that they have actually become revered conventions. Even when new elements such as parallelism, open closure, and regulated tonal

[65] *Ibid.*

structure are introduced, the intrinsic characteristics of the genre are left largely intact. It is possible for a poet to self-consciously attempt to destroy the conventions that have heretofore been regarded as intrinsic to the genre by introducing radical elements. We shall see later that Tu Fu was precisely the poet who did this to the *chüeh-chü* genre.

The T'ang period was truly a high point in the history of the quatrain. It was the culmination of the developments in the genre's aesthetics of simplicity, dynamic articulate energy, and sententiousness. These aesthetic principles were widely shared by poets such as Wang Ch'ang-ling 王昌齡 (?–756), Wang Wei 王維 (701–761), Li Po, Li I 李益 (c. 749–829), Liu Yü-hsi 劉禹錫 (772–842), Tu Mu 杜牧 (803–852), and Li Shang-yin 李商隱 (813?–858) who were considered by traditional critics as great masters of the quatrain. Even Tu Fu, who was not at all famous for his quatrains, wrote some which followed the dominant aesthetics. Genuinely great T'ang quatrains are too numerous to cite, so I shall restrict myself to a few representative works.

The Ming scholar Hu Ying-lin 胡應麟 considers the following poem "In the Mountains" ("Shan-chung" 山中), by Wang Po 王勃 (ca. 650–676) of the early T'ang, as "having entered the realm of marvels" of the T'ang quatrain:[66]

I grieve at having lingered by the Long River;	長江悲已滯
I long to return soon, over ten thousand miles.	萬里念將歸
What's more, in this evening when the wind is high,	況復高風晚
On mountain after mountain, the yellow leaves are flying.[67]	山山黃葉飛

The elegantly mannered diction of the first couplet, which is typical of the poetry of the early T'ang, reminds one of the equally mannered diction of Ho Hsün or Wu Chün, discussed in a previous

[66] Hu Ying-lin, *Shih-sou* 詩藪 (N.p.: K'ai-ming shu-tien, n.d.), *chüan* 6, p. 3.

[67] Kao Pu-ying 高步瀛, *T'ang Sung shih chü-yao* 唐宋詩舉要 (Taipei, I-wen-yin-shu kuan, 1958), vol. 2, p. 744. This translation is an adaptation from Stephen Owen's version in *The Poetry of the Early T'ang*, p. 128.

section. But the regulated tonal structure adds the "modern" T'ang rhythm to the poem. The first two lines constitute a perfectly parallel couplet, with the corresponding words matching each other neatly on tonal, semantic, and syntactic levels. Within this tightly knit parallel structure, however, Wang Po creates a sequential order by inserting the words *i* 已 (already) and *chiang* 將 (about to) into the respective lines. The "Long River," or the Yangtze, is where he has *already* lingered, and the "ten-thousand miles" are the distance he is *about to* travel in order to return home. This sequence in time generates a sense of progression and continuity within the couplet. It is interesting that the poet uses the word *chiang* or "about to" in the second line. The poet is obviously aware that he will not be able to return home soon because there is nothing in the poem to suggest that happy event. The word *chiang* is clearly used for the purpose of irony in order to intensify the poet's grief at being away from home, the theme of the quatrain, stated at the beginning.[68] The marvelousness of this poem comes primarily from the suggestive second couplet. Again the poet uses a phrase as a dynamic sequential element to connect the two couplets. This phrase is *k'uang-fu* 況復 or "what's more." A variant version has *k'uang-chu* 況屬 or "what's more [I am] facing" instead. In any case, the sense of having something worse added on top of something else is clear in both versions. This second couplet describes a scene of a late autumn evening in the mountains. It will be dark soon, and the wind is gusting. In this unpleasant situation, the yellow autumn leaves on mountain after mountain are being blown off the trees by the strong wind and are now flying in the air. Although the couplets are joined by "what's more," the precise connection is left to the reader to perceive for himself. In this way, the closure of the poem can be said to be open.[69] But of course, open closure is really an artifice of subtlety because all the elements of closure are implied in the poem. In Chinese poetry, autumn is all too often a grief-producing season in which lonely travelers long to go home,

[68] This has been noted by Hsiu Lung 秀龍 and Lu Tse 陸澤, in *T'ang Sung chüeh-chü hsüan chu-hsi* 唐宋絕句選注析, comp. Tien Chung 奠中 and edited with commentary by Hsiu Lung 秀龍 and Lu Tse 陸澤 (Taiyüan: Shansi jen-min ch'u-pan-she, 1980), p. 5.

[69] See Stephen Owen's fine analysis of this issue in *The Poetry of the Early T'ang*, pp. 127 and 133.

separated people desire reunion, and sensitive poets grieve over the cruelty of nature, which causes most plant life to wither. The gloomy and harsh late autumn evening scene in the quatrain thus intensifies Wang Po's homesickness. Moreover, a metaphorical relation between the poet and the flying yellow leaves can no doubt be established. Like the autumn leaves, the poet is being cut off from home, drifting in a foreign land to become haggard with grief and homesickness. Open closure is effective in extending the poetic spirit of a writer far beyond the physical confines of a poem. At the same time, it is also effective in inviting the sensitive reader into the poet's world of limitless imagination and feeling. It has been noted that open closure became one of the dominant forms of poetic closure in the eighth and ninth centuries.[70] As sententiousness is one of the defining characteristics of the quatrain, open closure is far more important in the quatrain than in any other verse form.

The next quatrain to be taken up is the "Song of Liang-chou" ("Liang-chou tz'u" 涼州詞) by Wang Han 王翰 who died in the late 720s, the beginning years of the High T'ang Era:

Fine wine of the grape, cup of phosphorescent jade,	蒲桃美酒夜光杯
About to drink, the *p'i-pa* plays on horseback, urging us to set off.	欲飲琵琶馬上催
If I lie drunk in the desert, don't you laugh at me—	醉臥沙場君莫笑
Since ancient times how many men who marched into battle have come back again?[71]	古來征戰幾人回

This poem is regarded by Hu Ying-lin as approaching the style of High T'ang poetry.[72] One distinctive quality of this quatrain is well brought out by Stephen Owen when he says, "what separates this poem from an Early T'ang border poem is the energy, the wildly unconventional behavior which incarnates the combination of desperation and carefreeness of the soldiers on campaign."[73] The

[70] *Ibid.*, p. 127.

[71] This translation is an adaptation from Stephen Owen's version in *ibid.*, p. 419.

[72] Hu Ying-lin, *Shih-sou*, p. 3.

[73] Owen, *The Poetry of the Early T'ang*, p. 419.

language of the poem is eminently simple and straightforward; the concluding line, in fact, even reads like a flat cliché. But it is hardly possible for any sensitive reader to fail to appreciate the strong feelings of desperation and heroic forbearance beneath this surface simplicity. The persona of the poem appears to abandon himself on purpose to drinking, but this only serves to hint subtly at his sense of desperation. There is no denying, however, that this quatrain is also charged with the expansive spirit of a man who is able to laugh in a hopeless situation. The sweeping continuous rhythm and the absence of statements of sorrow fully demonstrate the vast spirit of the poet.

The kind of vital human spirit observable in Wang Han's quatrain became an important new characteristic of High T'ang poetry. Part of the explanation for the immeasurable greatness of High T'ang resides in the fact that it is a poetry written by a group of extremely vigorous and exuberant men living at a high point in T'ang civilization. Relying on the solid foundations laid by centuries of poets and folk song writers before them, the High T'ang poets further infused the quatrain form with a new energy and vigor. The result was indeed astonishing. A few examples will suffice to illustrate this.

The poem titled "Bird Singing Valley" ("Niao-ming-chien" 鳥鳴澗) is one of Wang Wei's most often quoted great quatrains:

The man at leisure, cassia blossoms fall;	人閒桂花落
The night still, the spring mountain empty.	夜靜春山空
The moon rises, startling mountain birds—	月出驚山鳥
Time and again they sing in the spring valley.[74]	時鳴春澗中

Typical of Wang Wei's five-character quatrains, and especially of those in the *Wang-ch'uan-chi* 輞川集 (The Wang River Collection), this poem is deceptively simple.[75] Two characters—"spring" and

[74] Shen Te-ch'ien, *T'ang-shih pieh-ts'ai-chi*, vol. 2, p. 610.

[75] Stephen Owen has offered a useful discussion of Wang Wei's "artifice of simplicity" in his *The Great Age of Chinese Poetry* (New Haven: Yale University Press, 1981), pp. 27–51. Also see Pauline Yu's excellent discussion of Wang Wei's quatrains in *The Poetry of Wang Wei* (Bloomington: The University of Indiana Press, 1980), pp. 165–169, 200–205.

"mountain"—are even repeated in this short poem. This quatrain is one among many of Wang Wei's poems in which a Ch'an-like vision or awareness (*Ch'an-ching* 禪境) is expressed. Is it not more appropriate for us to say that the poem illustrates Buddhist quietude rather than High T'ang vitality? Wang Wei has also written a considerable amount of very dynamic and vigorous poetry. And there is a close relation between the two personae of the poet as expressed in two kinds of poetry. "Bird Singing Valley" is written by someone whose spirit is vast enough to thrust away all intellectual presuppositions in order to view nature in its pristine states of being. It captures two states of nature—one of quiescence and the other of dynamic motion—at the precise juncture of their interaction. The first couplet is a parallel one, consisting of four corresponding image clusters, juxtaposed side by side without any syntactic device to relate them. Therefore, it expresses an ideal state of being which is tranquil, self-contained, harmonious, and seemingly timeless. In this perfect state, the poet and nature are one. In contrast, the second couplet is one extended syntactic unit, in which a clear sense of passing time is observed. For the poet is keenly aware that the birds are calling time and again. The continuity from the first couplet to the second is maintained in this poem by the fact that the second state of nature is derived from the first. In this quatrain, not only is its language simple, but the situation is most ordinary as well. There is neither unusual imagery nor startling event. Yet no sensitive reader can fail to see the poignancy of Wang Wei's perceptual experience and its profundity. Embedding a wealth of meaning in the most ordinary poetic situation and using the simplest language to describe it has been one of the ideals in the history of the quatrain. In this quatrain by Wang Wei, we see a full realization of this aesthetic ideal. To achieve this realization requires the greatest skill and articulate energy.

The parallel couplet has been effectively used in Wang Wei's poem to bring out an ideal state of nature. We shall now look at a great "regulated quatrain" in which two perfectly parallel couplets are used. The following quatrain titled "Ascending the Heron Tower" ("Teng Kuan-ch'üeh-lou" 登鸛雀樓) was written by Wang Chih-huan 王之渙 (688–742), also a poet from the High T'ang period:

The white sun leans on the mountain, spent;
The Yellow River enters the sea, flowing.
If you want to exhaust your thousand-*li*
view,
You must climb one more story of the
tower.[76]

白日依山盡
黃河入海流
欲窮千里目
更上一層樓

Each of the couplets contains two lines which parallel each other word for word in both tonal and semantic aspects. But no reader through the centuries has ever complained that the poem is overly balanced and static. It resembles the middle two couplets of a regulated verse, but here strict parallelism is observed on the surface, and not in its deep structure. Of the couplets, only the first one, which consists solely of natural images, is organized in such a way as to create a self-contained world. But, unlike the opening couplet of "Bird Singing Valley," the lines here have syntactic unity. Hence continuity is preserved within each line, this couplet tersely presents a scene of overpowering vastness which can be viewed from the Heron Tower. Although in the second couplet strict parallelism is observed on the surface, conditional syntax underpins the lines as their deep structure. Thus the couplet is to be read as one continuous unit, serving as the unifying, closural device for the whole quatrain. The lofty aspiration expressed at the end of the poem is prompted by his experience of viewing the overpowering scenery. The desire to exhaust his thousand-*li* view tightly follows the sense of great distance described in the second line. The Heron Tower was situated in Shansi Province, far away from the ocean. The image of the Yellow River flowing into the ocean exists, then, only in the mind's eye of the poet. This fact helps us understand that the second line also serves as a vital link between the first couplet depicting the poet's perceptual experience and the second couplet describing his thought. The dynamic continuity so essential to the quatrain is thus kept intact by Wang Chih-huan's superbly crafted use of parallelism.

Concerning the seven-character *chüeh-chü*, Shen Te-ch'ien says, "It is most valuable for the seven-character *chüeh-chü* to use familiar language to express far-reaching feelings, and to conceal meaning

[76] Shen Te-ch'ien, *T'ang-shih pieh-ts'ai-chi*, p. 615.

without exposing it. It should use only immediate scenes and common everyday expressions, but at the same time it should contain overtones capable of causing the reader's spirit to reach far. Li Po is one who has achieved this."[77] These are useful and perceptive observations, applicable in fact to many other poets as well. Although examples illustrating Shen Te-ch'ien's observations can readily be drawn from the works of Wang Wei, Wang Ch'ang-ling, and other T'ang masters, I shall limit myself to the following quatrain by Li Po:

> *Thinking of the Past in Yüeh*
> When King Kou-chien of Yüeh came
> back after destroying the Wu,
> His warriors who returned home all
> wore embroidered clothes.
> Court ladies filled the spring palace like
> flowers,
> But now only partridges are flying
> there.[78]

> 越中懷古
> 越王勾踐破吳歸
> 戰士還家盡錦衣
> 宮女如花滿春殿
> 只今惟有鷓鴣飛

This quatrain was written when Li Po traveled to Yüeh-chou 越州 (modern Shao-hsing County 紹興縣 in Chekiang Province). The historical site reminded him of an ancient event that took place there. In 494 B.C., King Kou-chien of the State of Yüeh was defeated by King Fu-ch'ai 夫差 of the neighboring State of Wu.[79] After he returned home, Kou-chien reportedly lay on faggots and tasted gall (presumably some animal gall) every night to remind himself of the humiliating defeat while nursing vengeance against Fu-ch'ai. Nineteen years later he successfully conquered the Wu State. Li Po used the first three lines to recapture the past history and focuses his attention on Kou-chien's return in triumph. These images of past human glory contrast sharply with the bleak scenery described in the last line. This is certainly one level of meaning of the quatrain: the ultimate insubstantiality of human glory and achievement, compared to the eternal physical presence of nature. In this respect,

[77] *Ibid.*, p. 653.

[78] *Ibid.*

[79] Shen Tsu-fen, *T'ang-jen ch'i-chüeh-shih ch'ien-shih*, pp. 70–71.

Li Po has departed from the usual manner of implying a thematic contrast between the two couplets of the quatrain. The imbalance between the images of past glory and the description of the present scene—three lines against one line—ironically strengthens the point that Li Po is trying to get across. Upon closer scrutiny, deeper implications also reveal themselves. Despite the superb continuity in the first three lines and the obvious contrast between them and the last line, the quatrain also follows the conventional two-couplet structure. The first couplet is about King Kou-chien, returning home after having defeated the Wu. His warriors were all graciously rewarded because they were given embroidered clothes to replace their armour. The second couplet concerns Kou-chien's palace, the symbolic center of Yüeh culture to which he returned in triumph. In his palace, the beautiful court ladies were waiting for his return. Kou-chien's extravagant and decadent life after his conquest of Wu is subtly implied. And it is on this site of extravagance and decadence that partridges are now flying. In this way, the third line serves as the turning point in the poem. This quatrain, written in simple language, thus expresses the intricate web of Li Po's feelings and thoughts as he visited an ancient historical site.

I would like to close this essay with a look at a quatrain by Tu Fu, who, as noted earlier, brought some fundamental changes to the *chüeh-chü* genre. Tu Fu did not write many quatrains until late in his life, after he moved to Shu (modern Szechwan Province).[80] Therefore, most of his quatrains were written in a period of his life when he was self-consciously developing all kinds of startlingly new poetic techniques. He introduced strange rhythm and tonal pattern into the quatrain. He used this lyrical form for discursive and purely descriptive purposes. He enjoyed writing quatrains made up of two rigidly parallel couplets. I shall concern myself only with this last aspect because it bears particular relevance to the focus of this essay, the dominant aesthetics of the quatrain.

The following poem, one of four titled simply "Chüeh-chü," is a good example of his radical transformation of the new quatrain:

[80] Tseng Chien 曾緘, "Tu Tu-shih ch'i-yen *chüeh-chü* san-chi" 讀杜詩七言絕句散記, in *T'ang shih yen-chiu lun-wen chi* 唐詩研究論文集 (Chung-kuo yü-wen yen-chiu-she, 1969), pp. 55–56.

Two orioles sing among green willow trees;	兩個黃鸝鳴翠柳
A line of white egrets flies up into the blue sky.	一行白鷺上青天
A thousand autumns of snow on the western range are framed in my window,	窗含西嶺千秋雪
And the boats that will go ten-thousand *li* to Eastern Wu are moored at my door.[81]	門泊東吳萬里船

This quatrain was written in 764, when the poet had finally settled down in Szechwan. He was enjoying a period of relative peace in his life, after the chaotic years following the An Lu-shan rebellion. Previous scholars have criticized this quatrain for being like "broken embroidery and torn silk," lacking continuity and coherence.[82] These criticisms are justified only if we assume that Tu Fu has deliberately attempted to do away with the kind of dynamic continuity that so obviously exists between the two lines within the couplets and between the two couplets in all the examples we have examined above. Ching-hsien Wang has observed in his paper that the *chüeh-chü* is really closer to the "ancient-style poetry" than to the "modern style." This is certainly true in terms of the close relationship between the two lines of the couplets and of the transition from one couplet to the next. In the "ancient-style poetry," the second line in a couplet is usually sequential with the first in the unfolding of events, images, or ideas. Sequential order can usually be found in the overall progression of a poem as well. This sort of dynamic continuity, which, as I have argued, is intrinsic to the quatrain genre up until the High T'ang, is clearly lost in this poem by the great T'ang master. Tu Fu's quatrain presents a vignette of beautiful scenery as seen from his house. While in "Miscellaneous Poem Written in the Mountain," Wu Chün still "appears" to integrate the isolated lines, Tu Fu here appears to be a passive observer detached from the scene, even though the four sets

[81] Hung Mai 洪邁, *T'ang-jen wan-shou chüeh-chü* 唐人萬首絕句 (Hong Kong: Shih-chieh ch'u-pan-she, 1957), vol. 1, p. 5.

[82] Hu Ying-lin, *Shih-sou*, p. 20.

of nature images do revolve around him. This is not to say that there is no sense of continuity in this famous quatrain.

A careful reading reveals an important meaning from the visual surface which seems to constitute the whole poem. The poet is clearly in a happy and active sort of mood; he is drawn to nature to the extent that he wishes to take a boat and travel all the way down the Yangtze to the Wu region in eastern China. Although the four lines present four seemingly discrete, isolated sets of images, together they reveal a continuity in both spatial and temporal dimensions. The quatrain progresses from things close to his house to things higher up in the sky and finally to things in the far distances. With the exception of Eastern Wu, all the nature images refer to things that could be seen from inside a window of the poet's house. Therefore, the poem extends from the near to the far, and from the visually present to what exists in his mind only. Similarly, in terms of time, the poem also begins with what is close at hand: the lyrical moment of the present. The two events in nature, described in the first couplet, seem to be suspended in a kind of eternal present. The third line then expands this lyrical moment to a very long stretch of time in the concrete image of "snows of a thousand autumns," which obviously suggests a continuity from the past to the present and then to the future as well. The last line extends from the present to the future: the boats that will go ten thousand *li* to Eastern Wu are *now* moored at his door. It is interesting that Tu Fu should use this concluding line, which is actually concerned with his fantasy, to bring out a sense of *real* time. For, when the boats do set off, their long journey to Eastern Wu will take place in a real temporal framework. Thus the poem can be said to move from a time frame that is purely poetic to a more abstract sense of time and finally to that of real time, albeit this last stage is only suggested.

In one of his "Cedules," Peter A. Boodberg draws attention to possible associations with the seasons that may exist in the colors, images, and directions contained in Tu Fu's quatrain.[83] If indeed Tu Fu was self-conscious in implying the system of correspon-

[83] Peter A. Boodberg, *Cedules From a Berkeley Workshop in Asiatic Philology*, no. 022-550201. The analysis of the actual temporal progression in the quatrain is my own rather than Boodberg's.

dences among the "five elements," the "five colors," and the "five directions," then another level of temporal continuity can be discerned in his poem. In the first line the word "yellow" is associated with midsummer, while "green" (*ts'ui*) with spring. In the second line, the color "white" in "white egrets" is the color of autumn, while "blue" in "blue sky" is that of spring again. Since the yellow orioles are calling in the green willows and the white egrets are soaring up into the blue sky, perhaps the first couplet suggests a seasonal progression from spring to summer and then to autumn. In the crucial third line, the direction "west" corresponds to autumn, while the image of "snow" brings to mind the season of winter. Finally, in the last line, the word "east" in "Eastern Wu" is associated with spring. Therefore, the revolution of the seasons completes a full circle, and a well-integrated temporal continuity exists beneath the surface of a series of seemingly isolated sets of images.

The above discussion runs counter to the previously quoted view that this quatrain by Tu Fu is like "broken embroidery and torn silk." But the kind of spatial and temporal continuity which I have been describing is a far cry from the dynamic continuity found in all the other quatrains that we have looked at earlier. The quality of continuity in this quatrain is the product of a great master late in his life when he was intensely self-conscious about poetic craft. The language of this quatrain is still simple, the vast spirit of the poet can still be felt, and a subtle meaning is implied in his description of nature, but that readily perceptible sense of dynamic continuity so characteristic of earlier quatrains is now undeniably gone. Tu Fu's ingenuity has certainly opened up new possibilities for the *chüeh-chü* form, but at the same time it has also done violence to one aesthetic property which has heretofore been intrinsic to the genre.

Yu-kung Kao

The Aesthetics of Regulated Verse*

"Regulated verse" (*lü-shih* 律詩) is a highly schematized verse form which, after a period of incubation, emerged as a popular poetic genre in the seventh century. Even before that time, "regulated verse" had come to play a significant role in traditional Chinese society, not only as a literary form, but also as a political and social medium. In the normal usage of the term, "regulated verse" refers to a form containing eight lines of uniform length, with either five or seven characters per line, and conforming to a generally accepted code of phonetic and rhetorical rules. In this study, an exposition of these generally accepted rules serves only as the basis for my discussion of the less explicit and more controversial part of that code, which we, for lack of a better term, may call the "underlying aesthetics."[1] In reality, this aesthetics includes many diverse components, each of which underwent various stages of transformation; the components range from such technical factors as structural design to modes of philosophical speculation. I propose to examine only three versions of this aesthetics, covering the seventh and the first half of the eighth centuries, the period traditionally called Early and High T'ang. But in order to give a more complete picture of historical development of these aesthetic values, I shall include a brief survey of the early evolution of "five-character line verse" (*wu-yen-shih* 五言詩), which was the predecessor of "regulated verse."

Although any study of a schematized verse form naturally

* I wish to express my profound gratitude to Stephen Owen for making substantial stylistic improvements in my essay.

[1] "Aesthetics" has been used in several different ways in contemporary writings; here I follow Stephen Owen's usage in his *The Great Age of Chinese Poetry: The High T'ang* (New Haven: Yale University Press, 1981), p. 14.

should begin with its basic technical requirements, the study should not end there. A schematized form can be considered artistically significant only if its formal components contribute substantially to the total artistic effect of the poem. In its most powerful state, poetic form plays a necessary role in shaping the creative process. Consequently, in a successfully executed poem, the form is an integral part of the poet's intention and is inextricable from the realization of the poet's vision. Only then can the form be said to have its own "formal significance." It is the complex interaction between form and the poet which makes possible the emergence of formal significance. Behind this formal significance, there are such diverse issues as how a poet structures his poem within the limits of the form, what themes he chooses to express, and why one form is preferred over another. It is this nebulous area covering so many enigmatic but interesting questions which I refer to as "underlying aesthetics." It is "underlying" because, more often than not, it remains implicit and elusive; the practicing poet himself may not even be aware of its existence, let alone consciously recognize the complexity of the choices made. It is "aesthetics" because it is precisely this integral of choices which constitutes poetic beauty and value. Considering, for the sake of convenience, these choices as if they were fully conscious: they point to the poet's intention in relation to the form, to his understanding of the structural designs, his manipulation of rules to adapt to his creative imagination, and his effort of attaining his vision through this specific form. Form in the sense we are speaking of here is "received form," something the poet accepts from the literary community, something he continually recreates, something with which he must contend. Individual poets and critics may change some of the formal requirements, but no single person can create the aesthetics of a form.

This aesthetics is basically an interpretative code, through which a poet can go beyond the textual meaning and the reader can understand its contextual significance. Through this code, the poet and reader can communicate and exclude the uninitiated. This aesthetic code cannot be acquired as a mere set of rules, prescriptions, and proscriptions; it is learned only by internalizing models, with or without the assistance of explicit interpretation and prescription. Precisely because it always presents itself indirectly, it is difficult to articulate this aesthetics as a code, but the very fact that it never becomes fully explicit protects its power to suggest, to change, and to develop. The fact that I attempt to outline this implicit code in the following pages indicates that I do believe the code can be made explicit to a certain degree. Nevertheless, we should never forget the level on which this code always presents itself—submerged in and integrated with particular texts.

Five-Character Line Verse

The date for the beginning of "regulated verse" could be pushed back to the early sixth or late fifth century, when what I call "proto-regulated verse" began to make its appearance.[2] However, if one tries to understand the aesthetics behind the growth of "regulated verse," one must look at the continuity between the rise of "five-character line verse" and the subsequent establishment of "regulated verse." For this reason, I will offer a general outline of the origins of the aesthetics in the period predating "regulated verse," giving special attention to the problems which are most relevant to the later discussion. The group of "Nineteen Ancient Poems" (ca. second century A.D.) will be used as the model of the earliest stage of development of this verse form.

[2] In the introduction to the "Wu-yen lü-shih" 五言律詩 section of his anthology of T'ang poetry, *T'ang-shih p'in-hui* 唐詩品彙, Kao Ping 高棅 (1350–1423) suggests: "Although the flourishing of 'regulated verse' occurred during the T'ang, it evolved from the 'parallel line verse' [*li-chü* 麗句] begun in Liang and Ch'en times. Liang Yüan-ti's 梁元帝 poems of eight five-character lines were close to this form." See Kao Ping, *T'ang-shih p'in-hui* (rpt. Taipei: Shang-wu yin-shu-kuan, 1976), p. 47a. In recent years, the consensus was to place the beginning of conscious uses of tonal and parallel patterns as the start of "proto-regulated verse." This date can be as early as the last few decades of the fifth century. See Takagi Masakazu 高木正一, "Liu-ch'ao lü-shih chih hsing-ch'eng" 六朝律詩之形成, translated into Chinese by Cheng Ch'ing-mao 鄭清茂 and published in *Ta-lu tsa-chih* 大陸雜誌 13, no. 9 (1956), 287. Relevant to this problem, see also Wang Yün-hsi 王運熙, "Han-shan-tzu shih-ko te ch'uang-tso nien-tai" 寒山子詩歌的創作年代, in his *Han Wei Liu-ch'ao T'ang-tai wen-hsüeh lun-ts'ung* 漢魏六朝唐代文學論叢 (Shanghai: Ku-chi ch'u-pan-she, 1981), pp. 204–217; and Chien Chin-sung 簡錦松, "Mi-t'ien fa-lü hsi-t'an shih" 彌天法律細談詩, in *Chung-wai wen-hsüeh* 中外文學 11, no. 9 (1983), 22–50.

Metrical Rules of "Five-Character Line Verse"

The primary formal characteristic of the new verse form was the use of a new metrical pattern, which for the first time in the history of Chinese poetry was "character-based" or simply "syllabic." Prior to the appearance of "five-character line verse," Chinese poetry, from *Shih ching* 詩經 through *Ch'u tz'u* 楚辭 to the Han "ballad" (*yüeh-fu* 樂府), permitted a variable number of characters (or syllables) in each line and a variable number of lines in each verse. It is possible that metrical variation was determined by music, but that hypothetical relationship remains obscure. Simple as it may sound, this new form dramatically changed the fundamental rules of Chinese poetry. This new change may be summarized in the following four metrical rules: (1) each line has five characters, namely a pentasyllabic line; (2) each line has a caesura after the second character, with a secondary caesura occurring either after the third or fourth character, according to the semantic division; (3) a couplet forms an independent two-part metrical unit; and (4) the rhyme falls at the end of the second line of the couplet. These regular syllabic rules probably represented a response to the nearly complete disappearance of the musical element, providing a definite meter to compensate for lost musical rhythms.[3]

By definition, meter requires the repetition of pattern. In the earliest poetry, prior to the development of the regular pentasyllabic line, metrical pattern can be seen in the repetition of lines of variable syllabic length as defined by end rhymes, in the repetition of lines or stanzas with identical words, and in refrains, with some

[3] In his "Introductory Remarks on Orthodox Music" from the *T'ung-chih* 通志, Cheng Ch'iao 鄭樵 (1104–1160) comments on the change from "poetry with music" to "poetry without music." He states "Ancient poetry is called 'song-ballad,' while poetry of later times is characterized by both 'ancient' and 'recent' styles. 'Song-ballad' is composed for music, not for literature. Ancient people were profoundly interested in declamatory singing and resonant chanting. Now people no longer go for chanting, and have lost the secrets of song poetry. The words when regulated become poetry; poetry when given music becomes song. [In the past] one never wrote poems not to sing." See the Chinese text quoted in *Chung-kuo ku-tai yüeh-lun hsüan-chi* 中國古代樂論選集 (Peking, 1981), p. 227. See also Andrew Welsh's comments on the change from "song melos" to "speaking melos" in his *Roots of Lyric* (Princeton: Princeton University Press, 1978).

variations. Gradually, a tetrasyllabic line did become the dominant metrical pattern in the *Shih ching*, and here too we begin to find the joining of two lines in couplets and the joining of two couplets in quatrains.[4] These were merely tendencies and not strict rules. This possibly explains the failure successfully to continue and imitate this form in later periods; the imitators, assuming a regular syllabic line, dared not deviate from the "four-character line" norm.

In the "ballads" of the Han, the "five-character line" had already begun to achieve dominance. The "five-character line" had an inherent superiority over the "four-character line," and its internal complexity permitted variations hitherto achieved only by variable line length. A meter of single beat is theoretically possible, but its literal "monotony" precludes its popularity. Although from the earliest days Chinese words were predominantly monosyllabic, disyllabic compounds and phrases were already common. Since the time of the *Shih ching*, the basic metrical unit was definitely disyllabic, interspersed only occasionally with a single beat unit. The five-character line consists of an initial disyllabic unit and a final trisyllabic unit, which may be further divided into a monosyllabic unit and a disyllabic one. The points of caesura are not formally marked, but in reading they can be easily located by the natural semantic divisions of the line. The trisyllabic segment can therefore be either "two-and-one" or "one-and-two," according to the combination of characters. This shifting caesural point adds a complexity to the otherwise monotonous repetition of uniform pentasyllabic lines. If we remember that the earlier dominant rhythm was the even beat of the four-character line, we realize that the simple addition of one character was indeed a bold step, which meant that in the future Chinese poetic lines would have an odd number of syllables. Together with the shifting of the secondary caesura, the new rhythm seemed to offer possibilities for variety and fluidity.

The couplet repeats the "two-and-three" rhythm and is marked strongly as a unit by the end rhyme, regularly appearing as the last

[4] For a comprehensive review of the essential forms of Chinese prosody, see Hans H. Frankel, "Classical Chinese," in *Versification: Major Language Types*, ed. W. K. Wimsatt (New York: Modern Language Association, 1972), pp. 22–37.

syllable of each couplet. The two lines therefore can be read as two parts of an anthem with its verse and antiphon. As a complete musical line, both exposition and response form a self-contained cycle. This refinement, together with the sense of independence encouraged by the rhetorical rules, prepared the way to identify each couplet almost as an individual stanza. Later, the stanzaic couplet was to become the structural base of "regulated verse."

Rhetorical Rules of "Five-Character Line Verse"

Since the prosodic boundaries in Chinese poetry always coincide with the lexical and syntactic boundaries of ordinary language, the prosodic units within lines and their higher combinations naturally are also the lexical and syntactic units, whereas in a polysyllabic language the metrical boundaries may occur at any arbitary break between syllables within a single word. Hence, it is reasonable to suggest that the extension of rhetorical rules is as simple as that for metrical ones. But in contrast with the clear formulation of metrical rules, rhetorical ones evolved only gradually and were never as well defined. The following should probably be considered proprieties rather than rules: (1) function words (*hsü-tzu* 虛字) should sometimes be avoided; (2) noun-centered phrases may form the lines; (3) the couplet, with its two separate lines of equal length, becomes the most important independent superstructure while the individual line, the next intermediate structure, can only be considered complete in conjunction with the other line in the same couplet; (4) a single predicate may extend over two lines to form a continuous couplet, or two predicates may fill the two respective lines to form a discrete couplet; and (5) in special cases, the discrete couplet may consist of two parallel lines.

Chinese traditionally use the word *chü* (句) to refer to both a syntactic sentence in ordinary language and a line in poetic language.[5] This superficial overlapping often belies the profound dif-

[5] I have discussed in detail the essential features of Chinese poetic language in another article. See Yu-kung Kao, "Approaches to Chinese Poetic Language," in *Chung-yang yen-chiu-yüan kuo-chi han-hsüeh hui-i lun-wen chi: wen-hsüeh-tsu* 中央研究院國際漢學會議論文集:文學組(Taipei: Chung-yang yen-chiu-yüan, 1981), pp. 423–454.

ferences between the two. Obviously there is no clear-cut way to define a syntactic prose sentence in Chinese, but the use of sentence particles is one evident marker of a *chü*. The gradual elimination of function words, including particles, prepositions, conjunctions, demonstratives (but not adverbs and modal terms), may reflect a secret impulse to downgrade syntactic units. Correspondingly, among the favored constructions in poetry we often find the nominal expression, which is simply an expression with a noun as the center and a quality attributed to it. This effectively divides poetic language into two types of structures: one, the sentence with its subject and predicate; the other, the phrase with its noun and qualifier. This division came to have great influence on the development of style in Chinese poetry.

One consequence of these developments in poetic language is that the line can no longer be easily justified as a sentence. This structural dependence between the lines in a couplet should dispel any illusion of "line" as the equivalence of "sentence." In a discrete couplet, the relation between the two lines is often one of coordination, which is the foundation of parallelism.[6] Parallelism was always a prominent feature of Chinese poetry, but as coordinate relations in couplets became increasingly prevalent, the way was paved for the more sophisticated uses of parallelism in "regulated verse."

Early Lyrical Aesthetics and the "Nineteen Ancient Poems"

Already in the second century B.C., we find an explicit theory of lyric poetry that provides the basis of an interpretation of early poetry, particularly of the *Shih ching*. By the time the "Nineteen Ancient Poems" were being written (probably in the middle of the second century A.D. or later) this theory of the lyric was widely known and accepted by literati poets.[7] It is no surprise that once the formal components of "five-character line verse" were established,

[6] For an excellent discussion of coordination and parallelism in general, see Hans H. Frankel, *The Flowering Plum and the Palace Lady* (New Haven: Yale University Press, 1976), pp. 144–185.

[7] See James J. Y. Liu, *Chinese Theories of Literature* (Chicago: University of Chicago Press, 1975), esp. pp. 67–70.

the new poetry felt the influence of this theory of the lyric, which helped shape the emergence of a new and powerful lyrical aesthetics.

This lyrical aesthetics was based firmly in the oldest definition of poetry in the Chinese tradition: "poetry expresses intent" (*shih yen chih* 詩言志), a phrase which appeared repeatedly in the early classics and was most systematically elaborated in the "Great Preface," written no later than the first century, and appended to the Mao commentary to the *Shih ching*. This definition formed the basis of an "expressive theory of poetry," which has dominated the Chinese lyrical tradition until the present.

In its broader interpretation, this simple maxim implies that the poetic impulse arises from the desire to express the mental states and acts of the poet through artistic language.[8] To fully appreciate the implications of this seemingly innocuous statement of purpose, one has to consider several claims found in the Chinese humanistic tradition: (1) the understanding of one's own internal states by oneself and by others is of the highest priority among human endeavors; (2) the ideal and possibly the only way to achieve this understanding is to transcend surface and physical meanings and thereby capture the essence of the inner spirit; (3) ordinary language is an inadequate means of perpetuating and communicating this inner spirit, and only artistic language is capable of accomplishing this act of expression.

From such early sayings as "expression is to make intention complete; literariness is to make expression complete" (*yen i tsu chih, wen i tsu yen* 言以足志, 文以足言) to those of later days, such as "to see the nature through mind" (*i hsin kuan wu* 以心觀物), or "to capture the spirit through form" (*i hsing ch'uan shen* 以形傳神), a wide variety of statements on poetry are in some way extensions and applications of this primordial definition.[9] The interaction

[8] See Kang-i Sun Chang, "Chinese Lyric Criticism in the Six Dynasties," in *Theories of the Arts in China*, ed. Susan Bush and Christian Murck (Princeton: Princeton University Press, 1983), pp. 215–224.

[9] The first quote "yen i tsu chih, wen i tsu yen" 言以足志, 文以足言, from the *Tso-chuan* 左傳, if taken together with the idea of "attaining immortality by means of 'establishing oneself in words'" (also from the *Tso-chuan*) is the most fundamental premise on which later versions of Chinese poetics were built. See *Chung-kuo mei-*

between "interiority" (*hsin* 心) and its "expression" (*yen* 言) can be illustrated by such lines from the *Shih ching* as "my heart is grieved, no one knows my sorrow."[10] The objectification of an inner state through art allows both the expression of self and the recognition of the self. Central to this act of communication are two processes, internalization and formalization, which are essential to understanding the nature of this aesthetics.

In early poetry, both the narrative and descriptive modes were

---

hsüeh-shih tzu-liao hsüan-pien 中國美學史資料選編 (Peking: Chung-hua shu-chü, 1980), vol. 1, p. 3. The phrase "i hsin kuan-wu" 以心觀物 is from Shao Yung 邵雍, "Kuan-wu p'ien" 觀物篇, *Huang-chi ching-shih ch'üan-shu* 皇極經世全書. This remark can be found in the same convenient anthology noted above, vol. 2, p. 17. The remark "i hsing hsieh shen" 以形寫神 was made by Ku K'ai-chih 顧愷之, quoted in Chang Yen-yüan's 張彥遠 *Li-tai ming-hua chi* 歷代名畫記. It can also be found in *ibid.*, vol. 1, p. 175. Taken out of context, these two phrases have been subject to numerous interpretations. I follow the most popularly accepted interpretation of them as the summation of ideas in the development of Chinese aesthetic thinking, not necessarily that accepted by the speakers. "Mind" here does not refer to the concept of *wo* 我 or "I" in Wang Kuo-wei's 王國維 famous distinction between "i wo kuan wu" 以我觀物 ("to see nature through my self") and "i wu kuan wu" 以物觀物 ("to see nature through nature"). Wang Kuo-wei's remarks can be found in his *Jen-chien tz'u-hua* 人間詞話, ed. Hsü Tiao-fu 徐調孚 (Hong Kong: Chung-hua shu-chü, 1961). Wang Kuo-wei's ideas were also appropriated from Shao Yung, with his own interpretation added. "Mind" refers to the process of "internalization," which can be seen most distinctively in the theory of paintings, such as multiple perspectives, reliance on memory, and the synthesis of experience, all with specific emphasis on the importance of mind as a mediating *a priori* factor to the actual process of painting. Poetry certainly places the same emphasis upon this mediation, at least in theory. The formalistic language can be seen again in the structural and compositional design, the categorization of natural phenomena, themes and techniques, the systemization of learning of techniques, and the imitation of traditional models. In the center, there is the elusive concept of *shen* 神, which can be as simple as the "esssence" and "quality" of the object and as mysterious as the "divine spirit" of nature. Its complexity and changeability are understandable, as it basically denotes the intangible quality in lyrical experience, not possible to translate into ordinary language by definition, but profoundly moving and vivid for the ones who experience it. It is the quality of attaining the idealized state of beauty in arts. In every culture, the concept of beauty is resistent to analysis and has certain mysterious overtones.

[10] See for instance, Song No. 167. A text of the song can be found in *Kao Pen-han Shih-ching chu-shih* 高本漢詩經注釋, trans. and ed. Tung T'ung-ho 董同龢 (Taipei: Chung-hua ts'ung-shu pien-shen wei-yüan-hui, 1960), p. 434.

used side by side with the lyric or expressive mode. Descriptive poetry reached its height in the "rhymeprose" (*fu* 賦) of the Han, whereas narrative poetry continued to enjoy popularity in folk literature. However, with the development of the new "five-character line verse," the lyrical aesthetic became dominant. Further, the evolution of the formal characteristics of "five-character line verse" played a significant role in establishing lyrical aesthetics over other poetic modes. For example, the strong presence of independent couplets made it difficult to sustain linear continuity in narrative. The diminishing role of function words and syntactic structures hampered the internal cross-referencing of narrative and made it difficult to coordinate lines within a coherent temporal-spatial framework. The bipartite structure of couplets encouraged the use of parallelism not only within couplets but as a macrostructure of poetic amplification; this proved awkward and unnatural in the linear sequence of early narrative modes. The descriptive mode fared somewhat better: the new form seemed to encourage the presentation of a spatial dimension in a temporal artistic medium. In fact, the parallel relations in couplets lent themselves to a bipartite spatial relationship: the series of independent couplets easily suggested a corresponding juxtaposition in space. Looking through the "Nineteen Ancient Poems," we find none that are entirely narrative (although there are fragments of narrative sequence); two (Nos. 2 and 10) may be considered bona fide descriptive poems; the remaining seventeen poems are lyrical verses representing several structural types.

Poem No. 1 is probably the most typical example of a lyric poem dealing exclusively with the poet's internal state.[11] Each couplet embodies a relation between an "I" (the poet) and a "you" (his addressee) and presents some aspect of the mental states and acts of poet or friend. Virtually the entire poem is enacted in the poet's imagination, as he or she imagines the painful consequence of parting and the even more frightening possibility of betrayal. The entire poetic act is like a person examining various possibilities from multiple perspectives and under different conditions. Formal

[11] See Ma Mao-yüan 馬茂元, *Ku-shih shih-chiu-shou ch'u-t'an* 古詩十九首初探 (Hsi-an, 1981), pp. 105–111. Hereafter this book will be referred to as *Ch'u-t'an*.

repetition, a prominent feature of early poetry, is strikingly absent here. Yet repetition of an entirely different sort may still be present as the underlying structure; the lines of the poem are unified by a single state of mind and thereby possess a qualitative equivalence. As such, this poem captures that underlying equivalence as the lyrical quality of that moment.[12]

What is in question here is a deep interiority, often vaguely referred to as personality, the point where a personal history and philosophy reside, inaccessible to any outsider. This person comes into contact with the world only through his perception and expression, and these contacts occasionally open up this private world to the others. This interaction between the surface and the depth, perception and personality, generates the poetic act and unleashes expressions of feeling and thought, judgment and imagination, remembrance and expectation. From the time of the *Shih ching* on, it was the interest in precisely this conjunction between interiority and the exterior world which lent such weight to poetic *hsing* (興). *Hsing*, in this sense, was the "initial impression of natural objects" that served as a catalyst to precipitate poetic response. This tradition of the "affective image" continued to influence the opening lines of lyric poetry throughout the later tradition. Typical is the opening of the third of the "Nineteen Ancient Poems," in which the impressions of "green cypress" and "massive rocks" come and go abruptly, but still draw the poet's attention away from the mundane routine of life and ask the reader to share that movement.[13] The tone in which these impressions are presented is almost impersonal, and that impersonality marks a universal condition that can be shared by the poet and his readers alike. If the beginning of Poem No. 1 is overly personal by comparison, at least the action of "going on and on" is open for everyone to observe, not a private situation that only the poet has the privilege to know. In cases when the opening simply states a theme, it must be a generalized statement on life: no one can disagree that "one's living years do not exceed a hundred, but one

[12] See Chu Tzu-ch'ing 朱自清, "Ku-shih shih-chiu-shou shih" 古詩十九首釋, in his *Ku-shih-ko chien-shih san-chung* 古詩歌箋釋三種 (Shanghai: Ku-chi ch'u-pan-she, 1981), pp. 221–225.

[13] Ma Mao-yüan, *Ch'u-t'an*, pp. 49–54.

often has the worries of a thousand years" (the opening lines of the fifteenth of the "Nineteen Ancient Poems").[14] But most of the openings of the "Nineteen Ancient Poems" consist of impressions of natural objects ("bamboo") or parts of a scene ("bright moon" and "crickets"), either isolated from the rest of the poem or fully integrated as background. Poetry becomes the consequence of a confrontation between the poet and some external phenomenon, through which he voluntarily opens up his responses to you.

Lyric poetry is presented to us as if written by the poet for his privileged audience of one, with him or far away, while we eavesdrop.[15] But often the presentation is too obviously directed to the general audience to maintain this air of private conversation, especially when the poet assumes the stance of a teller, as in the fifth of the "Nineteen Ancient Poems," whose "melancholy music" from atop a tower is described in an objective manner. In this case, communication seems to be directed to the general public, a point of view more typical of writers of narrative. But the purpose of lyric poetry is to "move," to "influence" one's friend, a point we are constantly reminded of in the critical theory of *Shih ching* in the concept of *feng* (風). Thus in the end of the fifth of the "Nineteen Ancient Poems," the poet properly shifts to a direct address to his listener in a dialogic pattern. Likewise, the first poem of the series also concludes with a personal exchange. Here, despite the possible betrayal by his friend, the poet's final exhortation "to eat well" is a crucial reminder of the purpose of the poetic act. Of the seventeen poems in expressive mode (excluding the two descriptive poems in the series), only the endings of Poems Nos. 6 and 19 are simple descriptions of the poet's present or future state of mind, occasions when the poet's loneliness is so deeply entrenched that the presence of an audience is completely eliminated.[16]

It seems that the "beginning" and "ending" of a lyric poem in the expressive mode are defined in terms of human interaction. If the beginning of a poem can be described as the interaction between the poet and the world, then the conclusion can be described

[14] *Ibid.*, pp. 97–100.

[15] See Northrop Frye, *Anatomy of Criticism* (Princeton: Princeton University Press, 1957), pp. 249–250.

[16] Ma Mao-yüan, *Ch'u-t'an*, pp. 69–72, 101–104.

as the interaction between the poet and his friend (unless the isolation is so intense that the poet loses all sense of his audience). These two formal structural devices not only shape the design of future lyric poetry, but also point out the inaccessibility and private nature of an individual's interior life, a life only glimpsed at through brief interactions. While the language of the "beginning" is marked by its fragmentary nominal phrases and juxtaposed impressions, the language of the "ending" is the fully syntactic language, complete with demonstratives, with reference to time, and most often with modal constructions.

At the other end of the spectrum are two descriptive poems, one on the lonely lady left at home by her constantly traveling husband (No. 2) and the other on the forlorn couple, "Weaving Maid" and "Cowherd" (constellations), separated by the Milky Way (No. 10).[17] The frequent use of reduplicative descriptives strikes us as extraordinary; in other poems of the series these appear only infrequently. This form is strongly reminiscent of the traditional *hsing* style of the *Shih ching*, where such reduplicative descriptives commonly modify impressions of the external world. In these two descriptive poems the poet plays the role of an observer, but the series of impressions forms an extended version of the "beginning" in *hsing*-style poetry. Thus description is less an impersonal act than a series of highly impersonal impressions: the poet's reaction to nature and to the central character in the poem, be it the "lonely lady" or the "Weaving Maid." These poems are descriptive only on the surface, but in fact assume the voice of a persona to express a common lyrical quality that the poet and persona share. Even in the passages describing personal activities, feeling is hardly mentioned; we have only the objective comment "rain-like tears" or the thought "difficult to be alone in an empty bed." Through this formal poetic structure, emotions such as loneliness are given the objectification of art and presented to us, as if neutrally, for a response that cannot be neutral.

More frequently, description is incorporated in the expressive mode, as in the twelfth poem of the series. The section beginning with "In Yen and Chao, beautiful women abound" (*yen chao to*

[17] *Ibid.*, pp. 112–117, 128–132.

chia-jen 燕趙多佳人) comes as such a complete surprise that many editors prefer to treat it as a separate poem.[18] This editorial response to the mixing of modes suggests a clear recognition of their separate qualities. The first part of the twelfth poem is entirely in the expressive mode, concluding with a modal couplet that sounds like a clear marker of lyric closure. Thus a sense of fracture appears between the two parts of the poem, and the second, descriptive, section cannot be perfectly integrated into the whole. The descriptive mode is more successfully integrated in the eighteenth poem of the series, where a bolt of patterned silk is described and transformed into a metaphor that is embedded in the larger poetic act: an object from the outside world is integrated with feeling through an act of human imagination.[19] When the object of a description is no longer a simple object but an artistic one, as when the poet listens to music from a tower in the second poem of the series, the experience itself can be sustained through different phases of emotional response, and the poet can indeed be said to seamlessly fuse impression with expression. Such rendering of description of an external event to signify an internal state proleptically maps out one future direction of Chinese poetics.[20] The promise made by this mode is that if the interiority is secluded and inaccessible, if the language of interiority is inadequate for its truth, then the description of an external fact through formalistic language may provide an oblique route to the poet's inner world. The practical problem presented was the development of a formalistic language adequate to such a project.

The Aesthetics of the Six Dynasties: From "Landscape Poetry" to "Court-Style Poetry"

The period immediately following the production of the "Nineteen Ancient Poems" was one of the most creative times

[18] *Ibid.*, pp. 84–88. Chang Feng-i 張鳳翼, in his *Wen-hsüan ts'uan-chu* 文選纂注 was the first to divide the poem into two separate pieces. Yü Kuan-ying 余冠英 followed this suggestion in his *Han Wei Liu-ch'ao shih-hsüan* 漢魏六朝詩選 (Peking: Jen-min wen-hsüeh ch'u-pan-she, 1958), pp. 65–66.

[19] Ma Mao-yüan, *Ch'u-t'an*, pp. 141–144.

[20] *Ibid.*, pp. 62–68.

in Chinese poetry, a period known as Chien-an (建安, A.D. 196–220). In fact, during the hundred years from Chien-an till T'ai-k'ang (太康, A.D. 280–289), poetic experiments were carried out which foreshadowed most of the later modes of poetry. Nevertheless, the fundamental lyrical aesthetics of this period were a continuation of the earlier one. The descriptive mode tended toward what was called "poetry on objects," while the expressive mode turned to "poetry on inner states." However, the expressive *interpretation* of poetry was so widespread and firmly entrenched that in hermeneutics the distinction was blurred. The term *yung-huai* (詠懷) (expressing innermost feelings) may serve as a general category for expressive poetry, but we must also note that Juan Chi 阮籍 (210–263), the pioneer of *yung-huai* poetry, included in his collection of eighty-two *yung-huai* poems, many pieces in the descriptive mode.[21] Essentially, the term was used to indicate the use of a style following the model of "Nineteen Ancient Poems." If we look to some unifying characteristic of *yung-huai*, we would find it most readily in thematic treatment, in the predominant mood of foreboding, of frustration and loneliness, and in the voice of individual resignation in face of reality. If expression came from the innermost depths of individual feeling, then all surface joy was sooner or later overwhelmed by a pain and disappointment that filled the poet's world and was deeply rooted in his experience. Even hedonistic philosophy, occasionally articulated in these poems, was presented as the sole refuge from an extremity of pain. The major themes from the "Nineteen Ancient Poems" that continually recur in the work of these later poets were "separation" and "death" or *sheng-li ssu-pieh* 生離死別 ("separation from the living and from the dead"). The futility of earlier attempts to overcome death became increasingly apparent; elixirs of immortality no longer held quite the same trust, and poets often returned to the old consolation of future *ming* 名 ("recognition" or "fame") as a means of attaining immortality. Separation was even more painful, as the poets gener-

[21] See Ting Fu-pao 丁福保, "Ch'üan San-kuo shih" 全三國詩, in *Ch'üan Han San-kuo Chin Nan-pei-ch'ao shih* 全漢三國晉南北朝詩 (rpt. Taipei: Shih-chieh shu-chü, 1968), vol. 1, pp. 214–225. This reprint is divided into three volumes and organized into sections by dynastic period. Hereafter only the particular section, volume, and page numbers will be given.

ally felt that it should be possible to overcome man-made obstacles, whether they arose from external circumstance or a lover's betrayal. A strong sentiment of despair marked the majority of *yung-huai* poems.

It is interesting to note that the celebration of joyful occasions, from exciting trysts in the woods to the happy reunion of a married couple, had suddenly disappeared from works in the new verse form at the end of the second century, which heralded a century of rebellions, civil wars, foreign invasions, and conquests. Ironically, this is also a century of great productivity in "five-character line verse." For people of this age, escape from the misery and tragedy of this world could be possible only for an immortal. The early flowering of "poetry on the wandering immortal" (*yu-hsien-shih* 遊仙詩) depended heavily on objective description.[22] However, with the gradual rise of popular Taoism and alchemy, the observer assumed the active voice of an immortal, which allowed him, the alchemist-hermit, the would-be immortal, to speak in the desired voice of the fully realized immortal. The poetry of Hsi K'ang 嵇康 (223–262) and Kuo P'u 郭璞 (276–324) moves freely between the personae of immortals and hermits and the poet speaking of himself.[23] One significant change they brought to lyrical tradition was the introduction of an optimistic tone, a mood that in the past had always been shattered when reflection shifted from the present moment to the future.

Out of this trend grew a new lineage in the poetic tradition, passing through the so-called "philosophical poetry" or "discursive poetry" (*hsüan-yen-shih* 玄言詩), and eventually culminating in the "landscape poetry" (*shan-shui-shih* 山水詩) of Hsieh Ling-yün 謝靈運 (385–433). This lineage represents a distinctive transformation, but not a complete break, in the traditional *yung-huai* mode.[24] Eventually, there formed within this lineage the special

[22] See Ts'ao Chih's "On Immortals" 仙人篇 and "Ascending the Heavens" 升天行, in ibid., "Ch'üan San-kuo shih," vol. 1, p. 142. Although the poet has clearly introduced elements of imagination into both poems, he is not yet an immortal.

[23] *Ibid.*, "Ch'üan San-kuo shih," vol. 1, p. 209, and "Ch'üan Chin shih" 全晉詩, vol. 1, pp. 423–425. See especially Hsi K'ang's 嵇康 first poem on "Stating My Life Ambition" 述志, p. 209.

[24] *Ibid.*, "Ch'üan Sung shih" 全宋詩, vol. 2, pp. 632–654.

aesthetics of the Southern Dynasties (fourth through the sixth centuries) which developed into "court-style poetry" (*kung-t'i-shih* 宮體詩), where we find the prototypes of "regulated verse." Therefore, it is necessary to consider briefly the aesthetics of this particular poetic lineage.

We may trace this lineage back to the early years of the third century, when Ts'ao P'i 曹丕 (186–226) had written of his delight in social gatherings and visiting friends.[25] On reading Chang Hua's 張華 (232–300) poem "On the Third Day of the Third Month," we realize that these sensuous and social pleasures were open affairs, if not to every one, at least to the upperclass literati.[26] Chang Hua's poem is one of the earliest works presenting a picture of a joyful banquet set in a beautiful natural setting, complete with the performance of music and dance. Celebration here had a definite philosophical dimension, with repeated references to Confucius' vision of the good life. It is significant that on the most renowned occasion in the *Analects*, where we see Confucius' vision of happiness, the Master asks his disciples to "state [their] life ambition" (*yen chih*), the same exact wording as *yen chih* in "[poetry] expresses intent." Confucius was profoundly moved by Tseng Tien's answer that he only hoped to sing and dance with friends near I River in a fine spring day.[27] Here, with Confucius' endorsement, "life vision" is simply an artistic experience, and it could well be taken as the best illustration of the underlying philosophical basis of the future "landscape poetry."

In the hands of Hsieh Ling-yün, "landscape poetry" acquired its own identity in both its formal and thematic components. The journey itself became its own purpose rather than some fixed destination, and thus the visual and auditory pleasures of the journey were enjoyed for their own sake. The writing of the poem was simply the presentation of these pleasures; the poem itself became a series of still pictures arranged along the axis of forward movement in the journey. And there was corresponding pleasure in the meticulous description of each stage, a loving care given to capturing

[25] *Ibid.*, "Ch'üan San-kuo shih," vol. 1, p. 132.

[26] *Ibid.*, "Ch'üan Chin shih," vol. 1, pp. 281–282.

[27] See D. C. Lau, *Confucius: The Analects* (Baltimore: Penguin Books, 1979), pp. 110–111.

each significant moment. Out of this care taken to find artistically adequate correlatives for those special moments of lived experience, great impetus was given to the rhetorical aspect of composition.

In the years between the "Nineteen Ancient Poems" and those of Hsieh Ling-yün, the technique of parallelism had made great progress, but Hsieh made use of this new form to serve his special vision. As he moved through the landscape, his appreciation seemed to be punctuated by a series of stops. At each of these stops he appeared to take a breath and consider the surrounding view as a whole. Hence the parallelism presents to us two simultaneous pictures of a diptych and, even more importantly, the picture given in the couplet has a totality in itself that can be considered in isolation as one frame in a long handscroll. Even taken out of context, the couplet retains its aesthetic value. This impression of completeness was greatly strengthened by his extensive use of a parallelism which allowed no duplication of words in the two lines; this evolved into the new "regulated parallelism" which I shall discuss in the next section. In the absence of repeated words, elements from both lines were given as complementary parts, facing each other across a space, with the observer in the center, but remaining outside.

However, Hsieh Ling-yün was also strongly influenced by "discursive poetry." Hsieh could never give himself over entirely to the sensuousness of his descriptive world, and he invariably chose to end his poems with a passage of meditation on the meaning of life that was seldom perfectly integrated with the passages of description. Unable to resolve this problem of unity, he left it, along with his contributions to the poetry of "visiting landscapes," to the poets of the second half of the fifth century. His immediate successors, Hsieh T'iao 謝朓 (464–499) and Chiang Yen 江淹 (444–505), felt the shaping power of his vision of "landscape poetry," but they were probably influenced equally by another poet, Pao Chao 鮑照 (415–466), a younger contemporary of Hsieh Ling-yün.[28] Thus

[28] Ting Fu-pao, "Ch'üan Sung shih," vol. 2, pp. 664–708, for Pao Chao 鮑照; "Ch'üan Ch'i shih" 全齊詩, vol. 2, pp. 798–830, for Hsieh T'iao 謝朓; "Ch'üan Liang shih" 全梁詩, vol. 2, pp. 1,032–1,054, for Chiang Yen 江淹. See also John Marney, *Chiang Yen* (Boston: Twayne, 1981).

they inherited not only the heritage of "landscape poetry," but also through Pao Chao the older tradition of "expressing innermost feelings" directly traceable to the "Nineteen Ancient Poems." As such they were able to reconcile these two opposite, but complementary, traditions. Their achievements lay in a movement toward a more compact form which gave focus to the richness of sensory experience and at the same time sought to present that experience as *response* to the impressions of nature, as expression of their feelings. More than Hsieh Ling-yün's work, many of these poems may be properly called "poetry to describe the scenery" (*hsieh-ching-shih* 寫景詩), because their acts consist more of "looking from one point" than of "moving and looking" as if on a journey. They were also prolific in writing "poetry on objects" (*yung-wu-shih* 詠物詩) in a leaner and purer style than previous poetry in this mode, most of them in "ballad form" (*yüeh-fu*).

Their creative efforts, together with experiments in new euphonic patterns, paved the road for the establishment of "court-style poetry" as a popular genre.[29] In a number of ways, the aesthetics of the new genre did not encourage continuing experimentation; the advent of "regulated verse" was delayed another century. "Court-style poetry" had its thematic limitations as well as its formal constraints. Nevertheless, central to all these components was the tacit acceptance of sensuality as the sufficient and possibly necessary condition of artistic experience. The "interiority" of poetry began as "intent," or "vision" and, passing through various metamorphoses, it could only be defined as "thought" and "feeling." In "court-style poetry" it degenerated into "sensation," and "sensation" of only the most pleasant sort. Here at last, Ts'ao P'i's self-satisfaction in the happy feast of senses came to be a daily event set in a controlled environment, often a cultivated garden or a sumptuous banquet. No longer natural and drastically limited in

[29] For a discussion of "court-style poetry," see Anne Birrell, *New Songs from a Jade Terrace* (London: George Allen and Unwin, 1982), especially the "Introduction," pp. 1–28, and John Marney, *Liang Chien-wen Ti* (Boston: Twayne, 1976), pp. 76–117. For a discussion of the development of "court-style poetry" in the T'ang, see Stephen Owen, *The Poetry of the Early T'ang* (New Haven: Yale University Press, 1977), pp. 3–13.

scale, the minute details of experience were finely tuned to a sensitive, but delicate, year of the new aesthete. Imperceptibly, the place of expressive music from a disturbed mind, appearing so often in early poetry, was taken by a pictorialism where visual beauty and harmony reigned. Even when the voice of a persona appeared, it was a non-intrusive sentiment, designed not to draw attention but to provide the human interest in an otherwise objective picture. The voice of the pining lady or melancholy poet also replaced meditation on ethical and metaphysical issues. This new ending at least partially overcame the dichotomy between impression and expression in presenting a unified tableau. It is no wonder that this particular style continued to rule the literary scene long after the end of the Southern Dynasties in 589. But it was the persistent undercurrent of *yung-huai* which eventually brought a new life to poetry.

Regulated Verse

The movement toward determinate poetic form seemed to gather momentum in the second half of the fifth century with the new awareness of the tonal nature of Chinese language. In the following period of gestation, the two important formal techniques, tonal pattern and parallelism, underwent further refinement and provided the basis for the initiation of true "regulated verse" in the beginning of the seventh century.

This development really had two separate, though interrelated, aspects. The rhetorical rules developed steadily from the earliest days of "five-character line verse" and took control imperceptibly and unannounced. By contrast, the phonic rules attracted considerable attention during their initial stages and stirred up sporadic opposition during the sixth and seventh centuries. These rules firmly laid the foundation for the transformation of contemporary "descriptive poetry" into the more structured "regulated verse." Keeping in mind that these rules underwent a long formative period, we shall now describe the final established version of these rules.

New Metrical Patterns

The earlier discussion of metrical rules involved only syllabic ones. Another set of rules began to develop in the second half of the fifth century, when philologists and poets noticed the tones in their language, probably stimulated by the introduction of Sanskrit and its linguistics, brought into China by Indian Buddhists.[30] They immediately tried to apply this new discovery to poetry and created the new "tone-based rules" or tonal patterns.

Chinese had probably been a tonal language from the very beginning, even though the nature of earlier tones (say during the fifth century B.C.) is still unknown. The tonal qualities of Chinese during the inception of tonal regulation during the fifth century A.D. was very close to that of the T'ang period (618–907), thus insuring an easy transition from "court-style poetry" to "regulated verse." Shen Yüeh 沈約 (441–513), generally credited as the discoverer of tones, was probably only one of many from the poetry circle which concerned itself with tonal rules. Hsieh T'iao and Wang Jung 王融 (467–493) also belonged to this group.[31] But the most significant contribution was the simplification of the tonal system from a quadripartite division into a bipartite one, which made the marriage of tones and poetry a reality. This new division of "level" and "oblique" tones may appear trivial, but, as John Lotz points out in his study of versification in many cultures, in all the metrical systems he examined: "the phonological elements are

[30] The following discussion of tonal patterns is based primarily on the study in Wang Li's 王力 *Han-yü shih-lü-hsüeh* 漢語詩律學 (Shanghai: Chiao-yü ch'u-pan-she, 1965), pp. 41–131. Although I had consulted Ch'i Kung's 啓功 *Shih-wen sheng-lü lun-kao* 詩文聲律論稿 (Peking, 1978), I finally rejected his interesting but problematic analysis of these patterns. See also Stephen Owen, *The Poetry of the Early T'ang*, pp. 429–431; and Hans H. Frankel's development of G. B. Downer and A. C. Graham's theory in W. K. Wimsatt, *Versification*, pp. 29–32.

[31] See Hsiao Tzu-hsien 蕭子顯, *Nan-Ch'i shu* 南齊書 quoted in *Liang-Han Wei-Chin Nan-pei-ch'ao wen-hsüeh p'i-p'ing tzu-liao hui-pien* 兩漢魏晉南北朝文學批評資料彙編, ed. K'o Ch'ing-ming 柯慶明 and Tseng Yung-i 曾永義 (Taipei: Ch'eng-wen ch'u-pan-she, 1978); and Liu Shan-ching 劉善經, "Ssu-sheng lun" 四聲論, quoted in *Chung-kuo li-tai wen-lun hsüan* 中國歷代文論選, ed. Kuo Shao-yü 郭紹虞 (Shanghai: Ku-chi ch'u-pan-she, 1982), vol. 1, pp. 225–228. For Shen Yüeh's 沈約 poetry, see Ting Fu-pao, "Ch'üan Liang shih," vol. 2, pp. 987–1,029; for Wang Jung's 王融 poetry, see "Ch'üan Ch'i shih," vol. 2, pp. 778–795.

grouped into only two base classes, never into more . . . although in principle much finer gradations would be possible."[32]

Unfortunately, the exact nature of this new tonal division remains a matter of speculation. But reducing a more complex but realistic division into the simple binary system inevitably involves some strong phonic distinction to distinguish clearly the two contrastive classes. Without going into technical details, most hypotheses of the physical nature of these tones support a distinct contrast, either in duration between long and short tones, pitch between low and high, or in contour between level and deflected.[33] It is also possible that two or even all three of these categories of distinction were combined, which would have provided an even stronger contrast for the contemporary ears. As a working hypothesis, I propose only to see their contrast as between "lax" and "tense." The alternation of relaxation in the "level" tone and tension in the "oblique" tone will sufficiently illustrate the form and function of this new meter. The upbeat of urgency and momentum alternates with the downbeat of resolution and finality. This adequately explains the sense of anticipation in the closing of the first line of a couplet, usually in an oblique tone, and the sense of response and finality in the level tone which concludes the second line. Thus oblique tone suggests an urgency (and anticipation) unsuitable for closure.

This newly added element of tonal contrast allowed poets to experiment with the construction of an auditory design of some complexity, rather than building a simple repetition rhythm, as was the case in most other poetic traditions. The superimposition of a set of tonal patterns on the old syllabic meter resulted in what may be viewed as a system of contrasts based upon an underlying principle of symmetry. From this principle, factors of balance and dynamism, equivalence and opposition, stillness and movement, were meticulously distributed to achieve the maximum effect.

[32] W. K. Wimsatt, *Versification*, p. 15.

[33] Concerning the tones in T'ang Chinese, Wang Li proposes a contrast between long (for the "level" tone) and short (for the "oblique" tone). See his *Han-yü shih-lü-hsüeh*, pp. 6–7. But many linguists disagree with him on this hypothesis. For example, see Tsu-lin Mei, "Tones and Prosody in Middle Chinese and the Origin of the Rising Tone," *Harvard Journal of Asiatic Studies* 30 (1970), 86–110.

The resulting patterns discussed below were unsystematically incorporated into the final code in a series of stages. The first set of line patterns made its appearance in several variations during the middle of the fifth century; by the end of that century, many poets evidently began to treat them as the basic meter. The second set of couplet patterns began to be formulated at the same period, but its full adaptation into the system did not occur until the middle of the seventh century. Finally, possibly in the middle of the eighth century, the verse patterns were accepted widely as the prerequisite of a "regulated verse." Ironically, it was at this time that the most innovative poetic period, the High T'ang, had already come to its end.

(1) TONAL PATTERNS FOR LINES

The basic metric unit in "regulated verse" remains the disyllabic segment, which is assigned a tonal class according to the tone of the second, accented syllable. Theoretically, a typical example will have both syllables belonging to the same tone, but in reality instances in which they use opposite tones are almost as frequent. The combination of these tonal segments reflects the principle of maximum contrast. Hence, the normal four-character line will have two simple patterns: "- - / ' '" and "' ' / - -" with "-" standing for a "level" tone, "'" standing for an "oblique" one, and "/" standing for the cesura. (I will not discuss the variations of these patterns, such as "- / -" based mainly upon the disyllabic tonal class with opposite tones.)

(2) TONAL PATTERNS FOR COUPLETS

According to the principle of maximum contrast, on a higher level the natural opposition of "- - / - (' ')" is obviously "' ' / ' (- -)," and that of "' ' / (- -) '" is "- - / (' ') -"—its mirror image. Since the rhyme is supposed to be confined to the level tone, the only possible combinations for couplet patterns are the two pairs whose second line ends in a level tone. As in earlier poetry, the rhyme falls at the end of each couplet (x a x a x a x a). If one could draw the distribution of these patterns in color, the visual sense of balance would become immediately apparent. The enclosed design, with each part balanced by its opposite, creates a symbol of totality and self-containedness. The symmetry suggests a mini-system independent from the larger whole. The couplet's sense of independence is now doubly reinforced by phonic enclosure.

(3) TONAL PATTERNS FOR VERSE

To obtain contrast on the highest level, for a four-couplet verse one would naturally alternate the two sets of couplet patterns to form a quatrain, then repeat the quatrain to complete the pattern. If the concept of "opposition" (*tui* 對) is the operating principle between the two lines within the same couplet, then the line operating between the two couplets involves a new concept of "connection" (literally "gluing together," *nien* 黏). Connection is achieved through the use of units of the same tonal class in the initial positions of two neighboring lines from two different couplets. This reinforces the coherence of the poem by balancing the greater independence of each closed couplet. The alternation of the two sets results in the "connection" between two sets, whereas the repetition of the same set would break this connection. Since the same pattern will be repeated after each quatrain, this procedure can be extended indefinitely, which is precisely what occurs in the "extended form" (*p'ai-lü* 排律) of "regulated verse." But in normal "regulated verse" the quatrain is repeated only once. If the mirror image between lines suggests "opposition," the alternation between couplets creates "variations," and the second quatrain is the "transposition" or "development" that follows the completion of the "exposition" of the first quatrain.

One exception to the rhyme rule is the possible use of rhyme at the end of the first line in the first couplet, yielding a rhyme scheme a a x a x a x a. This variation permits the early establishment of the sense of rhyme, but it also disturbs the mirror image in the first couplet, demanding the use of the only other line pattern ending with a level tone. However, the remaining patterns of the whole verse will continue unchanged. The first line will be repeated in the fourth and last lines, preserving the principle of maximum contrast by keeping the greateat possible distance between lines with identical patterns. To conclude our observations on phonic patterns, I would like to compare the new code, no longer a linear pattern with a forward-moving momentum, with the blueprint of design of four independent, but related, quarters, each made with building blocks of two contrastive colors. They are fitted together snugly as one level of a symbolic system, to be completed by other components.

New Rhetorical Patterns

As in the case of metrical rules, the development of rules of rhetoric was continuous and gradual, with no perceptible break. However, one may still recognize the codification of a type of structure later known as the "regulated parallel couplet" (*lü-lien* 律聯), which came to play a central role in shaping the design of "regulated verse."[34] The concept of "regulated parallelism" is again based upon the principle of symmetry, in contrast to the earlier "duplicated parallelism" which was based upon the principle of repetition. "Parallelism" is essentially the extension and variation of the principle of equivalence, basic to lyric poetry. In the extreme case, equivalence becomes repetition, as in the early folk songs from the *Shih ching*. The old "duplicated parallelism" uses partial repetition in order to accentuate the difference of variable elements. As a prohibition against lexical repetition gradually became part of the new aesthetics, "parallelism" moved to the other extreme.

The new "regulated parallelism" operated primarily on the level of couplet; the two lines within a couplet are organized as corresponding parts of a balanced and enclosed system, in which each component in one part is matched by a similar, yet different, component in the corresponding position of the other part. Similarity occurs through an identity of word class in parallel components; difference occurs by the prohibition of repetition and the opposition of tones. This new requirement could perhaps only be realized in a non-inflected language that was essentially monosyllabic, where position and word boundaries can be strictly limited. Only in a language not dependent on function words can duplication be completely eliminated. Even more important is that

[34] Wang Li, *Han-yü shih-lü-hsüeh*, pp. 142–183.

in Chinese each semantic segment contains either one or at most two syllables. Any longer segment is seen as the combination of these minimum monosyllabic and disyllabic ones, and, as mentioned earlier, the phonetic boundaries of a compound are also its semantic boundaries. This assures the relatively effortless attainment of perfect correspondence between two parallel components.

Word class began as simple grammatical classification, with noun to match noun, and so on. But as Chinese generally considered this classification a semantic system, matching tended to occur in categorical groupings, preserving matching by word class, but semantically more determinate. Categories such as "celestial," "terrestrial," "architectural," "botanical," etc., absorbed grammatical categories into a semantic encyclopedia of all phenomena. Words from the same specialized category obviously share certain qualities, while maintaining some semantic identity. Consequently, every pair of parallel objects has certain degrees of underlying equivalence, with sharply contrastive surfaces. This restored the lost concept of repetition, at least on the level of the couplet, and made the parallel couplet even more enclosed than before.

Reacting to this strong presence of parallel couplet, the nonparallel verse structure seems to share the common characteristic of linearity and continuity. This marked the further demarcation of two types of poetic diction, which I shall not go into here. If one considers the mastery of parallel couplets (albeit without strict tonal patterns) by Hsieh Ling-yün as the beginning of the evolution of new rhetorical patterns, the culmination of that evolution can be found in its final establishment, probably in the middle of the eighth century. By this time, both tonal and rhetorical patterns were firmly in place, and any violation was considered a serious error. In other words, codification was also the beginning of fossilization. In the following pages we will give a brief survey of the impact of the "regulated couplet" and its influence on different levels of verse.

(I) PARALLEL PATTERNS IN LINES AND COUPLETS

Parallelism favors nouns for several reasons. One of the most obvious is that matching two elements often depends on two headnouns from the same word class. The proliferation of noun categories reflects the emphasis placed upon the nominal world. Another reason is that the parallel couplet's most effective function is to record the poet's impressions of the world, directly and objectively. In a parallel couplet, the poet's act of observation is typically implicit, and in this case even verbs of perception, such as "see" and "hear" may be considered superfluous. Therefore, a nominal expression linking a concrete noun and its most characteristic quality is used to describe one's impression of the natural world, with little interference from the mediating observer. This impression is also of a particular moment, because parallelism generally avoids explicit reference to relative time. Nevertheless, space is implied here as simultaneous existence, interacting with the poet in the center.

Once established, these characteristics of the parallel couplet readily had consequences on the level of the line. The increased use of nominal expressions, together with the implied structure of juxtaposition, gradually influenced poetic diction and intensified an earlier tendency in the treatment of nouns and function words. First of all, "content words" or "lexical words" (*shih-tzu* 實字) are practically the only ones allowed in the parallel couplets.[35] Among these content words, the noun of course is the center, but, in fact, quality words, with their own special categories, including "colors," "numerals," and "directions," subtly dominate the scene. On the other hand, the number of function words diminishes greatly. By definition, a series of juxtaposed nominal expressions excludes the use of function words. In parallel couplets, certain categories, such as "particle" and "preposition," were used only occasionally, when a poet wanted to create special effects. Other

[35] One famous example of the use of "function words" in the middle couplets can be found in Wang Wei's "Drifting on the Front Pond" with two particles, *i* 以 and *chih* 之. See Pauline Yu, *The Poetry of Wang Wei* (Bloomington: Indiana University Press, 1980), pp. 193–194, 230. But the exceptions were rare before the end of the sixteenth century. The popularity of the Kung-an 公安 and Ching-ling 竟陵 Schools at the beginning of the seventeenth century prompted numerous experimentations with the use of "function words" in "regulated verse." This practice was denounced by both Wang Fu-chih 王夫之 (1619– 1692) in his *Chiang-chai shih-hua* 薑齋詩話 (Peking: Chung-hua shu-chü, 1981), pp. 112–113 and Wang Shih-chen 王士禎 (1624–1711) in his *Tai-ching-t'ang shih-hua* 帶經堂詩話 (Peking: Chung-hua shu-chü, 1982), p. 759.

categories with much influence on lexical meaning, especially "modal words" and "adverbs," were used with discretion. All in all, this resulted in lines with rich meanings on the lexical level and dense in texture. In a parallel couplet, the juxtaposition could work in two different directions, as internal relations within the line and as lateral relation between the two lines. This naturally further intensified the overall texture; whatever syntactic structures were left in the line were relegated to the background.

(2) CONTINUOUS PATTERNS IN LINES AND COUPLETS

In contrast to the fragmented lines and couplets, another type of poetic diction, marked by linearity and continuity, continued to assert itself in "regulated verse," leading eventually to a structural design which made a clear division between these two types of diction and assigned each its special position in verse. In a verb-centered language, each verse line is normally continuous, with subject and predicate. Despite the dominance of "nominal expressions" (including "topic and comment"), Chinese lyrical poetry still uses the continuous line with frequency. Even the absence of a subject could not change the force of the verb, which, whether transitive or intransitive, often moved forward along the continuous line of a sentence. This sense of transitivity provided the momentum to carry the reader to the end of the poem.

Neighboring lines are linked together by an explicit or implicit temporal progression, by causal or logical interpretation, and most powerfully by syntactic structure. This forms a continuous couplet, either in coordination or in one integral structure. The coordinated couplet includes "question and answer," "condition and statement," and many other structures. The integral couplet can have the subject in one part, the predicate in another, or the subject and verb in one part and the object in another. In both cases, only one verb is involved. The most interesting case is the use of the pivotal object-subject construction, where the object of the verb in the first line serves at the same time as the subject of the verb in the second line. The transitivity is carried by the first verb through the pivotal noun onto the second verb and finally ends with the terminal object.

Not all parallel couplets are discrete; a particular type of parallelism popularly known as "on-rush flowing water couplet" (*liu-shui-tui* 流水對) describes the continuous but parallel couplets frequently used by the Early T'ang poets. The surface parallelism is supposed to disguise the undercurrent of continuity, thereby merging two different perspectives.

(3) PATTERN FOR VERSE

The two types of diction gravitated toward two modes of expression, the descriptive and the expressive. Even if this distinction is not absolute, the former favors continuous couplet and the latter a parallel one. After the middle of the eighth century, the distribution of parallel and continuous couplets in a verse eventually became a hard-and-fast pattern. No poet claiming to write in the norm of "regulated verse" would deviate from this pattern without some special reason.

This pattern, simply stated, has the two outer couplets continuous and the two inner ones parallel. In the early period, continuing the practice of "court-style poetry," the first couplet was often used to introduce the initial act through the presentation of impressions; therefore, they often appear in parallel structure. Later, the poet always had a choice between the two forms of initial couplet. Before the middle of the eighth century, often only one of the two inner couplets was parallel, particularly when the first couplet was parallel. In rare cases, none of these couplets used parallelism. However, these poems are borderline cases, sometimes considered to be in the "ancient style" (*ku-t'i* 古體), but using the phonic patterns of "recent style" (*chin-t'i* 近體), a category comprising both "regulated verse" and "quatrain verse" (*chüeh-chü* 絕句). This phenomenon sometimes reflected the fluidity of the pattern in its early stages, but in other cases it marked a preference by many poets for continuity over parallelism. The prevalence of this latter technique is attested to in the poems of Li Po 李白 (701–762) and Meng Hao-jan 孟浩然 (689–740), who, in effect, used the "continuous parallel couplet" to achieve the same thing. This departure did not apply to the last couplet, where the demands of poetic ending required it to be in continuous form. The practice of using a parallel couplet to end a poem in the Six Dynasties was seldom imitated. In later years, a master like Tu Fu 杜甫 (712–770) might conclude a poem in a continuous form, but close examination of the ending couplet reveals that the rules of parallelism were in fact rigorously followed. This device is exactly opposite that of "continuous parallelism," but it would seem that this remarkable disguise of the underlying parallelism is a *tour de force.*

To conclude my discussion on these technical aspects of "regulated verse," I would like to note that even with all these formal components at last in their places, the form remains an empty shell.[36] It is in the various interpretations of the form in particular poems that we find the underlying aesthetics which give it life. One ironic note should not escape our notice: our three versions of aesthetics cover the first one hundred and fifty years of the development of "regulated verse" until the eve of the Middle T'ang, when the process of codification of "regulated verse" was completed and the vitality of the form depleted.

The Artistic Vision of Early T'ang Poets

Poets of the seventh century were often credited with the invention of "regulated verse," a myth most of us no longer believe. My earlier sections present instead a sense of the gradual formulation of the verse form over the preceding century and a half and its continual evolution during the first fifty years of the seventh century. Why, then, is the seventh century singled out for this distinction? I believe that although any point during the first three hundred years of this evolution can be chosen as the beginning, the seventh century, particularly the seventies and eighties, is significant because of the emergence of the "four rhyme" format from the earlier "open-ended" format to become an independent genre. In other words, before this period, poets wrote poems in the new conventions with no specified number of couplets. Beginning at this time, poets had to decide between the "long form" (*ch'ang-p'ien*

[36] For an imaginative discussion on the formal components of Chinese poetry, particularly those of "regulated verse," see François Cheng, *Chinese Poetic Writing*, translated from the French by Donald A. Riggs and Jerome P. Seaton (Bloomington: Indiana University Press, 1982), pp. 23–68.

長篇), later called "extended form," and the "four couplet" form. To be sure, even earlier the four-couplet format was generally favored over other lengths, but it contended for popularity with other forms with five and six couplets. Yü Hsin's 庾信 (513–581) group of twenty-five poems on "paintings on screens" contains twenty-three in four couplets, and T'ang T'ai-tsung's 唐太宗 (597–649) ten-poem cycle on the "imperial capital" has nine in four couplets. However, the ending poems (two in Yü Hsin's group and one in T'ai-tsung's) are in the open-ended format.[37] The decision to placc a different forin as the closure of a long cycle signifies at least a partial awareness of their difference as genres.

Earlier, poets often felt free to ignore the conventions of the new meter and parallelism. Again, the choice between "ancient" and "recent" style was not a conscious one. But from the time of the "Four Talents of the Early T'ang," a clear division appeared between poems in the "regulated verse" form and poems in the "ancient style." The fluctuation of the new form, of course, produced many "borderline" cases, which were later classified under "ancient style" because of their violation of the strict patterns. However, both the loose interpretation of these patterns at the time these poems were written and their infusion with the spirit of the new form mark a point of departure from the "ancient style." It is therefore interesting to observe that in a Ming edition of T'ang poetry, the editors place the poems by T'ang T'ai-tsung, Yü Shih-nan 虞世南 (558–638), and Hsü Ching-tsung 許敬宗 (fl. mid-seventh century) under the category of "diverse styles" (*tsa-shih* 雜詩), while those by the "Four Talents" of the mid-seventh century were more strictly divided under the categories of "ancient style," "regulated verse," and "extended form." These divisions suggest the editors' awareness that by the time of the "Four Talents" these genres had become fully distinct.[38]

This claim of independence is important in my discussion of the

[37] For Yü Hsin's 庾信 "Yung hua p'ing-feng shih" 詠畫屏詩, see Ting Fu-pao, "Ch'üan Pei-Chou shih" 全北周詩, vol. 3, pp. 1,602–1,604; for T'ang T'ai-tsung's 唐太宗 "Ti-ching p'ien" 帝京篇, see *T'ang wu-shih-chia shih chi* 唐五十家詩集 (rpt. Shanghai: Ku-chi ch'u-pan-she, 1981), pp. 36–39.

[38] See *T'ang wu-shih-chia shih-chi*, pp. 27–46, for T'ang T'ai-tsung; pp. 57–70, for Yü Shih-nan 虞世南; and pp. 83–96, for Hsü Ching-tsung 許敬宗.

underlying aesthetics. Only with the establishment of a definite formal design can a poet begin to explore its various possibilities. The quadruple structure, trivial to casual observation, shall loom large in the following discussion. The reuniting of the two modes, descriptive and expressive, seemed to be a conscious choice made by poets in the seventies of the seventh century. It is probably more appropriate to say that these poets, especially the "Four Talents," sought to reintroduce the aesthetics of the earlier *yung-huai* tradition into the new descriptive tradition, known as "court-style poetry."[39] This integration, probably part of the general movement of "opposition poetics," can be seen as an attempt to return to the *yung-huai* techniques of the "beginning inspiration" and the "dialogic ending."[40] The compactness of the new format made sudden confrontation with the natural setting a more appropriate technique than a slow unfolding of the poetic act. Even more unusual is the direct statement of inner feeling at the very beginning of a poem, as in the opening couplet in the following poem by Yang Chiung 楊炯 (650–695), when the poet immediately and directly confronts feelings in the depths of his heart.[41]

Sorrow entangled—confused as hemp fibers; 愁結亂如麻
Endless sky—shine the setting rose clouds. 長天照落霞

This abrupt opening, which unequivocally declares the theme of the poem, is an idiosyncratic interpretation of the concept *hsing* by the "Four Talents," in this case Yang Chiung.

In poetic closure, the poet's effort to communicate a strong sentiment unique to the occasion had been natural in the works of earlier poets of "five-character line verse." However, the two centuries of "court-style poetry" had developed an objective mode of presentation of sense-impressions, an impersonal perspective in which the poetic act became more self-retrospective, with a general and hidden audience far removed from the poet. As a result, with the exception of the most intimate exchanges between friends in "parting poems," a perspective of "monologue" took over; the

[39] Stephen Owen, *The Poetry of the Early T'ang*, pp. 79–150.

[40] *Ibid.*, pp. 14–26.

[41] *T'ang wu-shih-chia shih-chi*, p. 231.

closing became more the poet's interaction with the reality, rather than with friends. Lo Pin-wang 駱賓王 (ca. 640–684) ended his poem for a social gathering with the revelation:

Only take [feeling] limpid as water,	唯將淡若水
To bow to the spirit of the ancients.	長揖古人風

This general statement on his idea of a true friendship, pure and with no flavor added, an echo of the ancients' ideal, was essentially an impersonal address to anyone willing to listen.[42]

In a compact poetic form with only four couplets, the beginning and the end (though assigned to the first and fourth couplets, respectively) were indeed too powerful to support a tripartite structure. The dichotomy between descriptive and expressive more often suggests a bipartite division, with the former occupying the first three couplets and the latter the last couplet. The concise form and precise structure helped enormously to consolidate the two pillars of support in this new aesthetics: internalization of the external and formalization of the internal, two traditional concepts imbued with fresh applications.

When a form extends to an indefinite length, the poetic voice gradually loses its control over the content; the present moment is stretched beyond the limits of maintaining a credible illusion of an arrested moment of the present.[43] This type of extended lyrical poetry, as Hsieh Ling-yün's "landscape poetry," encourages the tendency to create descriptive poems for the sake of description. When the form is condensed to four couplets, with only three of them recording the poet's impressions, the presence of the "lyrical voice" returns and the framework of the poetic act is assigned its special function; in this case, the poet is to observe and internalize the world and to express his inner states, including his internalized impression of the world. Together with the resurgence of the "lyrical self," the "lyrical moment" also made a powerful comeback. This short form was designed to capture a momentary glimpse into the mind of the poet; physical time and space, either in the medium or in the referential world, are entirely irrelevant in

[42] *Ibid.*, p. 409.

[43] See Wang Fu-chih, *Chiang-chai shih-hua*, p. 57.

this new context: the internal world of the "lyrical self." Every element in the first three couplets, as the content of the mind, has no dimension in space and in time, and belongs only to the particular "lyrical moment." Anything more complex than the simple relation between internalization and poet probably cannot be accommodated by this form. The elaborate description of a prolonged visit, the complicated development of a plot, or the painstaking introspection of one's own psychological problems—all need a fuller, more extended, and less structured form than "regulated verse." Only in a sudden inspiration, a penetrating insight, when an abrupt thought or image strike and catch one's attention for a moment, is the use of this form natural. But short as it is, it is still twice as long as "quatrain form." Therefore, the form still allows and demands "development" according to a formal design, which goes beyond the simple structural requirements listed in the last section and inspires at least one kind of interpretation popular among these early T'ang poets.

In this new formalistic language, the dichotomy between impressive and expressive, or between the first three couplets and the last, becomes the division between two stages in the poetic act: "exposition" and "reflection." If we want to describe them as two psychological phases, the terms "extroversion" and "introversion," which define the turning of mind outward to things outside and inward upon oneself, would suffice. The process of extroversion, though directed toward the outside, is nevertheless a psychological act in the process of internalization. Although the two may seem contradictory, both are marked by spontaneity and impersonality. As the poet responds to phenomena, the spontaneous response belongs to unmediated objective perception, which is neutralized by the poet's personal interference. It is this quality of impersonality which gives objectivity even to the treatment of internal subjective experience.[44] This seeming paradox provides an interesting addition to the original scenario of "landscape poetry"; the poet may now observe disinterestedly his own inner feeling and

[44] This quality of objectivity probably was the reason why Wang Kuo-wei suggested that one way of observing nature is to see it through nature itself ("i wu kuan wu"). See n. 9 above.

thought. This anatomy of interiority is structured along the same design as the description of impression, with parallelism in each of the inner couplets, with the juxtaposition of nominal expressions within each line, and with suggestive interaction and interdependence between the couplets. The following poem by Lo Pin-wang provides an example in which all three beginning couplets state the inner experiences:

Lonesome, dejected—preoccupations linger late;	寂寞心事晚
Shivering, falling—time of year, autumn.	搖落歲時秋
Together with this—lament aging hair;	共此傷年髮
Look at each other—regret going and staying.	相看惜去留
Listen to songs—should stop the tears;	當歌應破涕
Pity our fates—return to extreme sorrow.[45]	哀命返窮愁

All three couplets are parallel; the terms in parallel relation: "lonesome, dejected" and "shivering, falling," "late" and "autumn" are equated in an underlying metaphorical relation sustained by that parallel relation. The linear relations also convey parallels: "lonesome" is the "preoccupation" and "falling" the "time of the year." The texture of the inner couplets is thickened by a series of actions pregnant with emotive meanings, but the emotional being of the poet is presented in balanced form as an abstract painting on "feeling." The lament over their aging appearances, regret over parting, listening to songs and pitying each other's fates, do not appear in sequence; these acts probably happen again and again and possibly sometimes simultaneously. This simultaneity forces the converging of diverse movements into one. The qualities of the individual act blend with the qualities of time, place, and the poet's other emotional states. This many-sided view of the central event, "parting," should automatically remind us of the first poem from the "Nineteen Ancient Poems." Both share the same theme and have the same internalized content, but Lo's poem presented his inner world in a precisely demarcated design, with the strong presence of "lyrical self" and "lyrical moment" controlling the

[45] *T'ang wu-shih-chia shih-chi*, pp. 406–407.

whole poetic act. The binary structure within each line, within each couplet, within the inner couplets, and finally within the entire first section (between the setting of time and place and the inner couplets), creates a complex, but symmetrical, layered sculpture. This new structure demands a new process of reading. As the ordinary reading is linear and forward, the reading of parallel structure constantly diverts the reader's attention to the side, demanding that he pay attention to the corresponding lateral line. The onrushing forward movement is stopped in order to look backward and sideways, generating a retrospective lateral movement, dwelling within an enclosed space, and forming a circle. This form, or rather this form of reading, may serve as the most perfect illustration for depicting "spatiality" and "circularity" in poetry.

Earlier I claimed that the new form defines the time of an extended present as the lyrical moment. But the form in fact dictates the moment in two stages, or two separate moments in the lyrical act. If the first stage of extroversion is the moment of spontaneous impressions, the second introverted stage comes with the last couplet, to create a moment of reflective introspection. The separation of these two moments is a vital part of the design. Through this separation, the self can step away from momentary forgetfulness and return to the normal flux of realistic time. Of course, the appearance of objectivity is also replaced by the reappearance of the subjective self, no longer in the background; the poetic "I" will now be able to reflect upon his earlier internalized world and try to relate this reflection to the real "I." The subject of this introversion is the content of that lyrical moment, and the context that of the larger referential world, to which the poet must eventually return. To conclude his poem, Lo faces the future and his friend, stating:

> After parting can [you] remember? 別後能相憶
> At Tung-ling, there is the former marquis. 東陵有故侯

The modal construction (interrogative, probability, future) and the reference to himself and his friend bring the poet back to reality. The continuous couplet and its indefinite reference to the future and to the probable also returns the reading to a linear progression. What these poets achieved remains an open question. But if one can characterize the artistry of the poets of the Six Dynasties by its sophisticated depiction of sensory pleasure and sentimentality, one must probably also concede that the aspirations of the Early T'ang "Four Talents" lie far beyond this limited vision. Within the convention of "regulated verse," these poets attempted and succeeded in attaining an artistic vision to fill perception with meaning and form and to unite this meaning and form with personal expression. Therefore, the adoption of this form by later generations of poets such as Ch'en Tzu-ang 陳子昂 (661–702), Chang Chiu-ling 張九齡 (673–740), even Li Po, marked the ease with which it fulfilled their purposes.

The Life Vision of "Landscape Poets" of the High T'ang

The aesthetics discussed in the last section continued to serve as the central poetics of "regulated verse" throughout the history of the form, though it went through many revisions and variations. All later versions of the aesthetics, including some discussed in this essay, built upon the theory and practice of this version of the Early T'ang. Its interpretation of "intent" remained basically faithful to that of the Six Dynasties, that is, as personal "thought and feeling" at a certain moment, though a more exalted one, to be sure. The High T'ang, the first half of the eighth century, was a time of prosperity, not only in political and economic development, but also in literary refinement, with poetry as its most glorious achievement. With confidence and exuberance, the poets of the High T'ang seized "regulated verse" as an ideal form; they also began to see the potentiality for its further expansion. One of these directions was a new interpretation of "intent," which they took from its more original meaning of "purpose" and "vision" in life, a sense which Confucius and many others would surely have approved. Together with this recovery of its higher meaning, the dilemmas of "expression" and "language" reappeared. If the problem of "inadequacy of ordinary language" could be solved by the use of artistic language, this artistic language must have broader applications, including its possible use as a means to understand and even realize the elusive significance of life. In their search for a new vision in their poetry, the rediscovery of T'ao Ch'ien 陶潛 (365–427)

drew this new generation of poets back to the simple life and to nature.

T'ao Ch'ien, born two decades before Hsieh Ling-yün, was neglected both during his lifetime and afterward. His near-contemporary, Hsieh Ling-yün, entirey eclipsed T'ao and was hailed as the paragon of "landscape poetry."[46] However, T'ao was well-known as a distinguished hermit and was recognized as the predecessor of "hermit poets." Much of his work can be classed as "farmland poetry" (*t'ien-yüan shih* 田園詩), which was only occasionally appreciated by his immediate successors. During the Early T'ang period, Wang Chi 王績 imitated his casual style and farmland theme.[47] But it was not until Wang Wei 王維 (701–761) of the High T'ang that T'ao Ch'ien enjoyed his due recognition, which has never since declined.

From the time of the pre-Ch'in philosophers, two central concerns of Chinese thought were the distrust of language and knowledge and the exaltation of intuition, associated with a free mind and the simple life. Lao Tzu and Chuang Tzu were considered the early advocates of intuitive living, and even Confucius admired Tseng Tien's ambition to fully realize his values through the experience of living, as our earlier example on "stating life's purpose" has revealed. These concerns reveal a central dilemma in the history of Chinese thought, for which many philosophers offered solutions. Simply stated, the dilemma lies in the conflict between the need "to know the meaning of life" and the need "to abandon knowing in order to live." Every man has the need to understand himself and also the need for others to understand him. Through this understanding, in its private and public aspects, one may reach the understanding of the meaning of one's life. However, the process of knowing occurs primarily through analytic understanding, with techniques of reference, inference, reduction, and conceptualization. These techniques only destroy intuitive experience and block the attainment of true understanding. In other words, understanding the meaning of life depends upon knowing oneself,

[46] See Ting Fu-pao, "Ch'üan Chin shih," vol. 1, pp. 603–640, and James R. Hightower, *The Poetry of T'ao Ch'ien* (Oxford: Oxford University Press, 1970).

[47] Stephen Owen, *The Poetry of the Early T'ang*, pp. 60–82.

but that knowing may kill precisely the essence of living which is the purpose of knowing. "Inadequacy of language" in poetic theory is just one of a host of problems derived from this dilemma, which also encourages one to "forget language" (*wang-yen* 忘言) and to "uproot knowledge" (*ch'ü-chih* 去智), or in the positive direction to "follow one's nature" (*shuai-hsing* 率性) and "return to simplicity" (*fan-p'u* 返樸). Ever since antiquity, many attempts were made to find an "intuitive understanding" which could be integrated with the "intuitive life." In the Six Dynasties, the Neo-Taoists certainly made some contributions to this form of "intuitive knowledge." During the T'ang dynasty, the new wave of Buddhists, particularly those of the Ch'an School, again revived this issue, though theirs was one of practice, not discussion.[48] As did Confucius, Taoists and Buddhists saw the possibility of "living meaning" in "realizing the meaning of life not in words, but in living in accordance with a meaningful form." This suggests that in life a certain form of living contains the meaning itself; if this form can be spontaneously recaptured again and again, one may indeed reach an intuitive understanding. This seems to promise that if the form of artistic experience itself promises the meaningful structure for self-realization, intuitive understanding may be found in its purest and simplest form.[49]

For the poet T'ao Ch'ien, life embodies meaning; he experiences life. This embodiment may be manifest in artistic creation not limited to understanding on the level of self-reflection, but reaching the level of communication. But the poetic experience must reflect life in a state of contentment, in its simplicity and sincerity. If the simple acts of "plucking chrysanthemums," "seeing mountains at a distance," and spontaneous impressions of "fresh mountain air"

[48] Recognition of the opposition between intuitive knowledge and analytical knowledge is prevalent in many cultures and thus lacks the mysterious qualities some would ascribe to it. To anyone interested in this opposition in the philosophy of the West, I recommend Hao Wang's "The Formal and the Intuitive in the Biological Sciences: Use and Misuse," forthcoming.

[49] One important view of this debate can be found in Yüan Hsing-p'ei 袁行霈, "Wei Chin hsüan-hsüeh chung te yen-i chih pien yü Chung-kuo ku-tai wen-i li-lun" 魏晉玄學中的言意之辨與中國古代文藝理論, collected in *Ku-tai wen-hsüeh li-lun yen-chiu ts'ung-k'an* 古代文學理論研究叢刊 (Shanghai: Ku-chi ch'u-pan-she, 1979), vol. 1, pp. 125–147.

and "returning birds in pairs" contain meaning from intuitive understanding, it is perfectly understandable that any articulation will completely destroy it. T'ao's sudden forgetfulness of expression is the only way to assure his possession of this knowledge.[50]

In T'ao's poetry, the narrative structure completely withdraws into the background; description is aimed at the ordinary objects and events in his life, now reemerging in his imagination. The description is seen not through his physical eyes, but through his mind's eye. He does not observe a panoramic view from a particular vantage point, nor does he need to embark on a journey to search for truth or beauty. If there is truth or beauty, it should be in his life and familiar to him through memory or imagination. This perspective shifts with his mental attitude, not with his physical movement. This approach was to have great influence on the perspective of future landscape painters; apparently both are determined by the process of "internalization," whereby parallelism is used to realize the sense of completeness of a total picture of life at any moment, from any angle. The inner couplets of the first poem in his cycle, "Returning to Country Farming Life," follow the parallel pattern fairly closely, as the scenes from his farming life turn over in his mind slowly.[51] On the other hand, the inner couplets in the fifth poem of the "Drinking Wine" group suggest a continuous sequence, but the accidental progression without premeditated plan is important in conveying the casual quality of a tranquil life. The acts come and go as if mental images suddenly appear and disappear. To act without intent is only one aspect of this poetic act; more remarkable is that every act fits perfectly with T'ao's implicit and broad intent of life. Every casual movement reveals new beauty in nature.

The thematic content of T'ao Ch'ien's poetry was only one of the minor aspects of Wang Wei's attraction to T'ao's work. His poems on the farmland theme are few, and those on actual farming fewer still. What attracted him most in T'ao's work were the qualities of naturalness and casualness and the aspiration to a contented and self-contained world. In his couplet:

[50] Ting Fu-pao, "Ch'üan Chin shih," vol. 1, p. 472.

[51] *Ibid.*, p. 462.

Walking to the water's end; 行到水窮處
Sitting, watching the clouds rising. 坐看雲起時

Wang captures an effortless transition from one act to another without intended direction, but each act falls beautifully into its proper place within the total experience, as the world is complete in itself and meaningful in every moment.[52] Casualness in the temporal flow of events and completeness in the spatial extension of one's field of perception can be easily blended with the existing aesthetics of "regulated verse." The juxtaposition of independent couplets suggests an accidental continuity, and the self-containedness of each parallel couplet may be used to depict this moment of a complete world. In his aesthetics, each set of images carries its simple, natural, and symbolic meaning. Though this inner world is only an idealized one generated from an instantaneous and spontaneous experience, it is also a world to which the poet hopes to return or within which he hopes to remain forever. Because this world exists in nature, without artificial effort and artful manipulation, return to it can occur only through the poet's will. The symbolic meanings and vision associated with the natural objects and the whole landscape make the presentation of inner feeling and thought unnecessary, as was also true of T'ao Ch'ien's poetry. On entering this world in the first three couplets, one must be immersed in a state of reverie, with time suspended and self forgotten, and imagination alone assuming the entire burden of the poetic act. This self-realization has nothing to do with analytical knowledge, though the poetic form of this understanding may also have its own symbolic connotations, which are given by the tradition or by the poet, consciously or unconsciously. In this reflection of poetic content, although the ending couplet leads the poet away from his temporary moment of self-contentment, the world of reverie in this new aesthetics remains the focus of the poem. The poet will look backward fondly and try to fix his mind on the ideal; forgetful of all that is temporal, he remains hopeful for the eventual return. There lurk no surprises or disappointments. The poet is

[52] Pauline Yu, *The Poetry of Wang Wei*, pp. 157, 171, 224, and Stephen Owen, *The Great Age of Chinese Poetry*, pp. 34–35. See also Pauline Yu's discussion on Wang Wei's philosophical background and poetic theory, pp. 1–42.

confident of his control of the situation; he knows nature will stand fast, the season will return.

Long ago the late Professor Hsü Fu-kuan perceptively observed that Chuang Tzu's philosophy has profoundly influenced the poetic tradition in China, particularly its interpretation of enlightenment in terms of artistic experience.[53] The aesthetic values of T'ao Ch'ien and Wang Wei, along with those of Meng Hao-jan, are perhaps the most outstanding examples. Since poetic creation is mediated by sensation and perception, no poet can truly reach the state of "void" or "nothingness." But he can imagine the state, as an experience; this is exactly what Wang Wei, in a moment of inspiration, achieves. In his couplet:

River flows—beyond heaven, earth;	江流天地外
Mountains' color—between being, non-being.	山色有無中

Wang Wei skillfully used "abstract nouns" to create "a sense of elusive otherworldiness," and indeed he "opposed the danger of falseness of feeling by its true negation."[54] As a technique of objective presentation, Wang Wei thoroughly mastered the "negation of feeling"; in its most extreme form, the feeling of complete self-negation approximates the feeling of nothingness. In this tableau, the poet is not the only one to recede into background; even the river and mountains are on the very margins of the perceptual field. This world is empty for sure, but the world beyond or the "otherworld," though elusive, can still be imagined. With proper understanding of its many Buddhist associations, one can grasp the layers of symbolic structure in this simple couplet, where the picture is about to dissolve, the river flows with its temporal movement rapidly disappearing into the other world, and the surface color of the seemingly stationary mountains extends in spatial dimensions finally into infinity and void. In Chinese, "being" and "non-being," the proper translation of the more

[53] Hsü Fu-kuan 徐復觀, *Chung-kuo i-shu ching-shen* 中國藝術精神 (Taichung: Tunghai University, 1966), particularly the article "Chung-kuo i-shu ching-shen chu-t'i chih ch'eng hsien" 中國藝術精神主體之呈現, pp. 45–143.

[54] Pauline Yu, *The Poetry of Wang Wei*, pp. 156–157, 170–171, 224, and Stephen Owen, *The Great Age of Chinese Poetry*, p. 41.

idiomatic verbs, "have" and "have not," are both abstract and extremely concrete, not as nouns, but simply as verbs of possession and existence. It is through the perceptible and imaginable that the imperceptible and unimaginable can be intuitively understood. Therefore, this couplet probably says far more than the direct use of the abstract term, "to have no life" (*wu-sheng* 無生) in some of Wang Wei's concluding couplets.[55]

In conclusion, I should first point out that Wang Wei wrote the greater part of his poetry in the more traditional aesthetics, and many of his "regulated verses" simply do not fall into this type. Second, as in all artistic creation, the perfection of the vision depends upon successful execution and, consequently, the failure of vision in some of his works are simply the failure of the artist. Third, many of his works on this particular life vision involve the mixture of different modes and styles and should be considered hybrid cases. Finally, this life vision descends directly from T'ao's poetry, which was written in what a T'ang poet would have called the "ancient style." In many ways, a life vision transcends the limitations of any specific genre. If Wang Wei's aesthetics lie in the incorporation of "farmland poetry" into the orthodox aesthetics of the "regulated verse" of the Early T'ang, then it is equally valid to identify variations and mutations by different poets and genres. Wang Wei's use of a "farmland" poetry technique in "ancient-style poetry" and Wei Ying-wu's 韋應物 (ca. 736–791) adaptation of the same are two outstanding examples.

In this connection, a few words of explanation on the development of later poetics are necessary. Not bound by Wang Wei's aesthetics of an idealized world, many critics consider the essence of this style, "naturalness" (*tzu-jan* 自然), to be the highest artistic ideal in Chinese poetry.[56] From this central value, a group of terms developed, ranging from "limpid-unaccented" (*ch'ung-tan* 沖淡), to "refined-elegant" (*tien-ya* 典雅), "lofty-unconventional" (*ch'ing-ch'i* 清奇), and "rustic-primitive" (*chih-p'u* 質樸). Given the

[55] For example, see *T'ang wu-shih-chia shih-chi*, pp. 1,643 and 1,647.

[56] The most famous statement on *tzu-jan* 自然 is probably Ssu-k'ung T'u's 司空圖 poem in his *Shih-p'in* 詩品 which can be found in *Chung-kuo li-tai wen-lun hsüan*, vol. 2, p. 205; see also his "Letter to Mr. Li" on pp. 196–197 of this anthology. See also Wang Shih-chen's comment in *ibid.*, vol. 1, pp. 72 and 91.

poet's distrust of language, the concept of "meanings beyond the words" (*i tsai yen wai* 意在言外) also gradually evolved into a central ideal in Chinese poetry. This seminal idea certainly admirably suits the compactness of "regulated verse" and the aesthetics of "farmland poetry," but it belongs more to the aesthetics of the whole poetic tradition than to this particular version of aesthetics.

Tu Fu's Cosmic Vision at the End of the High T'ang

Tu Fu is the acknowledged master of "regulated verse," but, like T'ao Ch'ien, he was not fully appreciated during his lifetime; recognition came to him gradually in later ages. His contribution to "regulated verse" lies in his works in the "seven-character line" form written during his last few years, particularly the three poem cycles of 766, four years before his death. But this part of his heritage was to be neglected for at least another century, until its rediscovery by such late T'ang poets as Li Shang-yin 李商隱 (813–858) and Han Wo 韓渥 (844–923).

Tu Fu, an admirer of many of the sixth-century masters, began his career with "regulated verse" in the style of the late Six Dynasties with a thorough mastery of the aesthetics of the Early T'ang.[57] However, after years of wandering as a young poet, as a struggling petty official he could never abide comfortably with the life-vision espoused by some of the High T'ang poets. Among his early works in "regulated verse," mostly in "five-character line," the few poems on animals, such as "Horse from Hu" and "Falcon in a Painting," are works foreshadowing his later experiments with the use of allusion, textual and topical, to introduce deeper symbolic meanings and complex cultural associations to individual lines in a poem.[58] Therefore, the eagle depicted in his poem is no longer a specific eagle, but a generalized specimen, the essence of all eagles, with historical and textual images enriching the simple formal presentation. Huang T'ing-chien 黃庭堅 (1045–1105) of the

[57] Tu Fu's admiration for these masters can be found in the famous lines, "Pure and refreshing like Yü Hsin/Elegant and free like Pao Chao" 清新庾開府/俊逸鮑參軍 as highest praise to offer to Li Po. See Ch'iu Chao-an 仇兆鰲, *Tu shih hsiang-chu* 杜詩詳注, 5 vols. (rpt. Peking: Chung-hua shu-chü, 1979), vol. 1, pp. 52–54.

[58] *Ibid.*, vol. 2, pp. 11–12.

Northern Sung claimed that "every word from Tu Fu's poetry has its precedent in earlier texts." Clearly this exaggeration was meant to serve his personal purpose, but the gist of this statement confirms our general impression of Tu Fu's poetry: his erudition and passionate love of the classics, which eventually played an important part in his later experimentations.[59] He had creatively and imaginatively exploited this erudition in his search for some deeper essence or divine quality in understanding the world.

However, Tu Fu's foremost concern was not the art of poetry, but the political and cultural destiny of his country, the T'ang empire. In his early poetry, this concern surfaced in the form of social-political poems. The collapse of the T'ang court in 755 and the subsequent decline of the central government changed Tu Fu's life dramatically. After a period of flight as a refugee, he finally settled in Ch'eng-tu in 760. This relatively peaceful period from 760 to 766 was crucial to his later development. While the tranquility of his own garden-house outside the city afforded him the opportunity to live the life of T'ao Ch'ien or Wang Wei, he remained constantly concerned with the political and military developments of the court. Thus his poetry during this period was marked, not with the satisfaction of an ideal life, but only with a few moments of happy oblivion to the world's larger problems. It further prepared him to explore various possibilities in the form of "regulated verse," leading to the crowning achievement of his last period.

The year 766 is significant in the history of Chinese poetry for several reasons: leaving Ch'eng-tu, Tu Fu wrote several experimental poems, including his three monumental poem cycles. It was also the first year of the Ta-li 大曆 (766–779) period, which marks the transition from the High to the Middle T'ang. Ironically, Tu Fu's work from this period did not really affect the poetic circles of the Middle T'ang. During these few years, his traditional "five-character line" form of *lü-shih* underwent some change, his interests focusing on autobiographical reflection and frequent looks back-

[59] In his letter to Hung Chü-fu 洪駒父, Huang says, "It is most difficult to create one's own diction; when Tu Fu composed poems and Han Yü wrote prose, not one of their words lacked a history of its own." See *Chung-kuo li-tai wen-lun hsüan*, vol. 2, p. 316.

ward and homeward from his self-imposed exile and wandering.[60] Even in his poems on objects, the subjects were no longer the stallion and falcon, but the sickly old horse, the lone wild goose, or the fluttering sand gull. This type of metaphor served as a mirror to reflect his faded ambition and unflagging, but unappreciated, loyalty. He surely sensed that the time of reckoning was approaching; his heroic vision of himself had faded completely, abandoning even the simple hope that he might leave behind him a reputation in poetry. It was at this time he wrote:

In literature my name will not be known; 名豈文章著
Sickness, old age demand resignation of post, 官應老病休

the perfect balanced picture which summarized his life.[61] But his greatest achievements in poetry were yet to be written.

His most impressive achievement in poetry, in my opinion, lies in deepening and broadening the limited vision of "regulated verse" in the "seven-character line" form (*ch'i-lü* 七律). Yeh Chia-ying has proved conclusively that the maturity of the seven-character line regulated verse was achieved only after Tu Fu's extensive experiments during the sixties of the eighth century.[62] His experimentation took many directions. One was his attempt to formulate new phonic patterns, diction, and structure to accommodate a vision freer than what had been offered previously. But what I shall focus on here is the cosmic vision in his new works in the "seven-character line." The tragedy of Tu Fu is that after he left government service in 759, his mind never left the court far behind. As a passive observer of the dynasty's decline, he was genuinely involved in the whole political drama played out on the stage of Ch'ang-an; his vision was too much a cultural and historical one

[60] See Liu K'ai-yang 劉開揚, "Tu Fu wu-lü li-chieh" 杜甫五律例解 from his collected essays on T'ang poetry, *T'ang-shih lun-wen-chi* 唐詩論文集 (Shanghai: Ku-chi ch'u-pan-she, 1979), pp. 159–176.

[61] Stephen Owen, *The Great Age of Chinese Poetry*, p. 224.

[62] Yeh Chia-ying 葉嘉瑩, *Tu Fu ch'iu-hsing pa-shou chi-shuo* 杜甫秋興八首集說 (Taipei: Chung-hua ts'ung-shu pien-shen wei-yüan-hui, 1966), pp. 7–23. See also her discussion on the different stages of development of Tu Fu's *ch'i-lü* 七律 on pp. 23–52. The same point is also made by Ma Mao-yüan in his *Wan-chao-lou wen-chi* 晚照樓文集 (Shanghai: Ku-chi ch'u-pan-she, 1981), pp. 138–153. Ma also discusses the general contribution of Tu Fu to the *ch'i-lü* tradition.

to be accommodated by the limited form of "regulated verse." If momentary enlightenment and the self-contained world are some of the central features in this form, these were exactly what Tu Fu wanted to escape. The last four years of his life, from 766 until 770, were spent in a life again on the road, which led him farther and farther away from his dream, the return to Ch'ang-an.[63] To embrace this personal tragedy which was inextricably interwoven with the dynastic destiny, he had to expand the potential of the traditional form, "seven-character line regulated verse."

For illustration, I choose here a poem written at the beginning of his experimental period, in the last two years of his residence in Ch'eng-tu. Compared with his later poems, particularly his three cycles of 766, it demonstrates most of the features of his new aesthetics, while at the same time being more straightforward. The poem, entitled "Ascending the Tower," was composed upon his return to his Ch'eng-tu home after fleeing the outburst of local war in the area.[64] In the autumn of 763, Tibetan armies captured the capital, Ch'ang-an, for fifteen days. During their occupation, they established a temporary government with its own puppet emperor. Shortly afterward, the emperor in exile returned; the Tibetans withdrew from the capital area and invaded the western border districts, including Hsi-shan 西山 (West Mountains) county. In the spring of 764, Tu Fu came home and ascended a tower to enjoy the spring view:

Blossoms approaching high tower—
  grieves traveler's heart;
Ten-thousand places, troubles abound—
  this [occasion of] ascending.
Brocade River spring colors—
  appearing Heaven, Earth;
Jade Fort [Mountain] floating clouds—
  transforming the Past, the Present.

花近高樓傷客心
萬方多難此登臨
錦江春色來天地
玉壘浮雲變古今

[63] For Tu Fu's works in this last period, see Liu K'ai-yang, "Tu Fu tsai Ssu-ch'uan te shih-ko ch'uang-tso huo-tung" 杜甫在四川的詩歌創作活動 and "Tu Fu liang-Hu wan-ch'i shih-tso shu-p'ing" 杜甫兩湖晚期詩作述評, *T'ang-shih lun-wen-chi*, p. 316.

[64] Ch'iu Chao-ao, *Tu-shih hsiang-chu*, vol. 3, pp. 1,130–1,132.

North Star, imperial court—
  after all did not change;
Western Mountains, bandits-enemies—
  do not invade us.
Pity, Last Ruler [of Shu] still keeps his
  temple;
Sunset time I as pastime undertake to
  sing Song of Liang-fu.

北極朝廷終不改
西山寇盜莫相侵
可憐後主還祠廟
日暮聊爲梁甫吟

The allusion to contemporary events is obvious. Allusion to history is closely linked to the local history of the Shu 蜀 Kingdom from 221–263, located in the territory of today's Szechwan, with its capital at Ch'eng-tu. It was there that Tu Fu wrote this poem, exactly five hundred years after the fall of this local kingdom. The Last Ruler (*hou-chu* 後主), the second ruler of this short-lived kingdom, actually ruled more than forty years until his surrender to the invading Wei army. The "Song of Liang-fu" belongs to a genre of dirge, which Chu-ko Liang 諸葛亮 (181–234) was reputed to have been fond of singing. Brocade River is the main river running through this provincial capital; Jade Fort Mountain stands in the vicinity of Ch'eng-tu. Both are local geographical names (contrasting with names of broader scale like "North Star" in the sky), symbolizing the court and "Western Mountains" in the western border area of the province then occupied by the Tibetan armies. The proper names in this poem are relatively few compared to Tu Fu's later poetry, but by the standard of earlier poetry this type of special reference represents an increase not only in quantity, but also in density and intensity. Juxtaposition of simple images was no longer adequate to convey his complex ideas. He purposely chose to structure an imagistic world through private and communal allusions, which introduced dimensions of meanings that a simple image could not. "History," in a broad sense, was the object of his meditation. For Tu Fu there were three aspects of the past that he could not separate. The first aspect of his sense of "history" was a personal one, which was autobiographical and involved reflection on his past and often contemplation of his future. For Tu Fu this aspect of history was entwined with the second: contemporary history or the history of his country, particularly of the turbulent decade beginning with the An Lu-shan Rebellion in 755. The third aspect was an ancient one: the history of the cultural tradition, possibly of the remote past. But it was immediate and relevant for the poet because of his intimate relationship with the past through his education and through his immersion in the texts of the tradition. Chinese poets had always considered both memory and imagination to be the basis of poetic experience. In Tu Fu's mind, all three aspects of history were internalized in a personal memory that was rooted in the humanistic tradition and preserved in voluminous ancient texts. The meanings of contemporary actions, both personal and political, could be understood only through the prism of the remote past. Though the three levels of history were inseparable for him, during the writing of his three cycles his mind still shifted between levels according to the nature of the topic. The eight poems of "Autumn Meditations" were autobiographical accounts of contemporary history; the five poems "On Generals" concerned themselves with contemporary history through focusing on a few powerful generals; and the five poems "On Ancient Ruins" take us directly back to the historical context of the remote past, in which Tu Fu found a mirror to reflect his present fate.[65]

With this understanding of Tu Fu's uses of the past, one can immediately see the three different aspects operating simultaneously in the poem "Ascending the Tower." The first half of the poem is personal experience, but its references to the past are also explicit and direct. Place names like "Brocade River" and "Jade Fort" site the poet geographically, but their respective natural phenomena, "spring colors" and "floating clouds," link them as symbols to define the cosmos and to reveal changes in history. The second half shifts the focus to the immediate history of the court and the borderland; both were related to the Tibetan invasions and to the remote history of the Shu court, which foreshadowed contemporary events. However, if we take the inner couplets together, the

[65] *Ibid.*, "Autumn Meditations," vol. 4, pp. 1,484–1,499; "On Ancient Sites," vol. 4, pp. 1,499–1,503; and "On Generals," vol. 3, pp. 1,363–1,372. The cycle of "Autumn Meditations" was translated by A. C. Graham in his *Poems of the Late T'ang* (Baltimore: Penguin Books, 1965), pp. 51–56, and that of "On Ancient Sites" was translated by Hans H. Frankel in his *The Flowering Plum and the Palace Lady*, pp. 115–124.

two levels of reference suddenly take on a new significance. The coming of spring from every direction suggests the momentum of a continuity which may collide with the poet to stir his grief. This continuity underlines again the possible invasion by Tibetans from the Western Mountains, against which the poet tries to issue a warning. On the other hand, the transformation of the clouds and of history is marked by disruption. Similarly, the ephemeral puppet court disrupted historical continuity, but happily the restoration of the legitimate emperor ended the drama on an optimistic note. Both lines in the third couplet are in modal structures; the confident statement on the past leads into the hopeful statement on the future through the use of a continuous parallel couplet. As a result, the two inner couplets are related in three possible combinations: first, each pair of parallel lines; second, each pair of initial lines and that of the closing lines; and third, the third and sixth lines, and the fourth and fifth lines. If High T'ang aesthetics used symbols from nature to convey personal feeling, in Tu Fu's aesthetics the symbols of proper names or other coded words were used to convey a historical context and meanings. Here, the symbols were treated as constituents of a complex symbolic system; each person reading this poem should construct his own system of symbols to approximate that of Tu Fu: the natural, the personal, the historical, the cultural, and so on. Many critics attacked the reliance on allusion and symbol in Tu Fu's later period; yet it would be hard to imagine any other means to capture the depth and intensity of the symbolic world he constructed. This is a coded language to refer to information in memory and imagination; and hence a condensed language, which uses minimum words to convey the maximum amount of information. Since it is coded to specific historical or personal acts, sometimes involving specific texts, it requires the reader's willingness to learn this language, and sometimes to search for the hidden meanings.

The structure of the line in Tu's poem has been described as "indefinite," which can be seen in the uncertain relation in the first two couplets.[66] To organize fragments with indefinite relation requires one to grasp Tu Fu's interpretation of historical forces: continuity and disruption, momentum and resistance, or simply

[66] Stephen Owen, *The Great Age of Chinese Poetry*, p. 213.

"connection" 連 (*lien*) and "cutting" 斷 (*tuan*). We can analyze many of his poems in this context, including the one just discussed. Earlier poets' concept of continuity generally lacks the force and dynamism capable of making the act of connection a forceful and purposeful movement; consequently, the disruption is never violent and irretrievable. When history was introduced into poetic content, the contiguity and separation in space were complemented by the continuity and interruption in time. The past is interrupted, but hopefully the continuity may resume; the capital is separated from the poet, but he tries in his imagination to reunite with it. A new map of different symbolic forces can almost be charted in spatial and temporal terms, but this is not a map of the historical and realistic world, but of the symbolic and formalistic one.

Tu Fu's new aesthetics also demanded revisions in the treatment of the frame or the outer couplets of this new form. For Tu Fu, the writing of poetry was a serious act of devotion. He felt no qualms in revealing the painstaking efforts devoted to his works and preparation for each poetic act. The premeditated opening of the initial couplets is deliberately announced, without pretense of spontaneity, with the scope and subject laid out in public view. As in the beginning couplet mentioned above, the contrast between the immediate intent of "ascending" to view and enjoy the spring view and the ultimate intent of expressing the "grieved heart" of a traveler seeks to define the entire poetic act and content. The immediate perception of luxuriant and bursting blossoms reaching toward the poet on the tower is only a surface temporarily disguising the troubles everywhere in his world. The symbolic relation between these two unrelated phenomena is determined by his sense of history and serves as the basic structure of the whole poem. The external act of ascending finally ends in the internal act of grief; in the middle is placed the symbolic structure of his internalized states of mind. The indefinite and convoluted relations among phrases, usually limited to the middle couplets, now prevails in the opening and closing couplets to offer a new frame to the imagistic center. The most interesting opening is probably the kind of "reverse sequence" (*tao-ch'a* 倒插), which critics claimed to be Tu Fu's trademark, which switches the normal sequence of sentences, as in the beginning of "Ascending the Tower." Possibly Tu Fu was not even conscious of his use of a reversal; when he was ready to write the poem, he was simply seeing the world through his strong emotive eyes. Likewise, the so-called "surprise leap" generally attributed to his ending couplet was merely stating the facts of his "imaginative landscape."[67]

To end a poem was no longer a reflection and reiteration of an idealized state of being; the first three couplets represent no perfect state, nor do they suggest the condition of revery. If the poet was ever mesmerized, it was because of the intensity and complexity of his overpowering vision of the past and present. To redirect the poet's attention to his present personal situation was a painful reminder of his predicament. Tu Fu would frequently offer an objective assessment of the relation between this lyrical self and the cosmos or the larger historical and cultural context. In this particular poem, Tu Fu's admiration of Chu-ko Liang, who was one of the very few literati who truly attained their limited vision in political sphere, was expressed through his singing Chu-ko's favorite dirge. After all, the Last Ruler of Shu, to whose support and protection Chu-ko had devoted his life, still had his own temple in Ch'eng-tu, a reminder of the survival of the regime. The couplet points to the precarious state of the new emperor, Tai-tsung 代宗, who in his reign of less than two years had already once been forced to leave Ch'ang-an. Could this new emperor be like the Last Ruler, entrusting his government to some loyal and intelligent statesman like Chu-ko? By this time, Tu Fu had lost his heroic dream of becoming a responsible official, but his identification with Chu-ko had in no way diminished. On the contrary, this identification became all the stronger, centering on the contrastive circumstances between the two, particularly in the trust Chu-ko received from the two rulers he assisted and in the complete ignorance of Tu Fu's value on the part of his contemporaries. Through this contrast, Tu

[67] Wang Shih-chen 王世貞 (1526–1590) is quoted by Hu Chen-heng 胡震亨 as saying, "The inner structure of a couplet can be either 'direct continuation' [*chih-hsia* 直下] or 'reverse sequence.' The latter is extremely difficult, only Tu Fu mastered it." See Hu Chen-heng, *T'ang-yin kui-ch'ien* 唐音癸籤 (rpt. Shanghai: Ku-tien wen-hsüeh ch'u-pan-she, 1981), p. 21. Wang Shih-chen also declares, "in *ch'i-lü*, the inner couplets are not difficult; the hardest are the beginning and the ending couplets."

Fu painted a self-portrait in a historical context. Existence is bleak, the tone poignant; but nevertheless the ending imagery still directs the reader to look on him in a scale larger than life. The poem closes with a temporary resolution which obliterates the tragic voice. It is probably not coincidental that, though the eight poems of "Autumn Meditations" have been severely criticized for their obscurity and artificiality, each of the ending couplets is widely circulated and memorized, perhaps one of the most profound and noblest expressions of Tu Fu's predicament. Deprived of their inner couplets these endings may lose their complexity, but the projection of one's commitment to life and subsequent disappointment in concrete imagery are indeed Tu Fu's strength—one which no one in the whole lyrical tradition of China can rival.

In the past, critics often referred to this historical dimension in Tu Fu's later poetry as the embodiment of cosmos, which I translate as his "cosmic vision." Stephen Owen explains that Tu Fu's use of cosmogeny and creation "suggest not only an analogue to the generative forces of nature, they also point to a unifying poetic identity that transcends its particular manifestations."[68] In this sense, in his later words Tu Fu certainly deserves the title of the poet with "cosmic vision."

From this point on, Li Shang-yin brought the art of allusion and symbolism to another plateau, which directly influenced the development of many Sung schools of poetry. But that topic lies beyond the scope of this study. Rather, in conclusion I would like to discuss briefly a unique term in Chinese poetic criticism, *ching-chieh* 境界, which has been translated as "world," "realism," and so on. This concept was the offspring of the development of "landscape poetry" and "regulated verse," which centered on the issue of the union of *ch'ing* 情 (feeling) and *ching* 景 (scenery), or *ch'ing-ching chiao-jung* 情景交融 (blending of feeling and scenery) and, in my own terms, the integration of "impression" and "expression." In the three versions of aesthetics discussed here, this integration remained central to the problem of form and content, though each version placed the emphasis differently. As the early T'ang poets might be satisfied with the incidental and abrupt coalescence of

[68] Stephen Owen, *The Great Age of Chinese Poetry*, p. 184.

impression and inner state of mind, Wang Wei would like to see the contact symbolizing an idealized existence and an enlightenment. But it was Tu Fu alone who insisted that this integration was the converging point of all natural and historical forces. For these diverse possibilities of *ching-chieh*, I offer to translate the term "inscape," as defined by Jonathan Culler, who suggests it as a "moment of epiphany," "a moment of revelation in which form is grasped and surface becomes profundity."[69]

[69] Jonathan Culler, *The Structuralist Poetics: Structuralism, Linguistics and the Study of Literature* (Ithaca: Cornell University Press, 1975), p. 175.

Contributors

Kang-i Sun Chang is Assistant Professor of Chinese Literature at Yale University. She received her Ph.D. from Princeton University. Her publications include *The Evolution of Chinese* Tz'u *Poetry* (Princeton, 1980), *Six Dynasties Poetry* (Princeton, 1986), and a number of English and Chinese articles on Chinese literature. She is currently working on Ming and Ch'ing poetry.

François Cheng holds two doctorate degrees, the Doctorat de l'Université de Paris VII and the Doctorat d'Etat. He is now Professeur titulaire à l'Institut des Langues et Civilisations Orientales, Université de Paris III. His publications include *Analyse Formelle de l'Oeuvre Poétique d'un Auteur des Tang: Zhang Ruo-xu* (Edition Mouton, 1970), *L'Ecriture Poétique Chinoise* (Edition du Seuil, 1977), and *Vide et Plein, le Langage Pictural Chinois* (Edition du Seuil, 1979). His 1977 book has been translated into English by Donald A. Riggs and Jerome P. Seaton under the title *Chinese Poetic Writing* (Indiana, 1982).

Hans H. Frankel was born in Berlin, Germany, in 1916. He attended the Gymnasium at Göttingen. He graduated from Stanford University in 1937 and continued his studies at the University of California, Berkeley, where he received an M.A. in 1938 and a Ph.D. in 1942. During World War II he worked for U.S. government agencies in San Francisco, New York, and Washington. He was Associate Professor of Western Languages at National Peking University in 1947–1948. Following a period of research and teaching at the University of California, Berkeley, from 1951 to 1959, he was Assistant Professor of Chinese at Stanford University (1959–1961) and then Associate Professor of Chinese Literature at Yale University (1961–1967). Since 1967 he has been Professor of Chinese Literature at Yale. He has taught as Visiting Professor at Hamburg University (1964), Columbia University (1966–1967), Bonn University (1974), and Munich University (1980 and 1981). In 1983 he lectured in English, French, and German at the Tianjin Foreign Languages Institute. His publications include *The Flowering Plum and the Palace Lady* (Yale, 1976) and numerous articles on Chinese poetry. He is presently writing a book on the history and methodology of western-language translations of Chinese poetry.

Yu-kung Kao received his Ph.D. from Harvard University and is currently Professor of Chinese Literature at Princeton University. He is the co-author of several long articles on T'ang poetry. His other publications include articles, in both Chinese and English, on Chinese aesthetics, literary criticism, fiction, and poetic language.

Paul W. Kroll is Associate Professor of Chinese and chairman of the Department of Oriental Languages and Literatures at the University of Colorado, Boulder. He has written widely on medieval (especially T'ang) poetry, cultural history, and Taoist literature. He is currently working on a book that will deal with divine poetry, verse revelations, and songs of transcendence in medieval China.

Shuen-fu Lin received his Ph.D. from Princeton University and is presently Professor of Chinese Language and Literature at The University of Michigan. He is the author of *The Transformation of the Chinese Lyrical Tradition: Chiang K'uei and Southern Sung* Tz'u *Poetry* (Princeton, 1978) and several articles on Chinese aesthetics, fiction, and poetry. He is currently working on a book on early Taoist philosophical literature.

Lin Wen-yüeh is Professor of Chinese Literature at National Taiwan University. She has written several books and numerous articles in Chinese on medieval Chinese literature, including *The Poetry of T'ao Yüan-ming* and *The Poetry of Hsieh Ling-yün*. She has also published a complete Chinese translation of the Japanese monument of fiction, the *Tale of Genji*.

James J. Y. Liu (1926–1986) was Professor of Chinese Literature and Comparative Literature at Stanford University until his recent death. He received his education at Fu Jen University and Tsing Hua University in Peking, China, and at University of Bristol and Oxford University in England. In addition to teaching at Stanford, Liu had taught at the University of London, Hong Kong University, New Asia College in Hong Kong, the University of Hawaii, the University of Pittsburgh, and the University of Chicago. One of the most productive and internationally well-known scholars in the field, James Liu has bequeathed to us innumerable articles and a number of important books on Chinese literature, including *The Art of Chinese Poetry* (Chicago, 1962), *The Poetry of Li Shang-yin* (Chicago, 1969), *Major Lyricists of the Northern Sung* (Princeton, 1974), *Chinese Theories of Literature* (Chicago, 1975), and *The Interlingual Critic* (Indiana, 1982).

Stephen Owen received his Ph.D. from Yale University and is presently Professor of Chinese and Comparative Literature at Harvard University. He is the author of various books on Chinese poetry, the most recent being *Traditional Chinese Poetry and Poetics: Omen of the World* (Wisconsin, 1985) and *Remembrances: The Experience of the Past in Classical Chinese Literature* (Harvard, 1986).

Tu Wei-ming is Professor of Chinese History and Philosophy and chairman of the Committee on the Study of Religion at Harvard University. He received his Ph.D. from Harvard University and taught at Princeton University and the University of California, Berkeley, before he joined the Harvard faculty. His publications include *Neo-Confucian Thought in Action: Wang Yang-ming's Youth* (Berkeley, 1976), *Humanity and Self-Cultivation: Essays in Confucian Thought* (Berkeley, 1978), and *Confucian Thought: Selfhood as Creative Transformation* (SUNY, 1985).

Ching-hsien Wang majored in English at Tunghai University, Taiwan, and attended the Writers' Workshop at the University of Iowa after he came to the United States in 1964. He obtained his Ph.D. in Comparative Literature from the University of California, Berkeley, in 1971. He has taught at the University of Massachusetts, National Taiwan University, and Princeton University. He is presently Professor of Chinese and Comparative Literature at the University of Washington in Seattle. Since 1960 he has published more than thirty books, including critical and creative writings.

Zhou Zhenfu is currently a Senior Editor at the Chung-hua Publishing House in Peking, China. Trained in traditional Chinese scholarship, he is a well-known scholar specializing in classical poetry and literary criticism. His books (published in Chinese) on Chinese poetry, prose, and poetics include *Discourses on* Shih *Poetry and* Tz'u *Poetry* (*Shih-tz'u li-hua*) and an annotated edition of the *Wen-hsin tiao-lung*, a canonical text in Chinese literary criticism.

Index

A New Account of Tales of the World, 14, 23, 150–151
actuality, 24
aesthetics, 16; of concentration and subtlety, 311, 317, 319; of farmland poetry, 375; High T'ang, 381; insight, 25; lyrical, 338–345, 346; of regulated verse, 332–385; of simplicity, 320–321; Six Dynasties, 345–351; Southern Dynasties, 348
aging, 268, 280
"Ai Ying" ("Lament for Ying"), 270
alchemy, 347
allegorical narrative, 236
allegory, 219
allusion, 279–280, 381, 384; to contemporary events, 379; to history, 379; and symbol in late Tu Fu, 381
An Lu-shan Rebellion, 47, 240, 290, 329, 380
analogical thinking, 19
An-ch'i, 211
animals, 270, 280
art connoisseurship, 17, 18
asceticism, 27
autobiographer, 74; poet, 79f., 91, 93, 101; poetic, 75, 78; sage, 90
autobiographical account, 380
autobiography: Augustinean tradition of confessional, 72, 73; non-narrative, 73; poetry as, 71–102; western narrative, 73

balance and dynamism, 353
ballads, 24; of the Han (*yüeh-fu*), 335, 336
barbarians, 258, 261, 265, 284
Battle of Ch'i-pi, 140–141
beautiful women, 284
Becoming, process of, 34, 35
being, 3, 4, 11, 16, 373; theories of, 6; unity of, 88
Belpaire, Bruno, 67, 68
Bildung, 73, 74; Confucian, 73
binary structure, 367
biographer, 74
biography, 72
bird, 275, 277, 284
Boodberg, Peter A., "Cedules," 330–331
Book of Changes, 12, 14, 26, 56. See also *I ching*
Book of Lord Shang, 269
Book of Songs, 128, 133 (also *Book of Poetry*, 133); "Great Preface" to, 106. See also *Shih ching*
border poem, Early T'ang, 323
boundaries: metrical, 337; phonetic, 357; prosodic, 337; semantic, 357; word, 356
brevity of life, 268; and the desire to prolong it, 284
Brooks, Cleanth, 64
Buddhism, 21n46; Buddhist and Taoist philosophy, 235; Buddhists of Ch'an School, 370; Indian, 352; quietude, 325

caesura, 335, 336, 354
centeredness, 19, 21, 22
Chan, Wing-tsit, 3, 4, 6, 8, 9, 10, 11, 17, 31n69
Ch'an-ching ("Ch'an-like vision or awareness"), 325
Chang Chiu-ling, 45, 368

Chang Chü-chün, 197
Chang Chung, 197
Chang Heng, 181n44
Chang Hsieh, 107, 108, 111–114, 118, 120, 121, 148
Chang Hua, 114, 146, 171; "On the Third Day of the Third Month," 348
Chang Jo-hsü: "Ch'un-chiang hua-yüeh yeh" ("Night, Flower, and Moon on the River in Spring"), 41; ("Spring River in the Flower Moon Night"), 226–229, 241; ("Spring River Blossom Moon Night"), 289–290
Chang Lu, 270, 273
Chang Shou-chieh, 198
Chang Tsai, 146
Chang Tzu-jung, 227
Chang Yüeh, 183, 184
Ch'ang-an, 246ff., 377f., 383
ch'ang-chia, 285. *See also* professional singers and musicians
"Ch'ang-ko hsing" ("Song in Long Meter"), 280
Chao-ming wen-hsüan, 146. See also *Wen hsüan*
chao-yin-shih ("poetry summoning the recluse from or into reclusion"), 145ff.
Chavannes, Eduard, 167
chen jen ("Realized Persons"), 190, 192, 195, 214
Chen kao, 197, 214
Ch'en Lin, 139, 142; "Two Poems on Sightseeing," 142
Ch'en Tzu-ang, 130, 131, 162, 163, 165, 368; "Hsiu-chu p'ien-hsü," 131n3, 162; "A Song on Climbing the Gate Tower at Yu-chou," 163–164; "Thirty-eight Responses to Experience," 163
Ch'en Yin-k'o, 30, 241
Cheng Ch'iao, 335n3
Cheng-shih: period, 148, 149, 150; style of, 131, 151, 152
Ch'eng, François, 45n13; *Chinese Poetic Writing*, 36, 43, 48
Ch'eng I, 39
Ch'eng-tu, 376f., 383
Chi Yün, 145
ch'i, 56
Ch'i chien, 270
ch'i-yen shih ("heptasyllabic verse"), 224, 230
ch'i-yün ("rhythmic breath"), 38
Chia I, 98, 224
Chiang Yen, 349
Chiao-jan, *Models of Poetry* (*Shih-shih*), 66
Chien-an era, 130f., 135, 147, 148, 152, 156, 158f., 251, 288; poetic circle of, 136–145
Ch'ien Ch'i, 87
Ch'ien Chung-shu, 51, 58, 60–61
chih ("intent"), 74, 339–340
Ch'ih Sung Tzu ("Red Pine"), 191
chin i ("liquor of gold"), 212
chin-t'i shih ("modern-style poetry"), 221, 223, 229, 231, 236, 296, 298, 315, 316, 317, 329, 360
"Ch'in Nü-hsiu hsing," 285
Ch'in Shih Huang, 169, 212
Chinese grammar, 37
Ching Shan, 189
ching-chieh ("world," "realism," or "vision"), 384–385
ch'ing ("emotion" or "subjective disposition"), 74
Ch'ing t'ung ("Azure Lad"), 205ff., 214. *See also* Tung Wang Fu
ch'ing-ching ("landscape of feelings"), 45
Chu Hsi, 39, 217, 218
Chu Seng-lang, 198
Chu-ko Liang, 379, 383
Chu-ko Ying, 227
chü-yen ("the eye of the line"), 124–125
Ch'u Kuang-hsi, 153
Ch'u tz'u, 146, 219, 221, 222, 235, 251, 284, 288, 335; *Chiu chang*, 270; *Chiu*

ko, 219, 220; "Lament for Ying," 247
Ch'ü Yüan, 29, 78n12, 98, 219, 220, 291
Chuang Chiang, 291
Chuang Tzu, 4, 12, 13, 52–55, 61, 62, 65, 369, 373; Chuang, 152f., 157; Chuang Chou, 50; *Chuang Tzu*, 3, 12, 14, 26, 49, 51–52, 62, 69, 98
chüeh-chü ("broken-off lines"), 221, 231, 360, 365; ancient, 303; nature of, 296–331; origin of, 299–302; regulated, 320; "ultimate verse," 231f. *See also* quatrain
Chung Hsing, 138
Chung Hui, 18
Chung Hung, 17, 18, 107, 111, 113, 123, 131, 135, 145, 148, 151, 152; *Shih-p'in*, 107, 131, 136, 150, 153
ch'ung-ch'i ("mediating Breath" or "mediating Emptiness"), 34
circularity, 367
Classic of the Supreme Profundity (*T'ai-hsüan ching*), 6
climbing high, 259, 284
closural device, 305
closure, 353, 363; open, 314, 320, 322–323
cloud of unknowing, 9
cognition, discriminative, 13
commander of a military campaign, 269, 273, 284
Confucius, 12, 13, 53, 55, 56, 63, 76, 88, 92, 144, 166, 183, 203, 348, 368, 369; *Analects* (*Lun yü*), 183, 348; humanism, 239
coordination, 338, 359
cosmic vision, 384; of Tu Fu, 375
cosmological constructing, 31; Han thinking, 10, 25; images, 14
cosmology, 6, 24, 33, 44; Chinese, 33ff.
cosmos, creative process of, 35; embodiment of, 384
couplet, 304, 337, 338, 355; closing, 382; continuous parallel, 360; initial, 382; inner, 384; as metrical unit, 335; middle, 382; parallel, 312, 315, 322, 325, 328, 357; regulated parallel, 356; stanzaic, 337
court-style poetry, 345, 350, 360, 363. See also *kung-t'i-shih*
Cowherd, 344
Cowley, Abraham, 74
creativity, 10
Culler, Jonathan, 385

Dante, *Divina Commedia*, 236
de Saussure, Ferdinand, 50
dead words (*ssu-tzu*), 37, 38
death, 259, 270, 280, 284, 346
deer, white, 190, 203, 204
Demiéville, Paul, 168
description: descriptive language, 12; of landscape, 105–129; mode, 107, 110, 111, 340, 341, 345, 346, 363; poetry, 343, 344, 351; realism, 109, 111, 119, 124, 125, 129, 158; similitude, 105, 108, 127 (*see also* verisimilitude); word painting, 26
Dictung, 239
distrust of language, 369, 375
doubleness of self, 75ff., 86
dream experience, 234, 236
Duke of Chou (Chou Kung), 141, 166
dynamic continuity, 305, 307, 310, 312ff., 321, 326, 329, 331; words (*tung-tzu*), 37, 38
dynamism, 19, 22, 320

elegies for the dead, 310
embody nothingness (*t'i-wu*), 11ff; the thing (*t'i-wu*), 31
empathetic appreciation, 19
Empress Wu of the T'ang, 198
Emptiness, and Fullness, 33–37, 39, 43; degree of, 39; mediating, 41, 43; true, 39
empty words (*hsü-tzu*), 37–42. *See also* function words
enfeoffment of mountains, 184–185n53

enjambement, 257, 259, 279
enlightenment, 373, 378, 385
epistemic era, 5, 16, 23
epistemological: enterprise, 8; level, 24; system, 24
epistemology, 235
equality of potential, 14; principle of, 9
equivalence, 357; and opposition, 353; principle of, 356
eremitism, 147
Essay on the Four Fundamentals (*Ssu-pen lun*), 18
ethics, 16
Euripides, 241
exotic places and people, 258, 268, 270, 284
expansive spirit of man, 324, 325
experience: artistic, 348, 373; intuitive, 369; poetic, 370, 380; sensory, 350
experiential encounter, 20, 21, 27, 29; understanding, 21
exposition, 365
expression, 365; expressive mode, 343ff., 363; theory of poetry, 339
external phenomenon, 343
extrametrical head phrases, 257
extroversion, 365, 367
eye word (*tzu-yen*), 38

faithful woman rejected by husband or lover, 282, 284
Fan K'uang, 231
Fan Wen, 165
Fan Ying-yüan, 34–35n3
Fan Yün, 264
Fang, Achilles, 110n12, 115n23
Fang, Thomé H., 29
fang-shih, 168
farmer, 76–79; recluse, 86, 87
feast, 280, 284
feeling of nothingness, 373
feng, concept of, 343
feng and *shan* rites, 170, 171, 173, 174, 183, 184
Feng Hao, 245, 294
Feng-kao, 186f.
feng-ku ("wind and bone"), 130–166
feng-li ("wind and strength"), 131, 132, 145
fictional characters and situations, 282
five-character verse, 26, 129. See also *wu-yen shih*
five elements (*wu-hsing*), 45. *See also* five phases
five phases, 7
folk songs, 24, 299ff., 310, 317
foreigners, 261, 285
form and spirit, 11
form of reading, 367
formalization, 340; of the internal, 364
formula, 268
"Four Talents of the Early T'ang," 289, 362, 363, 368
Frankel, Hans H., 123n34
Frodsham, J. D., 23, 111n15
fu ("rhymeprose"), 24, 109f., 120, 221–222, 341; as genre, 220; in the sense of "display," 218; in the sense of "narration," 218; secondary, 222ff., 229, 235, 251
Fu Hsüan, "Song of Ch'in Nü-hsiu," 250
full words (*shih-tzu*), 37, 38, 42
function words, 39, 341, 356, 358

general leading army, 258, 268
generativity of the Tao, 11
"Ground" star, 213, 215
Graham, A. C., 52
"Great Preface" to Mao edition of *Shih ching*, 106, 217
Greek drama, 86
grief, 280, 284

Hamon, Philippe, 107
Han River, 307
Han shu, 264
Han Wo, 375
Han Wu Ti (Emperor Wu of Han), 169, 170, 174, 188, 203, 256, 257, 295

Han Yü, 165; "Mountain Rock," 230, 236
Han-fei Tzu, 273
Hao-li, 171, 172
hardships: caused by war, 284; of travel, 273, 284
Heaven (*t'ien*), 3, 57; Confucian concept of, 56; Earth, and Man, 33, 36, 45f.; the way of, 7
hermeneutics, 346; hermeneutic procedure, 26
hermit poets, 369
High T'ang vitality, 324–325
Hightower, James R., 30, 62, 154nn66, 67, 68, 155nn69, 70, 369n46
Hirsch, E. D., 297
historian, 71–72
Ho Hsün, 321; "A Farewell," 313–314
Ho Yen, 16, 131, 150; depiction of the Tao, 17
holism, 19, 21, 22
homesickness, 270, 284
Hsi Hsi, "In Reply to Hsi K'ang," 150
Hsi K'ang, 16, 26, 148, 150, 274, 347; "Song of Ch'iu Hu," 149
Hsi Wang Mu ("The Royal Mother in the West"), 189, 191, 203, 206; ("Queen Mother of the West"), 292, 294
Hsiao Kang, 158, 161; Liang Chien-wen-ti, 160–161; "Looking at a Lonely Flying Wild Goose," 318–319
hsiao-lü-shih ("little regulated verse"), 298
Hsiao Shui-shun, 68n64
Hsiao T'ung, 156
Hsi-ch'ü ko ("Songs from the Western Region"), 307, 311
Hsieh An, 151
Hsieh Hsüan, 119
Hsieh Hui-lien, 155
Hsieh Ling-yün, 66, 81, 107f., 111, 118–129, 153, 155, 157, 161, 173f., 177, 179f., 235, 301, 312, 347ff., 357, 364, 369; "I Follow Chin-chu River, Cross the Mountain, and Go Along by the Stream," 121–123; preface to "Eight Poems in Imitation of the Poems of the Wei Crown Prince's Gathering in Yeh," 144
Hsieh Tao-yün, 176–180, 182
Hsieh T'iao, 120, 129, 155, 349, 352; "Grievance of the Jade Stairs," 315
hsieh-ching-shih ("poetry to describe the scenery"), 350
hsien ("transcendent"), 189, 190, 195, 196, 198, 204, 213
hsin ("interiority"), 340
Hsin Yen-nien, 261, 285; "Yü-lin lang" ("Imperial Guard Officer," "Officer of the Guard," or "Palace Guard Officer"), 280, 285–286, 291
hsin yüeh-fu ("new *yüeh-fu*"), 93, 292–293
hsing ("affective image," "incitation," "indirect metaphor," or "initial impression of natural object"), 45f., 162–163, 217, 221, 284, 342, 344, 363
Hsü Chin yang-ch'iu, 150
Hsü Ching-tsung, 362
Hsü Chün, 197
Hsü Fu-kuan, 7n12, 18n41, 29n61, 245, 373
Hsü Hsün, 150, 151
Hsü Ling, 161, 300, 302
Hsü Shao, 18f.
Hsü Shen, 175, 178
hsüan-yen-shih ("discursive poetry," "philosophical poetry," or "poetry of Taoist discourse"), 123, 145, 149ff., 154, 158, 161, 347, 349
Hsün Tzu, 280
hsü-tzu ("empty words" or "function words"), 337, 338
Hsü-tzu-shuo (Interpretations of Empty Words), 39
Hu Shih, 237
Hu Ying-lin, 287, 321, 323; *Shih sou*, 132

Huai-nan Hsiao-shan, "Invitation to a Gentleman in Hiding," 146
Huai-nan Tzu, 34n3; *Huai-nan Tzu*, 270
Huan T'an, 192
Huang Ch'ao, 246
Huang Chieh, 284
Huang K'an, 134
Huang Ti, 170n11, 174, 188, 189
Huang T'ing-chien, 375
Hung-lou-meng (*Dream of the Red Chamber*), 73

I ching, 33, 267, 301; "Discussion of the Trigrams," 35; "Hsi-tz'u" ("Appended Words"), 56. See also *Book of Changes*
ideal situations and persons, 264, 284
idealized existence, 385
ideographic script, 44
image: clusters, 314; beyond images, 47
immanence, 4
immortality, 346
immortals, 284
impersonality, 365
impression, 365f.; integration of and expression, 384; of nature, 350; of the world, 344, 358
inadequacy: of language, 370; of ordinary language, 368
indeterminacy of human nature, 87
inscape, 385
insomnia, 273, 284
intellectual intuition, 13, 21
intent, 350, 368
intentionality, 35
interior life, 344
interiority, 342, 345, 350, 366
internalization, 340, 365, 371; of the external, 364
interpretative code, 333
interrogative form, 304, 305
intrinsic, aesthetic principles, 305; genre, 298–299
introversion, 365, 367

jih ching ("Germ of the sun"), 188
journey, 348
Juan Chi, 29, 117, 148–149, 150, 159, 346; "Poems Expressing My Feelings," 117, 149
Judgments on Poetry. See *Shih-p'in*

Kao, Yu-kung, 36
Kasyapa, 49
knowledge of the Tao, 13
Ko Hung, 168–169, 212
Ku K'ai-chih, 25
Ku Yen-wu, 161
ku-chüeh-chü ("ancient *chüeh-chü*"), 300
ku-i, 225
ku-t'i-shih ("ancient-style poetry"), 223, 229, 232, 252, 296, 329, 360, 374; *ku-shih*, 221f., 226, 229, 232, 251
Kuan chui pien (*Collection of Limited Views*), 51
K'uei-chou, 92, 97
K'un (fish in the *Chuang Tzu*), 98
Kung-an poets, 93
kung-t'i-shih ("court-style poetry"), 146, 156–159, 165, 348, 352
K'ung Jung, 138, 142
Kuo Hsiang, 3ff., 8ff., 27
Kuo Mao-ch'ien, 300
Kuo P'u, 112, 148, 159, 201, 236, 347
Kuo Shao-yü, 69
Kuo T'ai, 15

landscape, 81; imaginative, 383; painters, 371; poetry, 110, 123, 146, 364f., 369, 384 (see also *shan-shui-shih*); poets of the High T'ang, 368–378
language: artistic, 339, 368; inadequacy of, 49ff., 58; ordinary, 32, 44; poetic, 33, 36, 44, 61, 64; poetry as, 32; and politics, 16; temporal progression of, 44; verb-centered, 359
langue, 51
Lao Tzu, 4, 12, 49–58, 152f., 157, 264,

369; *Lao Tzu*, 5, 14, 26, 51. See also *Tao te ching*
Legalism, 140
leviathan, 210
lexical level, 36, 42, 44
lexicography, 37
Li chi, 264, 270
Li Ho, "Loud Song," 293–294
Li I, 321
Li P'an-lung, 223
Li Po, 29, 46, 86, 96, 130f., 162f., 191f., 199ff., 203–215, 251, 264, 291, 317, 321, 360, 368; "Farewell to a Friend," 40; "Fifty-nine Old Style Poems," 164; "Hardships of the Road to Shu," 287–288; Infinite Separation," 287, 290; "Question and Answer in the Mountains," 65; "Setting Out from Po-ti City at Dawn," 232; "Stairs of Jade," 48; "Thinking of the Past in Yüeh," 327–328; "Valediction: A Journey through Mount T'ien-mu in Dream," 234–236
Li sao, 219, 220, 236, 270, 291, 294
Li Shan, 60
Li Shang-yin, 321, 375, 384; "Eastern Fields," 249; "Goddess of Ch'ang-O," 42; "Lady Li," 294–295; "Poem in One Hundred Rhymes Written on a Journey through the Western Fields," 243–247; "Western Fields," 249
Li Yen-nien, "Song," 256–257, 275
Liang-fu, 171, 172
Liang Hung, "Alas Five Times," 259
Liang ku chüeh heng-ch'ui ch'ü (*Liang Dynasty Songs Accompanied by Drums, Horns, and Horizontal Flutes*), 307
Liao Wei-ch'ing, 134, 135
lien-chü ("linked verse"), 299–300
Lin Wen-yüeh, 239–240
linearity, 367; and continuity, 357, 359; of unitary meaning, 40
Ling-hu Ch'u, 244
Ling-pao, 193
Ling-shu tzu-wen (*Purple Text of the Numinous Writ*), 202
literary criticism, 17–18
Liu An, 147
Liu Ch'ang, 311f.
Liu Hsi, 175
Liu Hsieh, 17, 52, 118, 120, 135, 137, 149ff., 162f.; *Wen-hsin tiao-lung* (The Literary Mind and the Carving of Dragons), 109f., 114, 128, 131ff., 143f.; chapters in *Wen-hsin tiao-lung*: "Emotion and Literary Expression," 134; "Exegesis of Poetry," 143; "Intuitive Thinking," 62; "Physical World," 105–106; "Relating My Intention," 63
Liu I-ch'ing, 23
Liu, James, J. Y., 52, 69
Liu Shao, 18
Liu Yü-hsi, 321
liu-hsia ("fluid aurora"), 200, 202
living words (*huo-tzu*), 37, 38
Lo Ken-tse, 299
Lo Pin-wang, 364, 366; "Composition on the Imperial City," 222–226
Lo-fou Shan, 167
looking down from height, 259, 284
Lotz, John, 352
loyalty to emperor, 277
Lo-yang, 224, 247f., 259
Lu Chao-lin, 183, 184; "Hardship of Traveling," 247; "Reminiscence of Old Ch'ang-an," 223–226
Lu Chi, 117, 146, 148, 173, 177; preface to "Wen-fu" or "Rhyme-prose on Literature," 59–61; "T'ai shan yin" (A Chant of Mount T'ai"), 170–171; "Wen-fu," 115
Lü Ch'iu-ch'ung, 146
Lu Lun, "Songs Below the Frontier," 232–233
Lu Shih-yung, 123n36
Lu Ssu-tao, "Song on Picking Lotus Blossoms," 289
lü-shih ("regulated verse"), 42, 161,

lü-shih (cont.)
221, 231, 296, 326; aesthetics of, 332–385; five-character line, 376; four rhyme format in, 361–362; open-ended format, 361–362; *p'ai-lü* (extended form of regulated verse), 355; seven-character line, 377f. *See also* regulated verse
Lun yü, 188, 273, 280
lute (*ch'in*), 26
Lynn, Richard John, 68n65
lyric: closure, 345; mode of self-disclosure, 26, 341; moment, 366; poetry, 343; self, 364ff., 383; voice, 364
lyricism, 26, 28, 217, 222, 236, 239, 288; Pindaric, 219

Ma Ch'i-ch'ang, 54, 55
Ma Yüan, "The Wu Stream Is Deep," 258–259, 261
Mao Shan, 167, 197
"Mao-shih hsü" ("Preface to the Mao edition of the *Shih ching*"), 133
mask, 86
Mather, Richard B., 5n7, 15n35, 30
maximum contrast, principle of, 354, 355
meaning, 12; beyond images, 47; beyond words, 375
Mei, Tsu-lin, 353n33
Mencius, 56; *Mencius*, 21n46, 203, 264
Meng Ch'i, 164
Meng Chiao, 72n3
Meng Chien, "A Song in Narration of the Story of Ou-yang Hsing-chou, with Preface," 242–243
Meng Hao-jan, 167, 178n36, 360, 373
metamorphosis, 93–101
metaphor, 31, 46–47; and pun, 309
metaphysical: discussion, 15; projects, 4; verse, 23 (see also *hsüan-yen-shih*)
metaphysics, 17; Han, 7; Wei-Chin, 7; western, 6
metonymy, 31, 46–47
metrical pattern, 336; rules, 335–337, 356; unit, 354
microcosm, 35
military campaign, 258, 265, 270
Milky Way, 211, 215, 344
mimetic approach, 27
Ming-t'ang ("Hall of Light"), 174
modal construction, 367
models from history, 284
Monthly Comments (*Yüeh-tan p'ing*), 18
moralism and scholasticism, Eastern Han, 26
mortuary objects as imagery, 310
Mou Tsung-san, 12, 20
multiplicity, 10, 12, 15
music, 262, 270, 284; celestial, 214; of Heaven, 3, 26, 29
musical setting, 301
mythological figures, 292, 294
mythographer, 78

Nan-shih (History of the Southern Dynasties), 311
narrative, 72, 288; autobiographical, 238; *fu* as display, 217, 220–224, 226, 229, 241, 243, 252; mode, 340; nature of, 217–252; poetic, 241
narrativity, 229, 234
naturalism, 15n35, 27, 31
naturalness: and casualness, 371–372; as highest ideal in Chinese poetry, 374; theories of, 30
nature, 258, 268, 284; of all things, 9; discovery of for its own sake, 23; poetry, 23, 120; rhythm of, 26
negation: of feeling, 373
negative method, 20
Neo-Confucian thinkers, 33
Neo-Taoists, 370
New Critics, 215
nien ("connection"), 355
"Nineteen Ancient Poems" or "Nineteen Old Poems," 24, 113–114, 116, 148, 334, 338–346, 349–350, 366
non-being, 3, 4, 11, 16, 20, 373
non-Chinese people, 285, 286
nominal expression, 338, 358, 366

noun, 357
noun-centered phrases, 337

objective presentation, 373
"Of Grief and Indignation," 250
old age, 270, 284
omission: of conjunction or term of comparison, 40–41; of empty words, 40; of personal pronoun, 40; poetic, 40, 41; of preposition, 41–42
one, 33, 34; and many, 4, 11, 20
ontological: alienation, 28; assertion, 16; mode of questioning, 6; reflection of the Tao, 18, 24; thinking, 10; turn, 11, 14, 24, 25; unearthing, 31
ontologist, 27
ontology, 6, 24, 235; Wei-Chin, 10
opposition poetics, 363
oral poetry, 257
Orchid Pavilion, 27, 152, 153
original substance (*pen-t'i*), 7
otherworldliness, 373
Ou-yang Chien, 13; "Words Do Exhaust Meaning," 57–58
Owen, Stephen, 109, 323, 384

palace-style poetry, 295. See also *kung-t'i-shih* ("court-style poetry")
Pao Chao, 107, 108, 111, 120, 129, 155, 157, 247, 349; "In Imitation of 'The Difficult Journey,'" 302; "Listening to the Singing Girls at Night," 302
Pao-p'u tzu. See Ko Hung
paradox, 28; of hermeneutics, 57; of language, 49–58, 61–64; of poetics, 49–70
parallel couplets, 44, 95, 120, 124f., 313
parallelism, 42–43, 109, 111, 113, 123–129, 298, 299, 314, 317, 320, 326, 328, 341, 351, 357–359, 361, 362, 366, 371; action-oriented, 124–125; in *chüeh-chü*, 231; continuous, 361; duplicated, 356; in *lü-shih*, 237; object-oriented, 124–125, 127; regulated, 349, 356
parole, 50, 51
peerless beauty, 258, 261
P'ei Tzu-yeh, 106, 107, 135; "Discourse on the Carving of Insects," 106, 132
P'eng (bird in the *Chuang Tzu*), 98f.
P'eng-lai, 130, 164, 200, 201, 208ff., 212, 214
perception, hierarchy of, 11, 14
perceptual experience, 325, 326
personal knowledge, 18–23
personality, 342; appraisal, 17–21, 23, 24, 127, 133; traits, 21
philosophical inquiry, 24
phonetic patterning, 210, 214, 356, 360
physiognomical analysis, 19
pi ("comparison" or "direct metaphor"), 45–46, 162–163, 217, 221
pictorialism, 351
Pien (Ts'ao Ts'ao's consort), 286
plants, 270
Po Chü-i, 93, 126, 240; "Catching Locusts," 293; "His Own Portrait," 101–102; "On Reading the *Lao Tzu*," 51; "On Reading the Poems by Hsieh Ling-yün," 156; "Preface to the New Yüeh-fu," 292; "Song of Everlasting Sorrow," 239–241, 242; "Song of the P'i-p'a," 241–242; "The Whitehead of Shang-yang," 292
P'o Ch'in, 285
poet-autobiographer, 86
poetic act, 343, 345, 364, 365, 371, 372, 382; knowing, 24; vision, 24, 28, 30
poetics, of paradox, 49–70; Wei-Chin style of, 23
poetry, with music, 335n3; without music, 335n3
point of view, 218–219
politics, 15, 16, 28, 29, 191, 198
primal Breath (*yüan-ch'i*), 34, 45
Primordial Way, 33, 34

principal mode of Chinese narrative poetry, 218
principle, 7–8
process: creative, and transformation of the universe, 9; of detachment, 11
professional singers and musicians, 256, 261, 284, 285
profound learning (*hsüan-hsüeh*), 5–7, 11, 14ff., 23, 26
prose essay on travel (*yu-chi*), 119
prosodic rules, 298; and structure, 299
psychic scope, 234–236
punning as a poetic device, 307–311
pure conversation (*ch'ing-t'an*), 14–16, 18, 23, 149, 151

quatrain, 355; ancient-style, 298; dynamic, 232–233, 252; five-character, 302, 316ff., 324; nature of, 296–331; regulated, 298, 318, 325; seven-character, 302, 318f., 326; Six Dynasties, 231; static, 315. See also *chüeh-chü*

reality, 9, 11, 20, 24, 26, 27, 30, 62; holistic nature of, 62; permanent embodiments of, 50, 53; social, 23; ultimate, 11, 49–50, 58
reduplicative compounds, 128, 129
reflection, 365
reflective introspection, 367
refrain, 259, 268
regulated verse, 40, 95, 236–239, 312, 315; expanded, 239; prototypes of, 348; true, 351. See also *lü-shih*
repetition, principle of, 356; of lines, 273
reversibility, process of, 40
reverse sequence, 382
rhetorical rules, 337, 351
rhyme, 335, 354; patterns, 301–302
role, 86, 87, 95f.

sage, 4–5, 7ff., 21, 26, 29, 56, 57, 63, 75, 88; mind of, 9; of poetry 89; spirit of, 9, 10; Taoist, 93
sagehood, 9
Sakyamuni, 49
Sanskrit, 352
san-ts'ai ("Three Entities of Heaven, Earth, and Man"), 35
Schafer, Edward H., 167
Schipper, K. M., 194
self, 71, 86; double, 75; and other, 26–27; and role, 88, 101; true, 79; union of and role, 88
self-awareness, 7, 21; contentment, 372; cultivation, 28; examination, 75; forgetfulness, 22; knowledge, 19; negation, 373; portrait in historical context, 384; realization, 372
selfhood, 27
semiology, 32; semiotic order, 33
sense perceptions, 4, 7, 13
sentence, 313
sententiousness, 310, 320, 321, 323
separation, 346
sequence of structurally and verbally similar statements, 257, 262
sequential order, 313–314, 322, 329
Seven Worthies of the Bamboo Grove, 16, 27, 30, 152
Shang-ch'ing ("Highest Clarity"), 193, 196, 197, 207, 208
Shan-hai ching, 198
shan-shui-shih ("landscape poetry"), 111, 119–129, 153, 157, 161, 347–351
Shao Yung, 93
Shen Ch'üan-ch'i, 160
Shen Kua, 297n4
Shen Nung, 174
Shen Te-ch'ien, 123n37, 316, 320, 326–327
Shen Yüeh, 109, 132, 151, 152 352; "On the Biography of Hsieh Ling-yün," 150
shift of viewpoint, 262
Shih chi, 198, 264
Shih ching (*Book of Songs/Book of Poetry*), 61, 133, 188, 217, 220ff.,

250, 251, 287, 288, 292, 335, 336, 338, 342–343, 356; Mao Commentary to, 339; Poems: No. 2, 217; No. 57, 291; No. 58, 218–219; No. 65, 247; No. 70, 280; No. 94, 275; No. 113, 178n37; No. 164, 284; No. 167, 280; No. 169, 280; No. 197, 280; No. 202, 280; No. 237, 219; No. 259, 172, 179; No. 281, 219; No. 264, 257; No. 297, 219
Shih ming. *See* Liu Hsi
Shih, Vincent Yu-chung, 106n1, 109n9, 110n14, 129, 132n5, 133n10, 134n12, 143n36, 145n42, 148n49, 149n51, 150n58, 152, 162, 163, 163n88
shih yen chih ("poetry expresses intent"), 339
shih-hua ("remarks on poetry"), 38
Shih-lü ("Stone Wicket"), 174
Shih-p'in. See Chung Hung
Shih-shuo hsin-yü, 150–151. See also *A New Account of Tales of the World*
shih-tzu ("content words" or "full words"), 358
Shu, 379f.; Last Ruler of, 383
Shu ching (*Canon of Documents*), 169, 264
Shun, 169
Shuo-wen chieh-tzu. *See* Hsü Shen
significance, contextual, 333; formal, 333
signification, 32, 33, 42, 43
simplicity of diction, 303, 307, 310
singing girl, 306
soldier, 268, 270, 284
"Song of Liang-fu," 379
"Song of Mu-lan," 250
"Southeast Fly the Peacocks," 241, 243, 250
Soymié, Michel, 167
spatial dimension, 44
spatiality, 367
spiritual orientation, Wei-Chin, 11
spontaneity, 27
Spring and Autumn period, 301
Ssu-k'ung T'u, 47, 69, 297; "A Letter to Mr. Li on Poetry," 296; *The Twenty-four Modes of Poetry*, 67–68
Ssu-ma Ch'eng-chen, 185n53
Ssu-ma Ch'ien, 166
Ssu-ma Hsiang-ju, 109, 214
Ssu-ma Kuang, 34n3
stillness and movement, 353
substance, 13, 20; and function, 11
suffering of the common people, 259, 268, 284
Sui Yang-ti (Emperor Yang of the Sui), 227, 228
Su-jan ("Solemn State"), 173, 174
Sun Ch'o, 131, 151, 180, 235; "A Piece in Reply to Hsü Hsün," 151; "Wandering on Mount T'ien-t'ai," 120
Sung Chih-wen, 160
Sung poets, 94
Sung Wen-ti (Emperor Wen of the Liu Sung), 311
"Sung-pieh shih" ("A Parting Poem"), Sui dynasty anonymous quatrain, 318–320
Supreme Emptiness, 34, 36
Supreme Profundity, 6, 7
symbolic interchange, 23, 27; level, 44
symbolism, 384
symmetry, 355; principle of, 353, 356
synchronic structure of the discourse, 16
syntactic level, 42
syntax, 44
system of correspondences, 330–331

Ta Tai li chi, 264
Tai Tsung, 174, 178, 179
Ta-tung chen-ching ("Realized Scripture of the Grotto"), 208
T'ai Ching-nung, 136n16
T'ai ch'ing ("Grand Clarity"), 186, 187
t'ai-chi diagram, 43
T'ai-shang chiu-ch'ih pan-fu wu-ti nei-

chen ching (*Most High Scripture of the Dappled Talisman of the Nine Incarnadines and the Interior Realization of the Five Thearchs*), 195–196
T'ai-wei ("Grand Tenuity"), 171
T'ang Hsüan-tsung (Emperor Hsüan-tsung of T'ang), 170, 183, 184, 185n53, 200, 240, 291
T'ang Hui-hsiu, 157
T'ang Kao-tsung, 170, 183
T'ang T'ai-tsung (Emperor T'ai-tsung of T'ang), 160, 362
T'ang Yung-t'ung, 6–7, 11
Tao, 8, 10, 11, 12, 14, 16, 17, 20, 21, 23, 26, 28, 29, 30, 31, 34, 50, 53, 54, 56, 66, 69, 148, 151, 152; experience of, 14; manifold function, 21
tao ching ("inverted luminescence"), 208, 209
Tao te ching, 33. *See also* Lao Tzu
Tao tsang, 184n52
T'ao Ch'ien, 30, 61–62, 76–88, 120, 148, 153, 224, 236, 368–373, 376; "Drinking Wine," 80–81, 83, 93; "Imitations," 154; "Returning to Dwell in My Fields and Gardens," 77, 83, 154–155; "Untitled Poem," 154
T'ao Hung-ching, 206
Taoism, 21n46, 131, 140, 147, 150ff.; immortals, 268, 273; occult, 152; popular, 347; Taoist from Lin-ch'iung, 240
thought: binary mode of, 48; fundamental laws of Chinese, 32; Wei-Chin style of, 3ff., 17, 23, 24
Three Kingdoms, 17
Three, Taoist idea of, 35
Ti chu ("Presider of Earth"), 172
Tibetan armies, 378, 379
Tibetan invasions, 380, 381
T'ien-ch'i wang ("Prince Equal to Heaven"), 184
T'ien-t'ai Shan, 180
T'ien-ti sun ("the grandson of Heaven's Thearch"), 171
T'ien-t'ing ("Heaven's Court"), 171
T'ien wen, 294
t'ien-yüan-shih ("farmland poetry" or "rural poetry"), 146, 153–154, 369, 370–371, 374
time and space, 29–31
TLV mirror, 192
tones: level, 352, 354; level and oblique contrasted, 353; oblique, 352, 354; structure, 320–322; tonal pattern, 298, 299, 312, 315ff., 320, 351
Treatise on Personalities (*Jen-wu chih*), 18, 20
tsa-chüeh-chü ("miscellaneous *chüeh-chü*"), 300
tsa-shih ("miscellaneous poems" or "unclassified poems"), 82, 112, 114, 115, 118, 121
tsao hua ("Shaping Mutator"), 180
Ts'ao Chang, 286
Ts'ao Chih, 29, 142, 148, 186–191, 199, 247, 255, 269, 274, 280, 282, 285, 286; "Composition on the Famed Capital," 225; "Floating Duckweed," 282; "Presented to Piao, the Prince of Po-ma," 148; "Seeing Off Mr. Ying," 139, 143; "Some Famous Cities," 280–282
Ts'ao Jui, 255, 268
Ts'ao P'i, 71–72, 82, 85, 255, 274–277, 285, 286, 348, 350; "Command," 138–139; "Good!" 274–275; "I Look Down from the High Terrace," 275–278; "Song in Short Meter," 279; "Song of Shang-liu-t'ien," 278; "Song on Breaking a Willow Branch," 147–148; "Song on the Glorious Capital Lo-yang," 141; *Tien lun*, 137f.; "Yen-ko ho-ch'ang hsing," 142
Ts'ao Ts'ao, 19, 136, 139, 147, 201, 255, 262–274, 279–280, 282, 285, 286; "Cantos on the Pneuma Emerging," 191–192; "Dew on the Shallots," 137–138; "I Drink," 262–

264, 282; "Passing through the Mountain Passes," 140; "Shan-tsai hsing" ("Good!"), 278; "Short Songs," 140–141; "Songs of Ch'iu Hu," 147; "Song on the Village of the Dead," 137–138; "Song on Walking Out of the Eastern and Western Gates," 141; "Stepping Out of the Hsia Gate," 265, 268
Tseng Tien, 348, 369
Tso chuan, 339n9
Tso Ssu, 115, 146, 149, 159; "Invitation to a Gentleman in Hiding," 153
Tso Yen-nien, 285
Tsu Pao-ch'üan, 69
Ts'ui Ling-en, 175–176
Tsung Ping, 123n34, 154
Tu Ch'üeh, 165
Tu Fu, 40, 89–101, 165, 178–183, 203, 224, 236–239, 292, 315, 321, 328, 361, 375–385; contribution to *lü-shih*, 375; interpretation of historical forces, 381–382; new aesthetics, 382; works: "Ascending the Tower," 378–384; "Autumn Meditations," 92, 236–239, 380; "Autumn Wastes," 92; "Ballad of Beautiful Ladies," 290–291; "Ballad of the Army Carts," 288; "Barren Palm," 93; "Chüeh-chü," 328–331; "Empty Purse," 89–92; "Gazing Afar at the Marchmount," 178–179; "Journey to the North," 242, 245, 247; "Lament on the River Bank," 288; "Moon Night," 47; "Mooring Beneath Yüeh-yang," 99; "No Home to Take Leave of," 288; "On Ancient Ruins," 380; "On Generals," 380; "Recruiting Officer at Hsin-an," 288; "Recruiting Officer at Shih-hao," 288; "Separation of the Newlyweds," 288; "Spending the Night at White Sands Post Station," 100–101; "Yangtze and Han," 95, 97, 99, 100
Tu Mu, 223, 321
tuan-chü ("broken-off lines"), 300, 303, 311
"Tuan-ko hsing" ("Song in Short Meter"), 280
"Tu-ch'ü ko" ("Plain Songs"), 306–309, 311
tui ("opposition"), 355
Tun-huang, 246, 249, 295
Tung Chung-shu, 6, 7, 35
Tung Wang Fu ("The Royal Father in the East"), 189. *See also* Ch'ing t'ung
Tung-fang ch'ing-ti chün (Lord Azure Thearch of the Eastern Quarter), 195
Tung-fang Ch'iu, 130–131, 163
Two (Yin and Yang), 34
typology of personality, 86
Tzu-kung, 55
Tzu-lu, 76
"Tzu-yeh ko" ("Tzu-yeh Songs"), 288, 294, 305–309, 311
tz'u, 302
Tz'u Hai, 68

ultimate verse, 231–233, 252
understanding, 22; intuitive, 370, 371
union: of *ch'ing* and *ching*, 384; of yin and yang, 9
unitary principle, 44
universal resonance, 45
utopia, 262, 264, 282; Confucian, 140

"Variation on the Songs of the East and West Gates," 268
verisimilitude, 108, 124
view from the terrace, 277
visualizations, 195, 196, 208

Wang Ch'ang-ling, 64, 66, 321, 327
Wang Chi (a Han general), 277
Wang Chi (an Early T'ang poet), 369
Wang Ch'i, 199
Wang Chih-huan, "Ascending the Heron Tower," 325–326
Wang, Ching-hsien, 329

Wang Fu-chih, 297n4, 312
Wang Han, "Song of Liang-chou," 323–324
Wang Hsi-chih, 27
Wang Jung, 156, 352
Wang K'ang-chü, 146
Wang Kuo-wei, 340
Wang Li, 298n10, 353n10
Wang Pao, *Chiu huai*, "Tsun chia," 284
Wang Pi, 4ff., 34n3
Wang Po, "In the Mountains," 321–323; "Return from Picking Lotus Blossoms," 289–290
Wang Shih-chen, 287, 383n67
Wang Ts'an, 247; "My Lord's Feast," 143; "Seven Sorrows," 139
Wang Wei, 86, 87, 153, 321, 327, 369, 370–375, 376, 385; "Bird Singing Valley," 324–325, 326; "Preface to Poems on Flowers and Medicinal Herbs by the Reverend Master Kuang of Chien-fu Monastery," 65; "Villa on Chung-nan Mountain," 42; *Wang River Collection*, 324
Wang Yün-hsi, 302, 308, 310
Wang-tzu Ch'iao, 192
Watson, Burton, 55
Weaving Maid (star), 213, 215, 344
Wei Chuang, 250; "Lament of a Ch'in Woman," 246–250
Wei Hua-ts'un, 209
Wei Wen-ti (Emperor Wen of the Wei), 274. *See also* Ts'ao P'i
Wei Ying-wu, 374; "Coming Across Feng Chu in Ch'ang-an," 230
Wei Yüan, 34–35n3
"Wen fu" ("Rhymeprose on Literature," "Exposition on Literature," or "On Literature"), 59–61
Wen-hsin tiao-lung (*The Literary Mind and the Carving of Dragons, The Literary Mind: Elaborations*, or *Refinements of the Literary Mind*), 18, 52, 148. *See also* Liu Hsieh
Wen hsüan, 222
Westbrook, Francis A., 123n34
whistling, 201
Wilde, Oscar, 86
wish to be a perfect ruler, 273, 284
wish to be a perfect subject, 273, 284
woman triumphant, 261, 284–285
words, 12; exhaust meaning, 13; and meaning, 27–28; of stasis (*ching-tzu*), 37, 38
writing system, 32
Wu Chün, 314, 322; "Miscellaneous Poem Written in the Mountain," 314–315, 317, 329
Wu-sheng-ko ("Songs in the Wu Dialect"), 307, 311
wu-yen shih ("five-character line poetry"), 117, 230, 332, 334–338, 341, 347, 351
Wu-yüeh chen-hsing t'u, 193

Yang Chiung, 180n43, 363
Yang Hsien-yi and Gladys Yang, 67, 68
Yang Hsiung, 6, 56–57, 226; underlying structure of metaphysics, 7
Yang Kuei-fei, 240, 292
Yang Kuo-chung, 292
Yang Shen, 164
Yang Shih-yüan, 311
Yang Wan-li, 73
Yangtze, 97, 98, 307
Yeh, 135f., 142
Yeh Chia-ying, 377
Yeh Hsieh, 165; *Yüan shih*, 165
yen ("expression"), 340
yen chih ("state life ambition"), 348
Yen Yen-chih, 107, 108, 111; "Song of Ch'iu Hu," 250
Yen Yü, 64, 136; *Ts'ang-lang shih-hua*, 132, 135
"Yen-ko ho-ch'ang hsing," 277
yen-yüeh ("banquet music"), 302
Yin and Yang, 33, 35f., 42f., 45
Yin Fan, *Ho-yüeh ying-ling chi*, 290
Ying Shao, 175
Ying Yang, 139; "Cockfight," 144

Ying-chou, 200, 208, 209, 234
Yip, Wai-lim, 67, 68
Yü ch'ing ("Jade Clarity"), 187n55, 197
Yü Hsin, 247, 362; "Parting Again from Grand Secretary Chou," 315–317
yü i ("liquor of jade"), 212
Yü Kuan-ying, 267
Yu, Pauline, 67, 68
Yü Shih-nan, 362
Yüan Chen, 292
Yüan Jen-lin, 37n5, 39
"Yüan yu," 202n97
yüeh-fu, 24, 82, 137, 147, 220f., 226f., 229, 232f., 245, 300; development in Han and Wei, 255–286; development in T'ang, 287–295; Han, 250, 251, 275, 284, 302, 350
Yüeh-fu-shih-chi (*A Collection of Yüeh-fu Poetry*), 232, 255, 261, 262, 280, 300
yu-hsien-shih ("poetry on wandering immortals"), 82, 111f., 146ff., 151f., 159, 201, 347
Yung-chia era, 131, 151f.
yung-huai shih ("poetry expressing one's innermost feelings"), 82, 114, 346, 347, 351, 363
yung-shih ("poetry on historical events"), 241, 242
yung-wu-shih ("poems on things or objects"), 82, 146, 156, 158, 350
Yü-t'ai hsin-yung (*New Compositions from a Jade Terrace*), 161, 300, 303
Yü-t'ai-chi, 161

Zurcher, Erik, 5n7

Studies on China

The Origins of Chinese Civilization
Edited by David N. Keightley
University of California Press, 1982

Popular Chinese Literature and Performing Arts in the People's Republic of China, 1949–1979
Edited by Bonnie S. McDougall
University of California Press, 1984

Class and Social Stratification in Post-Revolution China
Edited by James L. Watson
Cambridge University Press, 1984

Popular Culture in Late Imperial China
Edited by David Johnson, Andrew J. Nathan, and Evelyn S. Rawski
University of California Press, 1985

Kinship Organization in Late Imperial China, 1000–1940
Edited by Patricia Buckley Ebrey and James L. Watson
University of California Press, 1986

The Vitality of the Lyric Voice: Shih *Poetry from the Late Han to the T'ang*
Edited by Shuen-fu Lin and Stephen Owen
Princeton University Press, 1986

Library of Congress Cataloging-in-Publication Data

Main entry under title:

The Vitality of the lyric voice.

Papers presented at a conference on the "Evolution of Shih poetry from the Han through the T'ang" at Bowdoin College in York, Me., June 9–14, 1982.
Includes index.
1. Chinese poetry—221 B.C.–960 A.D.—History and criticism—Congresses.
I. Lin, Shuen-fu, 1943– II. Owen, Stephen, 1946–
PL2313.V58 1986 895.1'12'09 85-30755
ISBN 0-691-03134-7